Teaching Geography in Secondary Schools

The Open University *Flexible* Postgraduate Certificate of Education

The readers and the companion volumes in the *flexible* PGCE series are:

Aspects of Teaching and Learning in Secondary Schools: Perspectives on practice

Teaching, Learning and the Curriculum in Secondary Schools: A reader

Aspects of Teaching Secondary Mathematics: Perspectives on practice

Teaching Mathematics in Secondary Schools: A reader

Aspects of Teaching Secondary Science: Perspectives on practice

Teaching Science in Secondary Schools: A reader

Aspects of Teaching Secondary Modern Foreign Languages: Perspectives on practice

Teaching Modern Foreign Languages in Secondary Schools: A reader

Aspects of Teaching Secondary Geography: Perspectives on practice

Teaching Geography in Secondary Schools: A reader

Aspects of Teaching Secondary Design and Technology: Perspectives on practice

Teaching Design and Technology in Secondary Schools: A reader

Aspects of Teaching Secondary Music: Perspectives on practice

Teaching Music in Secondary Schools: A reader

All of these subjects are part of the Open University's initial teacher education course, the *flexible* PGCE, and constitute part of an integrated course designed to develop critical understanding. The set books, reflecting a wide range of perspectives, and discussing the complex issues that surround teaching and learning in the twenty-first century, will appeal to both beginning and experienced teachers, to mentors, tutors, advisers and other teacher educators.

If you would like to receive a *flexible* PGCE prospectus please write to the Course Reservations Centre at The Call Centre, The Open University, Milton Keynes MK7 6ZS. Other information about programmes of professional development in education is available from the same address.

Teaching Geography in Secondary Schools
A reader

Teaching Geography in Secondary Schools: A reader introduces and explores a broad range of contemporary issues and key ideas and will provide a useful background for those teaching and training to teach this exciting subject.

The book is concerned with exploring the bigger picture of geography education. Divided into sections to help structure reading, it covers:

- Changes and challenges to geography education
- Curriculum planning and course development
- Continuity and progression
- Teaching styles and strategies
- ICT and geography
- Fieldwork
- Citizenship and geography
- Geography and multiculturalism
- The role of research

The *Teaching in Secondary Schools* series brings together collections of articles by highly experienced educators that focus on the issues surrounding the teaching of National Curriculum subjects. They are invaluable resources for those studying to become teachers, newly qualified teachers and more experienced practitioners, particularly those mentoring students and NQTs. The companion volume to this book is *Aspects of Teaching Secondary Geography: Perspectives on practice*.

Maggie Smith is a lecturer at The Open University and has responsibility for the Open University *flexible* Geography PGCE course.

Set book for the Open University *flexible* PGCE, Geography course EXG880.

Teaching Geography in Secondary Schools

A reader

Edited by Maggie Smith

London and New York

First published 2002
by RoutledgeFalmer
11 New Fetter Lane, London EC4P 4EE

Simultaneously published in the USA and Canada
by RoutledgeFalmer
29 West 35th Street, New York, NY 10001

RoutledgeFalmer is an imprint of the Taylor & Francis Group

© 2002 Compilation, original and editorial matter,
The Open University

Typeset in Goudy by Bookcraft Ltd, Stroud, Gloucestershire
Printed and bound in Great Britain by The University Press,
Cambridge, United Kingdom

British Library Cataloguing in Publication Data
A catalogue record for this book is available from the British Library

Library of Congress Cataloging in Publication Data
A catalog record has been requested

ISBN 0–415–26078–7 (hbk)

ISBN 0–415–26079–5 (pbk)

Contents

Figures

Tables

Abbreviations

ARG	Assessment Reform Group
BECTa	British Educational Communications and Technology Agency
CASE	Cognitive Acceleration in Science Education
CEE	Council for Environmental Education
CSIE	Centre for Studies on Inclusive Education
DES	Department of Education and Science
DfEE	Department for Education and Employment (now Department for Education and Skills, DfES)
FSC	Field Studies Council
GA	Geographical Association
GCSE	General Certificate of Secondary Education
GNC	Geography National Curriculum
GSIP	Geography, Schools and Industry Partnership
GYSL	Geography for the Young School Leaver
IBG	Institute of British Geographers
ICT	Information and communications technology
IGU	International Geographical Union
INSET	In-service education and training
NCC	National Curriculum Council
NGfL	National Grid for Learning
Ofsted	Office for Standards in Education
QCA	Qualifications and Curriculum Authority
RAE	Research Assessment Exercise
RGS	Royal Geographical Society
SCAA	School Curriculum and Assessment Authority
SEU	Standard and Effectiveness Unit
TLF	Teaching and Learning in the Foundation Subjects
TTA	Teacher Training Agency

Sources

Where a chapter in this book is based on or is a reprint or revision of material previously published elsewhere, details are given below, with grateful acknowledgements to the original publishers.

Chapter 1   This is an edited version of a chapter originally published in Kent, A. (ed.) (2000), *School Science Teaching: The History and Future of the Curriculum*, Kogan Page, London.

Chapter 2   This is based upon a paper entitled 'The Politics and Practicalities of Curriculum Change 1991-200: Issues Arising from a Study of School Geography in England', originally published in the *British Journal of Educational Studies*, 49(2), Blackwell, Oxford (June 2001).

Chapter 4   This is an edited version of a chapter originally published in Naish, M., Rawling, E. and Hart, C. (1987), *The Contribution of a Curriculum Project to 16-19 Education*, Longman, Harlow.

Chapter 5   Originally published in Tilbury, D. and Williams, M. (1997), *Teaching and Learning Geography*, Routledge, London.

Chapter 6   This is an edited version of a paper originally published in *Teaching Geography*, 20(2)(April 1995), The Geographical Association, Sheffield.

Chapter 7   Originally published in Kent, A. (ed.) (2000), *Reflective Practice in Geography Teaching*, Paul Chapman Publishing, London.

Chapter 8   Originally published in Tilbury, D. and Williams, M. (1997), *Teaching and Learning Geography*, Routledge, London.

Chapter 9   This is an edited version of a chapter originally published in Kent, A. (ed.) (2000), *Reflective Practice in Geography Teaching*, Paul Chapman Publishing, London.

Chapter 10   Originally published in Williams, M. (ed.) (1996), *Understanding Geographical and Environmental Education: The Role of Research*, Cassell, London.

Chapter 11   Originally published in Fisher, C. and Binns, J. A. (eds) (2000), *Issues in Geography Teaching*, RoutledgeFalmer, London.

Chapter 12   Originally published in Gerber, R. and Chuan, G. K. (eds) (2000), *Fieldwork in Geography: Reflections, Perspectives and Actions*, Kluwer Academic Publishers, Dordrecht.

Chapter 14   Originally published in Tilbury, D. and Williams, M. (1997), *Teaching and Learning Geography*, Routledge, London.

Chapter 15   Based upon two papers originally published in *Teaching Geography*, 23(4) and 24(1), The Geographical Association, Sheffield (October 1998) and (January 1999).

Chapter 16   Originally published in Grimwade, K., Reid, A. and Thompson, L, (eds) (2000), *Geography and the New Agenda: Citizenship, PSHE and Sustainable Development in the Secondary Curriculum*, The Geographical Association, Sheffield.

Chapter 17   This is based upon edited versions of a chapter originally published in Kent, A. (ed.) (2000), *Reflective Practice in Geography Teaching*, London: Paul Chapman Publishing and a paper originally published in *Teaching Geography*, (23)3, The Geographical Association, Sheffield (July 1998).

Chapter 18   Originally published in Tilbury, D. and Williams, M. (1997), *Teaching and Learning Geography*, London: Routledge.

Chapter 19   This is an edited version of a paper originally published in *Geography*, 84(3)(1999), The Geographical Association, Sheffield.

Chapter 20   Originally published in the *Journal of Geography in Higher Education*, 25(1)(2001), Carfax Publishing, Abingdon.

Chapter 21   Originally published in Kent, A. (ed.) (2000), *Reflective Practice in Geography Teaching*, Paul Chapman Publishing, London.

Chapter 22   This is an edited version of a paper originally published in *Geography*, 83(1)(1998), The Geographical Association, Sheffield.

Chapter 23   Originally published in Kent, A., Lambert, D., Naish, M. and Slater, F. (eds) (1996), *Geography in Education*, Cambridge University Press, Cambridge.

Acknowledgement

Special thanks are due to John Morgan of the Graduate School of Education at the University of Bristol for his invaluable assistance in the editing of the articles used in this book. His professionalism, commitment and unfailing enthusiasm for the task were much appreciated.

Foreword

The nature and form of initial teacher education and training are issues that lie at the heart of the teaching profession. They are inextricably linked to the standing and identity that society attributes to teachers and are seen as being one of the main planks in the push to raise standards in schools and to improve the quality of education in them. The initial teacher education curriculum therefore requires careful definition. How can it best contribute to the development of the range of skills, knowledge and understanding that makes up the complex, multi-faceted, multi-skilled and people-centred process of teaching?

There are, of course, external, government-defined requirements for initial teacher training courses. These specify, amongst other things, the length of time a student spends in school, the subject knowledge requirements beginning teachers are expected to demonstrate or the ICT skills that are needed. These requirements, however, do not in themselves constitute the initial training curriculum. They are only one of the many, if sometimes competing, components that make up the broad spectrum of a teacher's professional knowledge that underpin initial teacher education courses.

Certainly today's teachers need to be highly skilled in literacy, numeracy and ICT, in classroom methods and management. In addition, however, they also need to be well grounded in the critical dialogue of teaching. They need to be encouraged to be creative and innovative and to appreciate that teaching is a complex and problematic activity. This is a view of teaching that is shared with partner schools within the Open University Training Schools Network. As such it has informed the planning and development of the Open University's initial teacher training programme and the *flexible* PGCE.

All of the *flexible* PGCE courses have a series of connected and complementary readers. The *Teaching in Secondary Schools* series pulls together a range of new thinking about teaching and learning in particular subjects. Key debates and differing perspectives are presented, and evidence from research and practice is explored, inviting the reader to question the accepted orthodoxy, suggesting ways of enriching the present curriculum and offering new thoughts on classroom learning. These readers are accompanied by the series *Perspectives on practice*. Here, the focus is on the application of these developments to educational/subject policy and the classroom, and on the illustration of teaching skills, knowledge and understanding in a variety of school contexts. Both series include newly commissioned work.

This series from RoutledgeFalmer, in supporting the Open University's *flexible* PGCE, also includes two key texts that explore the wider educational background. These companion publications, *Teaching, Learning and the Curriculum in Secondary Schools: A reader* and *Aspects of Teaching and Learning in Secondary Schools: Perspectives on practice*, explore a contemporary view of developments in secondary education with the aim of providing analysis and insights for those participating in initial teacher training education courses.

Hilary Bourdillon – Director ITT Strategy
Steven Hutchinson – Director ITT Secondary
The Open University
September 2001

Preface

This reader, together with two other geography texts and two generic texts, provide in-depth discussion to the subject matter covered in the on-line modules which are the 'teaching blocks' of the Open University *flexible* PGCE course. The reader forms a useful collection of up-to-date articles, written by the most prominent teachers and teacher educators in the UK today and will be valuable to trainee teachers on any Geography PGCE course.

Some articles focus on long-standing issues; fieldwork activities and assessment methods, while others relate to new initiatives; citizenship and sustainability. The authors' views and opinions deliberately challenge readers and ask them to critically reflect on their work with pupils.

Sheila King
Director of Training Partnerships and
Lecturer in Geography Education
Institute of Education, University of London.

Introduction

Teaching Geography in Secondary Schools forms part of a series of readers designed to accompany the new Open University *flexible* PGCE course. It, and its partner book, *Aspects of Teaching Secondary Geography: Perspectives on practice,* will be the set books on the secondary geography course, as will the two generic readers *Teaching, Learning and the Curriculum in Secondary Schools* and *Aspects of Teaching and Learning in Secondary Schools,* and one further recent publication – *Learning to Teach Geography in the Secondary School* by David Lambert and David Balderstone. Together this set of books will provide the core academic text-based materials for the new geography course. They will be fully integrated with the web-based study modules and other web-based resources, and will also be integrated into the blocks of school experience undertaken by the students. School-based activities will use the texts as a platform, and the electronic conferencing environment in which the students will work will draw heavily on the texts as a resource.

The aim of this particular book, as its title suggests, is to bring together a wide range of articles and extracts, some new, but most from existing publications, that discuss the key ideas, debates and issues in geography education today. Students will be challenged to reflect critically on these issues in order to develop their own understanding of the complexity of many of the issues, and to consider the implications for their classroom practice. Most of the chapters include reference lists so that individual concerns and personal interests can be followed up in more detail.

The book is divided into four sections. The first puts the development of geography as a school subject into a historical perspective. It identifies the influences on and changes in the geography curriculum through the last century; it looks particularly closely at developments within the last decade; and sets out ideas about what we might want to see in the geography curriculum of the future.

The second section looks at some of the issues connected to the teaching and learning of geography in (and out of) the classroom. It provides an informed background to these issues so that beginning teachers can set their own classroom experiences into context and can start to develop their own ideas on how the issues might be addressed. A range of broader concerns – issues for geography in the twenty-first century – are featured in section three. As in all the sections, restrictions on the length of the book have meant that only a limited number of issues facing geography education could be selected for discussion here. We hope that the issues chosen reflect the diversity of the challenges ahead – ranging as they do from pedagogy, to content, to the future of geography.

In the final section, the theme is the important one of research and continuing professional development. The role of research is highlighted, the value of the teacher as a learner is explored, and the importance of practitioners becoming involved in the research in order to ensure that geography teaching continues to move forward to meet the new demands of the twenty-first century is stressed.

The chapters selected for this book have been written by respected authors, researchers and practitioners of geography education. The large volume of excellent material that exists on geography education, while clearly an advantage for the well-being of the subject, has certainly posed a major problem for the editor and advisory team in terms of the selection of articles for inclusion in the book. Inevitably some issues will have been left out. In all cases, however, the overriding consideration in deciding which articles to include was their relevance to the course objectives and to the needs of the Geography PGCE students who would be working in a flexible way and in a distance-learning situation on this Open University course.

Many of the authors of chapters have offered encouragement and suggestions – all of which were very gratefully received. The course team, course managers, editors and geography advisory group at the Open University have provided a constant source of support and advice, which was very welcome.

We hope that the discussions and debates raised in this book will provide PGCE students with much to think about as they prepare for the challenges of a career in teaching. Many of the issues raised, however, will also be issues facing more experienced geography teachers, and we hope that they too will benefit from the stimulus provided by the range of ideas presented in this book.

Maggie Smith

Section 1

Geography in the school curriculum

This section puts the development of geography as a subject in the school curriculum into its historical perspective and examines the influence of social, economic and political influences on the subject. It is hoped that the discussions in the three chapters that make up this section will encourage students to understand better what they see happening in school geography departments, and to develop their own personal views on the role and purpose of teaching geography in secondary schools.

In Chapter 1, Ashley Kent, writing from a personal viewpoint as head of the Education, Environment and Economy section at the Institute of Education, University of London, provides an overview of the development of geography education through the twentieth century. In particular he draws out the historical roots of many of the contemporary challenges facing the subject in schools. His chapter sets the scene for this book: it covers changes in pedagogy, content, resources, fieldwork and research, and he concludes by setting out some of the broad issues and challenges that face teachers of geography in the years ahead.

Eleanor Rawling, in Chapter 2, focuses more particularly on developments that have affected the geography curriculum in the last decade from the first National Curriculum for Geography and through the two subsequent revisions. She highlights more general issues about ideology and the politics of curriculum change during this period and she raises a number of issues and topics that provide a stimulus for further debate and research. For beginning teachers, this chapter will help in understanding the thinking behind the curriculum developments and initiatives with which they will be working in the classroom.

The last chapter in this section is one that encourages students to keep an open mind about what constitutes school geography. John Morgan traces the conflicts and debates that have characterised the various 'geographies' of the last 150 years, and notes that traces of many of these viewpoints still survive in the geography curriculum. He suggests analytical frameworks that students can use to make sense of the various types of 'geography' that they will encounter in their teaching.

Geography in the
school curriculum

1 Geography

Changes and challenges

Ashley Kent

The story of Geography's development as a popular subject in English schools is both fascinating and complex. This author's view is that it is both worthwhile and useful to have some historical perspective on contemporary challenges. This chapter attempts a personal overview of the evolution of geography education and this inevitably is influenced by the writer's long-standing involvement with the Institute of Education as both student and member of staff.

A number of publications have discussed the history of geographical education but probably the most succinct and accessible are the four articles by Boardman and McPartland (1993a, 1993b, 1993c, 1993d) in successive issues of *Teaching Geography*, to mark the centenary of the Geographical Association (GA). Marsden too has written about the history of geography education in various places, for instance 1995, 1996 and 1997. The most recent and substantial work is that of Walford (2000) and unsurprisingly Balchin's history of the Geographical Association (1993) is a story closely intertwined with the subject's evolution.

Curriculum development

During most of this century regional geography has been the dominant paradigm in school curriculums. A key influence was Herbertson, former Director of the School of Geography, Oxford University, whose seminal paper in 1905 divided the world into major natural regions. 'It is probable that his influence on what was taught in British schools was enormous and has since been unsurpassed' (Graves 1975: 28). This was not only because he used modified natural regions in his successful series of school textbooks (written with his wife), but because the concept was used in textbooks written by schoolteachers. For instance Brooks, Pickles and Stembridge produced a textbook series covering continent by continent. Indeed the prolific textbook writer Dudley Stamp acknowledged his debt to Herbertson and the natural region concept in 1957. A good illustration of the longevity of the regional framework underpinning syllabuses was the success of Preece and Wood's *The Foundations of Geography* (1938), which was still in print 50 years later having sold more than 2 million copies.

'The dominance of the regional framework in syllabus design continued during the post-war years', according to Boardman and McPartland (1993b: 65). As recently as 1960 the Ministry of Education lauded the regional framework, which it claimed lay at the 'very heart of geography' (1960: 38). The main criticism of this approach was its lack of intellectual challenge and that it tended 'to degenerate into the repetitive learning of factual information' (Boardman and McPartland 1993a: 5). Some argued that the sample studies approach was introduced as a counter to the disadvantages of the regional approach. The argument went that such a detailed study of any geographical unit such as a farm, village, valley or factory required the knowledge and understanding of ideas and concepts that could be generalized and 'was grounded in the lives and occupations of real people in real places, giving it the sanctity of authenticity' (Boardman and McPartland 1993b: 65). The 'study' element of sample study implied data description, analysis and evaluation. So successful was this approach that its popularity ranged from Fairgrieve and Young's *Real Geography,* the first of six books to be published in 1939, to the *Study Geography* series of five books by Rushby, Bell and Dybeck (1967).

Over the years, books written for geography teachers have been influential on practice and have reflected the content and pedagogies of their times. One particular early moment was James Fairgrieve's *Geography in School,* first published in 1926 and running to a fourth edition in 1937. He had left William Ellis School in 1912 to become a lecturer in the London Day Training College (later to become the University of London Institute of Education). The book presented his views on geography as developed over 20 years at the Institute and contains the well-known remark that 'The function of geography is to train future citizens to imagine accurately the condition of the great world stage and so help them to think sanely about political and social problems in the world around' (Fairgrieve 1926: 18). *Geography in School* remained the 'bible' on geographical education for several decades and a flavour of his thoughts is included in the following.

Geography is at once one of the most important of school subjects and one of the most difficult to teach.

There is a claim from geography for a place in the curriculum, not because it pays, but because we cannot have an education worth the name without geography.

Geography enables man to place himself on the world and to know where he stands with regard to his fellows, so that he will neither exaggerate nor diminish his own importance; it enables us to understand other people, to some extent, by comparison with ourselves. By a study of geography we are enabled to understand facts without a knowledge of which it would be impossible to do our duty as citizens of this very confusing and contradictory world.

There is not one single thing which stands so much in the way of social and international advance as a lack of knowledge of geography. The function of geography in school is to train future citizens to imagine accurately the conditions of the great world stage, and so help them to think sanely about political and social problems in the world around.

(Fairgrieve 1926)

His influence on geography teachers through teacher educators at the Institute continues through the generations. So Scarfe was a student of Fairgrieve, Honeybone a student of Scarfe and Graves a student of Honeybone, each respectively head of geography at the largest university school of education. Incidentally Long and Roberson were students of Scarfe! Perhaps it is no accident that generations of Institute (and wider) students (including this author) can recall one of his maxims that one should teach:

- from the known to the unknown;
- from the simple to the complex;
- from the indefinite to the definite (an unexpected reversal here);
- from the particular to the general.

Perhaps the zenith of Fairgrieve's approach and the regional framework underpinning curriculums came with the publication of Long and Roberson's *Teaching Geography* in 1966 in which the authors significantly remarked, 'we have nailed our flag to the regional mast, and those who would not place the main emphasis on regional geography in school must justify themselves with some other viable philosophy' (1966: 24).

Already the 'new geography' of higher education in the USA and the UK with its emphasis on theoretical models, conceptual frameworks and quantitative techniques was influencing a new generation of teachers unhappy with the idiographic regional approach. Seminal publications of the time were *Frontiers in Geographical Teaching* (Chorley and Haggett 1965); *Locational Analysis in Human Geography* (Haggett 1965); and *Models in Geography* (Chorley and Haggett 1967). Their messages were new, challenging and difficult. 'The books ... contained ideas of baffling abstruseness and exciting novelty in about equal parts' (Walford 1989: 310). Bringing this new 'content' into schools was no easy task and a key role was played by the Geographical Association Models and Quantitative Techniques Committee set up in 1967 and the special edition of *Geography* (January, 1969) focusing on such developments. Everson and FitzGerald, two young London teachers (and subsequently HMIs), had a considerable influence especially through the first A level textbook on the new geography, *Settlement Patterns* (1969).

Arguably within ten years a paradigm shift had occurred in terms of changed syllabuses and textbooks in the direction of the 'new geography'. Examples of key textbooks of the time were the *Oxford Geography Project* (Rolfe *et al.* 1974) and the work of Cole and Beynon (1968), Briggs (1972), Dinkele, Cotterell and Thorn (1976) and Bradford and Kent (1977).

Already by the 1960s there had developed in higher education (HE) a backlash against the positivistic, spatial science paradigm. Behavioural geography, welfare geography, radical geography, humanistic geography, post-modern geography and new cultural geography have all had their adherents but there is, in this author's view, no longer the relatively coherent 'feel' for approaches at HE level that if nothing else the positivistic geographers gave. Johnston's concluding comment in *Geography and Geographers* (1979) that 'human geography will continue branching towards anarchy' (p. 189) some could argue has some present-day validity.

The content of school curriculums, it has been argued, remains more directly linked to the 'new geography' of the 1960s than some of the latest HE developments. This author would argue that is generally true for recent GCSE and A level cores and syllabuses as well as the three versions of the National Curriculum.

The evolution of ways of teaching and learning geography through the century can be traced via a number of important publications aimed at the geography teacher. Fairgrieve's *Geography in Schools* (1926), and the UNESCO *Handbook of Suggestions on the Teaching of Geography*, edited by Scarfe (1951), and its successors in 1965, edited by Brouillette, and in 1982, edited by Graves, were significant contributions. Probably most influential in the 1960s were the *Handbook for Geography Teachers* (Long 1964) and *Teaching Geography* (Long and Roberson 1966). These probably represented the last of a particular approach to the content and pedagogy of geography. The 1970s saw an explosion of new books reflecting both the 'new geography' and newer pedagogic approaches. These included Walford (1973), DES (1972, 1978), Graves (1975), Hall (1976), Boden (1976), Marsden (1976) and Graves (1979). At the same time began an influential series of GA handbooks for the geography teacher. The first was *Geography in Secondary Education* (Graves, 1971), followed by Graves (1980), Boardman (1986) and Bailey and Fox (1996). As important was the publication of the *Geographical Teacher* in 1901 by the GA, to become *Geography* in 1927, much regretted by Fairgrieve who feared the dominance of the university world in the affairs of the GA, and in 1975 the first issue of *Teaching Geography*, edited by Patrick Bailey. This professional journal actively sought articles written by practitioners sharing successful classroom experiences and that tradition has been maintained by the GA in its ever widening range of publications geared to supporting teachers. Particular strategies have been well considered by GA publications, for instance enquiry learning (Roberts 1998); simulations (Walford 1996); fieldwork approaches (Job, Day and Smyth 1999); information technology (King 2000); critical thinking (Leat and McAleavy 1998); and values education (Reid 1996).

The 1990s have seen another mini boom in publications aimed at the geography teacher's reflective practice. These include Walford (1999), Battersby (1995), Hacking (1992), Kent, Lambert and Slater (1996), Naish (1992), Slater (1993), Tilbury and Williams (1997), Lambert and Balderstone (2000) and Kent (2000).

A microcosm of changing teaching strategies in geography education is represented by fieldwork developments. In chronological order three distinctive models of fieldwork emerged:

1   field teaching/field excursion;
2   hypothesis testing;
3   framework fieldwork.

Field teaching, sometimes pejoratively called 'Cook's tour' fieldwork, has a long and established tradition. Associated with Wooldridge (1955), the objective of such field teaching was 'to develop an eye for country – i.e. to build up the power, to read a piece of country'. It is to do with a knowledgeable, skilled and often charismatic field teacher, leading a group of students to an area with which he or she is intimately associated. Field notebooks, mini lectures, field sketching and question-and-answer sessions are typical teaching strategies used. Its strengths as an approach include a direct (through the soles of one's feet!) experience of a new environment and having it interpreted in a holistic fashion by an expert. On the downside this can become a tedious and passive exercise.

The hypothesis testing tradition emerged in schools in the 1960s and 70s and is still arguably an entrenched and accepted approach. It reflected the quantitative, spatial-scientific nature of Anglo-American geography of the time. Particularly influential on schools were the writings of Everson (1969, 1973) and Chapallaz *et al.* (1970). Its strengths included a focusing of activity around a testable hypothesis and the rigour of statistical techniques used. On the other hand too much emphasis can be given to data collection focused round highly specific and sometimes socially and environmentally irrelevant statements.

Another approach to emerge has been that of 'framework fieldwork', a term first coined by Hart in 1983 and formalized in the Geography 16–19 project teachers' handbook (Naish, Rawling and Hart 1987). It is to do with fieldwork being 'framed' around a specific people-environment question, issue or problem. Its strengths are that the fieldwork centres on questions and issues of social and environmental concern and appropriate techniques of data collection are utilized where and when appropriate. However, this does not allow for a holistic look at and appreciation of environments nor does it allow specific studies of physical and/or human environments (and related processes) for their own sakes. Other approaches to fieldwork have been of a more sensory nature as proposed by Van Matre (1979) and colleagues, a part of the earth education movement in the USA. Hawkins (1987) echoes some of these suggestions.

Discussions of the evolution of fieldwork strategies are found in Kent (1996), Kent and Foskett (2000) and Job (1999). Job especially challenges fieldworkers to engage the senses of students and to consider fieldwork exercises incorporating the dimension of sustainability.

This author's argument is that overall pedagogic developments in geography education have been similar to those in fieldwork. Each has gone through the regional/descriptive-didactic, spatial-scientific, issues-oriented approaches with the beginnings of an appearance of more critical value-laden geographies. Slater's work in values education while based at the Institute illustrates the engagement of this institution in current movements and debates (for example Slater 1992, 1994a, 1996).

Following new curriculums and related pedagogies there have been equally momentous changes in assessment strategies and styles. The establishment of the 'Assessment Matters' section in *Teaching Geography* reflects the importance of such developments … . Key influences on assessment have been the beginning of GCSE courses incorporating coursework and project work, often fieldwork-based; the influence on assessment schemes of the three Schools Council Geography projects; and the impact of the National Curriculum (as it has evolved in its three forms) on formative assessment and in particular identifying the levels that pupils have attained. For instance, the impact of the Geography 16–19 Project, funded for nine years from 1976 to 1985 and based at the University of London Institute of Education, had its greatest direct impact on the related A level syllabus run by the (then) University of London Examinations Board. At its peak in the mid-1990s, it generated an annual candidature of over 12,000 students. Arguably most innovative has been its decision-making paper first set in 1982.

Geography has always been well supported by a bewildering array of curriculum resources including textbooks, curriculum packs, audio-visuals and ICT resources. The latest *Geography Teachers' Handbook* has a whole section devoted to resources and their use and for many years now the annual GA conference has exhibited an extraordinary array of resources. Recently there has been rapid uptake by geography teachers of information technology. Unusually well financed by governments, there has been an energetic involvement of some geographers in this innovation and an ongoing commitment from the GA. For instance, it published a landmark book in 1980 by Shepherd, Cooper and Walker, who stated that it was their view 'that the computer can make a uniquely varied contribution to the teaching of geography. It can motivate in difficult areas of the curriculum, it can emancipate from the tedium of repetitious manual operations, and it can illuminate concepts and principles in a variety of ways.' The computer page in *Teaching Geography* first appeared in 1983 and its value has been most recently demonstrated by the compilation by King (2000) of a range of articles from what is firmly established as the publication's information and communications technology section. The fascinating story of these ICT developments has been told in various places, for example Kent (1982, 1992) and Freeman (1997). More troubling is the slow pace of uptake of even the most seductive elements of ICT such as multimedia equipment, e-mail and the Internet. Research into the process of uneven take-up includes those by Watson (1997, 2000) and Kent (1997a). Unlike other aspects of curriculum development in geography education, central funding has been available for the new technologies. Several curriculum projects have been based at the Institute of Education and in order have been: Learning Geography with Computers Project (1986–8); Project HIT – Humanities and Information Technology Project (1988–93); Remote Sensing in the Geography National Curriculum Project (1992–5); and Eurogame Project (1998–2000).

As discussed earlier, textbooks tend to reflect the pedagogic and content 'era' of their appearance and in England we have been fortunate to benefit from a wide range of publications though from a declining number of publishers. Some, however, including HMI, have expressed disquiet at the recent Waugh phenomenon whereby a number of textbooks produced by the same author have dominated the market. 'Many schools relied on a limited, and sometimes limiting, single textbook series' (Ofsted 1995). A welcome resurgence of research interest into the ways textbooks are written, purchased and used has occurred recently, for example Kent (1998), Walford (1989), Wright (1996), Marsden (1988), Lidstone (1992) and Graves (forthcoming).

The three major geography projects also produced curriculum resources but it was the Geography for the Young School Leaver (GYSL) Project that published in

1974/5 three theme-based packs. The boxes consisted of pupils' resource sheets, filmstrips, overhead transparencies, audiotapes and teachers' guides. The 'man, land and leisure', 'cities and people' and 'people, place and work' packs were, it was claimed, in over 200 schools within five years, a remarkable achievement. The Geography 14–18 Project did produce curriculum resources, as did the Geography 16–19 Project but they, unlike GYSL, were not fully blown materials production exercises.

Audio-visual aids and now their modern guise of videos, TVs, multimedia machines, slide projectors, data projectors and digital cameras have rightly been a key concern and resource for geography teachers from the earliest days. Some of the earliest audio-visual equipment was used by Fairgrieve in his own designed geography room at William Ellis School; Price used lantern slides at Ruabon Grammar School (Price 1929); and later there was a use of film as described by Fairgrieve (1932). Interest in the visual image was maintained later at the Institute by Long who reported on her research into use of photographs in geography classrooms in her presidential address to the GA in 1970. Most powerful and recent has been the emergence of televisual resources (Durbin 1996), that is, television programmes, whether live broadcasts, recorded or bought on video. As ever such resources, as is true of all teaching resources, need careful monitoring for ideological underpinnings and likely biases.

Research matters

Although strictly curriculum research and development projects, the three main geography projects (GYSL, and 14–18 from 1970 to 1975 and Geography 16–19 from 1976 to 1986) were under much more pressure to 'develop' than 'research'. Their lasting memorial lies in the changes they brought about in assessment styles; new geographies they proposed, i.e. the content including a social and environmental concern geography; engagement of large numbers of pilot school teachers; and various forms of enquiry learning. Although examination candidature for the GYSL and 14–18 courses was limited, their indirect impact on geography education was considerable, not unlike the earlier American High School Geography Project, which though it sold minimal numbers of 'curriculum packs' had considerable indirect impacts. Geography 16–19, based at the Institute with its original team of Naish, Kent and Rawling, had more success in attracting large numbers of candidates to its A level course. Under the leadership of Naish it benefited from the supportive role of Graves, then chair of the geography committee at the Schools Council and head of geography at the Institute. The teachers' handbooks produced by the 14–18 Project (Tolley and Reynolds 1997) and the 16–19 Project (Naish, Rawling and Hart 1987) built on earlier curriculum process concepts and literature and had considerable indirect influence on geography teachers. Boardman's work (1988) evaluates the impact of the GYSL Project, and other pieces of research have evaluated the 16–19 Project (e.g. Stephens 1988) and 14–18 Project (Lane 1980).

Monitoring the geography education research work undertaken has become a much more challenging and large-scale task as research activity has grown over the years. Consequently the first bibliography of British sources (Lukehurst and Graves 1972) describes 1,402 items in 78 pages between 1870 and 1970. The most recent equivalent (Foskett and Marsden 1998) extends over 27 years between 1970 and 1997, contains 5,708 items and is a 209-page publication. As Graves remarked in its foreword:

> ... in 1970 there were probably no more than four general books in print on geographical education that had been published in the UK. Today there are far more. Further, there has been an explosion in the number of articles in specialized journals, and in the number of university theses, dissertations and short monographs in this field. This is a reflection of the increasing number of university tutors specializing in this area and of teachers who have pursued a higher degree and explored educational problems in geography.
>
> (Foskett and Marsden 1998: v)

Started in 1968 by Graves, the Institute of Education MA programme has generated a great deal of MA dissertation research, not to mention academic reflection and professional development (Graves *et al.* 1989) and is arguably the greatest concentration of specialist MA dissertations anywhere in the world. The benefits of undertaking such a course explains why to an extent similar programmes and modules have been developed at the University of Southampton and most recently at the University of Waikato in New Zealand and at the recently established Centre for Geographic Education at Southwest Texas State University. Slater (1999) describes the nature of such higher education and implies its worth. 'The concept of geography education develops from the conversations which arise from teachers teaching geography, thinking about teaching geography, having time to be aware of the many contexts in which they and it are embedded, investigating their teaching and researching and re-searching their beliefs and practices' (p. 299).

Publications sharing research findings and debating methodologies and the like have experienced a mini boom in the last few years. Examples include: *Understanding Geographical and Environmental Education: The role of research* (Williams 1996); a series of monographs, *Reporting Research in Geography Education,* (Slater 1994b); and a *Research Forum* series (Kent 1998). Also there have been a number of research-oriented chapters in a number of recent books or journals, for instance Roberts (2000); Gerber and Williams (2000); Williams (1999); and Marsden (1996). Perhaps more interesting is the direction geography education research might take in the future. Marsden (1996: 21) lists his 'possible agenda':

- ideologies of geographical education;
- the nature of geographical knowledge;
- geography's interface with
    - other National Curriculum subjects; and
    - cross-curricular areas;
- connecting geography at the frontiers with Geography in school;
- systematic historical studies of aspects of geographical education;

- applications of relevant research in other curriculum areas;
- systematic comparative research in aspects of geographical education.

In his chapter Marsden argues for a 'return to the values and rigours of fundamental research' (1996: 15). Indeed Williams (1998) argues that the culture of research in geographical education is only at the 'incipient stage', given his model. Gerber and Williams (2000) argue for 'greater networking amongst geographical educators around the world thus promoting a global geographical education community of scholars'.

Most significantly, in Britain today the government and others are asking how research evidence can inform and has informed practice. Worryingly this author could not think straightaway of examples of pieces of research that had directly influenced practice yet feels that most completed research could influence practice. On reflection, however, the thesis of Biddle, 'An investigation into the use of curriculum theory in the formation of a systems model for the construction and evaluation of secondary school curriculums in England and Wales' (1974), influenced the Geography 16–19 Project; Graves's book on curriculum planning in 1979; and curriculum developments in Australia (Biddle 1976). More recently the research carried out by the Thinking Through Geography Team led by David Leat at the University of Newcastle has led to a publication (Leat 1998) that is actively changing classroom pedagogies (see Bright and Leat 2000). Roberts (2000) has helpfully considered the role of research in supporting teaching and learning.

Subject associations

Since the meeting held at Christ Church, Oxford in 1893 when a resolution was approved to form an association 'for the improvement of the status and teaching of geography', the Geographical Association (GA) so founded has been the leading national subject-teaching organization for geographers. With the aim of 'furthering the study and teaching of geography', it has become an organization with nearly 11,000 members and 60 local branches in England, Wales and Northern Ireland. As recorded in Balchin (1993) the GA over the years has represented the subject, provided support for teachers, and encouraged and published curriculum and subject innovations.

It has successfully undertaken a particularly important role in the era leading up to and including the National Curriculum by making the case for geography in a number of quarters, particularly the political. For instance in the early 1980s it became clear that there would be a national curriculum and Sir Keith Joseph indicated that any subject wishing to be included would have to justify itself. The GA invited Sir Keith to a gathering of its members at King's College, London on 19 June 1985. His address was well received in spite of a highly sceptical audience and he concluded with a request to geographers and the GA to answer seven questions. A first and initial response was sent to Sir Keith in August 1986 and a fuller response published in 1987, both edited by Bailey and Binns. A small delegation of GA officers met with the subsequent secretary of state, Kenneth Baker, in June 1987 by which time he had read the more considered response. These proactive overtures to secretaries of state probably secured Geography's position in the upcoming National Curriculum. Such GA involvement with political actors has continued since the early 1980s with positive effects. A recent example of this is the GA's position statement (1999a), which is clearly of value to the community of geographers, as well as a useful political statement.

The GA's trio of publications, *Primary Geography, Teaching Geography* and *Geography,* support the work of geographers at all levels as does the burgeoning publications list of the Association. In the latest catalogue (1999/2000), for instance, there are categories on: curriculum planning and delivery; fieldwork; information technology; international studies; mentoring; photo resources; place studies; professional development; promoting geography; quiz books; research; and statistics and data.

The GA offers a number of other services to its members including activities at the sixty local branches, a worldwise quiz system, a quarterly newsletter and its three-day annual conference with its major publishers' exhibition, lectures, seminars and workshops. Given the ongoing challenge to the subject of maintaining its place in the curriculum and its popularity with students, some of its recent initiatives have been particularly opportune. Geography Action Week was first launched as an annual event in November 1996. Based on the USA's Geography Awareness Week, it gave schools the chance to give the subject a high profile and show its educational value and interest. In 1996 the week focused round the Land-Use UK Survey; in 1998 round Geography Through the Window; and in 2000 round Coastline 2000 (Spooner and Morron 2000). This initiative has certainly generated a host of original and creative activities upon which schools have engaged (Walford 1997). The Land-Use UK Survey of 1996 (Walford 1999) and the Coastline 2000 survey have rightly given considerable publicity to the involvement of thousands of students in worthwhile survey activities and follow on from the proud traditions of the first and second Land Utilisation surveys directed by Stamp and Coleman respectively.

Membership of the GA has traditionally been from across the constituencies of geography with an ongoing majority from secondary schools. However, in spite of Fairgrieve's fear in the 1920s of the dominance of the university world in the affairs of the Association, the worry nowadays is that it is the exception to the rule when a university academic is a member.

The Royal Geographical Society (now with the Institute of British Geographers) has also played a key role in geography education in England through its various education committees, conferences and publications. Its latest director and secretary, Dr Rita Gardener, is particularly aware of the needs of geography education and has helped set up a number of initiatives, several of which are in partnership with the Geographical Association. Examples of geography education activities include: careers conferences and publications; update conferences for sixth formers with lectures from university geographers; help with expeditions and fieldwork advice particularly with expeditions abroad; a variety of prizes for schools and students; and production of resources based on research expeditions for schools such as Wahiba Sand Sea Slide Set and the Maraca Pack. Because of its strong political connections the RGS–IBG has been especially successful in campaigning for geography and consulting with government and related organizations.

Teacher education

Tutors in university schools of education with responsibility for initial teacher training in geography have over the years tended to plough a lonely furrow in their respective institutions. That was until 1964, when Norman Graves, recently arrived as head of geography at the Institute of Education (from the University of Liverpool), set up the first national-level tutors' meeting so that colleagues could share experiences and expertise. That meeting has now become an annual weekend conference, each year held in a different location. Now arguably one of the best attended and established of the tutors' groups, in recent years the agenda has reflected the twofold concerns of the age: firstly, the standards for the award of QTS as defined by law, how these can be 'delivered' and the related Ofsted inspection process; and secondly, sharing of research findings. The latter has always been an element of such annual meetings but this now assumes rather greater import with university academics subject to the four-yearly research assessment exercise (RAE).

In-service education and training (INSET) or, as it is now known, continuing professional development has had a patchy history. There have always been one-off lectures by academics at local GA meetings and the same local GA branches laid on popular workshop conferences at the time of the 'new geography' in the 1960s and 1970s. But most progressive and supportive INSET until the 1980s was under the auspices of the education authorities until the Thatcher government diverted funding away from them. This put greater pressure on individual schools or groups of schools to provide INSET opportunities for geography staff. It also did the same for the national, regional and local levels of the GA. Similarly institutions of higher education increased the number of short, one-day or half-day courses for teachers in their catchment areas. A particular yet important offshoot of that was the establishment in 1968 of an MA course at the Institute of Education, which was a genuinely critical, reflective higher degree with clear practical benefits to geography teachers. That continues and in 2001 also became a distance learning programme.

Sadly, however, it is this writer's view that such reflection and professional development are not sufficiently widespread for most geography teachers. I believe professional development of teachers should be ongoing, well resourced and of a top priority. It is not! Teachers should be regularly offered the refreshment and renewal a sabbatical or teacher-fellowship brings. They are not! Well-resourced in-service education and training are fundamental to developing teacher expertise and boosting morale. Sadly, such developments happen all too rarely. The extreme difficulty faced by teachers wishing to undertake vital and ongoing professional development is damaging to both their health and that of the system. There is insufficient 'space' for teachers to allow them to develop professionally (Kent 1997b:

301). Perhaps recently announced National Standards for Subject Leaders (TTA 1998) and their concomitant for Geography (GA 1999b) might provide a boost for a better resourced continuing professional development.

International developments

Geography educators (particularly university staff) in Britain, partly through colonial legacies, have had strong research and academic links with other parts of the English-speaking world, especially North America, Australasia, parts of South and South-East Asia and parts of Africa. But it was the establishment of the Geography Education Commission of the International Geographical Union (IGU) in 1952 by Neville Scarfe that formalizes relationships between colleagues world-wide by the holding of major four-yearly commission conferences as well as a number of intervening regional conferences. So, for instance, the main commission meetings in the last few years have been in Brisbane (1988); Boulder (1992); The Hague (1996); and Kyongju (South Korea) (2000).

The chair of the Commission has played a key leadership role in the organization so Scarfe (1952–56) and Graves (1972–80) were influential as result. As a subset of the Commission (usually consisting of 10 commissioners), Graves established in the 1970s the British Sub Committee, which ran conferences and engaged in research activities. The chair's position was taken over by Naish in 1984 and by Kent in 1997. Recent conferences run by the British Sub Committee were those in 1997 on 'values in geography education' and in 1999 on 'geography and environmental education'. Publications of the group include, for example: teaching materials (Butt *et al.* 1998); bibliographies (Foskett and Marsden 1998); conference proceedings (Kent 2000) and research findings (Naish 1990).

The history of the IGU Commission on Geography Education is told by Wise (1992), too late to relate the important achievement of the Commission under Haubrich's leadership (1988–96) of the publication (in 1992) of the *Journal of International Research in Geographical and Environmental Education* (IRGEE), edited by Gerber and Lidstone. British geography educators have written a good deal in their new academic journal. For instance, the Forum in Volume 8, Number 3,1999 was co-ordinated by Marsden in which seven other British geographers report on 'Geographical education in England and Wales: the state of play at the end of the millennium'.

Probably the most significant achievement of the Commission was the publication of the *International Charter on Geographical Education*, first published in 1992 and later in 21 languages in 1994. It was published in the April 1995 issue of *Teaching Geography*. Its significance is that it offers a curriculum framework and justification for those colleagues around the world attempting to establish or at least strengthen geographical education in their system. In some senses it 'spread the word' about geography education in the way that the UNESCO source books did in 1965 (Brouillette) and 1982 (Graves).

Challenges for the subject

Relatively recently Bailey suggested that 'Geography has never before achieved such a high status in the British curriculum' (1991: 2) but it can be argued that since then its position is far from firmly secured and established. The subject needs to meet a number of challenges successfully, some of which have been identified in other places (for example Kent 1997b; Marsden 1997; and Carter 1999). Some of these challenges include:

- maintaining its popularity in all levels of the system;
- making the case effectively for the value and study of geography;
- communicating more effectively the nature of modern geography, offsetting stereotypical and ill-informed images (Kent 1999);
- improving communications between geographers (Kent and Smith 1997);
- maintaining the fieldwork tradition;
- bringing curriculums and school-based geographers up to date with the latest geographies at HE level;
- improving the quality of thinking in geography classrooms (see Leat 1998);
- raising the quality and standards of KS3 geography since there are some suggestions from recent Ofsted inspections that geography does less than well (Ofsted 1998);
- to ensure future curriculums satisfy the needs of 5–19-year-olds (such as in the GeoVisions Project – Robinson, Carter and Sinclair 1999);
- geography's contribution to a rethought 14–19 curriculum with a stress on numeracy, literacy, citizenship, sustainable development and personal, social and moral development;
- for Geography courses to move beyond the strictures of National Curriculum Geography (the observant reader will have noticed minimal reference to it in this chapter since the author feels it has almost obsessively been fully considered in other places);
- that future Geography curriculums learn the lessons from 100 years' experience of teaching the subject in schools – the lessons from history, some of which are outlined in Boardman and McPartland (1993a, b, c and d: 161) and indeed in this chapter.

It is to be hoped geography and geographers rise to these changes and challenges. They have so far.

References

Bailey, P. (1991) *Securing the Place of Geography in the National Curriculum of English and Welsh Schools*, Sheffield: The Geographical Association.
Bailey, P. and Binns, T. (eds) (1986) *A Case for Geography*, Sheffield: The Geographical Association.
Bailey, P. and Binns, T. (eds) (1987) *A Case for Geography*, Sheffield: The Geographical Association.

Bailey, P. and Fox, P. (1996) *Geography Teachers' Handbook*, Sheffield: The Geographical Association.

Balchin, W.G.V. (1993) *The Geographical Association, The First Hundred Years 1893–1993*, Sheffield: The Geographical Association.

Battersby, J. (1995) *Teaching Geography at Key Stage 3*, Cambridge: Chris Kington Publishing.

Biddle, D. (1974) 'An investigation into the use of curriculum theory in the formation of a systems model for the construction and evaluation of secondary school curricula in England and Wales', unpublished PhD thesis, Institute of Education, University of London, London.

Biddle, D. (1976) *Translating Curriculum Theory into Practice in Geographical Education: A systems approach*, Victoria: Australian Geography Teachers Association.

Boardman, D. (ed.) (1986) *Handbook for Geography Teachers*, Sheffield: The Geographical Association.

Boardman, D. (ed.) (1988) 'The impact of the Curriculum Project: geography for the young school leaver', *Educational Review*, Occasional Publications, 14, Birmingham: University of Birmingham.

Boardman, D. and McPartland, M. (1993a) 'Building on the foundations: 1893–1945', *Teaching Geography* 18(1): 3–6.

Boardman, D. and McPartland, M. (1993b) 'From regions to models: 1944–69', *Teaching Geography* 18(2): 65–9.

Boardman, D. and McPartland, M. (1993c) 'Innovations and change: 1970–82', *Teaching Geography* 18(3): 117–20.

Boardman, D. and McPartland, M. (1993d) 'Towards centralisation: 1983–93', *Teaching Geography* 18(4: 159–62.

Boden, P. (1976) *Developments in Geography Teaching*, London: Open Books.

Bradford, M.G. and Kent, W.A. (1977) *Human Geography: Theories and their applications*, Oxford: Oxford University Press.

Briggs, K. (1972) *Introducing Transportation Networks*, London: University of London Press.

Bright, N. and Leat, D. (2000) 'Towards a new professionalism', in W.A. Kent (ed.) *Reflective Practice in the Teaching of Geography*, London: Sage.

Brouillette, B. (1965) *Source Book for Geography Teaching*, Paris: Longman/UNESCO.

Butt, G. *et al.* (1998) *Living and Working in Berlin*, Sheffield: The Geographical Association.

Carter, R. (1999) 'Connecting geography: an agenda for action', *Geography* 84(4): 289–97.

Chapallaz, D. P. *et al.* (1970) 'Hypothesis testing in field studies', *Teaching Geography*, 11, Sheffield: The Geographical Association.

Chorley, R. J. and Haggett, P. (eds) (1965) *Frontiers in Geographical Teaching*, London: Methuen.

Chorley, R. J. and Haggett, P. (eds) (1967) *Models in Geography*, London: Methuen.

Cole, J. P. and Beynon, N. J. (1968) *New Ways in Geography*, Oxford: Basil Blackwell,.

Department of Education and Science (DES) (1972) *New Thinking in School Geography Education*, Pamphlet 59, London: HMSO.

Department of Education and Science (1978) *The Teaching of Ideas in Geography Matters for Discussion: Some suggestions for the middle and secondary years of education*, London: HMSO.

Dinkele, G., Cotterell, S. and Thorn, I. (1976) *Harrap's Reformed Geography*, London: Harrap.

Durbin, C. (1996) 'Teaching geography with televisual resources', in P. Bailey and P. Fox (eds) *Geography Teachers' Handbook*, Sheffield: The Geographical Association.

Everson, J.A. (1969) 'Some aspects of teaching geography through fieldwork', *Geography*, 54(1): 64–73.

Everson, J.A. (1973) 'Fieldwork in school geography', in R. Walford (ed.) *New Directions in Geography Teaching*, London: Longman.

Everson, J.A. and FitzGerald, B.P. (1969) *Settlement Patterns*, London: Longman.

Fairgrieve, J. (1926) *Geography in School*, University of London Press, London.

Fairgrieve, J. (1932) 'The use of film in teaching', *Geography*, 17: 129–40.

Fairgrieve J. and Young, E. (1939) *Real Geography*, London: Philip.

Foskett, N. and Marsden, B. (eds) (1998) *A Bibliography of Geographical Education 1970–1997*, Sheffield: The Geographical Association.

Freeman, D. (1997) 'Using information technology and new technologies in geography', in D. Tilbury and M. Williams (eds) *Teaching and Learning Geography*, London: Routledge.

Geographical Association (1999a) 'Geography in the curriculum: a position statement from the GA', *Geography* 84(2): 164–7.

Geographical Association (1999b) *Leading Geography: National Standards for Geography Teachers in Secondary Schools*, Sheffield: The Geographical Association.

Gerber, R. and Williams, M. (2000) 'Overview and international perspectives', in W.A. Kent (ed.) *Reflective Practice in the Teaching of Geography*, London: Sage.

Graves, N.J. (1971) *Geography in Secondary Education*, Sheffield: The Geographical Association .

Graves, N J. (1975) *Geography in Education*, London: Heinemann Educational Books.

Graves, N.J. (1979) *Curriculum Planning in Geography*, London: Heinemann,.

Graves, N.J. (1980) *Geographical Education in Secondary Schools*, Sheffield: The Geographical Association,.

Graves, N.J. (1982) *New UNESCO Source Book for Geography Teaching*, Paris: Longman/The UNESCO Press.

Graves, N.J. (1995) *Geography in Education*, London: Heinemann Educational Books.

Graves, N.J. (forthcoming) *Two Hundred Years of Geography Textbooks*, publisher unknown.

Graves, N. *et al.* (1989) *Research in Geography Education: MA dissertations 1968–1988*, Institute of Education, London: University of London.

Hacking, E. (1992) *Geography into Practice*, Harlow: Longman.

Haggett, P. (1965) *Locational Analysis in Human Geography*, London: St. Martin's Press.

Hall, D. (1976) *Geography and the Geography Teacher*, London: Allen and Unwin.

Hart, C. (1983) *Fieldwork the 16–19 Way*, Geography 16–19 Project Occasional Paper, Institute of Education, London: University of London.

Hawkins, G. (1987) 'From awareness to participation: new directions with the outdoor experience', *Geography* 72(3): 217–22.

Herbertson, A. J. (1905) 'The major natural regions', *Geographical Journal*, 25.

Job, D. (1999) *New Directions in Geographical Fieldwork*, Cambridge: Cambridge University Press.

Job, D., Day, C. and Smyth, T. (1999) *Beyond the Bikesheds: Fresh approaches to fieldwork in the school locality*, Sheffield: The Geographical Association.

Johnston, R.J. (1979) *Geography and Geographers*, London: Arnold.

Kent, W.A. (1982) 'The challenge of the microcomputer', in N. Graves *et al.* (ed.) *Geography in Education Now*, Bedford Way Papers, 13, Institute of Education, London: University of London.

Kent, W.A. (1992) 'The new technology and geographical education', in M. Naish (ed.) *Geography and Education, National and International Perspectives*, London: Institute of Education, University of London.

Kent, W.A. (1996) A strategy for geography fieldwork, in Van der Schee *et al.* (eds) *Innovation in Geographical Education*, 167–77, Utrecht/Amsterdam: International Geographical Union.

Kent, W.A. (1997a) 'Process and pattern of a curriculum innovation', unpublished PhD thesis, Institute of Education, London: University of London.

Kent, W.A. (1997b) 'Challenging geography: a personal view', *Geography*, 82 (4).

Kent, W.A. (1998) *Research Forum 1: Textbooks*, International Geographical Union with the Institute of Education, London: University of London.

Kent, W.A. (1999) 'Image and reality – how do others see us?', Guest editorial in *International Research in Geographical and Environmental Education* 8(2): 103–7.

Kent, W.A. (ed.) (2000) *Reflective Practice in the Teaching of Geography*, London: Sage.

Kent, W.A. and Foskett, N. (2000) 'Fieldwork in the school geography curriculum – pedagogical issues and development', in P. Gerber and G.K. Chuan (eds) *Fieldwork in Geography: Reflections, Perspectives and Actions*, Dordrecht: Kluwer Academic Publishers.

Kent, W.A. and Jackson, S. (eds) (2000) *Geography and Environmental Education: International perspectives*, International Geographical Union with the Institute of Education, London: University of London.

Kent, W.A., Lambert, D.M. and Slater, F.A. (eds) (1996) *Geography in Education: Viewpoints on teaching and learning*, Cambridge: Cambridge University Press.

Kent, W.A. and Smith, M. (1997) 'Links between geography in schools and higher education', in A. Powell (ed.) *Handbook of Post 16 Geography*, The Geographical Association, Sheffield.

King, S. (ed.) (2000) *High-Tech Geography ICT in Secondary Schools*, Sheffield: The Geographical Association.

Lambert, D.M. (1996) 'Assessing pupils' attainment and supporting learning', in W.A. Kent, D.M. Lambert and F.A. Slater (eds) *Geography in Education: Viewpoints on teaching and learning*, 260–89, Cambridge: Cambridge University Press.

Lambert, D.M. (2000) 'Using assessment to support learning', in W. A. Kent (ed.) *Reflective Practice in the Teaching of Geography*, London: Sage.

Lambert, D.M. and Balderstone, D. (2000) *Learning to Teach Geography in the Secondary School*, London: Routledge.

Lane, J. A. (1980) 'An evaluation of some aspects of the Kent Consortium 14–18 Geography Project', unpublished MA dissertation, Institute of Education, London: University of London.

Leat, D. (1998) *Thinking Through Geography*, Cambridge: Chris Kington Publishing.

Leat, D. and McAleavy, T. (1998) 'Critical thinking in the humanities', *Teaching Geography*, 23(3): 112–14.

Lidstone, T. (1992) 'In defence of textbooks', in M. Naish (ed.) *Geography and Education: National and international perspectives*, 177–93, Institute of Education, London: University of London.

Long, M. (ed.) (1964) *Handbook for Geography Teachers*, Methuen, London.

Long, M. and Roberson, B. S. (1966) *Teaching Geography*, Heinemann Educational Books, London.

Lukehurst, C.T. and Graves, N.J. (1972) *Geography in Education: A bibliography of British sources 1870–1970*, Sheffield: The Geographical Association.

Marsden, B. (1996) 'Geography', in P. Gordon (ed.) *A Guide to Educational Research*, London: The Woburn Press.

Marsden, W.E. (1976) *Evaluating the Geography Curriculum*, London: Oliver and Boyd.

Marsden, W. E. (1988) 'Continuity and change in geography textbooks: perspectives from the 1930s to the 1960s', *Geography*, 74(4): 327–43.

Marsden, W.E. (1995) *Geography 11–16: Rekindling good practice*, London: David Fulton.

Marsden, W.E. (1996) 'The place of geography in the school curriculum: an historical overview, 1886–1976', in D. Tilbury and M. Williams (eds) *Teaching and Learning Geography*, 7–14, London: Routledge.

Marsden, W.E. (1997) 'On taking the geography out of geographical education: some historical pointers', *Geography*, 82(3): 241–52.

Ministry of Education (1960) *Geography and Education*, London: HMSO.

Naish, M.C. (ed.) (1990) *Experiences of Centralisation*, International Geographical Union with the Institute of Education, London: University of London.

Naish, M.C. (ed.) (1992) *Geography and Education: National and international perspectives*, Institute of Education, London: University of London.

Naish, M.C., Rawling, E. and Hart, C. (1987) *Geography 16–19: The contribution of a curriculum project to 16–19 education*, London: Longman.

Ofsted (1995) *Geography: A review of inspection findings, 1993/94*, London: HMSO.

Ofsted (1998) *Secondary Education: A review of secondary schools in England, 1993–97*, London: HMSO.

Preece, D.M. and Wood, H.R.B. (1938) *The Foundations of Geography*, London: University Tutorial Press.

Price, E.S. (1929) 'The lantern and the geography room', *Geography*, 15: 294–8.

Reid, A. (1996) 'Exploring values in sustainable development', *Teaching Geography*, 21(4): 168–72.

Roberts, M. (1998) 'The nature of geographical enquiry at Key Stage 3', *Teaching Geography*, 23(4).

Roberts, M. (2000) 'The role of research in supporting teaching and learning', in W.A. Kent (ed.) *Reflective Practice in the Teaching of Geography*, London: Sage.

Robinson, R., Carter, C. and Sinclair, S. (1999) 'Wiser people – better world?', in *Teaching Geography*, 24(1): 10–13.

Rolfe, J, *et al.* (1974) *Oxford Geography Project*, Oxford: Oxford University Press.

Rushby, J.G., Bell, J. and Dybeck, M.W. (1967) *Study Geography*, London: Longman.

Scarfe, N.V. (1951) *A Handbook of Suggestions on the Teaching of Geography*, Paris: UNESCO.

Shepherd, I.D.H., Cooper, Z.A. and Walker, D.R.F. (1980) *Computer Assisted Learning*, London: CET with the Geographical Association.

Slater, F.A. (1992) ' … to travel with a different view', in M. Naish (ed.) *Geography and Education: National and international perspectives*, 97–113, Institute of Education, London: University of London.

Slater, F.A. (1993) *Learning Through Geography*, Indiana: National Council for Geographic Education.

Slater, F.A. (1994a) 'Education through geography: knowledge, understanding, values and culture', *Geography*, 79(2): 147–63.

Slater, F.A. (ed.) (1994b) *Reporting Research in Geography Education*, Monographs, 1, Institute of Education, London: University of London.

Slater, F.A. (1996) 'Values: towards mapping their locations, in a geography education', in W.A. Kent, D.M. Lambert and F.A. Slater (eds) *Geography in Education: Viewpoints on teaching and learning*, 200–30, Cambridge: Cambridge University Press.

Slater, F.A. (1999) 'Notes on geography education at higher degree level in the United Kingdom', *International Research in Geographical and Environmental Education*, 8(3): 295–99.

Spooner, D. and Morron, M. (2000) 'Coastline 2000: a survey for the new millennium', *Geography*, 85(l): 69–70.

Stamp, L.D. (1957) 'Major natural regions: Herbertson after 50 years', *Geography*, 42: 201–16.

Stephens, P. (1988) 'An enquiry into the extent to which the Geography 16–19 Project has fulfilled its objectives with regard to its enquiry approach to learning and its distinctive approach to geographical education', unpublished MA dissertation, Institute of Education, London: University of London.

Teacher Training Agency (TTA) (1998) *National Standards for Subject Leaders*, London: TTA.

Tilbury, D. and Williams, M. (eds) (1997) *Teaching and Learning Geography*, London: Routledge.

Tolley, H. and Reynolds, J.B. (1997) *Geography 14–18: A handbook for school-based curriculum development*, Basingstoke: Macmillan Education.

Van Matre, S. (1979) *Sunshine Earth – An Acclimatisation Program for Outdoor Learning*, American Camping Association.

Walford, R. (ed.) (1973) *New Directions in Geography Teaching*, Harlow: Longman.

Walford, R. (1989) 'On the frontier with the new model army: geography publishing from the 1960s to the 1990s', *Geography*, 74(4): 308–20.

Walford, R. (1991) *Viewpoints on Geography Teaching*, Harlow: Longman.

Walford, R. (1996) 'The simplicity of simulation', in *Geography Teachers' Handbook*, eds P. Bailey and P. Fox, The Geographical Association, Sheffield.

Walford, R. (ed.) (1997) *Land Use – UK. A Survey for the 21st Century*, Sheffield: The Geographical Association.

Walford, R. (1999) 'The 1996 Geographical Association Land-Use Survey: a "geographical commitment"', *International Research in Geographical and Environmental Education*, 8(3): 291–4.

Walford, R. (2000) *Geography in British Schools 1850–2000: Making a world of difference*, London: Woburn Press.

Watson, D. (1997) Information technology in geography classes: the appearance and reality of change, unpublished PhD thesis, School of Education, King's College, London: University of London.

Watson, D. (2000) 'Issues raised by research into ICT and geography education', in W.A. Kent (ed.) *Research Forum 2: Information and communications technology*, International Geographical Union with Institute of Education, London: University of London.

Williams, M. (ed.) (1996) *Understanding Geographical and Environmental Education: The role of research*, London: Cassell Education.

Williams, M. (1998) 'Review of research in geographical education', in W. A. Kent (ed.) *Research Forum 1: Textbooks*, 1–10, Institute of Education, London: University of London.

Williams, M. (1999) 'Research in geographical education', *International Research in Geographical and Environmental Education*, 8(3): 301–04.

Wise, M.J. (1992) 'International geography, the IGU Commission on Education', Chapter 15, in M. Naish (ed.) *Geography and Education: National and international perspectives*, Institute of Education, London: University of London.

Wooldridge, S. W. (1955) 'The status of geography and the role of fieldwork', *Geography*, 40: 73–83.

Wright, D. (1996) 'Textbook research in geographical and environmental education', in M. Williams (ed.) *Understanding Geographical and Environmental Education*, 172–82, London: Cassell.

2 School Geography in England 1991–2001

The politics and practicalities of curriculum change

Eleanor Rawling

Why 1991?

1991 was a key year for school Geography. In that year the Statutory Order for Geography in the National Curriculum was published. To achieve Geography's acceptance as a NC subject and its 'place in the sun', the Geographical Association (GA) had campaigned vigorously and many hailed this as a significant triumph for the subject community (Bailey 1991). In fact, geographers paid a high price for this victory. With its five traditionally focused attainment targets and 183 content-based statements of attainment, the 1991 Geography Order seemed to signal a move back to the kind of informational/utilitarian tradition from which Goodson (1998) claims the geography community had worked so hard to break away since 1950. The overlapping programmes of study did not make a workable curriculum framework and the Order seemed to ignore features such as key ideas, geographical enquiry and issue-based investigations in Geography, characteristic of the previous twenty years of curriculum development (Rawling 1992; Lambert 1994; Roberts 1991). Stephen Ball (1994), in his work on the influence of the New Right, commented on the consequences of this repositioning of the Geography curriculum as he saw it:

> With its undertones of assimilation, nationalism and consensus around the regressive re-establishment of fictional past glories, restorationist National Curriculum geography isolates students in time and space, cutting them off from the realities of the single European market, global economic dependencies and inequalities, and the ecological crisis.

This experience of complete curriculum upheaval was shared by many other curriculum subjects, as a result of the processes set in motion by the Education Reform Act. Ball (1990) examines the conflicts which characterised the production of the Mathematics and English Orders, and other authors have investigated the experience of non-core subjects (e.g. Evans and Penney 1995 for PE; Phillips 1998 for History). In each case, as Ball points out, contestation over the detail of subject knowledge represented a power struggle for domination and for prestige by different communities and groups within the educational state. Specifically, in the 1988–93 period, the dominant group influencing educational policy was the 'New Right'. In the case of geography, the government-appointed Geography Working Group was steered towards a political solution (Rawling 1992). Thus geography had won the status battle but apparently lost the ideological arguments to the 'New Right' and to what Ball and subsequent writers have called 'cultural restorationism' with its emphasis on discrete and traditional forms of subject content and a pedagogy of didactic transmission.

It can be argued that the subsequent curriculum history of school Geography in the 1990s reveals the substantial cost of this ideological defeat. The subject community suffered a blow to its confidence and morale, particularly those curriculum projects and individuals which had moved into more progressive modes of operation. It also had to devote considerable creative energy to supporting teachers and to redressing this formulation, with some success, as this paper will show. It might also be argued that, as a consequence of its residual image as merely a utilitarian and informational subject, school Geography in the 1990s has not been recognised as a significant 'frontline' contributor to the curriculum. It is always the first candidate for reduction, optional status or dis-application when more important initiatives require space, as recent policy decisions over KS1, 2 and 4 reveal. It has also been constrained from playing its full part in debates about broader initiatives – for example, citizenship, sustainable development education and thinking skills.

Given this situation, it is tempting to assume that all subsequent curriculum changes have been minor. In both the Dearing Review (1993–5) and the QCA Review (1998–9) the emphasis has been on reduction, simplification and improving manageability and there has not been the opportunity for a major rethink, certainly for any non-core subject (though the Literacy and Numeracy strategies have necessitated reformulation for English and Maths). Much of the New Right ideology (subject-based curriculum, emphasis on content) has remained embedded in the NC structure. Indeed Kelly (1999) suggests that curriculum change in the 1990s has been 'no more than tinkering with content, attainment targets, profile components, levels and so on ...' (p. 101). Neverthless, the Geography Order has undergone significant restructuring, and seen the re-emergence of progressive educational features such as geographical enquiry, values and a global dimension (though significantly geography has not managed to improve its curriculum status, particularly at KS4). Helsby and Mc Culloch note that

> disputes over detail (of the NC) should not be seen as simply teething problems, as the sponsors of the National Curriculum would no doubt have preferred to think, but as continuing contestation over the principles and practices involved.
>
> (Helsby and McCulloch 1996: 8)

The remainder of this chapter will analyse the continuing contestation over the Geography curriculum. In so doing it will also raise more general issues about the politics and practicalities of curriculum change in this period since 1991. Many studies of educational policy-making (Dale 1989; Ball 1990; Ball 1994; Carr and Hartnett 1996) have focused on analysing aspects of the 1988 Education Reform Act, particularly the National Curriculum, and in this way have elucidated the characteristics and impacts of policy-making for the period from the mid-1980s to about 1993. Studies of other National Curriculum subjects (Evans and Penney 1995; Phillips 1998) have also tended to focus on the construction and implementation of the original National Curriculum documents. This chapter will seek to move the debate forward by looking at the processes and impacts of two National Curriculum Reviews and the changing policy trends and structures becoming apparent under 'New Labour'.

The policy cycle applied to the changing Geography curriculum

Bowe, Ball and Gold (1992) warn of the dangers of following a linear approach to policy studies in education, explaining that this leads to a separation of policy generation from policy implementation, as if policy is merely 'what gets done to people'. They propose instead recognition of a continuous policy cycle, comprising three policy contexts: the context of influence, in which interested parties struggle to dominate the prevailing discourses; the context of text production in which the official policy texts (e.g. NC Order, non-statutory guidance) are produced; and the context of practice, in which the official policy is received and subject to interpretation and to some extent 're-creation'. Evans and Penney (1995) have traced the sequence of policy text production for a National Curriculum subject (PE) but it has not been used before to analyse and compare the subsequent impact of two National Curriculum Reviews. Table 2.1 (overleaf) shows in overview how the policy contexts can be applied to Geography and should be referred to, alongside the text of this section. The overlapping nature of each context is significant – effectively the context of practice for one National Curriculum is the context of influence for the next. Note that the dates are notional – the 'contexts' are not precise periods.

The first review of the National Geography Curriculum

The 1991–3 period (the context of practice for the first NC and the context of influence for the Dearing Review) was dominated by the pragmatic realisation that the national Geography framework, as outlined in the 1991 Order, was virtually unworkable in curriculum and assessment terms. Initial reactions both of the geography community as a whole and of individual teachers, focused on the sheer weight of prescription, on the limiting nature of the 'information about the world' view of geography, and on the apparently alien ideology it incorporated. However, as more evidence became available about implementation from Ofsted (1993a and b), so deeper structural concerns assumed greater significance. Despite the conclusion that – 'the way in which the AT/PoS structure has been interpreted makes it difficult to plan good quality work' (NCC 1992), neither the National Curriculum

Table 2.1 The Policy Cycle Approach applied to the Geography National Curriculum

	Original Geography NC (1991 Order)	Dearing Review of NC (1995 Order)	QCA Review of NC (1999 Order)	Future Curriculum Review/Change?
Context of influence	New Right 'discourse of derision' Geography gains a place in the curriculum but unresolved issues about process/content	Overwhelming evidence of faulty Order (NCC/Ofsted) Political imperative to 'rescue' the NC and Dearing special para 3.49 about geography	Relief at structural changes and flexibility Re-emergence of progressive educational influence via SCAA/QCA publications	Government priorities at KS1/2/4 constrain Geography further? 'Command curriculum' approach threatens teacher professionalism?
Context of text production	Direct political control over Geography Working Group and intervention by Secretary of State with Draft Order Subject professional influence marginalised	Pragmatic single-focus exercise – 'simplify' SCAA runs subject advisory groups, with strong central control of task + outcomes Subject community has constrained influence	Multi-focus exercise – simplify + new agenda QCA subject teams given freedom to draw on subject task groups + consultants Labour's new agenda is a 'no-go' area for QCA	Rolling programme of projects instead of 2005 review – Geography included from 2001 Existing strategies (e.g. Literacy KS1/2, KS3 Strategy) preempt decisions?
Context of practice	Severe implementation problems especially primary KS4 curriculum never implemented and Geography optional after 1993–4	Improvements in practice noted by SCAA/Ofsted Subject associations raise profile and membership and work together	Big issues will be: Re-establishing high quality geography at KS1, 2 and 3 Supply of geography teachers Changing 14–19 curriculum context	Either Creative interpretation of NC by geography community ensures contribution to curriculum priorities Or continued decline in quality/status
Overall message	An imposed political solution produces a 'culturally restored' Geography curriculum	A pragmatic solution results in an improved simplified Geography curriculum framework	Professional influence allows consolidation in curriculum detail but fails to improve status	?

Note
The 1991 and 1995 Geography requirements were both implemented in the same year that they became statutory (i.e. September 1991 and September 1995). The 1999 requirements received statutory status in 1999 but were not implemented until September 2000. Hence they are often referred to as the National Curriculum 2000.

Council (NCC) nor the Schools Examination and Assessment Council (SEAC) were able to provide much immediate support. As Ball points out (1994, p. 28) the New Right actually tightened its grip on policy-making in the 1991–3 period. NCC's 1991 non-statutory guidance for Geography was the subject of bitter conflicts between the Geography Task Group (professional geography educationalists called in to advise NCC) and the right-wing-dominated NCC Council members. It was later rated by an independent evaluation as 'the least useful' of NCC's INSET materials (Social Surveys, Gallup Poll 1992). In SEAC, under Lord Griffiths' chairmanship, there was a continuing push from the centre to extend bureaucratic control, in the form of national assessment instruments. For geography, work began on optional KS1 SATs, KS3 tests, KS4 National Curriculum-based GCSE criteria, despite SEAC Geography Committee's own recognition of the intractable problems the requirements provided for assessment (1990). In the event, both KS3 tests and the NC-related GCSE criteria were abandoned in 1993, but for political rather than curriculum reasons.

It would have been difficult to ignore the mounting evidence in 1991–3 of the structural inadequacies of the Geography Order. The Geographical Association (GA), whilst explicitly recognising these faults, took the line that constructive support to geography teachers on making the most of the National Curriculum (Rawling 1991) was the best way to maintain and promote good geography, at the same time as campaigning for change. Both the GA and the Council of British Geography (COBRIG) made strong representations to Sir Ron Dearing, attempting to read the political climate by accepting that major change to content was not on offer, but suggesting that reformulation of the AT/PoS relationship was a necessary first step, before slimming could be addressed. Such lobbying, backed by Ofsted evidence, proved effective. The Final Dearing Report (1993) contained a separate paragraph (4.39, p. 36) which gave special dispensation for structural amendments to be made to the Geography Order, despite the fact that the whole exercise was publicised as merely 'slimming down'.

The process of text production in the Dearing Review (December 1993–September 1995) was handled not by the Department for Education (DfE) but by the School Curriculum and Assessment Authority (SCAA) newly created in October 1993 as a direct result of the Dearing recommendations. Teacher discontent 1992/3 meant that, for negative reasons, the brief was slimming down the over-weighted National Curriculum structure and enhancing flexibility for teachers. For geography, there was the added necessity for structural change. Subject advisory groups were set up to undertake the threefold task of identifying essential knowledge, understanding and skills from the original subject orders, redrafting the programmes of study more simply and writing the new level descriptions (SCAA 1993). SCAA was anxious to keep a tight rein on individual subject enthusiasms (seen by many as a problem of the original exercise) and to maintain overarching consistency and coherence. Hence there were also powerful Key Stage Advisory Groups acting in a cross-checking and supervisory capacity at every stage of the work. Although subject officers were nominally in charge of the development work, control was also exerted centrally from SCAA by means of: set guidelines for membership of the subject advisory groups; chairing of each subject advisory group by an assistant chief executive of SCAA (in Geography's case, Keith Weller – also responsible for Science and the KS4 groups); common proforma for undertaking and reporting the development work; and the existence of a SCAA Council observer on each subject advisory group (for Geography, Shawar Sadeque). The work was all tightly managed and controlled within the short timescale (Jan–March 1994), before the proposals went to the Secretary of State (April) and out for consultation in May 1994. Although some subjects may have chafed under these restrictions, for Geography the situation could only improve from the low point of 1991. The subject advisory group, with strong GA and teacher representation, was fully supportive of the thrust towards simplification and may even be said to have gained from the tightly focused task, given the clear recognition of the Geography Order's problems (Battersby 1995). The revised Geography Order may be described as a pragmatic solution to the 1991 Order. It provided a new structure for the programmes of study, clarified the relationship between the ATs and PoS and gave partial recognition to geographical enquiry (though, significantly, this politically sensitive term was not actually used in the Order).

The second review of the National Geography Curriculum

The context of practice for the 1995 Order was also the context of influence for the QCA Review, and for the subject community the emphasis was on professional consolidation. Roger Carter, Chair of the GA's Education Standing Committee, expressed the relief of much of the profession:

> The revised National Curriculum for geography is good news. Most of the problems identified in the earlier Order have been addressed, although some with more success than others. Teachers will now be able to work with programmes of study that are more realistic in content terms, more straightforward in presentation, and clearer about the relationship between Key Stages.
> (Roger Carter, *TES*, November 1994)

For the National Curriculum as a whole, the Dearing Review had shifted the emphasis away from 'delivery' and towards teachers' responsibilities for developing a minimum national framework. Given this, SCAA was able to play a very different role to that of SEAC and NCC pre-1993. The appointments of Sir Ron Dearing as its first chair (from April 1994), Gillian Shepherd as Secretary of State for Education (from July 1994), and Nick Tate as Chief Executive of SCAA (from October 1994) signalled the beginning of a period in which the curriculum and assessment body was able to give greater stress to curriculum matters and, as Dainton (1996) suggests, to operate more consultatively. Significantly, the Corporate Plan for 1995–8 (SCAA 1995a) recognised, in Aim 1, the need to identify and undertake 'development work to support the National Curriculum'. The SCAA (and later QCA) Geography Team was able to develop a strategy for subject support and an increasingly fruitful relationship with the subject associations and the geography teaching community. This was reflected during the 1994–9 period in regular updating meetings, publication of a termly subject 'Update', and involvement of subject experts and consultative groups in all its work. SCAA/QCA officers also attended subject association committee meetings as observers. Another result was the production of a whole range of curriculum-focused guidance publications. Exemplification of Standards for Geography at KS3 (SCAA 1996a), Expectations in Geography at KS1/2 (SCAA 1997a), and Optional Tests and Tasks for Geography at KS3 (SCAA 1996b) all incorporated a strong element of curriculum planning and a framework of geographical enquiry, despite their rather unpromising assessment-focused titles. Curriculum Planning at Key Stage 2 (SCAA 1997b) and Geographical Enquiry at Key Stages 1–3 (QCA 1998) were more ostentatiously focused on curriculum matters. Geography's high profile in more general SCAA publications (IT guidance 1995b; Use of Language 1996c) also proved useful as a way of emphasising geography's wider contribution. The significance of these publications is that, at national level, they laid the groundwork for further necessary structural changes and more progressive features to be added to the Geography Order in the forthcoming review. They also lifted the level of professional debate and raised the morale of the geography education community. It is not surprising to find that SCAA monitoring (1996d and 1997c) and Ofsted inspection evidence (1999a and b) charted a steady improvement in the implementation of school geography. There were, of course, continuing concerns (e.g. interpretation of enquiry, assessment) but by July 1997 when a pre-Review Consultation Conference was held, the SCAA geography team reported that manageability was no longer the big issue. A growing realisation that Geography's position in the school curriculum was steadily being diminished, particularly in the primary curriculum and at KS4, meant that 'the key issue in a review of Geography is its place in the curriculum' (SCAA 1997d).

In the 1998–9 Review, handled by the Qualifications and Curriculum Authority (QCA, newly-formed in 1997 from the merger of SCAA and the National Council for Vocational Qualifications, NCVQ), although the subject groups were given the more directive name of 'task groups', they were not as tightly constrained this time. QCA was keen as SCAA had been to maintain consistency and coherence across the whole exercise but, given the greater consultation and dialogue which had taken place in the 1995–8 period, it felt more able to involve and trust the subject communities to undertake the required work. Significantly too, QCA was much larger than SCAA, since it had taken over the vocational and general vocational qualifications work from NCVQ, and its Council, despite having stronger representation from the more progressive educational community, played a very different role to that of its predecessor. It was no longer possible after October 1997 to involve Council members in the minutiae of decisions about individual subjects. QCA's own subject officers were given responsibility for leading and managing the process. There was a small co-ordinating National Curriculum Review division and Key Stage/phase groups were established with a remit to overview the whole process. But the task groups were chaired by the QCA subject teams not by senior QCA officers and there were no QCA Council observers on subject task groups.

More significantly, despite their names, the subject task groups did not represent one single high profile group destined to carry out all the work. They were merely one part of a myriad of groups and individuals from which the subject teams sought assistance. For Geography, again, the style of development suited the situation, at least in terms of the work on the curriculum. The subject officers had built up a strong and positive relationship with the subject community, including not only the Geographical Association but also the Council for British Geography and the newly-merged (1995) Royal Geographical Society with Institute of British Geographers (RGS-IBG). The SCAA and GA publications of the 1995–8 period had established considerable agreement over the key aspects of the subject at school level. This all provided a sound professional basis from which to ensure that the review would make further improvements to the structure and detail of the Geography Order. The subject community was not as successful in effecting changes to geography's curriculum status. The KS4 curriculum requirements remained virtually intact, apart from additional new requirements in the form of citizenship.

The next curriculum review?

As far as providing a context of practice for teachers and an influence on the next review, the National Geography Curriculum 2000 (DfEE/QCA 1999) now provides a national framework for the subject which, after ten years, finally makes curriculum sense. It highlights Geography's wider contribution to the curriculum (including to education for sustainable development and citizenship) and leaves teachers considerable curriculum freedom to vary the content and develop varied teaching and learning approaches. More significantly, perhaps, a progressive educational ideology has emerged, thus to some extent contesting the 'cultural restorationism' of the 1991 Order. Of course, as Alexander has commented (1985, p. 158), 'ideologies do not come in single file, one replacing the other, but compete, interact and continue in juxtaposition'. The current National Geography Curriculum is a mix of residual and emerging ideologies, but it least it represents a better balance of what Marsden (1995) has called education-focused, society-focused and subject-focused emphases than at any time in the past twenty years. This combined with its minimal format means that there is freedom of interpretation. Arguably it is a 'post-modern curriculum' in this respect, although whether teachers will be willing or able to implement this newly found freedom is less clear (Rawling 2001).

However, since 1997, the educational discourse has been moving away from the details of curriculum frameworks – that was yesterday's struggle for which the QCA Review probably represented the last battle. Not only has the focus shifted to new policy issues (e.g. literacy, numeracy, thinking skills) but the conditions in the 1990s which allowed increasing influence from professional geography educators are already changing. As Power and Whitty (1999) have shown, New Labour educational policies do not so much present 'a Third Way' as a continuation of right-wing policies with an even harder-line approach to implementation, apparent in targets, performance indicators and specific curriculum strategies (e.g. the Literacy and Numeracy Strategies). Bell (1999) refers to the post-1997 period as a distinctive 'excellence phase' in educational policy-making, with a strong emphasis on outcomes and controlled strategies. Geography has not gained from these approaches in the 1997–2001 period. The stress on literacy and numeracy and the 1998 announcement that the programmes of study were no longer compulsory for the 'non-core six' have caused a decline in access to geography for pupils in many primary schools. The KS4 review decision leaves Geography as an optional subject alongside an ever-expanding compulsory curriculum, so it will not be able to improve its position, despite the wider disapplication possibilities now available (QCA 2000). Geographers are also anxious about the possible impact of the Labour Government's desire to create room for its new agenda of citizenship, personal, social and health education, education for sustainable development and creative and cultural education. The new Citizenship requirements, compulsory from 2002 at KS3 and 4, provide particular concerns because of their separate subject format. Implementation details have been left to schools and so it is not clear yet to what extent the existence of another set of requirements will be interpreted as a totally new subject on the timetable, or as an opportunity to extend and develop the contribution of existing subjects like Geography.

For all curriculum subjects, the experience of Geography also reveals the growing impact of new groups of people and new structures which have been brought into policy-making by New Labour. The recommendations about the 'new agenda' topics (citizenship, personal, social and health education, sustainable development education, creativity and cultural education) were made by government-appointed task groups working throughout 1998–9. Although they eventually fed into a joint DfEE/QCA Preparation for Adult Life overview group and so into the NC review, they were not an integral part of the review process. Thus the QCA subject teams were only able to feed appropriate curriculum requirements into revised orders at a late stage (e.g. environmental change/sustainable development and citizenship references into geography) and in some cases, a separate decision was taken (e.g. to create a Citizenship Subject Order) instead of considering what existing subject formulations had to offer.

Another example is the Standards and Effectiveness Unit (SEU), established as a separate unit at the DfEE. The SEU is large and influential (in numbers, SEU staff roughly equal numbers in SCAA pre-1997). The SEU has impacted directly on the work of QCA's subject teams. Although the decision was taken to produce joint SEU/QCA Schemes of Work for all subjects instead of non-statutory guidance to support the revised curriculum, the Maths and English teams were not allowed to produce KS1/2 Schemes of Work because of potential conflict with the Literacy and Numeracy Strategies. So far the impact on Geography has been slight but significant, involving debates over the extent to which the Schemes of Work for Geography were to be directive (the approved interpretation) or exemplary (a model for curriculum development). From 2001, SEU activities will impact more directly on geography departments as the Key Stage 3 Strategy extends the Literacy and Numeracy initiatives into secondary schools, promotes ICT and introduces a specific strand concerned with Teaching and Learning in the Foundation subjects (TLF). The TLF is being trialled in some pilot local authorities during 2000–1 and many geography departments are involved. Potentially the individual elements of TLF (including planning effective learning, thinking skills, motivation and continuity) offer the opportunity for geography teachers to be more creative and flexible with the National Curriculum. However, what it also reveals is that the centre of gravity of curriculum policy-making and management seems to be changing, with the SEU in the ascendant. Ministerial appointments and departmental changes resulting from the 2001 General Election (June) seem unlikely to cause major new directions at the Department for Education and Skills (DfES). With Estelle Morris as Secretary of State, the DfES is likely to continue the DfEE's proactive role in curriculum matters. Since October 2000, Professor David Hargreaves has taken over as the new Chief Executive of QCA. With future changes to the National Curriculum and the school curriculum in mind, it will be crucial to see how QCA and SEU divide up their respective responsibilities, what processes of continuing review and change might be envisaged and how centrally individual subjects will be involved in policy matters. Already, in 2001, the signs are that QCA, under Hargreaves' leadership, wishes to maintain a significant curriculum role – seen for example in the attention being given to the Creativity Across the Curriculum Project and to the development of Citizenship Schemes of Work. Geography is involved in both these initiatives. Equally however, QCA's regulatory and monitoring functions as an assessment authority are assuming greater importance as the number of academic and vocational qualifications grows and with the recently announced review of the functioning of the AS/A2 structure. Although no official pronouncements have been made about the next curriculum review, it now seems less likely that there will be a big National Curriculum review in 2005. The QCA curriculum projects, established after the last review (e.g. Science for the 21st Century, coherence in the 14–19 curriculum) effectively comprise a rolling programme of change and development. From April 2001, Geography and History are included in this process through the QCA Geography and History Curriculum Project. A small amount of funding is available for some reflection and rethinking about the appropriateness of existing curriculum frameworks (from 3–19 years) for the twenty-first century. What is not clear yet is what, if any, action will result from the project's findings and how significant these will be alongside the more directed and classroom-focused strategies being developed by the SEU's TLF activities.

Identifying some key conclusions and issues

The differing scale and character of curriculum change

The 1989–91 period was an example of the 'big bang' approach to subject change, with a high-profile working group developing a completely new curriculum in relative secrecy and isolation from the rest of the subject community. The Conservative government had chosen this approach deliberately, in order to promote what it saw as a 'fresh start' to the school curriculum and to reject previously accepted professional expertise and wisdom about the subject (Lawton 1994). By contrast, both reviews of the National Curriculum were necessarily smaller scale because they were starting from existing Orders and attempting to simplify and reduce them. In addition, and also inevitably because of problems caused both for the whole curriculum and for Geography by the first attempt, the process was less secretive and involved the subject community more directly. The Dearing Review may be seen, in retrospect, as a pragmatic single focus exercise, aimed at 'rescuing' the National Curriculum. In comparison, the QCA Review was a more multi-focused exercise, encompassing both continuing amendment and consolidation of the 'old' curriculum (inherited from the previous government), but more significantly, the introduction of New Labour's distinctive interests which tended to cut across the old subject framework. Some NC subjects benefited from this clash of interests – in Geography's case there were gains in the curriculum framework but losses in curriculum status. The Dearing and QCA Reviews now seem to represent the end of 'sorting out' the old curriculum; the signs are that New Labour's policy emphases and new ways of working herald a new era in which there is less interest in the details of curriculum input by subject (e.g. the Geography curriculum details) and more interest in curriculum output in certain defined areas (literacy targets, GCSE league tables). As already suggested, there is unlikely to be full-scale curriculum review in 2005 but instead a programme of separate 'projects' over the next few years. The Geography and History Curriculum Project provides one part of the context of influence for future changes, but so also do the Key Stage 3 Strategy and the promotion of citizenship.

Changing sites for struggles over subject knowledge

If the analysis is correct, then the 1990s have seen a significant shift in the location of subject power struggles. The 1990s for geography have been all about amending the detail of the 1991 Order to produce a workable curriculum framework and, in this respect, the 1994–2000 climate was favourable to change. Within the subject community it is now essential to support teachers in creatively implementing this framework and so to continue to be concerned with subject content details. However, at national level, the sites for promotion of and maintenance of the subject perspective have changed. Geography's future status and the contribution it will be allowed to make to the curriculum will depend, as for other subjects, on how it is seen to address the newer policy initiatives emerging since 1997. These include raising literacy and numeracy standards, contributing to ICT developments, participating in the TLF work, promoting citizenship and sustainable development education and, for 14–19, providing a range of accessible opportunities for young people. For many of these, Geography has relevant experience to share (e.g. thinking skills, Leat 1998), is already being asked to contribute (e.g. GA involvement in the literacy strategy at KS3), or can draw on new aspects of the Geography curriculum (e.g. environmental change and sustainable development; enquiry). This is not to suggest that school subjects like Geography should merely become servicing agents for continually changing national priorities. Geographers have gradually realised that the existence of a strong and interactive relationship between the subject in schools and in higher education is crucial to the status and well-being at all levels (Rawling and Daugherty 1996). It does not matter whether the context is a primary curriculum increasingly focused on the basics, coherence at 14–19, or Geography's role in key skills development in higher education. Most geographers agree that these are better dealt with from the base of a common and dynamically growing understanding of Geography's contribution to education for the twenty-first century (Unwin 1992; Morgan 2000). In the more diffuse policy arenas of the 2000s, one important weapon for geography educators may be a much clearer view of geographic entitlement – what aspects of geographical knowledge, skills and understanding are essential for young people at different ages, and particularly by the time they leave school. Power struggles over subject knowledge are likely to continue, even in an increasingly non-subject-based educational policy framework.

The growing importance of professional educators active within policy-making arenas

In 1986, Lawton drew attention to the different kinds of people involved in policy-making at the DES, then perceived as the central body in decision-making. He identified politicians, bureaucrats and professional educators, represented particularly by the 450 or so HMI, as holding different beliefs and values and hence making distinctive impacts on educational policy. As a result, policy decisions at the DES were rarely the result of consensus, but more often arose from compromise or negotiation within what Lawton called the 'tension system'. For geography pre-1988, the HMI had been particularly supportive of some of the more progressive developments initiated by the curriculum projects and this may, in part, explain why the geography subject community failed to recognise the dangers in the NC exercise.

After 1988, this delicately balanced tension system was destroyed and the impact of professional educators as a group was seriously constrained. The experience of geography shows that the influence of subject HMI, and of the newly created subject officers at NCC and SEAC, was marginalised in the National Curriculum production process. The evidence points overwhelmingly to the dominant influence of politicians in the 1991–3 period as far as policy affecting the Geography curriculum is concerned.

However, after 1993, one of the most significant features for Geography, and possibly for other subjects, has been the re-emergence of a professional educational influence. This is particularly noticeable through the work of the subject officers in SCAA and QCA, but supported by those remaining HMI able to play a subject role (e.g. the HMI National Geography Adviser and the HMI Teacher Education Inspector). The changed political climate and procedures in both reviews have enabled these people to work co-operatively rather than in conflict with the subject community and so to help effect considerable change to the Geography Order.

Significantly, the Labour administration has brought new groups of professionals into policy-making and policy management since 1997 – the task forces, advisory groups, special advisers, developers of literacy and numeracy strategies and staff of the SEU. The SEU, for example, now has five divisions (LEA Improvement, School Improvement, Pupils Standards, Diversity and Best Practice, Excellence in Cities) and many of its staff come from educational rather than a civil service or administrative background (see DfEE Standards website). High-profile educationalists such as Tim Brighouse (until 1999 Vice-Chair of the Standards Task Force), David Hargreaves (Vice-Chair of the Standards Task Force until 2000 and his appointment as Chief Executive of QCA) and David Reynolds (School Improvement Adviser) have been given positions where their voices can be heard. The National Education Research Forum is another initiative (from 1999) which intends to draw educationalists into the debate about using research findings to inform policy. Whilst these attempts at dialogue reflect Labour's belief that 'what matters is what works' (Blair 1998) and are to be welcomed generally because they bring a larger group of professional educators into the policy-making circle, they do raise wider issues. For example, how should some, at least, of these people be classified on Lawton's table? As a number of commentators have pointed out (Bell 1999; Power and Whitty 1999) the Labour government's approach promotes a strange mixture of autonomy and control. It is pragmatic and willing initially to incorporate ideas from different perspectives but, having decided on policy, then detailed implementation is set within a directive framework of targets and strategies. Thus the work of the SEU now focuses almost exclusively on specific strategies such as school improvement and raising standards, using the government's own interpretation of how this is to be pursued and, significantly for Geography, of which subjects will be included. For the moment, it might be more correct to see SEU staff as 'technocrats' acting in a tightly controlled policy management role, rather than as professional educators commenting on and influencing policy direction. Task groups and advisory groups may be less directed, and it is not yet clear, for instance, how much freedom will be exercised by the National Education Research Forum and whether it will have the genuine ability to influence rather than react to the policy agenda (Pring 2000). Given this situation, it becomes even more crucial that the geographic education community can act as a united and powerful professional voice for the subject at all levels in education.

Changing power structures inside the educational state

In the conclusion (Endnote) to his book about *Politics and Policy-making in Education*, Ball (1990) presented a diagrammatic representation of the contending influences inside the educational state (p. 212). It illustrates the struggles over school knowledge played out between the New Right 'cultural restorationists', who strongly influenced Number 10 and the Secretary of State's office, and the more progressive educationalists with their power base in the NCC and HMI. The DES, with its more traditional 'reforming humanist' ideology and openness to 'industrial trainer' ideas from business and industry lobbies, acted as a moderating influence.

The politics of the changing Geography curriculum throughout the 1990s suggests that this representation now needs to be amended (see Figure 2.1). The lines of ideological conflict are not so easily drawn in 2001. New Labour does not

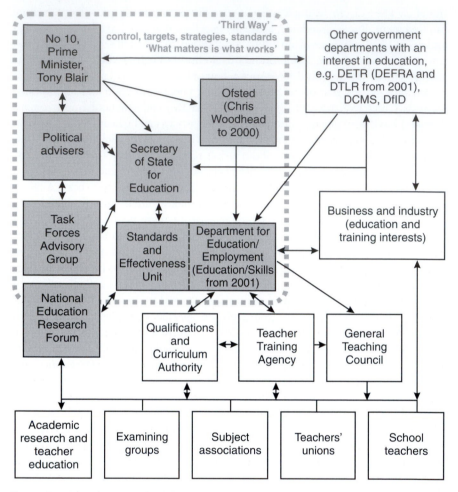

Figure 2.1 Struggles over school knowledge inside the educational state

Source: Ball (1990: 212).

define itself in old ideological terms, but draws on a mixture of ideas from across the full ideological spectrum. Targets, performance indicators and the basic and key skills represent a continuation of right-wing curriculum policies. Measures to promote citizenship, sustainable development education, personal, social and health education and values borrow from more radical, left-wing agendas. It might be suggested that it is not the curriculum policies themselves which represent New Labour's 'Third Way', but the approach and structures of control which have been introduced to implement these policies. New Labour seems to have built up a power bloc in which political advisers, task groups, Ofsted and, notably, the SEU, are focused directly on implementing stated government educational policies on a direct line from Number 10. Several political commentators have noted the growing influence and strong control exerted by the Prime Minister (Kavanagh and Seldon 1999; Hennessy 2000). Kavanagh and Seldon noted that Tony Blair increased the number of political advisers in Whitehall from 38 under John Major to 64 by January 1998 (and recent newspaper speculations suggest that the number is now nearer 78). He has taken on a more direct approach to setting and over-seeing strategy which frequently sidelines government departments. This is what Hennessy (2000) calls the 'command premiership'. Although designed to make things happen and to promote 'joined up policy' this strong control has implications for education, and specifically for curriculum policy-making. In the last six years, professional geography educators have been given considerable freedom within broad policy frameworks to manage the detail and make amendments to the subject order. This was true in SCAA and also in the first two years of QCA. However, once the official National Curriculum Review was finished and Labour's own actions started to take effect, QCA was faced with a whole range of new political advisers and a rival body. The SEU now provides not only advice to Ministers on QCA's policy management role but it actually implements new policy initiatives (e.g. the Literacy Strategy). So far the greatest impact of this has been felt by the core subjects. The SEU staff responsible for Literacy and Numeracy already duplicate to some extent the work of QCA subject officers, with consequences for the latters' independence. The appointment of a SEU Science Director for KS3 may overlap with the work of the QCA Science Team. New initiatives such as thinking skills and assessment for learning, both part of the Key Stage 3 strategy, seem to be led from SEU, though they could easily have been allocated to QCA's curriculum division. There is not necessarily any greater merit in QCA being the curriculum policy management body as compared to SEU. What is significant is that the government has not re-defined QCA's curriculum role but created new structures which are under its direct influence. These more restricted approaches to curriculum policy management are already bringing criticism from academics (e.g. Ball 1999; Goldstein and Woodhouse 2000) and seem set to continue under the new Secretary of State from 2001, despite talk of a toning-down of the 'control ethos'. It may be that the freedom of movement which has been enjoyed and the open dialogue which this has allowed between geography educators within and outside the official agencies, is threat-ened by the more rigid and managerialist approach of the 'Third Way'. The subject communities will need to be astute and watchful as to where the most powerful sites of curriculum policy-making emerge in the 2000s.

Phases of policy-making

Bell's study of educational policy in England (1990) suggested that the 1988–99 period divided into two main phases – the 'market phase' 1988–96 and the 'excellence phase', 1997 onwards. Although this may be appropriate as a broad framework for all educational policy, my analysis seems to suggest that, as far as curriculum policy-making is concerned, there needs to be three subdivisions, as follows:

- The 1988–93 phase, during which the National Curriculum subject Orders were developed. This was characterised by *strong political control of the curriculum content*, the pervasive influence of 'cultural restorationist' ideology, and the marginalisation of professional educators.
- The 1993–7 phase was a period of *pragmatic accommodation and negotiation*, in which New Right influence diminished and, because of the need to involve teachers more co-operatively in implementation, professional educators and teachers within and beyond the central agencies participated more in policy-making and management.
- The final phase, 1997 onwards, has been characterised by *less ideology and more control – a 'command curriculum'*. New Labour's Third Way is recognisable in the greater direction over outcomes and implementation strategies, with a new breed of 'technocrats' managing policy and even classroom interventions. The 2001 Labour election victory may result in some changes of emphasis, but it seems unlikely that there will be major changes in overall direction or any reason to talk of a new policy-making phase.

Conclusion

This chapter has focused on analysing the changing National Geography Curriculum 1991–2001. It has not dealt with the 14–19 curriculum where school Geography is heavily influenced by GCSE and AS/A level criteria and by awarding body specifications. However, the fortunes of Geography KS1–3 are inextricably linked to the character and status of the subject at 14–19. Recent declining numbers for GCSE and A level, whatever the causes (Westaway and Rawling 2001), are almost certain to have a negative effect down the curriculum (5–14) and also up the curriculum into higher education. The analysis in this chapter seems to suggest that if the geography community is to ensure the continuing growth and quality of the subject in primary and secondary schools, it will be necessary to maintain an awareness and understanding of the policy process and to recognise and use any opportunities which arise to strengthen the subject. A strong and cohesive geography subject community will be an important prerequisite so that geography can promote a positive image, revive and extend professionalism to deal with new initiatives, and present a united front to counter other powerful groups. Finally, an important weapon in the increasingly non-subject-based curricular struggles may be the recognition of a clear geographical entitlement, aiming to explain and justify the contribution of geography to education for the twenty-first century.

References

Alexander, R. (1985) 'Teacher development and informal primary education', in A. Blythe (ed.) *Informal Primary Education Today*, Lewes: The Falmer Press,

Bailey, P. (1991) *Securing the Place of Geography in the National Curriculum of English and Welsh Schools: a study in the politics and practicalities of curriculum reform*, Sheffield: Geographical Association.

Ball, S.J. (1990) *Politics and Policy-making in Education: Explorations in Policy Sociology,* London: Routledge.

Ball, S.J. (1994) *Education Reform: a critical and post structural approach,* Buckingham: Open University Press.

Ball, S.J. (1999) 'Labour, learning and the economy; a policy sociology perspective', *Cambridge Journal of Education,* 29(2): 195–206.

Battersby, J. (1995) 'Rationale for the revised curriculum' in Special Dearing Issue of *Teaching Geography,* 20(2): 57–8.

Bell, L. (1999) 'Back to the future; the development of educational policy in England', *Journal of Educational Administration,* 37(3): 200–28.

Blair, T. (1998) *The Government's Annual Report 1997–98,* London: The Stationery Office.

Bowe, R., Ball, S.J. with Gold, A. (1992 *Reforming Education and Changing Schools: case studies in policy sociology,* London: Routledge.

Carr, W. and Hartnett, A. (1996) *Education and the Struggle for Democracy,* Buckingham: Open University Press.

Carter, R. (1994) 'Feet back on Firmer Ground', Geography Extra, *Times Educational Supplement,* 18 November.

Dainton, S. (1996) 'The National Curriculum and the Policy Process', in M. Barber (ed.) *The National Curriculum: a Study in Policy,* Keele University Press.

Dale, R. (1989) *The State and Education Policy,* Buckingham: Open University Press.

Dearing, Sir Ron (1993) *The National Curriculum and its Assessment; Final Report,* London: School Curriculum and Assessment Authority.

Department for Education (1995) *Geography in the National Curriculum,* London: HMSO.

Department for Education and Employment and Qualifications and Curriculum Authority (1998 and updated 2000) *A Scheme of Work for Key Stages 1 and 2; Geography,* London: QCA.

Department for Education and Employment and Qualifications and Curriculum Authority (1999a) *The National Curriculum Handbook for Secondary Teachers, Key Stages 3 and 4,* London: DfEE/QCA.

Department for Education and Employment and Qualifications and Curriculum Authority (1999b) *Geography: The National Curriculum for England,* London: DfEE/QCA.

Department for Education and Employment and Qualifications and Curriculum Authority (2000) *A Scheme of Work for Key Stage 3: Geography,* London: DfEE/QCA.

Department of Education and Science (1991) *Geography in the National Curriculum: England,* London: HMSO.

Evans, J. and Penney, D. (1995) 'The politics of pedagogy: making a National Curriculum Physical Education', *Journal of Educational Policy,* 10(1): 27–44.

Goldstein, H. and Woodhouse, G. (2000) 'School Effectiveness Research and Educational Policy', *Oxford Review of Education,* 26(3): 353–63.

Goodson, I.F. (1998), 'Becoming a School Subject', in I.F. Goodson with C.J. Anstead and J.M. Mangan (eds) *Subject Knowledge: Readings for the Study of School Subjects,* Lewes: Falmer Press.

Helsby, G. and McCulloch, G. (1996) 'Introduction: teachers and the National Curriculum', in G. Helsby and G. McCulloch (eds) *Teachers and the National Curriculum,* London: Cassell.

Hennessy, P. (2000) *The Prime Minister; the office and its holders since 1945,* London: Allen Lane, The Penguin Press.

Jones, S. and Daugherty, R. (1999) 'Geography in the schools of Wales', *International Research in Geography and Environmental Education,* 8(3): 273–8.

Kavanagh, D. and Seldon, A. (1999) *The Powers Behind the Prime Minister*, London: Harper Collins.

Kelly, A.V. (1999) *The Curriculum: Theory and Practice*, 4th edn, London: Paul Chapman/ Sage Publications.

Lambert, D. (1994) 'The National Curriculum; what shall we do with it?' *Geography*, 79(1): 65–76.

Lawton, D. (1986) 'The Department of Education and Science: policy-making at the centre', in A. Hartnett and M. Naish (eds) *Education and Society Today*, Lewes: Falmer Press.

Lawton, D. (1994) *The Tory Mind on Education, 1979–94*, Lewes: Falmer Press.

Leat, D. (1998) *Thinking Through Geography*, Cambridge: Chris Kington Publishin.

Marsden, W.E. (1995) *Geography 11–16: Rekindling Good Practice*, London: David Fulton Publishers.

McGuiness, C. (1999) *From Thinking Skills to Thinking Classrooms: a review and evaluation of approaches to developing pupils' thinking* London: DfEE.

Morgan, J. (2000) 'To Which Space Do I Belong? Imagining citizenship in one curriculum subject' , *Curriculum Journal* 11(1): 55–68.

National Curriculum Council (NCC) (1992) Implementing National Curriculum Geography, unpublished report of the responses to the NCC Questionnaire survey, York NCC.

Ofsted (1993a) *Geography Key Stages 1,2 and 3; The First Year 1991–92*, London: HMSO.

—— (1993b) *Geography, Key Stages 1,2 and 3: The Second Year, 1992–3*, London: HMSO.

—— (1999a) *Primary Education 1994–98: A Review of Primary Schools in England*, London: HMSO.

—— (1999b) *Standards in the Secondary Curriculum 1997–98*, London: HMSO.

Phillips, R. (1998) *History Teaching, Nationhood and the State: A Study in Educational Politics*, London: Cassell.

Power, S. and Whitty, G. (1999) 'New Labour's Educational Policy: First, Second or Third Way?', *Journal of Educational Policy*, 14(5): 534–46.

Pring, R (2000) 'Educational research: Editorial', *British Journal of Educational Studies*, 48(1): 1–3.

Qualifications and Curriculum Authority (QCA) (1998) *Geographical Enquiry for Key Stages 1–3*, London: QCA.

—— (2000) *Guidance on Disapplication of National Currriculum Subjects at KS4*, London: QCA.

Rawling, E. (1991) 'Making the most of the National Curriculum' *Teaching Geography*, 16(3): 130–1.

Rawling, E. (1992) 'The making of a National Geography Curriculum', *Geography*, no. 337, 77(4): 292–309.

Rawling, E. (1993) 'School geography: towards 2000', *Geography*, 78(2): 110–16.

Rawling, E. (1996) 'The impact of the National Curriculum on school-based curriculum development in secondary geography', *Geography in Education*, Cambridge University Press, 100–32.

Rawling, E. (1999) 'Geography in England 1988–98: costs and benefits of National Curriculum change', *International Research in Geography and Environmental Education*, 8, Clevedon: Channel View Books/Multilingual Matters.

Rawling, E. (2001) 'National Curriculum Geography: new opportunities for curriculum development', in A. Kent *Reflective Practice in the Teaching of Geography*, London: Sage.

Rawling, E.M. and Daugherty, R.A. (eds) (1996) *Geography into the Twenty-first Century*, Chichester: John Wiley.

Roberts, M. (1991) 'On the Eve of the Geography National Curriculum: implications for secondary schools', *Geography*, 76(4): 331–42.

School Curriculum and Assessment Authority publications (all London: SCAA).

—— (1993) *Review Handbook for Subject and Key Stage Advisory Groups*, Internal SCAA document.

—— (1995a) *Corporate Plan 1995–1998.*

—— (1995b) *Key Stage 3; Information Technology and the National Curriculum.*

—— (1996a) *Consistency in Teacher Assessment, Exemplification of Standards – Geography at Key Stage 3.*

—— (1996b) *Optional Tests and Tasks; Geography Key Stage 3.*

—— (1996c) *Geography and Use of Language (KS1/2 and 3).*

—— (1996d) *Monitoring the School Curriculum: Reporting to Schools.*

—— (1997a) *Expectations for Geography at Key Stages 1 and 2.*

—— (1997b) *Curriculum Planning at Key Stage 2.*

—— (1997c) *Monitoring the School Curriculum: Reporting to Schools.*

—— (1997d) *Geography Position Statement*, Internal Geography Team paper for National Curriculum Review Conference, July 1997.

School Examinations and Assessment Council (1990) *The Feasibility of the Geography Working Group's Report for the Purposes of Assessment; Response from the SEAC Geography Committee to Council*, London: SEAC

Social Surveys (Gallup Poll) Limited (1992) *The Council's Role in Supporting Implementation of the National Curriculum*, York: NCC.

Unwin, T. (1992) *The Place of Geography*, Harlow: Longman Scientific and Technical.

Westaway, J. and Rawling, E. (2001) 'The rises and falls of geography', *Teaching Geography*, 26(3): 108–11

3 Constructing school geographies

John Morgan

The curriculum is avowedly and manifestly a social construction. Why, then, is this central social construct treated as such a timeless given in so many studies of schooling?

(Goodson 1992: 66)

Dominant social and cultural groups have been able to establish their language, and their knowledge priorities, learning styles, pedagogical preferences, etc., as the 'official examinable culture' of school. Their notions of important and useful knowledge, their ways of presenting truth, their ways of arguing and establishing correctness, and their logics, grammars and language as institutional norms by which academic and scholastic success is defined and assessed.

(Lankshear *et al.* 1997: 30)

Introduction

This chapter is written in the belief that beginning geography teachers should have an opportunity to reflect upon the history of Geography as a school subject. As the quotation from Goodson (1992) at the head of this chapter suggests, too often the Geography curriculum is simply presented as a given. It is written down and that's all there is to it. Lankshear *et al.*'s (1997) comment reminds us of why we should delve a little deeper into how the geography taught in schools came to be accepted as common sense. He suggests that there is nothing 'natural' about what goes on in school geography. Instead, what counts as geography reflects the interests of powerful social groups.

The first part of this chapter offers an account of the development of school Geography in Britain which stresses that the definition of what is to count as Geography has been a matter of struggle and conflict. Many accounts of the development of school Geography in England and Wales tend to take the form of 'uncritical narratives' (Ploszajska 2000), which chronicle the 'progressive evolution' of the discipline and the institutions that sponsor it. Writing about the development of Geography as an academic subject, Livingstone (1992) argues that these accounts are 'in-house reviews of disciplinary developments for the geographical community', in which the exploits of heroic figures and epic moments in the history of British Geography are related to the next generation of scholars (Boardman and McPartland 1993a, 1993b, 1993c, 1993d; Kent 2000; Walford 2000).

The second part of the chapter attempts to provide an analytical framework which can be used to make sense of the different forms of geography education discussed in this chapter. It is offered in the hope that, as you spend time in schools and talk to practising geography teachers, you can make sense of the debates and arguments about the purposes of school Geography that (hopefully) pervade the departments you work in.

Origins

Geography as a school subject is a relatively new subject. Boardman and McPartland (1993a) describe the development of school Geography in the period 1893–1943. They stress the role of Halford Mackinder in promoting the development of the subject at a time when Geography was 'virtually non-existent in the universities'. Mackinder 'realised that if geography teaching was to improve, many more geographers would need to be trained in the universities'. Boardman and McPartland consider that Mackinder's four-point strategy was an attempt by an early pioneer to 'improve the teaching of geography by ensuring that teachers had the necessary knowledge and skills'. The practical success of this strategy can be measured by the expansion of Geography as an examination subject in grammar schools after the 1902 Education Act and the inclusion of Geography in the 1904 Secondary regulations. Boardman and McPartland represent the means by which Geography came to be included in the school curriculum as a victory for common sense, a reflection of the inherent usefulness of the subject. However, Apple (1990) reminds us that any attempt at understanding whose knowledge gets into schools must be, by its very nature, historical. School subjects are the outgrowths of specific historical conditions and, as Lankshear suggests, reflect the interest of dominant groups. In the light of this, Ó Tuathail (1996) re-assesses the role of Mackinder, who, he suggests, saw the function of geography as maintaining an organic social order in the light of disorienting economic, social and political changes that were operating at the end of the nineteenth century. Ó Tuathail shows how Mackinder was a social conservative, and the form of the geography education that came to dominate took on the features of what might be called 'classical humanism'. According to this view Geography was established during a period of arrested imperial expansion and international competition in which many influential figures and associations took the view that greater 'social efficiency' required a renewal of cultural leadership at a national level. It was in this period that a group of intellectually 'second rate' subjects gradually specialised into the component parts of History, Geography and English Language and Literature, and each of these was established as a separate department of 'higher' knowledge with professorial status. In this way, the development of school Geography can be seen as a response to the material conditions of the late twentieth century. For Mackinder, geography had the potential to halt the relative decline of British power and renew the idea of Empire. While the 'old' geography was concerned with the collection of mere 'useless' information about places, the new geography was about 'training the faculty of sight in a detached pictorialisation of the drama of the world'. The geographical eye is panoptic, elevated, disembodied and able to roam freely over the globe. Mackinder imagined that this type of visualisation would allow British subjects to see the spaces of Empire, and render them meaningful to British interests. Ó Tuathail argues that this view of geography was nothing less than an 'ideological assault' on the minds of British children. Mackinder's geography was based on a 'modernism of reaction' which sought to place Cartesian perspectivalism at its centre. This common-sense or perspectivalist space has 'remained within our consciousness, knowledge, *and educational methods*' (emphasis added).

Ó Tuathail's argument is important since it stresses the contribution that geography made to broader projects of imperialism, and its political role in maintaining social order. Others have stressed this aspect of the development of geography. For instance, Eliot-Hurst (1985) argues that the 'fragments of social science as we now know them, history, economics, anthropology, geography, and so on, emerged as concomitants to the development of a new socio-economic system, capitalism' (p. 59). Similarly, Hudson (1977) noted that geography was 'vigorously promoted' to serve the interests of imperialism in its various aspects, including territorial acquisition, economic exploitation, militarism, and the practice of race and class domination. By 1870, geography acted as a gazetteer for the ruling class, explorer, and apologist for the inhumanities of the industrial revolution. Hudson's work prompted a range of studies of the intellectual origins of geography. Peet (1985) demonstrated how geography lent scientific legitimacy to imperialistic ideologies such as environmental determinism. Highlighting the importance of imperialism in the establishment of school Geography, Marsden (1996) considers that:

> In the nineteenth century European nations were completing their colonisation of places hitherto unknown to the western world. It was therefore regarded as an educationally valuable activity to learn the names of places, recognise where places were and, moreover, where the places ruled by Britain were.
>
> (p. 28)

These concerns with the origins of school Geography may seem far removed from the lives of teachers in schools today. However, this history is important for the argument in this chapter, since the forms of school Geography that were established in this period have continued to be influential. School Geography was established as a subject whose proper object of study was man and his environment. The gender was significant, as feminist historians of geography have argued, since the type of knowledge that was counted as valid was invariably 'masculine'. Forms of writing that reflected what Haraway (1997) calls the 'rhetoric of the modest witness' were favoured, requiring a way of writing that was naked, unadorned, factual and compelling, relying on 'hard' scientific evidence. In the intellectual division of labour, Geography came to be defined as a science, concerned with the description of the abundant diversity of the world. It is a testament to the power of this scientific model that school geography teachers will readily recognize this view of the subject. As Rose (1993) notes:

> Most geographers continue to believe that the true nature of the world can, in principle, be explored and revealed through objective study … [Livingstone] argues that the contemporary discipline continues to constitute itself as a search for foundational knowledge through the trope of discovery …
>
> (1993: 63)

In this way, school Geography established itself as a 'hard' subject, rooted in modernist notions of scientific method. This tradition of G
eography was based in the idea of 'classical humanism'. Skilbeck (1976: 17) argues that for classical humanists, it is:

> the task of the guardian class, including the teachers, to initiate the young into the mysteries of knowledge and the ways in which knowledge confers various kinds of social power on those who possess it … classical humanism has been associated with firm and clear discipline, high attainment in examinations, continuity between past and present, the cohesiveness and orderly development of institutions.

This was an approach designed to train the elite, and grew out of the training given to the children of the upper and middle classes in the late nineteenth century. By emphasising certain aspects of the subject, and in the process excluding other ways of understanding the world, school Geography was able to take its place in the academic curriculum. Sinfield (1985) notes that this idea of classical humanism as expressed through the 'competitive academic curriculum' was still dominant in 1944 when the Butler Act was passed, making secondary education compulsory for all children.

The regional method

In the period after World War Two, school Geography retained many of its 'traditional' features. Though the simple listing of places and features associated with 'capes and bays' Geography had been replaced by a concern to classify and describe 'natural regions', Marsden suggests that by the post-1945 period:

> … the presentation of material was equally inert and cumulative, and the learning procedures similarly concentrated on memorisation and recall.
>
> (p. 31)

Smith and Ogden (1977) described the features of the 'traditional approach': the human side of the subject was concerned with describing man's activities in the production of goods and the exploitation of natural resources, along with some facts on demography and settlement patterns. There was an emphasis on field observation as a method of data collection. The approach that developed in the post-war period has been described as one of 'enlightened traditionalism' (Beddis 1983; Walford 1981). School Geography provided students with knowledge of the physical and human environments. In relation to human geography, this was largely a description of patterns of population, settlement and economic activity, realised through the study of places and regions. Where explanations for these patterns were offered, these tended to be framed in terms of ideas about environmental determinism. Social issues were largely ignored, which reflected a number of factors, including ideas about the strict academic division of labour and the professional responsibility of teachers to avoid political discussions with pupils. Boardman and McPartland note that the dominance of the regional framework in syllabus design continued during the post-war years. They also note the developing popularity of 'sample studies', which were 'grounded in the lives and occupations of real people in real places, giving it the sanctity of authenticity' (p. 65). The focus in Boardman and McPartland's account of this period is the improved range of audio-visual aids developed to 'help the geography teacher to inject a greater sense of reality into lessons' (p. 66). This concern with 'bringing reality into the classroom' needs to be seen in a wider context. The description of the uniqueness of the national space and the activities contained within it was suited to a period in which the political geography of the UK was relatively stable and settled (Gamble 1989; Walford 2000).

The 1960s

The period from the 1960s onwards is characterised by what might be called the 'de-traditionalisation' of school Geography. School Geography was the subject of a series of important contests and debates which challenged the hegemony of the 'competitive academic curriculum'. The pressure for change came from both developments in the nature of Geography as an academic discipline, and from changes in the wider educational context, notably the broadening of educational provision to those groups who were previously excluded.

Taking the developments in the nature of Geography as an academic discipline first, Mitchell (2000) notes that, 'throughout the discipline of geography from the mid-1960s on, calls for greater "relevancy" were increasingly common' (p. 35). Similarly, Peet (1998) considers that the Hartshonian discourse of Geography as 'an exceptional, synthesising study of regional uniqueness', which had been a hegemonic disciplinary philosophy between 1939 and 1953, came to be challenged in this period. He suggests a number of 'frustrations' with Geography, including: the emphasis on regions; the lack of modern, scientific methodologies; the remoteness of the discipline from practical and social utility; and a lack of prestige on campus and in government and industry. A solution to these 'frustrations' was found in Schaefer's (1953) alternative programme. Regional geography was dismissed as 'ideographic' and geographers were to begin the 'nomothetic' task of finding methodological laws. Schaefer's work led to the development of Geography as a spatial science which involved a new theoretical structure and the acceptance of statistical techniques in the 'quantitative revolution'. The key to the development of Geography as a spatial science was relevance. From the 1960s, geographers increasingly made claims for their role as spatial planners, providing practical solutions to spatial problems that were well in line with the demands of the corporate state. In the context of broad consensus or 'one-nation' politics, supported by a background of economic growth and Britain's pre-eminence in world affairs, it is perhaps unsurprising that geography took on many of the assumptions and outlooks that characterised the wider polity, society and culture. For example, House's influential textbook *The UK Space* (1973) placed a considerable degree of faith in the capacity for planning. House spoke of the possibility of 'more comprehensive regional planning', and concluded that 'the necessary further management of the UK space ... will not be feasible without ... greater and more decisive public intervention to channel market forces in the national interest'. The faith in rational planning is also found in Chisholm and Manners' (1971) book, *Spatial Problems of the United Kingdom*. They discussed how 'geographical space' was becoming a new dimension of public concern and policy:

> the undoubted achievement of the welfare state in demolishing the principle bastions of inequality have exposed more vividly than ever before the causes for equalitarian public concern, amongst which are several characterised by their spatial as much as by their social nature.
>
> (p. 16)

The answer to solving these 'spatial problems' was planning, to provide a 'more relevant framework for the administration of public decisions' (p. 19). Harvey (2000: 77) has recently commented on the development of this 'pragmatic focus' in academic geography from the 1960s. He suggests that the 'attempt to reconstruct geographical knowledge as instrument of administrative planning in Britain' was linked to the political climate of the time characterised by the Labour Prime Minister Harold Wilson's rhetoric about the 'white heat of technology'. In this context, the goal of rational planning was linked to ideas of 'efficiency of regional and urban planning as a 'lever of social betterment for the whole population'. Smith and Ogden (1977: 50) commented on the interests served by the 'new' geography:

> Like most other scholars, geographers are creatures of their time ... we can now see that the quantitative revolution closely reflected the contemporary preoccupation with technological gymnastics, reverence for cybernetics, and the sense that human ingenuity in an era of general prosperity would automatically generate solutions to our problems.

Explaining the 'paradigm shift' in school geography

This shift away from the older regional-based approach to the systematic and positivist influenced approach was reflected in school Geography, though, as sociologists of education remind us, it is too simplistic to see this as simply the translation of ideas and concepts in academic geography to the school curriculum. The adoption of the 'new' geography in schools reflected the struggle for status and power amongst subject practitioners. Goodson's (1983) social history of the curriculum suggests that the struggle for geography has been a struggle for respectability. He sees developments in geography as part of a struggle on behalf of vested interests in the pursuit of resources and the career ambitions of individual academics and teachers.

One of the problems of Geography as a school subject faced in gaining status within schools was its expansiveness, its tendency to take on new vistas, with the result that the boundaries of the discipline were ill-defined. The solution to this problem was to hand over power to geographers in universities. This explains for Goodson the impetus behind the 'new' geography of the 1960s. Through its newly acquired methodological rigour, geography's position as a 'real' science could at last be assured. New geography, in its quest for hard data, represented a move to the technical rationality of positivist versions of the natural sciences. Thus, the key to understanding the adoption of the 'new' geography was status and resources. Goodson argues that there is a clear link between external examinations for the able student and the flow of status and resources. In other words there is a fundamental drive towards the attainment of academic status:

> Academic subjects provide the teacher with a career structure characterised by better promotion prospects and pay than less academic subjects. Most resources get given to academic subjects that are taught to able students. The conflict over the status of examinable knowledge is above all a battle over the material resources and career prospects available to each subject community or subject teacher.

The 'new' geography stressed the 'scientific' and theoretical side of the subject at the expense of 'fieldwork' and 'regional studies'. Goodson is clear about the motives behind these moves. The aspirations of school teachers was about the material gains to be made from having school Geography accepted as a fully-fledged academic subject that was able to command more resources and offer better career prospects for teachers. This meant that the needs of the students were placed behind the needs of the subject's teachers for status. Similarly, Huckle (1985) argues that the new geography was an elitist exercise, an attempt to render the schooling of a minority of pupils more technocratic and vocationally relevant. The new geography was experienced most by the more 'able' students, but elements of positivism infused all the major curriculum documents of the period. For Goodson it was the acceptance of the 'new geography' that allowed Geography to finish its 'long march' to acceptance as an academic discipline:

from now on its future would indeed be determined not in the school classroom but on the 'intellectual battlefields of the universities'.

(p. 79)

What we see here is the way in which a version of school Geography emerged that reflected the needs and interests of a small minority of the school population. However, the establishment of the 'new geography' with its new found status gained through the appliance of science is not the end of the story. For in *School Subjects and Curriculum Change*, Goodson notes another disruptive force on the horizon:

> But if by the mid-1970s the teachers of geography had accepted new geography because of its clear benefits in achieving high scientific status within the universities new dissenters were active.

(p. 81)

The so-called 'new' geography was adopted by many school teachers as a means of strengthening the subject's position in schools. However, there were also significant changes in the nature of educational provision which affected Geography as taught in schools. As Sinfield (1985) notes, a notion of education designed for the offspring of the gentry and the commercial bourgeoisie could not survive without adaptation in a society which proclaimed equality of opportunity. As a consequence, from the 1960s, Geography as taught in schools was subject to important changes. This was linked to a series of factors that there were influencing the school curriculum in general, including: government pressure for more and better scientists; the anticipated raising of the school leaving age to sixteen; the amalgamation of grammar and secondary modern schools into comprehensives; and the demand for increased student participation.

The period between 1945 and 1960 was one of continued growth of educational spending. In the 1960s successive governments held the conviction that the British economy, in order to compete on a world scale, needed a greater degree of state intervention in economic planning and a thorough overhaul of the social infrastructure of the country. One aspect of this overhaul was the expansion of further and higher education, which required the incorporation of children previously excluded from academic qualifications. These objectives lay behind the growth of comprehensive education. The 1944 Education Act committed the British state, for the first time, to the provision of free education for all. The reforms enshrined principles of equality and access in the political role of the public educational service. Teachers were entrusted both with sustaining a capitalist economy and society, and with providing an egalitarian and universally accessible public service. The contradictions in this role were not experienced on an abstract, theoretical level, but also through concrete, practical conflicts within their day-to-day working lives. As Bonnett (1990) argues, teachers are under pressure to produce a stream of trained disciplined and qualified students on the one hand, and to strive to treat students as equally valuable and valued members of society. Teachers are thus in a double bind: they are contributing to the reproduction of capitalism at the same time as being committed to values that come into conflict with capitalism. This experience of tension has been resolved through a variety of ideological forms. One of these is liberalism, which offers the hope that significant egalitarian change is possible within a modern 'free market' society. It holds out the possibility that capitalism and equality can go hand in hand. Bonnett identifies a number of strands of the liberal ideology in the work of many teachers. One of these is reformism, which represents a belief in the value of change within a system rather than an opposition to it. It is contrasted to conservatism because of its belief in progressive, egalitarian change, and to radicalism which sees change as coming from the challenge to the existing socio-economic system. Reformism has become a central part of the politics of public professionalism. This is because it brings together a commitment to both equality and to the reproduction of capitalism and thereby resolves the contradictions in public professionals' political experiences. This specific ideology made sense to public educators in the post-war historical context, a time when there was widespread optimism about the viability of Britain as a modernising and increasingly socially and economically mobile society. The economy was growing, universal welfare programmes were being expanded, social mobility was increasing. In all, the possibility of a politically progressive market society was, it seemed, being proved.

These ideals about the dominance of the liberal educational ideology that formed the common-sense world view of teachers are useful for thinking about the politics of the school Geography curriculum. In terms of school Geography the liberal educational ideology described here was reflected in the growth of what might be called 'progressivism'.

Progressivism was reflected in moves towards curriculum integration in the Humanities Curriculum Project which challenged the traditional subject boundaries which, it was argued, were in danger of becoming petrified, and subject-based approaches such as the Geography for the Young School Leaver (GYSL). These projects tried to accommodate the social changes of the 1960s and 1970s, for example, by addressing gender stereotypes and recognising the multicultural and multilingual nature of British society. These projects were largely materials-based, they developed materials for classroom use for students and teacher materials. Perhaps the most influential of these approaches was the GYSL project, which in many ways represented a challenge to the 'traditional' ways in which Geography was taught. Whilst GYSL sought to reform the discipline and effect changes in the everyday work of geography teachers, rendering the boundaries between subject disciplines less rigid and more open to influences from other subject disciplines, there also developed strong tendencies for what Marsden (1996) calls 'issues-based' approaches or 'adjectival' studies, approaches which were by definition multidisciplinary. In addition, these 'progressive' approaches reacted against many of the features of 'traditional' geography teaching.

The overall effect of these changes in educational provision, and the nature of Geography as a discipline was to increase the diversity of approaches to school

Geography and steadily erode the coherence and status that 'traditional' school Geography based on the tenets of classical humanism once had.

For example, whilst the 'new geography' allowed the perpetuation of a school Geography designed for and catering for the needs of the small number of school students, progressivism allowed some geography educators to address the needs of a larger group of students. Writing of the period from the 1960s to the early 1980s, Huckle (1985: 301) noted that:

> While the majority of school geographers were preoccupied with the 'new' geography, others were employing humanistic and structuralist philosophies to design lessons on such topics as environmental issues, global inequalities and urban redevelopment.

To varying degrees, these approaches had in common a revulsion against the abstraction, dehumanisation and retreat from social relevance that the positivism of the 'new geography' was supposed to represent (Smith 2000). This progressive geography drew upon a number of conceptual developments in the discipline linked to behavioural geography, environmental geography, welfare geography and radical geography. These sought to develop a geography education whose content was socially and environmentally relevant and which urged people to do something about their concerns.

In this section I have argued that school Geography underwent important changes in the period from the 1960s. In terms of the content, traditional regional approaches were joined (and in many cases replaced by) the systematic approaches associated with the 'new' geography. These changes in content reflected not just developments in academic geography, but changes in the nature of the school intake. The raising of the school leaving age, comprehensivization, and the incorporation of large numbers of working-class children had important effects on the nature of pedagogy (Bernstein 1971). These pedagogical shifts also reflected social and cultural changes, in response to changed expectations about the education of girls and, in large urban areas, the presence of large numbers of children of people from the New Commonwealth and Pakistan.

The 1980s and the 'return of tradition'

The changes described in the previous section were inevitably related to changes in the nature of educational thinking which is in turned linked to broader currents of social and cultural change. Another way of putting this is that school Geography became the site of political struggle over its meanings. In the 1980s the struggle over the meanings of school Geography intensified, amounting to what might be termed the 'politicisation of the Geography curriculum'.

The 1980s were characterised by tumultuous changes in the economic, social, political and cultural geographies of the United Kingdom. In these contexts it is perhaps unsurprising that previous representations of the UK space which stressed the continuity and essential harmony of the nation were challenged. In geography education this involved questioning the relevance of much of the school Geography curriculum to the lives of children living in increasingly stressed urban areas.

One manifestation of this economic and social 'crisis' was the call for the schools to prepare young people for the 'world of work'. The inauguration of the so-called 'Great Debate' after Prime Minister Callaghan's speech at John Ruskin College in 1976 led to a plethora of initiatives designed to increase the relevance of schooling to the 'world of work'. Jamieson and Lightfoot (1982) identified the pressures that were being placed on the school curriculum to reflect the needs of industry. These included:

1   Technological pressures and the feeling that schools neglected applied studies in favour of pure science.
2   Employment. Whilst careers education and guidance had been developed in schools in the 1970s, there was increased pressure to strengthen school-industry links. There was a feeling that pupils needed to have a more positive set of attitudes to work.
3   Industrial society. There was a widespread feeling that the school curriculum did not adequately prepare young people for life in a modern industrial society.

Thus, an important development in school Geography in the 1980s was an increased concern with the vocational aspects of geography education. Corney (1985) discussed the potential for geography education to contribute to school–industry initiatives. He suggested that it was in this area that geography could make the greatest contribution. There was a feeling that schools should show much greater concern with developing 'economic literacy' amongst students. This would require the possession of factual knowledge about the national economy, and the teaching of economic concepts which allow pupils to form balanced and informed judgements about economic matters. This would help pupils appreciate how the nation earns and maintains its standard of living, so that they can properly 'esteem the essential roles of industry and commerce to the process'. In short, pupils needed to acquire an understanding of the economic basis of society and how wealth is created.

Geography could also provide for skill development. These included basic skills such as literacy, numeracy and graphicacy, as well as social skills which would equip them for the world of work, such as flexibility, adaptability, working as part of a team, and taking initiative and responsibility. In addition, geography could provide study skills deemed essential for coping with the world of work, such as compre-hending arguments, the classification and analysis of data and time management. In developing economic literacy and developing appropriate skills, there was a need for teaching strategies and assessment procedures that reflect a variety of strategies, develop active pupil participation in the learning process. Corney notes that:

> Modern geographical education increasingly stresses knowledge and ideas which are relevant and up to date, and gives high priority to broader

educational aims such as the development of personal skills and capacities. It employs a variety of teaching strategies, emphasising active pupil involvement in learning, and attempts to assess through appropriate techniques the extent to which knowledge and skills can be used in a problem-solving situation.

(p. 10)

In terms of content, it was argued, Geography syllabuses contribute to pupils' developing economic literacy, technological awareness and ability to make informal judgements. For instance, they typically stress the factors that influence the development of industry and economic activities, involve the study of the impacts of changing technology on employment prospects in a locality or region, the influence of economic activity on the quality of life and environment, and an understanding of the planning system. This work is frequently local and involves fieldwork. The Geography, Schools and Industry Partnership (GSIP) was established with two main aims. First, to identify the contribution of geography teachers in helping pupils to understand the nature of modern industry and its role in society. Second, to involve geography teachers together with persons from industry in the development, dissemination and evaluation of activities designed to promote such understanding.

The calls for geography to play its part in the promotion of an 'enterprise culture' were ironic in the same decade that saw decline of much of Britain's industrial base. The 1980s saw the publication of a whole series of geographical texts that charted the 'break-up' of Britain. The titles of these are indicative of the mood of many geographers in this period: Hudson and Williams' (1989) *Divided Britain*, Lewis and Townsend's (1989) *The North–South Divide*, Cloke's (1992) *Policy and Change in Thatcher's Britain*, and Johnston *et al.*'s (1988) *A Nation Dividing?* These books can be read as part of the geographical Left's attempt to make sense of the changes that took place under successive Conservative governments. There were some important changes taking place here. The old Marxist political-economic approaches were rapidly merged with developments in other disciplines that were attempting to account for the decline of Labour politics and the new landscape of Britain. Much of this work was involved in mapping the changes, but some geographers were concerned to offer accounts of the changes, a task which meant engaging with social and political theory. These accounts pointed to the fact that the Conservative government inherited in 1979 a country divided in various ways – by class, gender, race and location. They argued that it was to become even more divided in the 1980s. However, these accounts tend to point to the political intent involved in the widening of these divisions. For example, Hudson and Williams, writing at the end of a decade of Thatcher's policies argued that 'the North–South divide has deliberately been redefined and enhanced as part of the political strategy of Thatcherism. It was and is intimately connected to its electoral prospects'.

There is insufficient space here to fully document the policies that were adopted under the Conservative governments. However, it is worth noting the ways in which the space economy was altered. Martin and Sunley (1997) argue that under the post-war consensus the national economy was the key geographical unit of economic organisation, accumulation and regulation. There was also a degree of spatial centralisation of the economy and integration via welfare policies designed to foster consistent national standards across the regions of the UK. The economic policies of the period were aimed at the redistribution of wealth with the effect of reducing inter-regional income differentials through public expenditure and public employment. The reversal of these policies in the 1980s had important consequences. The exposure of the national economy to external influences in the form of globalisation means that regions within Britain have been exposed to the intense competition and uncertainties linked with the global economy. Individual regions and localities are more prone to external shocks. The privatisation of public industries and the shake-out in public employment have exacerbated the problems and the shift in welfare ideologies has had serious implications for particular social groups in these areas.

'Radical' geography reflected a concern with four major areas. First, there was a sense of economic change. Britain's economy was subject to de-industrialisation and manufacturing decline, which was only partly offset by the development of new types of work. These changes were seen as important because of their uneven impact on regions and localities in Britain. Second, there was a focus on the changing political relations of the British state. There was a recognition of the pressures for devolution in the context of heightened economic division, attempts to reassert central political control at various levels of the state, and the moves to reduce public expenditure and open up areas previously dominated by state provision to market forces. Third, there was a focus on the social effects of these developments, with a focus on divisions along axes of race and gender. Finally, the environment was recognised as an important area of political tension and debate. Together, these amounted to a radical agenda for geographical study.

These academic writings had their educational corollary in the development of a radical school Geography. Building upon the tradition of 'progressivism' in school geography, radical geography educators advocated a form of 'socially critical' education that was less concerned with the defence of geography *per se* than with the development of a broader social education (Huckle 1983). The flavour of these alternatives can be seen in the issues of the journal *Contemporary Issues in Geography and Education* published by the Association for Curriculum Development between 1984 and 1987. The journal's concerns mirrored those of the geographical left: racism, sexism, wealth and poverty, environmental degradation, war and conflict. In participating in these debates geography teachers were engaging in wider debates about the nature of the schooling and how it differed from broader notions of education. For example, Huckle challenged what he regarded as the complacency of large sections of geography educators when he stated that boredom and alienation were the dominant responses of pupils to what was on offer in geography lessons.

As I have presented it here, the 1980s saw a struggle about the purposes of geography education in schools between those who saw education as a vehicle for social transformation and those who sought to stress its relevance to the economic renewal of the nation. These different versions of school Geography were the subject of critique by the New Right in the 1980s, in the form of calls for the 'return' of traditional subject-based teaching. In terms of geography, this 'discourse of derision' (Ball 1994) took the form of an attack on progressive teaching methods that meant that children no longer knew where places were. The place of Geography in the school curriculum became the subject of public debate in the 1980s when the Secretary of State for Education, Sir Keith Joseph addressed the Geographical Association. In relation to geography the argument was about the extent to which the teaching of content – by which was meant 'facts' – was being undermined by a focus on values and attitudes.

It is worth noting that these 'assertive' versions of geography teaching were limited in scope and influence. For many geography teachers, life in the classroom was 'business as usual'. Thus, in the 1980s – in the midst of profound economic, social and political change – geography continued to provide images and explanations of the world that relied on older models of environmental determinism, neoclassical economics and Whiggish versions of history (Gilbert 1984). Machon (1987) accounts for the failure of geography teachers to incorporate elements of political education into their teaching as a result of a combination of factors. These included: the stress on the importance of subject matter, the establishment of uniform and distancing patterns of authority and an acceptance that some issues are 'not suitable for the children'. Taken together, this means that many controversial issues, explanatory models and radical perspectives are off limits in the geography classroom. This 'slows the pace of change in political, economic and social processes and underwrites the status quo'.

The National Curriculum

The 'curriculum wars' of the 1980s gave way to an uneasy peace with the establishment of the National Curriculum in 1990. As Helsby (1999) notes, the introduction of central curriculum initiatives was contentious because of the strong postwar tradition of curriculum autonomy that had been associated with strongly ingrained notion of teacher 'professionalism'. In reality the curriculum autonomy of teachers was always relative. It was largely limited to what took place in their individual classrooms and teachers exercised little control over the wider context of their work. Teachers were always subject to external control over their work in terms of having to prepare students for public examinations. Thus a combination of inertia, lack of time and lack of incentive meant that few teachers actually exploited what freedom of action they did enjoy, tending to fall back on their own experiences and replicating traditional practices. There is something to be said for the idea that the notion of 'curriculum autonomy' took on the characteristics of a 'myth', a social construct that shaped understanding of reality and fuelled expectations of what could or could not be done by either teachers or the state. This myth remained largely unchallenged throughout the 1960s and early 1970s.

The National Curriculum represented the reassertion of central control over the school curriculum. The National Curriculum was compulsory for all teachers, offered little or no additional funding and had a high degree of detailed curricular prescription. The process of constructing the National Curriculum was complex and contested, though here I wish to note only that it must be seen as an attempt to overturn the perceived 'progressivism' of teaching in favour of more traditional knowledge-based approaches or what Ball (1994) has called the 'curriculum of the dead'. In the 'discourse of derision' that surrounded the implementation of the National Curriculum, teachers were often criticised for their failure to safeguard standards and were to be reduced to mere technicians, no longer making decisions about the curriculum but following orders devised elsewhere. The National Curriculum placed increased emphasis on a particular interpretation of subject knowledge and moved towards central prescription and enforcement of what was to be taught in schools (see Rawling (this volume) for a discussion of the National Curriculum).

The 'naturalisation' of school Geography

This chapter has provided an account of the development of Geography as a school subject. It has sought to relate important changes in the nature of school Geography to the values and interests of particular social groups. Even from this cursory examination of the development of Geography as a school subject, it would appear that Lankshear *et al.*'s assertion is correct. For most of the twentieth century, dominant views about the nature of the subject have held sway. Particular notions of important and useful knowledge, clearly defined ways of arguing and establishing correctness have formed the basis of school curriculums, examination syllabuses and the National Curriculum for Geography. However, this discussion of the changing and contested nature of school Geography suggests that despite the work of the National Curriculum to present a fixed structure for the subject in schools, there exists a variety of forms of Geography as a school subject, informed variously by 'traditional', 'scientific', 'humanist' and 'radical' versions of school geography. An important part of the argument in this chapter is that these versions of geography are inextricably tied up with questions of power. A useful way of analysing the relationship between geography and power is to adapt Ball *et al.*'s (1990) matrix. The horizontal axis – Self–Not self – concerns relationships between people, and portrays the distance between a focus on the personal, private needs of the individual and the formal, rule-governed situations to which the individual might be subject. In other words, individual versus collective need. The vertical axis concerns sources of power: Authority–Authenticity. The polarity of power lies in the fact that it can be 'top-down' or bottom-up – dictatorial or democratic.

The *geography as skills* version of the subject has as its goal the development of functionally literate individuals who are able to function in the workplace and earn an income. Geography is sponsored by the state education system as long as it functions to provide a skilled workforce of active consumers. Current developments in geography suggest that it is recognised as contributing to this project. Geography students have a range of skills including literacy, numeracy, graphicacy and ICT. In addition geography makes claims for its ability to contribute to vocational education. Through the hidden curriculum, it can be argued that school Geography promotes versions of active consumerism, as it indirectly markets the diversity of the world and highlights the naturalness of travel and tourism and the consumption of environments. The curriculum becomes carefully pre-specified in terms of grade-criteria, assessment items and levels of achievement. The attendant pedagogy rests on a strongly behaviourist notion of motivation by reward. There is little room here for the consideration of feelings or emotions. The focus is on presentation and performance.

The version of *geography as cultural heritage* is similarly constructed on direction and prescription. A selected elite agree the 'canon' of geographical knowledge into which educated members of society are inducted. The emphasis here is perhaps on a geography of awe and wonder, whereby students are to learn how to read and respond to places and environments through appropriate intellectual skills. This view of the subject is restated by Walford (2000) in his discussion of the 'issues for the future' facing geography. Walford argues that there is a need to defend the place of 'geography' in the curriculum in the 'present climate of uncertainty'. He is sceptical of the idea that recent moves to introduce 'Citizenship' and 'Education for Sustainable Development' are an opportunity for Geography to defend and expand its place in the curriculum. Instead, he argues that geographers should not be deflected from what they do better:

> providing a sound base of world knowledge, stimulating interest in places near and far, and getting pupils to appreciate the wonder and diversity of the world in both its physical and human manifestations. Pupil support for this educational enterprise is likely to be deeper and more constant.
>
> (p. 302)

Walford is clear here that it is the very nature of the subject of geography that is *intrinsically* interesting and stimulating and is worthy of study by all pupils:

> Given the wealth and range of lively material available to geography teachers and the richness of life in the real world, it ought to be rare for a geography teacher not to be able to interest or stimulate students in some part of the subject on its own merits.
>
> (p. 305)

The role of geography in a skills-based or utilitarian education is not given particular emphasis by Walford, who would prefer a form of geography which emphasised:

> The need to have a general understanding of patterns and processes, of the way the world works spatially and economically, of how landscapes and townscapes come to be the way they are, even more the need to feel wonder, awe and respect for the physical world.
>
> (p. 306)

In both these versions of the subject, the learner is passive – the individual is neither empowered nor invited to engage in the construction of knowledge. Instead, the focus is on conforming and adapting herself to the subject, learning a set of rules, a body of information that somebody has defined as worthwhile. In Walford's version, there is a need to 'appreciate' and 'respect' rather than to critique, and to acquire rather than actively generate knowledge. There is a real sense in which geography is something individuals 'have done to them':

> Geography teachers in Britain have, over the past hundred years, played a significant part in opening the eyes and widening the horizons of those who have sat in their classes.
>
> (p. 311)

Progressive geography, or the *geography as personal growth* model, places an emphasis on the development of the individual and the construction of meaning in the classroom. Teaching and the definition of geography is pupil-centred. This is reflected in the increased attention given to learning in the 'teaching and learning' equation. Here, the subject of Geography is the source for the development of a wide range of abilities and sensibilities. Personal responses to stimuli are valued and developed, and there is an attempt to connect with the 'experience' of pupils. This approach is best reflected in Lambert and Balderstone's (2000) *Learning to Teach Geography in the Secondary School*:

> The key assumption to understand is our fundamental 'pupil-centeredness' – our belief that good teachers develop a real feel for, and commitment to, the children they teach; it does not matter how good a geographer you are, if you cannot make connection with the children in your class you will not be able to teach them effectively.
>
> (p. 2)

In line with this Lambert and Balderstone's textbook has a humanistic feel about it. A wide range of more 'expressive' resources (music, literature, poems) are discussed alongside the more 'traditional' textbooks, maps and computers. The architecture of geography teaching – lesson plans and assessment strategies – is 'softened' to make the point that it is the quality of human relationships in the geography classroom that is the measure of 'good' geography teaching. Thus, in their hands, assessment becomes a means of developing a 'conversation' rather than a hard-edged tool for sorting and classifying children.

Finally, in the bottom right-hand sector, is 'socially critical geography' or *geography as critical literacy*. This version of geography is assertive, class-conscious and political in content. Social issues are addressed head on. The stance is oppositional, collective aspirations and criticisms become the basis for action. Children are taught 'how to read the world' (Huckle 1997).

It is important to recognise that each version of geography contains and informs a particular political epistemology, the geographical learner is placed differently in relation to subject knowledge, their teachers and the state. Each produces different kinds of students (and citizens) with different kinds of abilities and relationships with peers. In each version the paradigm of meanings within and about geography differs and conflicts. Since the mid-1970s geography teaching has been brought into the political arena.

Some conclusions

This analysis of the history of disputation in the field of geography teaching indicates how teachers have found themselves positioned in debates about the nature of economic and social change. In a period when questions of economic change, political and social order and national identity have been to the fore, Geography as a school subject has been unavoidably linked to projects to 're-imagine' the national space. This can be seen in both the content of school Geography and in its pedagogy – the ways in which it is taught. The classical humanist version of geography, designed to pass on the cultural heritage of the nation, and staunchly defended by Walford, strives to present the world independent of politics and history, as 'natural' and common sense. Certain forms of content and ways of looking at the world are presented as valuable and important for all children. This approach operates and seeks to present itself as 'disinterested' and 'non-political' – the focus is on what we share as a common geography, and entails a rejection of the idea that people have their own histories, cultures and geographies. The result is that the fractured experience of space and place that is rooted in changing political geographies is glossed over by notions of 'personal growth'.

It was perhaps the experience of the breakdown of the post-war consensus and the experience of increased social and economic division that led to the emergence of the more assertive versions of geography teaching that emerged in the 1970s and 1980s. These versions, which sought to address issues of class, gender, and race were engaged in a struggle over representation, over the meanings of geography. The reactions to and attacks upon these 'progressive' and assertive versions have been relatively successful in displacing them. The National Curriculum and the focus on assessment have served to reduce their presence even further. However, as Roberts (1994) suggests, geography teachers who have developed practical ideologies and distinctive ideas about what counts as 'good' geography have been able to maintain their practices. The result is that there are a variety of geographies taught in school, and that the construction of school Geography is an ongoing process in which all geography teachers are involved.

References

Apple, M. (1990) *Ideology and Curriculum*, 2nd edn, New York: Routledge.
Ball, S. (1994) *Education Reform: a critical and post-structural approach*, London: Routledge.
Ball, S., Kenny, A. and Gardiner, D. (1990) 'Literacy, politics and the teaching of English', in I. Goodson and P. Medway (eds) *Bringing English to Order*, London: Falmer Press.
Beddis, R. (1983) 'Geographical Education Since 1960: a personal view', in J. Huckle (ed.) *Geographical Education: Reflection and Action*, 10–19, Oxford: Oxford University Press.
Bernstein, B. (1971) *Class, Codes and Control. Volume 1*. St Albans: Paladin.

Boardman, D. and McPartland, M. (1993a) 'Building on the foundations: 1893–1945', *Teaching Geography*, 18(1): 3–6.

Boardman, D. and McPartland, M. (1993b) 'From regions to models: 1944–69', *Teaching Geography*, 18(2): 65–9.

Boardman, D. and McPartland, M. (1993c) 'Innovations and change: 1970–82', *Teaching Geography*, 18(3): 117–20.

Boardman, D. and McPartland, M. (1993d) 'Towards centralisation: 1983–93', *Teaching Geography*, 18(4): 159–62.

Bonnett, A. (1990) *Radicalism, Antiracism and Representation*, London: Routledge.

Chisholm, M. and Manners, G. (eds) (1971) *Spatial Policy Problems of the United Kingdom*, Cambridge: Cambridge University Press.

Cloke, P. (ed.) (1992) *Policy and Change in Thatcher's Britain*, Oxford: Pergamon.

Corney, G. (ed.) (1985) *Geography, Schools and Industry*, Sheffield: Geographical Association.

Eliot-Hurst, M. (1985) 'Geography has neither existence nor future', in R. Johnston (ed.) *The Future of Geography*, 59–91, London: Methuen.

Gamble, A. (1989) 'Thatcherism and the new politics', in J. Mohan (ed.) *The Political Geography of Contemporary Britain*, 1–17, London: Macmillan.

Gilbert, R. (1984) *The Impotent Image: Reflections of ideology in the secondary school curriculum*, Lewes: Falmer Press.

Goodson, I. (1983) *Social Subjects and Curriculum Change*, London: Croom Helm.

Goodson, I. (1992) 'On Curriculum Form; Notes toward a Theory of Curriculum', *Sociology of Education*, 65(1): 66–75.

Haraway, D. (1997) *Modest_Witness@Second_Millennium.FemaleManMeets_OncoMouse*, London: Routledge.

Harvey, D. (2000) 'Re-inventing Geography', *New Left Review*, 2nd series, July–August No. 4.

Helsby, G. (1999) *Changing teachers' work*, Buckingham: Open University Press.

House, J. (ed.) (1973) *The UK Space: Resources. Environment and the Future*, London; Weidenfeld and Nicolson.

Huckle, J. (ed.) (1983) *Geographical Education: Reflection and Action*, Oxford: Oxford University Press.

Huckle, J. (1985) 'Geography and Schooling', in R. Johnston (ed.) *The Future of Geography*, London: Methuen, 291–306.

Huckle, J. (1997) 'Towards a critical school geography', in D. Tilbury and M. Williams: (eds) *Teaching and Learning Geography*, London: Routledge, 241–52.

Hudson, B. (1977) 'The new geography and the new imperialism', *Antipode*, 99: 12–19.

Hudson, R. and Williams, A. (1985) *Divided Britain*, Chichester: Wiley.

Jamieson, I. and Lightfoot, M. (1982) *Schools and Industry*, Schools Council Working Paper No.3, London: Methuen.

Johnston, R. and Pattie, C. (1988) *A Nation Dividing? The Electoral Map of Britain 1979–87*, Harlow: Longman.

Kent, W.A. (2000) 'Geography: Changes and Challenges', in W.A. Kent (ed.) *School Subject Teaching: the history and future of the curriculum*, 111–31. London: Kogan Page.

Lambert, D. and Balderstone, D. (2000) *Learning to Teach Geography in the Secondary School*, London: RoutledgeFalmer.

Lankshear, C., Gee, P., Knobel, M. and Searle, C. (1997) *Changing Literacies*, Buckingham: Open University Press.

Lewis, J. and Townsend, A. (eds) (1989) *The North–South Divide*, London: Paul Chapman.

Livingstone, D. (1992) *The Geographical Tradition*, Oxford: Blackwell.

Machon, P. (1987) 'Teaching controversial issues; some observations and suggestions', in P. Bailey and T. Binns (eds) *A Case for Geography*, Sheffield: Geographical Association.

Marsden, W. (1996) *Geography 11–16: Rekindling Good Practice*, London: David Fulton Publishers.

Martin, R. and Sunley, P. (1997) 'The post-Keynesian state and the space economy', in R. Lee and J. Wills (eds) *Geographies of Economies*, 278–89, London: Arnold.

Mitchell, D. (2000) *Cultural Geography: a critical introduction*, Oxford: Blackwell.

Ó Tuathail, G. (1996) *Critical Geopolitics*, London: Routledge.

Peet, R. (1985) 'The origins of environmental determinism', *Annals of the Association of American Geographers*, 75: 309–33.

Peet, R. (1998) *Modern Geographical Thought*, Oxford: Blackwell.

Ploszajska, T. (2000) 'Historiographies of geography and empire' in B. Graham and C. Nash (eds) *Modern Historical Geographies*, 121–45, London: Prentice Hall.

Roberts, M. (1994) 'Interpretations of the Geography National Curriculum: a common curriculum for all?', *Journal of Curriculum Studies*, 27.

Rose, G. (1993) *Feminism and Geography: The limits of geographical knowledge*, Cambridge: Polity Press.

Schaeffer, K.F. (1953) 'Exceptionalism in geography: a methodological consideration', *Annals of the Association of American Geographers*, 43, 226–49.

Sinfield, A. (1985) 'Give an account of Shakespeare and Education, showing why you think they are effective and what you have appreciated about them. Support your comments with precise references', in J. Dollimore and A. Sinfield (eds) *Political Shakespeare: New essays in materialism*, 134–57, Manchester: Manchester University Press.

Skilbeck, M. (1976) 'Three Educational Ideologies', *Curriculum Design and Development: Ideologies and Values*, Buckingham: Open University Press.

Smith, D. (2000) *Moral Geographies: ethics in a world of difference*, Edinburgh University Press.

Smith, D.M and Ogden, P. (1997) 'Reform and Revolution in Human Geography', in R. Lee (ed.) *Change and Tradition: Geography's New Frontiers*, 47–58, London: Department of Geography, Queen Mary College, University of London.

Walford, R. (ed.) (1981) *Signposts for Geography Teaching*, Harlow: Longman.

Walford, R. (2000) *Geography in British Schools 1850–2000*, London: Woburn Press.

Section 2

Geography in (and out of) the classroom

Section 2 is the largest section in this book. Given the intended audience for the book, no apologies are made for this. Students on the PGCE course will be meeting many of these issues early in their school experience and the aim of this section is to help the students towards a fuller understanding of the background to and implications of the issues.

Clearly these are not the only issues that face geography teachers in the classroom at the present time. The task of selecting issues to explore in his section was not easy – those chosen are ones which are likely to pose the most immediate concerns to beginning teachers.

For most chapters in this section, there is a match in the companion volume, *Aspects of Teaching Secondary Geography: Perspectives on practice* where the practical side of the issues are explored and support the form of ideas that can be implemented in the classroom (and outside) is offered.

4   The enquiry-based approach to teaching and learning Geography

Michael Naish, Eleanor Rawling and Clive Hart

The Geography 16–19 Project proposes that the study of geography at 16–19 level should take place through enquiry-based teaching and learning. The term encompasses a range of teaching methods and approaches by which the teacher encourages students to enquire actively into questions, issues and problems, rather than merely to accept passively the conclusions, research and opinions of others.

It is important that the term 'enquiry-based' is further explained so that it is not misunderstood. One way in which to consider different approaches to teaching and learning is to envisage a continuum such as that shown in Figure 4.1. Exposition, narration and reception learning occupy one extreme of the teaching–learning continuum and are characterised by a relatively low level of pupil autonomy, since the teacher is dominantly in control of the situation. Moving along the continuum, other possible teaching strategies and learning activities are identified. These include close direction of question analysis and problem-solving activities, provision of advice and guidance in open-ended discovery situations, and finally, at the other end of the continuum, encouragement and support given to creative activity. In all these learning situations, an orientation towards enquiry may exist, if enquiry is defined in Dewey's terms as 'active, persistent and careful consideration of any belief or supposed form of knowledge in the light of grounds that support it and the conclusions to which it tends' (Dewey 1933).

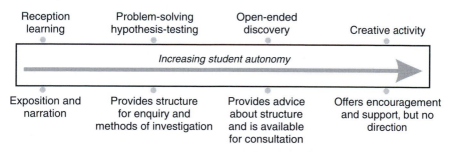

Figure 4.1 The teaching–learning continuum

Even in the most formal classroom where exposition is the dominant method used by the teacher, it is possible to be conducting an enquiry in the broad sense of the term. The term 'enquiry-learning' as currently used amongst educationalists and teachers tends to be more usually equated with the discovery learning and creative activities occupying the other end of the continuum. To avoid confusion, the Geography 16–19 Project has adopted the term enquiry-based learning. The list below shows that enquiry-based learning as developed by the Project is focused on the 'structured problem solving' and 'open-ended discovery' points on the continuum, with the facility to draw on expository methods or to expand into creative activity, if appropriate. The key features of the Geography 16–19 enquiry-based approach to learning are summarised in the following.

Characteristics of the enquiry-based approach to learning

An approach to learning which

- identifies questions, issues and problems as the starting points for enquiry
- involves students as active participants in a sequence of meaningful learning through enquiry
- provides opportunities for the development of a wide range of skills and abilities (intellectual, social, practical and communication)
- presents opportunities for fieldwork and classroom work to be closely integrated
- provides possibilities for open-ended enquiries in which attitudes and values may be clarified, and an open interchange of ideas and opinions can take place
- provides scope for an effective balance of both teacher-directed work and more independent student enquiry
- assists in the development of political literacy such that students gain understanding of the social environment and how to participate in it.

A clear enquiry focus

If a genuine enquiry sequence is to be followed in a teaching–learning activity, then it is a necessary prerequisite that study should begin with questions, issues or problems. The identification of a clear enquiry focus ensures that opportunities for the use of intellectual skills are presented in a meaningful way. This kind of satisfaction, derived from appreciating the link between 'question and answer', seems to be highly significant in learning. The work of psychologists like Ausubel, Bruner and Gagné all reinforce this idea in different ways. In her book, *Learning through Geography*, Frances Slater suggests that question identification is the key to successful learning through geography: 'Question identification can be usefully adopted as the first procedure in planning a learning activity. Questions are thus the initial and continually guiding signposts which help us to organise and plan pathways leading students to meaningful learning through geography' (Slater 1982).

A meaningful sequence of enquiry

The phrase referring to 'signposts which help us to organise and plan pathways ... ' draws attention to another important characteristic of an enquiry-based learning approach. A sequence of learning activities is implied, since an appropriate response to questions, issues or problems is to follow an enquiry route in finding answers, solutions or a personal response. Figure 4.2 presents a summary version of the route for enquiry. As presented here, it shows that following initial awareness of a question, issue or problem, an appropriate sequence of enquiry activity might

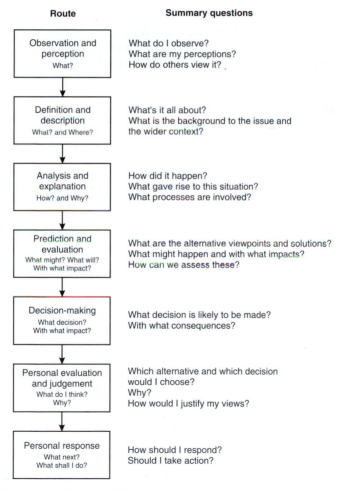

Route	Summary questions
Observation and perception What?	What do I observe? What are my perceptions? How do others view it?
Definition and description What? and Where?	What's it all about? What is the background to the issue and the wider context?
Analysis and explanation How? and Why?	How did it happen? What gave rise to this situation? What processes are involved?
Prediction and evaluation What might? What will? With what impact?	What are the alternative viewpoints and solutions? What might happen and with what impacts? How can we assess these?
Decision-making What decision? With what impact?	What decision is likely to be made? With what consequences?
Personal evaluation and judgement What do I think? Why?	Which alternative and which decision would I choose? Why? How would I justify my views?
Personal response What next? What shall I do?	How should I respond? Should I take action?

Figure 4.2 Summary of the route for enquiry

cover some of the following operations: definition, description, analysis, explanation, evaluation, prediction, generalisation, decision-making, personal evaluation and judgement and personal response. As will be explained later, such a route does not provide a rigid structure for enquiry, but merely acts as a reminder of the kinds of activities which are often present in enquiry. The route can then be used as a guide to lesson and course planning.

Active involvement of students in this kind of enquiry sequence is an important characteristic of the Project's approach, and one for which there is considerable justification. Experience seems to suggest that meaningful knowledge consists of more than just a body of content. R.G. Collingwood suggested as early as 1939 that the activity of knowing, in which one tries to find answers to questions, is of fundamental importance: 'A body of knowledge consists not only of "propositions", "statements", "judgements" or whatever terms logicians use in order to designate assertive acts of thought ... but of these together with the questions they are meant to answer.'

The Project's approach to learning depends on the view that learning which derives from active participation in seeking answers is likely to be more easily retained and more meaningful re-applied than knowledge taken in passively.

Opportunities for skill development

Another important consideration is that active involvement in the processes of finding out and of achieving understanding provides a wealth of opportunities for skill development. It may be suggested that in following a route for enquiry such as that in Figure 4.2, learning activities need to be structured, so that skills can be applied to resources and data in order to move towards answers, solutions and personal judgements. Figure 4.3 shows this relationship diagrammatically. Where

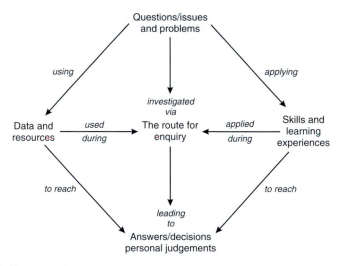

Figure 4.3 From questions to answers

the complete enquiry sequence is followed, students will be presented with opportunities for practising a wide range of intellectual, communication, social, practical and study skills.

Table 4.1 Coin Street: the battle for the inner city

Section of enquiry	Resources used	Main student activities
1 Coin Street		
The issue introduced	Tape–slide sequence, newspaper cutting, maps, photographs	Drawing out ideas from the impact material, class discussion, note-taking
2 The South Bank explored		
The Coin Street site, history and context	Planning documents, maps, articles, textbook material, slides/photographs/tapes	Interpretation of written material, charts, graphs, etc, writing summaries, producing maps, plotting data, deriving general ideas
3 Whose city?		
The current situation, people and processes	The Coin Street site and people, planning documents, maps	Role playing; observation and interpretation in the field; relating the map/ written material to reality; analysing a complex situation; talking to people; taking photographs; summarising issues
4 Decision-making and Coin Street		
Consideration of alternatives, the decision-making process	Own fieldwork data and impressions, transcript of actual public inquiry, articles, radio reports, textbook material.	Role playing, applying field observations to inquiry situation; handling alternative viewpoints; putting a viewpoint, arguing clearly; summarising
5 Inner cities: the wider context		
The inner city experience in other cities	Textbook material, articles, BBC Programme	Reading, interpreting and applying theories; generalisation, evaluation
6 Changing inner cities		
The future and my view	Own notes and impressions	Clarifying own values, thinking out own view, deciding on what action to take

Table 4.1 presents an analysis of the student activities which characterise a typical enquiry exercise. The diagram reveals both the overlapping nature of skills being practised at different stages in the exercise and also the extent to which a large number of opportunities for skill development can be provided in one piece of enquiry work. The way in which fieldwork activities form an integral part of the enquiry should also be noted. Inside or outside the classroom, the main focus is the question or issue, and so students perceive no artificial separation between fieldwork and classwork.

Open and closed enquiries

Enquiry-based learning may be either open or closed. Table 4.1 indicates that the Coin Street exercise is essentially an open-ended exercise. The issue of how to redevelop the Coin Street site and other similar South Bank sites is a complex one. There is no right or wrong answer. Students may find that role-playing the official public inquiry system leads them to one kind of decision. However, they will be aware of the influence of the values held by the participants in the process. They will also have begun to appreciate that power and status in society are reflected in strength in the decision-making system. Thus, the end stage of their own enquiry is not at the end of the public inquiry (stage 4) but is reached after due consideration and clarification of their own viewpoint (stage 6). The overall character of the enquiry is open-ended.

In such open-ended enquiries, students require encouragement and support from the teacher to identify the full range of possibilities, to clarify their own position and to decide on appropriate action. During open-ended enquiry, '16–19' work is located near the right end of the teaching–learning continuum. Opportunities also exist for work that lies even further to the right of the continuum (Figure 4. 1), in cases where the student enquiry is genuinely creative and is not directed or structured by the teacher.

On other occasions, it may be appropriate to run a more closed problem-solving or question-answering exercise, where perhaps there is one technically correct answer, obtainable through a clearly defined series of steps. As part of the Coin Street work, for instance, it is possible to envisage students carrying out technical feasibility studies as to the possibilities afforded by different sites. They may be involved in answering questions such as 'How many housing units might be built here?', 'Are there cost implications in providing access for cars?', 'Is it possible to build underground parking facilities for office blocks at these sites?'. Such questions provide the basis for closed enquiry work, typical of activities nearer to the left end of the teaching–learning continuum.

Partners in enquiry

Enquiry-based teaching and learning, as advocated by the Project, has the advantage of providing scope for a balance of teacher-directed work and more independent student enquiry. It is the responsibility of the teacher to plan out the teaching–learning activities as appropriate to the objectives of the particular piece of work and to the availability of resource material. On some occasions, it may be necessary to include a large element of formal class-teaching. At other times, it will be found appropriate to allow students to follow up independent lines of enquiry, referring back to the teacher only for advice and support. Whichever emphasis is taken, the students become involved in using their skills to undertake the enquiry. Teachers and students work in partnership to develop the geographer's craft and to enhance personal competence.

References

Collingwood, R.G. (1939) *An Autobiography*, Oxford: Oxford University Press.
Dewey, J. (1933) *How We Think: A re-statement of reflective thinking upon education processes*, Boston: Heath.
Slater, F. (1982) *Learning Through Geography*, Oxford: Heinemann Educational.

5 Curriculum planning and course development

A matter of professional judgement

Margaret Roberts

> There is a dilemma in describing a course of study ... it is only in a trivial sense that one gives a course to 'get something across', merely to impart information. There are better means to that end than teaching. Unless the learner also masters himself, disciplines his taste, deepens his view of the world, the 'something' that is got across is hardly worth the effort of transmission.
>
> (Bruner 1966: 73)

Introduction

Now that there is a Geography National Curriculum (GNC) for pupils aged 5 to 14 and detailed syllabuses for GCSE and A level, teachers might wonder whether their role in curriculum planning has been taken away from them. Clearly, the existence or nature of statutory requirements and examination syllabuses could be challenged. However, this chapter does not enter that debate but focuses on what teachers might do within the current educational context to plan the Geography curriculum in their schools and to develop their own geography courses.

The terms 'curriculum planning' and 'course development' encompass the thinking and documentation that occurs before, during and after teaching and learning takes place in the classroom. Teachers approach the task of planning in different ways, being influenced, consciously or subconsciously, by the models of planning they have encountered, by the GNC, by examination syllabuses, by textbooks, by colleagues and by experience. The way a curriculum is planned is a matter of debate and ultimately a matter of professional judgement. This chapter focuses on two models of curriculum development: an objectives model and a process model. It outlines the basic features and origins of each model, gives examples of their impact on geographical education and looks at the merits and criticisms of each approach. Finally, it highlights the dilemmas teachers face in adapting these models to their own use. Before looking at these models, however, it is worth distinguishing between a syllabus and a curriculum plan.

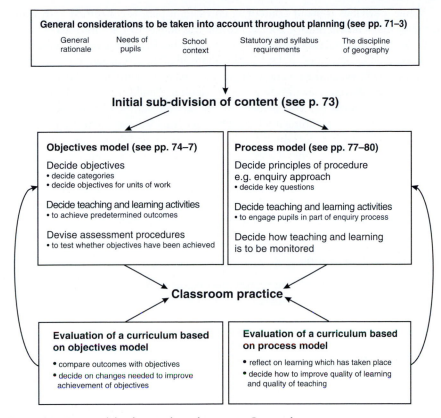

Figure 5.1 Two models of curriculum planning in Geography

From syllabus to curriculum

Before the impact of the Schools Council's curriculum development projects in the 1970s most geography teachers in England and Wales planned their courses by deciding what should be taught, and in what order. The documentation resulting from this simplest of planning models was a syllabus, i.e. a concise list of content stating what should he taught and when. The starting point for planning was the subject itself. It was taken for granted that planning the Geography curriculum meant thinking primarily about content. Issues of contention were largely limited to debates about what should he included and about the best ways to transmit the selected content.

A possible legacy of the syllabus model of curriculum planning is the tendency of most geography teachers to begin their planning, not with the kinds of considerations on which theoretical models are based, but with a rough plotting of content onto a grid. If the only consideration taken into account in completing the grid is the content of Geography then the result is a syllabus rather than a curriculum plan. From such a framework it is, however, possible to develop the Geography curriculum.

While a syllabus is about content, a curriculum plan is concerned with transforming that content into a course. To do this it has to take into account the complexity of the total educational experience in schools, its purposes, its content, its processes and its outcomes, and it must evaluate all of these. Further, it is concerned with the way in which these various elements of education are interrelated.

There are different views on how the curriculum should he planned and where the emphasis should be, as is evident in the models outlined below. Whichever model of curriculum planning is adopted by a geography department, there are two valuable preliminary stages which can be used in both models of planning. First, it has to be decided what general considerations need to be taken into account and, second, a rough outline of the course has to be drafted. Although these stages are shown at the top of the curriculum plan in Figure 5.1, general considerations need to be taken into account throughout the planning process and, moreover, the results of the initial drafting may he modified during the planning process.

General considerations

The general considerations are represented below in the form of questions. The order in which they are considered and their relative importance are matters of judgement.

Rationale

- What is the overall purpose of education in the school?
- What implications do these aims have for the Geography curriculum?
- In what ways can the Geography curriculum contribute to the school's general aims?

The pupils

- What experiences of learning Geography (from feeder schools and from outside school) do pupils bring with them and how can these be used?
- How can the interests and enthusiasms brought by pupils be used?
- What individual needs do pupils have in relation to their learning of Geography?

The school context

- What opportunities and constraints are provided by the economic, social and environmental context in which the school is situated?
- What opportunities are there for making use of the local and regional context, e.g. visits, fieldwork, links with the local community?
- What are the opportunities and constraints of the school buildings, the school grounds, and the school's resources?

- What links does the school have with other places in Britain and abroad?
- How can links with the feeder schools be built in to curriculum planning?

Statutory and syllabus requirements

- What are the requirements of the GNC and the selected examination syllabuses?
- To what extent can Geography courses contribute to statutory and examination requirements in other parts of the curriculum, e.g. through integrated courses, in developing literacy, IT skills and numeracy?

The subject of geography

- Within the constraints of the GNC and examination syllabuses, what aspects of geography and approaches to geography does the department want to emphasize, e.g. people/environment approach, a scientific approach, a geography of social concern?

Initial drafting

What is prescribed for schools now in the GNC and examination syllabuses is prescribed for long periods of time: two years (examination syllabuses); three years (Key Stage 1 and Key Stage 3) and four years (Key Stage 2). A useful initial task in curriculum planning is to divide these long courses into more manageable units, possibly varying from two weeks to one term in length. This process is similar to syllabus construction in its focus on what should be taught and when. It differs in that it takes into account the general considerations outlined above. It also takes into account the model of curriculum planning which will subsequently be used. Initial drafting involves consideration of the following questions.

- What units of work have been used previously in the school?
- Should these be maintained, modified or scrapped?
- What resources does the school have, in terms of staffing and physical resources?
- What should be the focus of the units: themes, places, issues, particular experiences (e.g. individual investigations) or a mixture of all four?
- What opportunities arise from the general considerations (pp. 71–3)?
- What opportunities are there for incorporating the use of information technology and fieldwork?
- What opportunities are there for liasing with work done in other subjects?
- What scope is there for progression in the units of work?

Initial decisions can be marked on a two-, three- or four-year plan depending on course length. Examples of such frameworks are found in several publications (e.g. Grimwade 1995).

The objectives model of planning

Characteristics

There are three essential characteristics of the objectives model of planning. First, decisions are made at the start of a course of study about the intended outcomes. These decisions are expressed first as broad aims and then as more detailed objectives, i.e. statements of what pupils ate expected to learn. Second, teaching and learning activities are designed so that the chosen objectives can he achieved. Third, the success of the course is determined by the extent to which the objectives have been achieved.

Origins

The objectives model of planning had its origins in the United States of America (Bobbit 1918; Tyler 1949; Taba 1962) where ideas related to behavioural psychology were applied to curriculum planning. There has been considerable debate about how specific objectives have to be. Some (e.g. Mager 1962) have argued that an objective must describe what a pupil has to be able to do in relation to a particular area of content, e.g. identify symbols on a weather map. This has been termed a 'behavioural objective' on the grounds that it indicates the intended behaviour. Other advocates of the objectives model of planning would argue against such detailed specification, saying that it would lead to proliferation of statements, but see value in general statements of objectives, e.g. the understanding of weather maps.

The use of objectives in curriculum planning in the USA encouraged thinking about different types of learning outcomes. The most influential categorization of learning outcomes was devised by Bloom (1956). He published a taxonomy of education objectives in two parts: the cognitive domain in which learning outcomes were defined by different types of thinking, and the affective domain in which learning outcomes were defined by different types of response and attitude. He subdivided each domain into a hierarchy of levels of achievement. Thus, for example, he subdivided the cognitive domain into knowledge (with emphasis on recall), comprehension, analysis, synthesis and evaluation.

Influence of the objectives model of curriculum planning on geographical education

Geographical education has been influenced by the objectives model of planning in several ways – in the use of both behavioural and more general objectives as a framework for planning, in the use of Bloom's 'categories' of objectives, and in the accountability of courses.

Examples of objectives taken from Geography curriculum documents, shown in the list below, range from one which could be easily transformed into a behavioural objective to one which gives no indication of what the pupil has to do in order to achieve the objective. In geographical education more general statements about learning outcomes have been used more frequently than highly specific behavioural objectives.

1   To draw an accurate cross-section from measurements taken outside the classroom (GNC. DES 1991: 5).
2   To analyse the effect on the environment of the development of two energy sources (GNC. DES 1991: 26).
3   To recall specific facts relating to the syllabus content and demonstrate locational knowledge within the range of small, regional, national, international and world scales (GCSE syllabuses. NEAB 1995).
4   To recognize alternative value positions and to relate these to the ideologies with which they are associated (Geography Avery Hill GCSE syllabus. WJEC 1995).
5   Key idea: Leisure activities often involve extensive use of land, sometimes in competition with other users (GYSL 1974).

Bloom's categorization of objectives has been very influential. The following are examples of different categorizations used in Geography.

1   Key ideas; skills; values (GYSL 1974).
2   Knowledge; understanding; skills; values (National Criteria for GCSE Geography. HMSO 1985).
3   Knowledge; understanding; application; skills and techniques (Core Criteria for GCSE. SCAA 1995).
4   Knowledge; skills; attitudes and values (NCC 1991).
5   Concepts; skills and techniques; values and attitudes; cross-curricular themes (Currie *et al.* 1994).

In geographical education, the categorization of objectives has focused attention on the relative importance of different types of learning in relation to an area of content. If, for example, a teacher is teaching a unit of work about the Lower Don Valley in Sheffield, what is the main purpose? Is it to enable pupils to recall specific facts, to increase understanding of the concepts of urban decay and regeneration, to increase understanding of the political processes involved in change, to teach skills in map-reading and resource interpretation, or a combination of all of these? There could be valid reasons for any of these purposes, but the teaching and learning activities would be different. Clarification of objectives provides some guidelines in deciding which teaching and learning activities should be used.

Categorization of objectives, as well as helping to clarify teachers' thinking, has enabled examination boards to give different weighting in assessing different types of learning. For example, the NEAB Geography GCSE syllabus D for 1996/7 has the following weighting: recall 20 per cent; understanding, application and skills 45 per cent; practical skills 24 per cent; values 11 per cent. Over the last twenty years the emphasis on recall has decreased while that on understanding, skills and values has increased.

Objectives have also become important in geographical education as a means of accountability. The success of a course of geographical education is for the most part measured publicly by the achievement of predetermined objectives. Examination results of geography at GCSE and A level are fed into national league tables. The Education Reform Act of 1988 emphasized the outcomes of learning. The terms of reference to the Geography Working Group stated that:

> There should be clear objectives, attainment targets, for the knowledge, skills and understanding which pupils of different abilities and maturities should be expected to have acquired by the end of the academic year in which they reach the ages of 7, 11, 14, and 16.
>
> (DES 1990: 93)

The expectation that curriculum planning involves the specification of objectives is reinforced by Ofsted inspection guidelines – 'purpose is demonstrated by effective planning, including the clarity of objectives' (Ofsted 1993: Section 4.7.1. p. 49).

If the objectives model of planning is adopted the following questions need to be considered:

- What categories of objectives should be included in the curriculum plan (taking into account what is prescribed and the department's professional judgements)?
- Using these categories, what should the objectives be for each unit of work?
- What teaching and learning activities would lead to an achievement of these objectives?
- What resources are available to support these teaching and learning activities?
- What means of assessment will the department use to assess the achievement of these objectives for each unit of work?
- What criteria will be used to establish levels of achievement?
- What degree of precision is needed in defining objectives for individual lessons?
- How can the objectives provide for progression throughout the course?

The answers to these questions are likely to result in the use of a planning framework for each unit of work, with different categories of objectives used as headings.

The merits of the objectives model

The objectives model encourages systematic thinking about outcomes of learning, types of learning, and the emphasis given in assessment to different types of learning. This can encourage activities which are deemed to be more worthwhile. The categories of knowledge and understanding, skills and values, have provided a useful and supportive framework for organizing Geography courses, textbooks and syllabuses during the last twenty-five years. The inclusion of objectives in a curriculum plan can provide a sense of purpose to the teaching and learning. The extent to which objectives have been achieved can be used in external accountability to parents and to society generally.

Criticisms of the objectives model

The objectives model has been criticized on several grounds. It is much easier to prescribe outcomes and define outcomes for the learning of simple skills than for the understanding of ideas or complex situations. Understanding develops rather than being reached. The fact that some objectives are more easily defined than others could lead to greater emphasis being given to these outcomes of learning which are easily defined and assessed, but which are not necessarily more worthwhile.

Pursuit of clarity in defining objectives can lead to proliferation of statements. For example, the 1991 GNC was criticized for the large number of Statements of Attainment, while being at the same time found fault with because some of these statements needed to be broken down into separate statements in order to clarify what was needed. It is burdensome to write the number of objectives needed for clarity and impractical to assess the achievement of them all. Yet general objectives used in Geography, such as statements of key ideas, are open to criticism for failing to state what pupils need to do to achieve them.

There have been objections to the emphasis on predetermined outcomes because there is little role for the pupils, apart from complying with the teacher's plans. If one of the aims of education is to encourage pupils to think, how can all the outcomes be predetermined? As Stenhouse wrote: 'Education as induction into knowledge is successful to the extent that it makes the behavioural outcomes of the students unpredictable' (Stenhouse 1975: 82).

The objectives model might focus too much attention on the final products of learning. This could encourage teaching to the test, leading to closed, limited activities rather than to activities with unpredictable outcomes. It could also discourage teachers from using the unpredictable opportunities for learning which may arise from topical events, or from opportunities which may emerge during the course of a lesson.

A strong focus on objectives can act as a blinker to what is really happening in a classroom, so that the teacher is unaware of learning taking place which is unrelated to the objectives.

A curriculum plan tends to have common objectives for all pupils. This tends to overlook individual differences and needs.

A process model of curriculum development

Characteristics

There are three essential features of the process model of curriculum development. First, decisions are made about the principles of procedure which should guide teaching and learning activities before detailed planning takes place. Second, teaching and learning activities are designed which are underpinned by the principles of procedure and, third, the course is evaluated by monitoring the processes as well as the outcomes of learning.

Origins

The process model of curriculum development grew out of a belief in the intrinsic value of the education process, and from criticisms of the objectives model of planning (Peters 1959; Bruner 1966; Raths 1971; Stenhouse 1975).

One of the first examples of curriculum development based on a process model was an American social science course, developed by Jerome Bruner in the 1960s. The course, 'Man: A Course of Study', expressed its aims as principles instead of objectives. The first of the seven principles was: 'To initiate and develop in youngsters a process of question-posing'. The principles were intended to underpin all classroom activity, instead of representing end points of learning. The first principle was built into the course by using a framework of questions: What is human about human beings? How did they get that way? How can they be made more so?

Another notable example of the use of the process model was the Schools Council Humanities Curriculum Project, directed by Lawrence Stenhouse in the 1970s. One of its principles was 'that the mode of enquiry in controversial areas should have discussion rather than instruction as its core' (Ruddock 1983: 8). The project applied this principle in the provision of resources and devising of strategies to promote discussion. Raths, writing generally about curriculum development, advocated using criteria for identifying worthwhile activities. An example of his criteria is: 'All other things being equal, one activity is more worthwhile than another if it asks students to engage in inquiry into ideas, applications of intellectual processes, or current problems, either personal or social' (Raths 1971: 716).

As the process model of the curriculum was developed, new ways of evaluating teaching and learning developed, including action research in which teachers investigated the processes taking place in their own classrooms. The process model is associated with types of evaluation which depend on teachers 'reflecting in action', i.e. while they are teaching (Schon 1983), and after action, considering different types of evidence collected during classroom experience. Planning and developing a curriculum using the process model became not only a means of providing a curriculum for pupils, but also a means of continuous professional development.

Application of the process model of curriculum planning to geographical education

The impact of the process model of curriculum development in Geography can be seen in the development of the enquiry approach and on research into classroom processes.

The principles of procedure implicit in the enquiry approach would emphasize first, the importance of both teachers and pupils asking questions and, second, the importance of the active involvement of pupils in the processes necessary to answer them.

The importance given to questioning in Geography has led to the use of key questions at an early stage of curriculum planning. Instead of starting curriculum planning by defining the end products of learning it has become common to start at the beginning point of learning, i.e. with questions. Examples include the Schools Council 16–19 Project and the 1995 GNC.

The Schools Council 16–19 Geography Project produced a sequence of questions to be answered in investigating any geographical issue, in its route to geographical enquiry: what? where? how? why? what might? what will? with what impact? what decision? what do I think? why? what next? what shall I do? (Naish *et al.* 1987). These questions were to provide a framework for use in any area of content.

The 1995 GNC also has a series of questions in the Programmes of Study: what/ where is it? what is it like? how did it get like this? how and why is it changing? what are the implications?

Many examination syllabuses are now set out as a series of questions, e.g. 'What is quality of life and how can it be measured?' (Geography Avery Hill GCSE. WJEC 1995).

The second implicit principle of the enquiry approach is the involvement of pupils in the processes needed to answer those questions, rather than being provided with answers by the teacher. The impact of this principle on geographical education is seen in the emphasis on the skills needed to process geographical information in the GNC and in some examination syllabuses.

The 1995 GNC lists the investigative processes in Section 2 of each Programme of Study. Furthermore, the Level Descriptors in the Statement of Attainment for Geography in GNC emphasize process skills rather than terminal points in learning.

Examination Boards encourage the development of enquiry processes by setting decision-making examination papers and by assessing the ability to construct and process geographical knowledge from given data. Individual coursework investigations required for some external examinations engage pupils in the process of constructing geography for themselves. Marking schemes for such investigations attempt to assess engagement in different parts of the process, albeit from a final product.

The process model of thinking about curriculum has encouraged research into the processes of teaching and learning taking place in the classroom, focusing particularly on teachers' and pupils' use of language to learn geography. Research on oracy (Carter 1991), written work (Barnes 1976) and reading (Davies 1986) has revealed the role that pupils can play in developing their own understanding of geography. The increase in the use of small group work, role play, simulations, different genres of writing, and learning diaries are all evidence of the acknowledgement of the pupils' role in the construction of geographical knowledge and their contribution to the curriculum.

If the process model of curriculum planning is adopted, then the following questions need to be considered.

- What key questions need to be asked to enable pupils to engage with this area of subject-matter?
- Which questions should be asked initially by the teacher?
- How can teaching and learning activities be devised to encourage pupils to ask their own questions?

- What resources are needed to enable pupils to answer these questions?
- How are these resources collected and selected?
- What geographical techniques and procedures could be used to answer these questions?
- How can these techniques and procedures be incorporated into pupil activities?
- Which parts of the enquiry process will pupils be engaged in during the course unit and which during individual lessons?
- How can the processes in which the pupils are engaged be evaluated during and after lessons?
- How can what has been learned from the evaluation be built into subsequent lessons and units of work?

Merits of the process model

The process model of curriculum development focuses on learning. It recognizes the role of pupils in shaping what they learn and in constructing geography for themselves. It recognizes the complexity of classroom interaction. It values the learning that takes place, whether it is intended, unintended or unexpected. It takes account of individual differences. It is based on the intrinsic value of education. The professional judgement of teachers is valued in evaluating courses and assessing individuals.

Criticisms of the process model

The principles underpinning courses planned using the process model are not sufficiently precise to be used objectively in evaluation or assessment. The understanding of what takes place during a course is a matter for personal interpretation and professional judgement. Such judgements are less valuable than those based on a curriculum plan which follows the objectives model when comparisons are needed for purposes of public accountability and national assessment.

Professional dilemmas in curriculum planning

How teachers plan the Geography curriculum and develop courses is a matter of professional judgement. The current educational context is pulling them in two different directions.

The 1995 GNC encourages the use of the process model in curriculum development, with its focus on questions, processes of learning, and professional judgement in making holistic assessments of the pupils' levels of learning. Yet Ofsted inspections expect every unit of work and every lesson to have 'clearly formulated objectives'. Should open-ended questions or predetermined outcomes be the starting-point for planning for the GNC? Should key questions be interpreted as not being open-ended but just another form of expressing content? If a department wants to use a process model, how can objectives be defined to satisfy Ofsted? How much scope is there in the GNC to allow for the unexpected and the unpredictable, and to value the variety of response from individuals and schools? If a department wants to use an objectives model, what categories should be used for the GNC? How can the general statements in the level descriptors be developed into more precise statements of objectives? What should the balance be between openness and prescription in departmental GNC plans?

In the examination years the dilemmas for teachers are different. External examinations inevitably have to state the end products of learning which they are going to assess. Objectives are clearly stated. Yet some examinations place emphasis on individual enquiries, and frame the syllabus with key questions. What emphasis should geography departments give during the development and teaching of examination courses to the processes of learning geography compared to the end products of learning? League tables and Ofsted inspections encourage geography teachers to teach to the test, to what is required at the end, and to what will achieve high grades for the pupils. There may well be a conflict between the aims of enabling pupils to achieve the highest possible grades in public examinations and enabling pupils to become critical, enquiring people.

We seem to have reached a point in geographical education when both the objectives model and the process model have to be taken into account in curriculum planning and course design. This is because both models have had an influence on present-day geographical education. It is important to be aware of their influence and of some of the dilemmas they present. Inevitably, there will be compromises. This may mean using different models for different units of work, having some units emphasizing questioning and the enquiry process, and others concentrating on the product of learning. It may mean modifying the process model so that enquiry is rarely open-ended but is to a large extent controlled by the teacher. It may mean attempting to define objectives which would assess, formatively, a pupil's ability to engage in the enquiry process.

Geography teachers have to make professional judgements about how to work within the current context. Curriculum planning models, objectives, principles, approaches, etc. are not given by law but have been devised to meet needs. They are ideas which teachers have used for support in the challenging task of developing a worthwhile curriculum. It is up to teachers and departments to decide how to use these ideas, and what decisions to make, in the best interests of the pupils, the school and, ultimately, society. Within the current context, there are still many important decisions to be made about the Geography curriculum.

References

Barnes, D. (1976) *From Communication to Curriculum*, Harmondsworth: Penguin.
Bloom, B.S. (1956) *Taxonomy of Educational Objectives*, New York: David McKay Co.
Bobbitt, J.F. (1918) *The Curriculum*, Boston: Houghton Mifflin.
Bruner, J.S. (1966) *Towards a Theory of Instruction*, New York: W.W. Norton and Company Inc.

82 *Teaching Geography in secondary schools*

Carter, R. (1991) *Talking about Geography: The Work of Geography Teachers in the National Oracy Project*, Sheffield: Geographical Association.

Currie, S., Battersby, J., Bowden, D., Webster, A. and Whittal, R. (1994) *Landscape and Water Resources*, Glasgow: Collins Educational.

Davies, F. (1986) *Books in the School Curriculum*, London: Educational Publishers Council and National Book League.

DES (1990) *Geography for Ages 5 to 16*, London: HMSO.

DES (1991) *Geography in the National Curriculum*, London: HMSO.

Grimwade, K. (1995) 'Revising courses', *Teaching Geography* 20 (2): 62–6.

Geography for the Young School Leaver Project (1974) *Man, Land and Leisure: Teachers' Guide*, London: Schools Council Publications.

Mager, R.F. (1962) *Preparing Instructional Objectives*, Belmont, California: Fearon Publishers.

Naish, M., Rawling, E. and Hart, M. (1987) *The Contribution of a Curriculum Project to 16–19 Education*, London: Longman.

NCC (1991) *Geography Non-statutory Guidance (England)*, York: National Curriculum Council.

Ofsted (1993) *Handbook for the Inspection of Schools*, London: HMSO.

Peters, R.S. (1959) *Authority, Responsibility and Education*, London: Allen and Unwin.

Raths, J.D. (1971) 'Teaching without specific objectives', *Educational Leadership*, April: 714–20.

Ruddock, J. (1983) *The Humanities Curriculum Project: An Introduction*, Norwich: University of East Anglia.

SCAA (1995) *GCSE Subject Criteria for Geography*, London: SCAA.

Schon, D. (1983) *The Reflective Practitioner*, London: Temple Smith.

Stenhouse, L. (1975) *An Introduction to Curriculum Research and Development*, London: Heinemann Educational Books.

Taba, H. (1962) *Curriculum Development: Theory and Practice*, New York: Harcourt Brace and World.

Tyler, R. (1949) *Basic Principles of Curriculum and Instruction*, Chicago: University of Chicago Press.

6 Continuity and progression

Trevor Bennetts

Continuity and progression are widely recognised as desirable qualities within a curriculum. The National Curriculum, with its programmes of study and attainment targets, was intended to strengthen both qualities within the education provided for pupils between the ages of 5 and 16. The revisions to the Order for Geography appear to be a mixed blessing, weakening some aspects of continuity while in other respects making it much easier to plan for progression in pupils' learning. Before delving into details, it may be useful to clarify the distinction between the two concepts.

The idea of *continuity* suggests the persistence of significant features of geographical education as pupils move through the school system. Such features could include aspects of content, particular types of learning activity or common assumptions about the nature of the subject. With strong continuity, it is possible to design courses which enable pupils to build upon their previous experience and learning; and, thereby, help them to acquire knowledge and develop their understanding, skills and competencies in a structured way. Continuity of provision and approach can be looked for both within and between schools.

The idea of *progression*, on the other hand, focuses on how pupils' learning advances. It can be applied both to the design of a curriculum, in particular how the structure of content and sequence of learning activities are intended to facilitate advances in learning, and to the gradual gains in knowledge, understanding, skills and competencies which pupils actually achieve. The idea of progression is complementary to that of continuity. While continuity of curricular provision provides opportunities for advances in learning, by itself it does not guarantee them. Progression has to be planned for and monitored, and the only effective way of doing the latter is by the use of assessment.

The scope for continuity

The inclusion of Geography as a foundation subject within the National Curriculum was itself an important step towards promoting continuity. While Dearing's recommendation that Geography should be allocated at least 36 hours per year in Key Stage 1, and 45 hours per year in Key Stages 2 and 3 may not satisfy everyone, it should ensure that all pupils have the benefit of a sustained encounter with the subject until the age of 14. It is no longer acceptable for geography teachers in secondary schools to ignore what pupils have learnt in primary schools, nor for secondary schools to design humanities courses in which geography is only a weak component. Whatever the title of the courses through which geography is to be delivered, the subject has to be there in a clearly identified form, and it has to meet the statutory requirements of the National Curriculum. The new programmes of study do contain recurrent elements which support continuity. Among the most prominent of these are:

1   the emphasis on the study of places;
2   the attention given to location, spatial patterns and the links between places;
3   the concern with physical and human geography, and with the relationships between people and their environments;
4   the use of maps; and
5   the investigation of places and themes.

Furthermore, Key Stage 3 maintains sufficient breadth to offer many opportunities for continuity with GCSE courses.

The scope for progression

The level descriptions should make it much easier for secondary schools to plan their Geography curriculums and assess their pupils' progress in learning. While the need to differentiate provision in order to cater for pupils of very different capabilities will remain, teachers will no longer have to contend with a structure which made that especially difficult.

SCAA's conception of progression in Geography within Key Stage 3 is stated in very clear terms in its draft proposals (SCAA 1994).

Through the Key Stage, pupils will increasingly:

• broaden and deepen their knowledge and understanding of places and themes;
• make use of a wide and precise geographical vocabulary;
• analyse, rather than describe, geographical patterns, processes and change;
• appreciate the interactions within and between physical and human processes that operate in any environment;
• appreciate the interdependence of places;
• become proficient at conducting and comparing studies at a widening range of scales and in contrasting places and environments;
• apply their geographical knowledge and understanding to unfamiliar contexts;
• select and make effective use of skills and techniques to support their geographical investigations;
• appreciate the limitations of geographical evidence and the tentative and incomplete nature of some explanations.

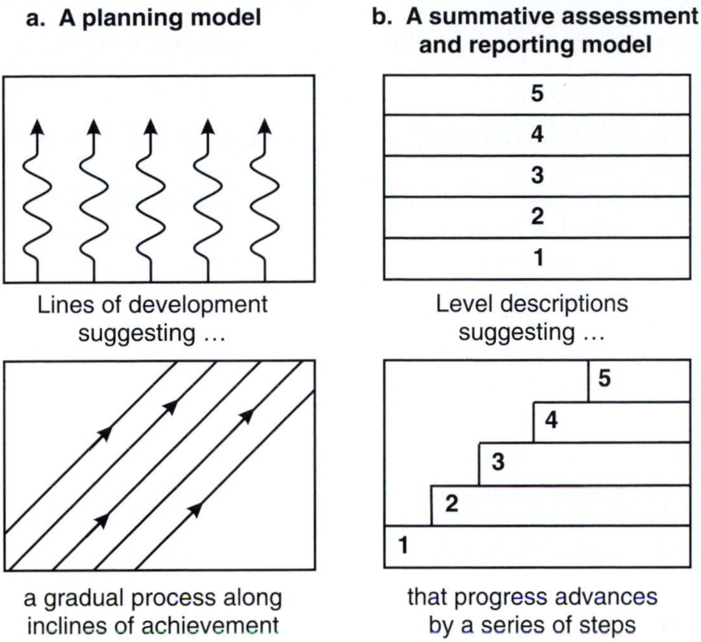

a. A planning model   **b. A summative assessment
                                             and reporting model**

Lines of development   Level descriptions
suggesting …   suggesting …

a gradual process along   that progress advances
inclines of achievement   by a series of steps

Figure 6.1   Contrasting images of progression

The statement suggests a gradual process, involving a wide range of elements which characterise attainment in the subject. These elements, which provide broad criteria for assessing pupils' progress, are in the main reflected in the level descriptions. However, the idea of levels of attainment is not entirely consistent with the notion of progression as a range of qualities which develop gradually through the Key Stages. Each level description is a cluster of interrelated elements, and while the boundaries between successive levels are not sharply defined, the image of progression which the levels present is more like a series of steps than gently sloping inclines (Figure 6.1).

The reasons for this difference are easy to understand. The level descriptions are designated to underpin assessment and reporting. While progression can usefully be analysed in terms of different elements or aspects of learning, represented in Figure 6.1 as lines of development, each level description is a generalised pen picture of the type of overall attainment which qualifies for a particular grade at the end of a Key Stage. Progression in learning is more complicated than either of these. Individual pupils may advance more rapidly in some aspects of the subject than others, and their progress is not always continuous. They may at times even regress. Furthermore, in practice, the quality of their performance has to be measured in relation to specific content and activities, and to the circumstances in which the activities take place.

Planning for progression

Among the principles which should influence planning for progression in Key Stage 3 are:

- teaching should build on pupils' existing knowledge and experience, whenever possible;
- learning tasks should be matched carefully to pupils' capabilities;
- particular attention should be given to those aspects of geography which not only interest pupils at the time of teaching but also provide satisfactory preparation for the next phase of education.

Planning for progression should, therefore, take account of the past, present and future: what pupils have already experienced and achieved; what they can reasonably be expected to do at the time; and what will best serve their future needs. Although some pupils will not continue with the subject beyond Key Stage 3, all must be given the foundation from which to advance should they decide to take the subject further.

It is useful to analyse the nature of the progression required for the Key Stage, in relation to:

- breadth of geographical knowledge;
- depth of geographical understanding;
- use of geographical skills;
- attitudes and values.

Breadth of geographical knowledge

Pupils' breadth of geographical knowledge is largely an outcome of the content of the curriculum, although it may also be related to the attention given to recall of knowledge as an educational objective. The study of the places and themes specified for the Key Stage should produce a gradual extension of pupils' knowledge of the variety of conditions and processes on the earth's surface. As they move through Key Stage 3, pupils should become increasingly well informed. The inclusion in the Programme of Study of a more developed and a less developed country; of physical, human and environmental themes; and of studies at a range of spatial scales and in a variety of geographical contexts, provides abundant scope for pupils to acquire a broad base of geographical knowledge. Such knowledge should support the development of their understanding.

Table 6.1 A content framework for progression in the theme of economic activities

Year	Relevant unit of study	Weeks	Aspects of economic activities to be studied
7	Short case studies: sparsely populated areas	6	Types of economic activity
			Influence on those activities of the environment, location, and, where relevant, the history of places studied
	farm studies	6	
	an industrial region	6	Links within and between economic activities
	a large commercial city	3	Causes of recent change
			(Concepts of primary, secondary and tertiary activities)
8	Tourism – theme focus	6	Geography of an economic activity
			Distribution patterns of different types of tourism
			Attractions and requirements: natural attractions and their development; accommodation, transport and other facilities
			Seasonal patterns and their effects
			(Concepts of supply and demand, price and cost; choice, resources and their development)
	Towns: internal characteristics and changing patterns	6	Economic and other factors influencing land-use and building patterns
			Development of out-of-town shopping centres and business parks
			(Concepts of conflicting land-uses, accessibility, land values)
	A 'more developed' country	12	Economic characteristics of the country
			International trade. Uneven distribution of population, economic activities and prosperity
			Comparison of two regions – causes of economic differences
9	A 'less developed' country	12	Economic characteristics of the country
			International trade; uneven distribution of population, economic activities and prosperity
			Comparison of two regions – causes of economic differences
			(Concepts of development, core and periphery)
	Movements between countries	6	International patterns of trade, migration and investment
			Relationships between rich and poor countries
			Causes of uneven development

When planning the Geography curriculum, teachers need to consider which information is intended to be used by pupils primarily as part of the process of learning, with no need for long-term recall, and which is intended to be memorised so that it can be recalled when required. This distinction has implications for teaching and assessment.

There is no single principle for determining the sequence in which specific knowledge should be acquired, as much is dependent on context and use. Obviously, to be of value the knowledge must be both accurate and meaningful to the pupils. The broadening of a pupil's knowledge is to a considerable extent a cumulative process, with the idea of progression becoming more pertinent when we consider how that knowledge is to be structured to develop understanding. Previously acquired knowledge is reinforced when pupils perceive it to be relevant to new learning, and long-term recall is usually helped by periodic revisiting.

Depth of geographical understanding

Progression in pupils' geographical understanding is closely associated with the development of their ability to describe and explain geographical conditions, patterns, relationships and changes. This is often dependent on them developing general geographical ideas (concepts, generalisations and models) and being able to apply these to new situations. Understanding is revealed by the ability of pupils to interpret, analyse, synthesise and evaluate information. There is, therefore, a close relationship between the development of understanding and more general intellectual capabilities. This is reflected in the level descriptions.

Thus, while for *Level 4* pupils are expected to:

- begin to describe geographical patterns and to appreciate the importance of location in understanding places …
- recognise and describe physical and human processes …
- begin to show understanding of how these processes can change the features of places, and that these changes affect the lives and activities of people living there.

For *Level 7* they are expected to:

- describe the interactions within and between physical and human processes …
- show how these interactions create geographical patterns and contribute to change in places and patterns …
- show understanding that many factors influence decisions made about places, and use this to explain how places change.

There are clear indications here that progression in geographical understanding in Key Stage 3 is envisaged in terms of pupils' increasing capacity to comprehend complex interactions, and to offer fuller and more sophisticated explanations. This implies that they must develop the general ideas which will enable them to structure and interpret information about places and themes. The fact that place studies at regional and national scales are not required until Key Stage 3 is largely because pupils' ability to develop a coherent view of a place at these scales is dependent on their capacity to make sense of generalised descriptions of conditions and processes.

To some extent, the abilities of pupils to deal with complex relationships and with generalisations go hand in hand. However, there are limits to how far it is reasonable to expect pupils of this age to think in abstract terms. While many will experience considerable intellectual development between the ages of 11 and 14 which will affect their style of reasoning and extend their abilities to form concepts and explore relationships, their thinking will for the most part be tied to concrete experiences. They still need to relate their ideas to particular objects, events and situations which have reality for them, even if the information on which their knowledge is based is derived from secondary sources. We should not underestimate the challenge presented by such concepts as spatial interdependence, development, sustainable development, stewardship and conservation, and need to be clear in our own minds about the essential meaning of such concepts before we consider how pupils' understanding of them can be developed.

The identification of key ideas and analysis of potential lines of progression can be approached through the themes specified in the Programme of Study. While some of the themes may be taught almost exclusively within single units of study, most of them can be planned as recurrent elements which will be relevant to a number of units, including those which are based on specific places rather than themes. Economic activities, for example, could be the focus for one unit and figure prominently in several others.

In the example presented in Table 6.1, the unit planned to be the focus for the theme of 'economic activities' is that of 'tourism', which is to occupy six weeks in Year 8. However, economic activities also figure prominently in many other units. The short case studies in Year 7 all have an economic dimension, and through these pupils are introduced to the differences between primary, secondary and tertiary industries. In Year 8, the study of towns includes an investigation of the changing distribution pattern of retailing and office development, and the place studies in Years 8 and 9 give particular attention to broad economic patterns and to regional contrasts. Finally, explicit attention is given to 'development', which, although specified in the PoS as a separate theme, is closely linked to economic activities.

In this scheme, progression in the treatment of economic activities is envisaged as involving the gradual introduction and development of economic and geographic concepts, and gradual increases in the spatial scale of studies and in the complexity of the relationships investigated. Although not indicated in Table 6.1, progression would also require the development and application of relevant techniques and skills.

Use of geographical skills

The types of learning that are often grouped together under the general heading of 'skills' are varied in character. The National Curriculum for Geography includes:

- specific techniques – such as those associated with fieldwork, the use of maps and diagrams, and the use of information technology;
- broad categories of cognitive activity – such as describing, interpreting, analysing, explaining and communicating; and
- strategies of enquiry – ways of structuring and carrying out investigations so as to arrive at valid conclusions which can be substantiated.

Although these three types of skills are different in kind, in practice it is often necessary to use them in conjunction. Furthermore, in geographical studies they have to be applied in contexts which have geographical content, and which therefore require knowledge and understanding on the part of the pupils.

Progression in learning geographical skills is most easily envisaged in relation to the more specific techniques. Useful advice on progression in the development of map skills has been provided by Boardman (1986). Appropriate map skills should be developed systematically over the Key Stage, rather than be taught in a single unit in Year 7 and then largely ignored.

When we turn to broader categories of cognitive activity, such as describing and interpreting, it becomes obvious that what we are including here as skills are competencies which are dependent on knowledge and understanding. To interpret the coastal relief depicted on a 1:50,000 Ordnance Survey map, it may be necessary to know something about coastal processes and coastal landforms as well as about map conventions.

Progression is not a simple sequence of activities which, for example, proceeds from identifying a feature to describing it and then explaining its characteristics. The nature and distinctiveness of the feature, and the quality of description and explanation are all relevant. A curriculum should be designed to give pupils opportunities to improve the quality of their descriptions and explanations; and to apply their understanding in increasingly sophisticated ways. Their explanations can reveal their understanding, and both will reflect their knowledge and their styles of reasoning.

Progression in geographical enquiry is also a complicated matter, for which pupils require opportunities to develop a range of skills. The level descriptions draw attention to the importance of pupils' growing independence in carrying out investigations, but the role of teachers must not be underestimated. Pupils will require considerable guidance over the Key Stage to continue to develop effective strategies for investigating places and themes.

Attitudes and values

Attitudes and values are implicit rather than explicit in the National Curriculum for Geography. However, they are present in both the programmes of study and level descriptions, especially in the requirement that pupils 'consider the issues which arise from peoples' interactions with their environments' and in the attention given to disparities of development. Values are deeply embedded within such topics as the causes and effects of population migration, conflicts over urban land use, and people's response to hazards; and within such concepts as development, quality of life, environmental management, sustainability, stewardship and conservation. Pupils need to develop understanding of how the goals, assumptions, attitudes and values held by people influence their decisions and actions. They also need opportunities to discuss and reflect on such matters, so that they can develop well-informed views of their own. Progression is linked to the extent to which pupils are sensitive to the views of others; can engage in rational discussion; can diagnose issues and responses; and understand that solutions sometimes require compromise.

Building progression into a scheme of work

Progression is an important dimension in a curriculum, but it is a less tangible component than others such as content and learning activities, and tends to be implicit rather than explicit in schemes of work. I have tried to show that it can be analysed in relation to various broad categories of learning, which are represented in the level descriptions for Geography and in the KS3 Programme of Study for the subject. As we have seen, these categories are complex and interrelated.

The visible structure of a KS3 scheme of work is likely to consist of a sequence of units of study, most of which focus on particular aspects of content. The content and skills specified in the KS3 Programme of Study can be arranged in many ways, producing alternative units and different sequences. Progression through such frameworks can be approached in two ways.

One is in the form of 'routes' or 'threads' which are planned to enable pupils to return periodically to significant elements of their geographical education, so that their learning can advance in a systematic way. Elements which can be planned as routes include: recurrent themes, such as weather and climate, settlement and economic activities; specific groups of related skills, such as those associated with mapwork and fieldwork, and even key concepts, such as relative location, place, development and environmental management. This is the approach which produces a 'spiral curriculum'.

The other approach, which is complementary to the first, is concerned with broader competencies, such as the ability to describe and explain, and with very general qualities associated with different levels of achievement, such as the extent to which pupils understand abstract ideas and complex relationships, use suitable strategies of enquiry, and reveal an appreciation of the significance of conflicting attitudes and values. This approach is more in line with the judgements which have to be made in relation to level descriptions.

Although much can be planned in advance, teaching has to take account of how pupils respond to particular learning tasks, and to the different rates of progress of groups and individuals. Assessment is essential to monitor pupils' progress and enable teachers to differentiate their provision to meet individual needs. As progress in learning cannot be taken for granted, the implementation of curriculum plans, especially at the level of lesson planning, has to be flexible: that is part of the art of teaching.

References

Boardman, D. (ed.) (1986) *Handbook for Geography Teachers*, The Geographical Association.
Curriculum Council for Wales (1991) *Geography in the National Curriculum (Wales). Non-Statutory Guidance*, CCW.
Geography Working Group (1990) *Geography for Ages 5 to 16*, Report of the National Curriculum GWG, DES.
School Curriculum and Assessment Authority (1994) *Geography in the National Curriculum, Draft Proposals*, SCAA.

7 Teaching styles and strategies

David Balderstone

Although there has been increasing standardisation in recent years of the aims and content of geographical education in England and Wales, teaching geography remains a very personal activity. Geography teachers can still exercise autonomy in their selection of teaching strategies and learning activities. Thus, it is easier to determine what geography teachers teach than to influence how they deliver this content (Roberts 1996: 237).

However, as Slater (1987: 55) asserts, the selection of teaching strategies is 'as important as selecting content'. Successful teaching involves knowing what to do to bring about the desired learning and being able to do it. One of our main professional concerns as geography teachers should be to learn how to set up learning activities and use different teaching strategies to bring about the aspects of learning in geography that we intend for our pupils. Thus geography teachers are also 'learners', developing their knowledge and understanding of processes of teaching and learning in the subject (Lambert and Balderstone 2000: 233).

We could be forgiven for thinking that teaching is now anything but a personal activity. In the late 1990s, the debate has shifted away from the content of the curriculum towards a focus on methods of teaching. The introduction of programmes for developing literacy and numeracy in the primary years based on the use of specific teaching strategies provides the clearest indication of this policy trend. However important this context, it is not the purpose of this chapter to analyse the influence of educational policy upon classroom practice in Geography. This author shares Margaret Roberts' belief that geography teachers still have considerable freedom to decide 'how they are going to teach and how their pupils are going to learn' (1996: 32).

We begin by considering some of the contexts shaping current discussions about teaching strategies, before outlining some of the frameworks that have been used to describe teaching strategies. Finally, some thoughts about the ways in which geography teachers might develop their pedagogic knowledge are explored in order to raise important professional development issues.

Contexts and concerns

What teachers do to ensure that pupils learn, the 'craft' of teaching, is often referred to as pedagogy. In defining pedagogy as 'any conscious activity by one person designed to enhance learning in another', Watkins and Mortimore (1999: 3) emphasise the importance of the relationship between teaching and learning. They contend that an emphasis on only the teacher's role and activity would be more appropriately described by the term 'didactics'.

In exploring different conceptions of pedagogy, Watkins and Mortimore (ibid.) suggest that there have been four main phases in the development of our understanding, but recognise that the transition between these has not represented a smooth progression:

1   A focus on different types of teachers which attributed impact to a teacher's personal style, the underlying purpose perhaps being to identify 'good' and 'bad' approaches.
2   A focus on the contexts of teaching which added organisational and managerial aspects of teachers' classroom work to the view of pedagogy. This view of pedagogy established a 'more sophisticated approach to understanding the complex interactions of pupils and teachers' (ibid.: 4) with the classroom being seen as an 'activity system'.
3   A focus on teaching and learning reflecting a shift away from 'transmission–reception' models towards a view of effective learners being able to develop a better understanding of their own learning. This view is partly the result of our 'increased awareness of the need to think of learners as active constructors of meaning' (ibid.: 7).
4   Current views of pedagogy which offer more complex and integrated models which specify relations between the different elements: teachers, learners, classrooms and other contexts, content, views of learning and learning about learning (Watkins *et al.* 1996). Central to such a conception is the creation of learning communities in which 'knowledge is actively constructed, and in which the focus of learning is sometimes learning itself' (Watkins and Mortimore 1999: 8).

We are starting to see a growing interest in pedagogy in education at the level of policy, practice and research. Some would argue that pedagogy has, until recently, been a neglected issue even though it affects the way in which learners are taught (Millet 1999; Mortimore 1999). Anthea Millet, the former Chief Executive of the Teacher Training Agency in England and Wales (herself a former geography teacher), argued that this is partly due to teachers' understandable fears of treading on each other's 'professional toes'. 'I am always struck by how difficult they find it to talk about teaching and how unwilling some of them are to talk about teaching at all. They prefer to talk about learning as if there is no relationship between the two' (1999: 4).

Hallam and Ireson (1999: 69) contend that the controversy about pedagogy is inevitable because there is a lack of understanding about the relationship between the 'learning of the individual' and the 'activities of the teacher'. For practical reasons, the assessment of teaching tends to focus on the skills of the teacher and pupils' learning outcomes. Hallam and Ireson (ibid.) also argue that research has tended to focus on either teaching or learning because of the 'difficulty of capturing the tenuous relationship between the two'. They conclude that to become an 'effective pedagogue', a teacher needs to acquire 'a complex body of knowledge, extensive practical skills and the means of evaluating them' (ibid.: 88).

Although there is a fairly extensive literature about approaches to the teaching of Geography, there seems to me to be an ill-defined body of pedagogic knowledge within geography education. In broad terms, most of the debate within geography education during the 1960s and 1970s focused on the nature of the subject discipline and its educational potential. Although there was interest in approaches to learning Geography and the creation of appropriate curriculum materials, little attention was given to the rationale for and principles guiding the effective use of different teaching strategies.

Graves (1971) did provide a discussion of teaching strategies in Geography stressing the importance of the relationship between teaching and learning when attempting to achieve geographical objectives. He argued that 'any method which is successful in reaching the objective is a good method. There is no point in being doctrinaire about a particular method, if in fact it is not resulting in pupils learning what they are supposed to be learning' (ibid.: 6). Graves distinguished between 'teaching methods', which he described as a 'series of procedures', and 'techniques of teaching geography' (see Figure 7.1). 'Techniques' refer to what we understand by teaching strategies whereas 'procedures' describe the general approach to teaching adopted by the teacher.

Methods of teaching Geography

A Verbal learning and real understanding
B Guidance and discovery in learning Geography
C Thinking in Geography

Techniques of teaching Geography

A Classroom techniques
    (i)   The oral lesson using a textbook and atlas
    (ii)   The non-oral working lesson
    (iii)   The use of medium- and large-scale maps
    (iv)   Using pictures and photographs
    (v)   The use of other audio visual aids
    (vi)   The case study approach
    (vii)   The transformation of data
    (viii) Games and stimulation
    (ix)   Programmed learning

B Fieldwork techniques
    (i)   Types of fieldwork in the lower secondary school
    (ii)   Investigations in the upper secondary school

Figure 7.1 The methods and techniques of teaching Geography

Source: Graves (1971).

The Schools' Council projects (Geography for the Young School Leaver 14–16, Geography 14–18 and Geography 16–19) made highly significant contributions to curriculum development in Geography in the 1970s and 1980s. One of the main aims of these projects was to encourage approaches to learning Geography that would enable pupils to develop a range of abilities and skills in the process of gaining knowledge and understanding. These projects advocated particular styles of teaching which reflected their educational aims and philosophy. Through this process of school-based curriculum development, they sought to influence the teaching styles and strategies used by geography teachers. Roberts (1996: 235) illustrates this point by quoting Renwick (1985), who suggests that the Geography for the Young School Leaver project

> encouraged the move away from didactic methods of teaching to experiential learning … the project particularly encourages the move towards a discovery/ investigative approach in situations well structured by the teacher. The teacher is encouraged to be a guide and stimulus, and to abandon the traditional expository approach in favour of more 'open learning'.

Through the late 1970s and the 1980s concern focused on the role of Geography as a medium for education. Frances Slater's (1982) *Learning Through Geography* was an influential text providing teachers with guidance on how to structure learning activities. The identification of key questions guided planning and the development of the learning process. Classroom activities and teaching strategies were suggested for working towards generalisations or the resolution of conflicting viewpoints. The important role of language in learning was also discussed.

In a similar way, *The Geography Teacher's Guide to the Classroom* (Fien, Gerber and Wilson 1984) provided examples of classroom activities as well as practical advice on specific curriculum issues and teaching strategies. Once again the emphasis was on Geography as a 'medium for education'. However, this was one of the first texts for geography teachers that explored the application of specific teaching strategies in Geography.

While the 'handbooks' produced for geography teachers by the Geographical Association (Boardman 1987; Bailey and Fox 1996) have provided guidance about some teaching strategies, the need to fulfil a variety of purposes means that they lack any in-depth discussion of many pedagogic issues. They consider approaches to teaching and learning in Geography and strategies for using different resources, but provide only limited guidance about different aspects of learning in Geography and little insight into relationships between teaching and learning in the subject. This is perhaps understandable given the need to address a multitude of other curriculum issues.

One of the most significant recent developments in teaching and learning in Geography has been the attention being given to the need to develop pupils' ability to think through Geography. Leat (1997: 143) argues that there has been 'too much emphasis on substantive aspects of geography and not enough on the intellectual development of pupils'. This author shares David Leat's concern about the preponderance of 'busy work' in many geography classrooms and about the failure of many geography textbooks, and much geography teaching to challenge pupils (ibid.: 143). This is due to a lack of attention being given to the nature of pupil learning through Geography and to pedagogic relationships between teaching and learning in the subject.

One of the consequences of the increasing standardisation of the curriculum is that the content of school Geography has changed little in recent years and we have also seen the emergence of the 'textbook as curriculum' in many schools. The danger is that such 'textbook curricula' require 'minimal skilled intervention' by the teacher and can thus diminish 'teacher professionalism' (Leat 1997: 144). The 'Thinking through Geography' project (Leat 1998) offers teaching strategies and learning activities designed to promote pupils' intellectual development through more stimulating and challenging Geography lessons. It also makes a significant contribution to our understanding of pedagogy in Geography through its focus on 'fundamental concepts' in Geography. Giving some attention to how pupils develop their conceptual understanding should help geography teachers to understand more about the use of teaching strategies that promote cognitive development. Geography teachers need to learn more about how certain strategies can provide appropriate challenge which is an essential prerequisite of intellectual development. They also need to develop debriefing skills that help pupils to explore their own thinking (metacognition).

Educational policy

The educational policy context also exerts a significant influence on how we view teaching. Watkins and Mortimore (1999: 13) comment on how politicians and policy-makers have been taking an increasing interest in the 'details of pedagogy'. More recently, the emphasis on the development of 'evidence-based policy' in education has led to a focus on actions which policy-makers claim will achieve particular results. This approach can be seen in the introduction of literacy and numeracy strategies in primary schools in England and Wales. The effectiveness of these strategies in achieving the desired improvements in literacy and numeracy will be monitored, creating some interesting relations between teachers, academic researchers and educational policy-makers.

'Standards' which define aspects of a teacher's work have been introduced. The *Standards for the Award of Qualified Teacher Status* in England and Wales (DfEE 1998a) outline the 'standards' that need to be achieved by trainee teachers if they are to gain Qualified Teacher Status. Initial teacher training courses are required to assess all trainees to ensure that they meet all of these standards. Within a section on 'Planning, Teaching and Class Management' there is a requirement for trainee teachers to demonstrate that they 'use teaching methods which sustain the momentum of pupils' work and keep all pupils engaged' (ibid.: 8). A range of objectives, related to different aspects of learning, are stated for these 'methods' but no strategies are specified. Trainee teachers are also required to 'evaluate their own teaching critically and use this to improve their effectiveness' (ibid.: 9). It remains to be seen whether subject-specific exemplifications of these standards will be developed and if so what they might say about teaching strategies in Geography.

In addition to this, an even more prescriptive 'initial teacher training National Curriculum' was introduced for the use of information and communications technology in subject teaching (DfEE 1998b). This curriculum requires that all trainee teachers are 'taught' and 'able to use' 'effective teaching and assessment methods' relevant to the use of ICT in their subject teaching. Their 'knowledge and understanding of, and competence with information technology' must also be developed. It is perhaps interesting that direct reference is made to pedagogy in this latter area. Trainee teachers are required to 'demonstrate that they are competent in those areas of ICT which support pedagogy' in their subject teaching and specific strategies or applications are set out.

National Standards for subject leaders have also been introduced (TTA 1998) but have yet to be made statutory. These standards are part of a policy which seeks to promote 'improvements in the quality of teaching and leadership which will have the maximum impact on pupils' learning' (ibid., p. 1). Subject leaders are seen as having a key responsibility for 'teaching and learning' in their subject. They are required to 'secure and sustain effective teaching of the subject, evaluate the quality of teaching and standards of pupils' achievements and set targets for improvement' (ibid., p. 10). The Geographical Association's (1999) guidance on these standards advocates that subject leaders in Geography should plan opportunities for a variety of teaching and learning styles and strategies. It identifies some questions that subject leaders should consider in relation to the use of these strategies (ibid.: 9):

- Which of these strategies do you use in your school/department?
- How often do you use these strategies?
- How do you know that they are used in other classes?
- Which are planned for, and which are followed incidentally?
- Are they planned with continuity and progression in mind?
- How can you make these accessible to all (noting, for example, gender, ethnicity, ability)?
- How might you plan to introduce a new approach?
- What constraints might there be to developing new strategies?
- How might you overcome these constraints?

It remains to be seen how the work of subject leaders in Geography will be judged against these standards. For example, there are undoubtedly subject leaders who can successfully evaluate teaching in their subject, identifying effective practice and providing guidance on the 'choice of appropriate teaching and learning methods to meet the needs of the subject and of different pupils' (TTA 1998: 11). However, what range of teaching styles and strategies will be deemed to be 'appropriate' and by whom? The standards also appear to require subject leaders to develop their own pedagogic knowledge and skills, but will there be a professional development culture, processes and support in place to enable this to occur?

Another new policy which could have important implications for teaching and learning is the introduction of the notion of 'Advanced Skills' teachers who are rewarded for their classroom expertise. Part of the role of being an 'Advanced Skills' teacher involves sharing this expertise both within and between schools. Although there appear to be fairly rigorous procedures for assessing teachers' capabilities, the criteria for awarding 'Advanced Skills' status in relation to pedagogy are unclear at the moment. What range of teaching strategies must teachers use effectively? To what extent do they understand the nature of the relationships between their teaching and their pupils' learning? Do they understand the principles underpinning effective use of particular strategies and are they able to communicate this understanding to the teachers with whom they are supposed to share such practice? Do they possess the skills and strategies needed to promote effective professional development for other teachers?

Effective teaching

There is already an extensive body of research literature about effective teaching. Some of this research has concentrated on identifying particular features of teaching and learning which contribute to school effectiveness (Mortimore 1994). Doyle (1987) argues that pupils achieve more when teachers employ a structured approach to their teaching, provide pupils with plenty of opportunities to practise, monitor progress and check understanding with frequent direct questioning, and provide continuous feedback on this progress. Research into 'effective' departments in secondary schools has also emphasised the importance of structuring and feedback in contributing to effective teaching (Harris, Jamieson and Russ 1995). This research also drew attention to the value of teaching strategies and learning activities that encourage cooperative learning as well as underlining the importance of using a variety of styles and strategies.

Evidence from the inspection of Geography lessons raises some important issues about teaching strategies. Reviews of this evidence have highlighted possible relationships between the use of particular teaching strategies and standards of achievement in Geography (Smith 1997; Ofsted 1998). Low standards of achievement often result from insufficient use being made of practical and investigative work (such as fieldwork), or of strategies and geographical contexts that promote thinking. Furthermore, Smith (1997: 126) suggests that in such situations:

> There is sometimes a narrowness in the range of teaching methods characterised by over-long expositions, over-directed styles inhibiting curiosity and initiative and discussions mediated by and through the teacher, all of which reduce opportunities for developing thinking in an uncritical context. Also, some teachers intervene too quickly and then provide an answer in their own words.

Such comments illustrate the importance of pedagogy, of the need for geography teachers to understand more about the principles underpinning effective use of different teaching strategies. They also highlight the need for effective subject leadership as well as the creation of a professional development culture and processes which enhance teacher professionalism and promote further improvements in the quality of geography teaching.

Frameworks for describing and analysing teaching styles

The term 'teaching style' is used to describe the way in which Geography is taught. It has an important influence on the educational experience of pupils in Geography because it affects how they learn Geography. A teacher's teaching style is determined by their 'behaviour' (their demeanour and the way in which they relate to pupils) and the strategy that they choose to bring about the learning intended.

Some teachers often feel that certain teaching styles and strategies are more appropriate for them because they suit their personality and reflect their philosophy of teaching. However, it is now generally accepted that teachers need to develop a repertoire of different styles and strategies. This is because they need to consider the characteristics and needs of their pupils (their attitudes, abilities and preferred ways of learning) and the intended learning outcomes, as well as their own preferred ways of teaching. They draw upon their own body of pedagogic knowledge about how teachers teach and how pupils learn. Teachers' personal qualities and their approaches to classroom management influence the way that they teach. The nature of the learning environment that they work in (classroom appearance and layout), the size of the class and the availability of appropriate learning resources will also have a significant influence on the decisions that they make about their teaching.

Many of the terms that are used to describe different ways of teaching are not always helpful. Terms such as didactic, teacher-directed, whole-class, practical and experiential provide what are at best only general descriptions.

When used to describe teaching styles, terms such as 'progressive' and 'traditional' are value-laden and stereotypical extremes. For example, one view of progressive teaching might be that it is enquiry-based, child-centred, concerned with problem-solving and therefore represents a forward-looking and effective approach to teaching. However, another view might be that it is 'trendy' and lacking intellectual substance. Traditional teaching may be seen as being old-fashioned, autocratic, didactic and lacking creative opportunities, or as being reliable and effective at maintaining academic standards. Opinions about the relative strengths and weaknesses of different styles of teaching vary and such descriptions only give a partial view of how a teacher may be teaching.

As mentioned earlier, research in the past has often focused on the relationship between different styles of teaching and the effectiveness of pupil learning. This often leads to more value being placed on one style than another because it is believed to be more effective or, as Roberts (1996: 235) also suggests, because it relates more to the researchers' 'particular educational aims and philosophy'.

The Schools Council projects described earlier set out to influence the styles of teaching used by geography teachers through the process of school-based

Teaching–learning relationships

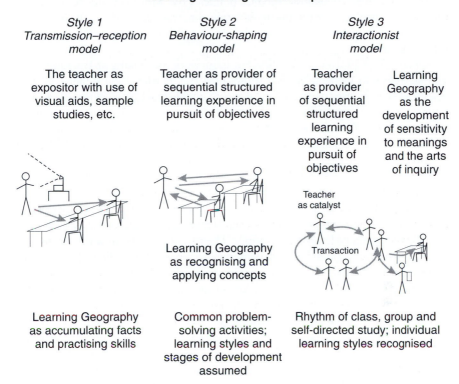

Style 1	Style 2	Style 3
Transmission–reception model	*Behaviour-shaping model*	*Interactionist model*

The teacher as expositor with use of visual aids, sample studies, etc.

Teacher as provider of sequential structured learning experience in pursuit of objectives

Teacher as provider of sequential structured learning experience in pursuit of objectives

Learning Geography as the development of sensitivity to meanings and the arts of inquiry

Teacher as catalyst

Transaction

Learning Geography as recognising and applying concepts

Learning Geography as accumulating facts and practising skills

Common problem-solving activities; learning styles and stages of development assumed

Rhythm of class, group and self-directed study; individual learning styles recognised

Figure 7.2 Alternative styles of teaching and learning Geography
Source: Tolley and Reynolds (1977).

curriculum development. The 14–18 Bristol Project, which sought to influence Geography for high achieving pupils during the 1970s, identified three styles of classroom interaction (see Figure 7.2) but indicated a strong preference for an interactionist style of teaching Geography. The weaknesses of the transmission and structured learning approaches were highlighted while greater emphasis was placed on the significance of values in decision-making and on the deeper learning processes inherent in the interactionist model.

Another influential curriculum development, the Schools Council 16–19 Geography Project, advocated an 'enquiry-based' approach to teaching and learning and envisaged a continuum of approaches (see Chapter 4). Although this provided 'scope for an effective balance of both teacher-directed and more independent enquiry' (Naish *et al.* 1987: 46), the projects view of enquiry-based learning focused predominantly on structured problem-solving and open-ended discovery.

It is clear that there is often a gap between the rhetoric and ideals espoused about teaching styles and what actually happens in the classroom. Pragmatism and an understanding of particular school contexts and cultures lead teachers to adapt the teaching styles and strategies that they use. However, this could lead to a belief that you cannot use particular styles or strategies with pupils in certain school contexts. This would of course deprive pupils of opportunities to learn in different ways.

Roberts (1996) introduced a different framework for looking at teaching styles and strategies in Geography. She shows how the 'participation dimension' (see Table 7.1) can be used as an analytical tool to enable teachers to 'engage critically' with their own practice. She has adapted this framework so that it can be used to interpret and analyse different styles of teaching and learning in Geography (see Table 7.2). Using this framework it is possible to imagine what geography lessons consistent with particular styles of teaching and learning might be like. She argues that teachers can adapt their strategies so that they operate across different styles depending on the context in which they are working (ibid.: 238).

In the closed style the learners are passive as the teacher controls the selection of content and the way it is presented to them. This content is presented as 'authoritative knowledge' to be learnt by the pupils. The teacher decides how this content or 'data' is to be investigated by prescribing the procedures to be followed. The pupils follow instructions presented in textbooks and worksheets or through whole-class teaching. The learning outcomes or key ideas and generalisations are predetermined by the teacher and accepted by the pupils as valid conclusions.

Framed styles of teaching and learning are guided by more explicit geographical questions. The focus of the geographical study or enquiry is still determined by the teacher, but pupils are encouraged to generate their own questions. Presenting pupils with questions, problems to be solved or decisions to be made creates a 'need to know' with pupils (Roberts 1996: 243). The resources and content are still selected by the teacher but they tend to be presented as 'evidence' to be interpreted.

In this framed style, teachers help pupils to develop their understanding of the processes and techniques involved in geographical enquiry. Evaluation is also important as pupils need to understand the strengths and limitations of different sources of information and techniques for presenting or analysing this data. Conflicting information or viewpoints should be explored so that pupils can come to different conclusions when analysing this information.

When using negotiated styles of teaching and learning, teachers identify the general theme to be studied but the pupils generate the questions that will guide their enquiry either individually or in groups. As well as negotiating these questions the teacher will provide guidance about the methods and sequence of enquiry, and about the suitability of proposed sources of information. The pupils collect this information independently and select appropriate methods to present, analyse and interpret this data. It is helpful to review the sources and methods selected because the processes of learning are often as important as the learning outcomes themselves.

Roberts' (1996) discussion of how this framework can be used to analyse different approaches to teaching and learning in Geography is illustrated with examples from a variety of geography lessons and fieldwork activities. Further

Table 7.1 The participation dimension

	◀— *Closed* ——	*Framed* ——	*Negotiated* —▶
Content	Tightly controlled by teacher; not negotiable	Teacher controls topic, frames of reference and tasks; criteria made explicit	Discussed at each point; joint decisions
Focus	Authoritative knowledge and skills; simplified, monolithic	Stress on empirical testing; processes chosen by teacher; some legitimation of student ideas	Search for justifications and principles; strong legitimation of student ideas
Students' role	Acceptance; routine performance: little access to principles	Join in teacher's thinking; make hypotheses, set up tests; operate teacher's frame	Discuss goals and methods critically; share responsibility for frame and criteria
Key concepts	'Authority': the proper procedures and the right answers	'Access': to skills, processes, criteria	'Relevance': critical discussion of students' priorities
Methods	Exposition; worksheets (closed); note-giving; individual exercises; routine practical work; teacher evaluates	Exposition, with discussion eliciting suggestions; individual/group problem-solving; lists of tasks given; discussion of outcomes, but teacher adjudicates	Group and class discussion and decision-making about goals and criteria. Students plan and carry out work, make presentations, evaluate success

Source: Barnes *et al.*, (1987).

examples illustrating how the framework might be applied when interpreting geographical fieldwork can also be found in Lambert and Balderstone (2000).

The choice of fieldwork approach and strategies to be used will depend on the purpose that the teacher has in mind for this fieldwork. The purpose may be to develop knowledge and understanding 'about' the environment or to develop practical skills and provide activity-based learning experiences 'through' the environment. Alternatively, the aim might be to promote education 'for' the environment with its agenda for social change leading to more sustainable lifestyles. Job, Day and Smyth (1999: 14) provide a summary of the purposes and strategies of local fieldwork (see Table 7.3). They contend that the 'best fieldwork teachers have an awareness of the full range of strategies and a clear view of the purposes of the fieldwork and can vary their approach according to the needs of students and the available environments' (ibid.:13). These approaches are certainly not mutually exclusive and it is clear that several draw upon elements from a variety of available strategies.

Table 7.2 A framework for looking at different styles of teaching and learning in geography

Stage of teaching and learning	Closed	Framed	Negotiated
Questions	Questions not explicit or questions remain the teacher's questions	Questions explicit, activities planned to make pupils ask questions	Pupils decide what they want to investigate under guidance from teacher
Data	Data selected by teacher, presented as authoritative, not to be challenged	Variety of data selected by teacher, presented as evidence to be interpreted	Pupils are helped to find their own data from sources in and out of school
Interpretation	Teacher decides what is to be done with data, pupils follow instructions	Methods of interpretation are open to discussion and choice	Pupils choose methods of analysis and interpretation in consultation with teacher
Conclusions	Key ideas presented, generalisations are predicted, not open to debate	Pupils reach conclusions from data, different interpretations are expected	Pupils reach own conclusions and evaluate them
Summary	The teacher controls the knowledge by making all decisions about data, activities, conclusions. Pupils are not expected to challenge what is presented	The teacher inducts pupils into ways in which geographical knowledge is constructed, so that they are enabled to use these ways to construct knowledge themselves. Pupils are made aware of choices and are encouraged to be critical	Pupils are enabled by the teacher to investigate questions of concern and interest to themselves

Source: Roberts (1996: 240).

Field teaching and field research can bring about a range of desirable educational outcomes. The practical nature of tasks such as observing, collecting and recording data helps pupils to acquire new skills and develop 'technical competency' in a range of fieldwork and data-handling skills. The use of focused investigations and carefully structured approaches to geographical enquiry can help pupils to transfer these skills and frameworks to their own independent investigations. There may also be some gains in conceptual understanding and the development of technical and specialised vocabulary will usually be strengthened.

Table 7.3 Fieldwork strategies and purposes

Strategy	Purposes	Characteristic activities
The traditional field excursion	Developing skills in geographical recording and interpretation Showing relationships between physical and human landscape features Developing concept of landscape evolving over time Developing an appreciation of landscape and nurturing a sense of place	Students guided through a landscape by teacher with local knowledge, often following a route on a large-scale map. Sites grid-referenced and described with aid of landscape sketches and sketch maps to explore the underlying geology, topographical features, the mantle of soil and vegetation and the landscape history in terms of human activity. Students listen, record and answer questions concerning possible interpretations of the landscape.
Field research based on hypothesis testing	Applying geographical theory or generalised models to real-world situations Generating and applying hypotheses based on theory to be tested through collections of appropriate field data Developing skills in analysing data using statistical methods in order to test field situations against geographical theory	The conventional deductive approach involves initial consideration of geographical theory, leading to the formulation of hypotheses which are then tested against field situations through the collection of quantitative data and testing against expected patterns and relationships. More flexible variants of this approach encourage students to develop their own hypotheses based on initial field observations, thereby incorporating an inductive element.
Geographical enquiry	Encouraging students to identify, construct and ask geographical questions Enabling students to identify and gather relevant information to answer geographical questions and offer explanations and interpretations of their findings Enabling students to apply their findings to the wider world and personal decisions	A geographical question, issue or problem is identified, ideally from student's own experiences in the field. Students are then supported in the gathering of appropriate data (quantitative or qualitative) to answer their key question. Findings are evaluated and the implications applied to the wider world and personal decisions where appropriate.
Discovery fieldwork	Allowing students to discover their own interests in a landscape (rather than through a teacher) Allowing students to develop their own focus of study and methods of investigation. Encouraging self-confidence and self-motivation by putting students in control of their learning	Teacher assumes the role or animateur, allowing the group to follow its own route through the landscape. When students ask questions these are countered with further questions to encourage deeper thinking. A discussion and recording session then identifies themes for further investigation in small groups. This further work has arisen from students' perceptions and preferences rather than those of teachers.

(*continued on next page*)

Table 7.3 Fieldwork strategies and purposes (cont.)

Sensory fieldwork	Encouraging new sensitivities to environments through using all the senses	Structured activities designed to stimulate the senses in order to promote awareness of environments. Sensory walks, use of blindfolds, sound maps, poetry and artwork are characteristic activities. Can be used as an introductory activity prior to more conventional investigative work or to develop a sense of place, aesthetic appreciation or critical appraisal of environmental change.
	Nurturing caring attitudes to nature and empathy with other people through emotional engagement	
	Acknowledging that sensory experience is as valid as intellectual activity in understanding our surroundings	

Source: Job, Day and Smyth (1999: 14).

However, much of the potential of fieldwork for generating pupil-centred learning can be lost if the focus of study, data collection techniques and sites have been predetermined by the teacher rather than arising from pupils' own field experiences and perceptions. Job (1999) argues that when hypothesis-testing approaches are used the development of conceptual understanding depends more on processed data rather than on direct field experiences. He draws attention to Harvey's (1991) research into pupils' experiences of fieldwork at A level which suggests that the quest for generalisations dominating the more heavily quantitative approaches to fieldwork can result in a neglect of 'sense of place'.

Job (1999) provides examples of a variety of less structured fieldwork activities that can be used to encourage deeper thinking about landscapes and environmental issues. These activities can provide starting points for fieldwork investigations raising pupils' awareness of an environment based on their own personal experiences and perceptions. The objective of this 'engagement with places at an emotional or sensory level' is to develop pupils' 'sense of care and concern about places and landscapes' (Job 1999: 156) which is a vital element of any deeper environmental perspective. Art, poetry and literature can all help to provide such sensory experiences and develop pupils' 'sense of place'.

Figure 7.3 is a graphical summary of the different approaches to geographical fieldwork outlined by David Job. Each approach is distinguished by its focus, and the extent to which it relies upon measurement and data collection or more qualitative forms of experience. A more comprehensive review of these different fieldwork styles and strategies can be found in Job (1999) and Job, Day and Smyth (1999).

Understanding different teaching strategies

One of the important features of successful teaching is variety. It is widely accepted that, to be effective, teachers need to develop a repertoire of teaching styles and strategies that they can use successfully in different situations. Teachers use different

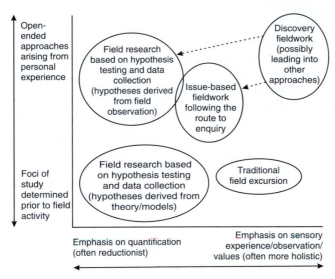

Figure 7.3 Graphical representation of fieldwork approaches

Source: Job (1999: 23).

strategies to achieve different learning outcomes, to promote different learning styles or processes, and to respond to the variety of ways in which pupils learn. Pupils will not thrive and achieve their potential on a monotonous diet no matter how it is presented. An important part of being a geography teacher involves finding out how these different teaching strategies foster different types of mental activity and the degree to which particular mental activities bring about learning in the subject.

Wragg (1997: 86) describes 'teaching' as 'whatever teachers do to ensure children learn'. Teaching strategies are the specific methods, techniques or procedures employed by teachers to bring about this learning. Over the years there have been many different approaches used to define, describe and classify these teaching strategies. Each approach has its limitations and drawbacks not least because of the complex variations between different school and subject contexts. Wragg (1997) identifies five general categories of teaching strategies:

- telling and explaining;
- discovery and invention;
- teachers' questions;
- feedback;
- group or team work.

Elsewhere, an attempt is made to explore in some detail the main groups of strategies used in the teaching of Geography (Lambert and Balderstone 2000). These groupings are certainly generic but they are felt to have particular relevance to geography teaching:

- exposition;
- questioning;
- collaborative strategies;
- games, simulations and role plays;
- values education strategies;
- problem-solving and decision-making;
- developing thinking skills.

This represents an attempt to identify some of the important principles guiding the effective use of different teaching strategies in geography education. It draws upon work already undertaken within geography education and elsewhere to provide advice for trainee teachers of geography. However, it recognises the need for more focused and illuminative research to be carried out to inform our understanding of the different strategies used to teach geography. To exercise the professional judgement that Roberts (1996) and others value so strongly, geography teachers need to understand how and when they can use different teaching strategies effectively.

Developing pedagogic knowledge in geography education

Geography in education has made considerable advances in the last thirty years or more. This discussion has tried to show how curriculum concerns, particularly in relation to the nature of the subject discipline and the planning of the Geography curriculum in schools, have dominated development efforts during that period. The 1980s saw a welcome shift in focus towards a concern for the learning that takes place through a geographical education and especially for developing the crucial role of geographical enquiry in this learning. Increasing standardisation of the Geography curriculum at all levels in schools has been centre stage over the last decade leading to calls from many for renewed curriculum development endeavours and innovation. Other important issues such as the contribution of a geographical education to global citizenship and the development of pupils' critical thinking skills are also deserving of our attention.

But geography teachers should not neglect their own professional practice and should continue the process of developing their pedagogic knowledge that they began during their initial training. Graves (1997) argues that teachers adapt an essentially pragmatic attitude towards teaching methods, selecting strategies that are in harmony with their objectives. But pragmatism should not be our only concern and, as Graves himself rightly warns, 'consolidation does not mean stagnation' (ibid.: 30).

There is a growing body of research on teachers' professional learning (Brown and MacIntyre 1993; Calderhead 1988) which needs to be extended and more fully utilised. Geography teachers need to develop their knowledge and understanding of processes of teaching and learning in geography. There are no short cuts to acquiring this pedagogic knowledge. Initially, trainees begin to develop this knowledge through observation of experienced practitioners at work in the classroom supported by advice from mentors and other teachers. However, there are dangers of oversimplification in this model of professional learning if these mentors and practitioners themselves have a limited understanding of pedagogic relationships. Teacher education could be enriched through further development of techniques of classroom observation and coaching which would enhance the pedagogic knowledge of both trainees and experienced teachers.

There is a growing awareness of the complexity of classroom processes and of the different ways of interpreting and influencing these processes. This usually begins during initial training as trainee teachers become less concerned with their own performance and start to recognise what Tony Fisher describes as a 'complex interplay of three specific types of knowledge': knowledge about learners, knowledge about geography and pedagogic knowledge (1998: 32). Fisher summarises these interrelationships between teaching and learning in geography in a useful dynamic model in which teaching is 'seen as both a causal and an enabling activity' (see Figure 7.4).

Central to the development of a geography teacher's pedagogic knowledge is the need to build up a broad repertoire of teaching styles and strategies. Receptiveness to ideas about different approaches and a willingness to be flexible, imaginative and take risks can help to enrich one's pedagogic knowledge, David Leat describes geography as 'an enormously eclectic borrower' with geography teachers being 'inclined to play fast and loose in applying ideas and techniques' (Leat and McAleavy 1998: 113). It also puts geography teachers in a better position to promote the intellectual development of their pupils and respond to the concerns reported earlier in this chapter about the lack of challenge in many geography lessons (Smith 1997). Leat and McAleavy (ibid.) assert that 'teaching thinking strategies and pedagogy can add substantially to the repertoire of teachers and schools to make changes in the classroom without which raising attainment becomes an end without a means'.

Teacher education implies something more than just 'training' and I have always felt that professional growth requires 'attitude' as much as 'knowledge, understanding and skills'. In this context, 'attitude' is appropriately summed up by Romey and Elberty Jr (1984: 315):

> Past successes pose a danger to person-centred education in geography. Once something 'works' we tend to want to use the techniques over again in order to repeat the success ... [I]f an approach works, rejoice, but then approach the next question freshly, on its own terms and seek a new perspective. Abandon 'techniques' that get to feel like formulas, and search for freshness as if you have had no past experience. Mistakes? Yes, mistakes must continue to be made if progress is to continue. Failure to make mistakes generally means failure to grow. Teachers must join their students in exploring all possible paths, including what may appear to be dead ends, if better paths are to be found. It is amazing how often a 'safe' path becomes a blind alley and an unlikely, overgrown trail leads to a previously unknown highway.

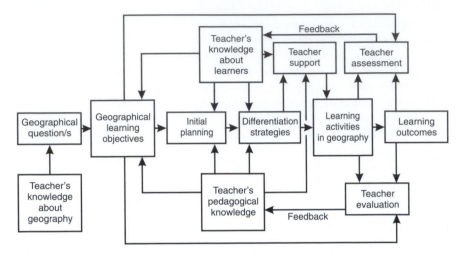

Figure 7.4 The 'teaching and learning complex' – a model of teaching for learning in geography

Source: Fisher (1998: 3).

There is also something about successful teaching that is difficult to put your finger on. The interplay between effective teaching and successful learning has sometimes been described as 'artistry'. The idea of artistry recognises that teaching is a highly creative and personal activity:

> There is a striking quality to fine classrooms. Pupils are caught up in learning; excitement abounds; and playfulness and seriousness blend easily because the purposes are clear, the goals sensible and an unmistakable feeling of well-being prevails.
> Artist teachers achieve these qualities by knowing both their subject matter and their students; by guiding the learning with deft control that itself is born out of perception, intuition and creative impulse.
>
> (Rubin 1985: v)

I hope that this brief discussion has outlined the nature of the challenge facing geography education in relation to pedagogy. There is a need to extend research into this important area and find ways of making such research accessible to classroom practitioners in a form that they can understand and value. Developments in teacher education – and by this I go beyond that of just initial teacher education – need to be underpinned by enquiry. Effective strategies must be found to disseminate the outcomes of such enquiry and ensure that they inform pedagogy in geography education in schools. Until they are it is unlikely that some of the concerns expressed about the value of educational research will be addressed.

References

Bailey, P. and Fox, P. (eds) (1996) *Geography Teachers' Handbook,* Sheffield: Geographical Association.

Barnes, D., Johnson, G., Jordan, S., Layton, P., Medway, P. and Yeoman, D. (1987) *The TVEI Curriculum 14–16: An Interim Report Based on Case Studies in Twelve Schools,* University of Leeds.

Boardman, D. (ed.) (1987) *Handbook for Geography Teachers,* Sheffield: Geographical Association.

Brown, S. and MacIntyre, D. (1993) *Making Sense of Teaching,* Buckingham: Open University Press.

Calderhead, J. (1988) *Teachers' Professional Learning,* London: Falmer Press.

DfEE (1998a) *Standards for the Award of Qualified Teacher Status in England and Wales,* London: HMSO.

DfEE (1998b) *Initial Teacher Training National Curriculum for the Use of Information and Communications Technology in Subject Teaching,* London: HMSO.

Doyle, W. (1987) 'Research on teaching effects as a resource for improving instruction', in Wideen, M. and Andrews, I. (eds), *Staff Development for School Improvement,* Lewes: Falmer Press.

Fien, J., Gerber, R. and Wilson, P. (1984) *The Geography Teacher's Guide to the Classroom,* Melbourne: Macmillan.

Fisher, T. (1998) *Developing as a Geography Teacher,* Cambridge: Chris Kington Publishing.

Geographical Association (1999) *Leading Geography: National Standards for Geography Leaders in Secondary Schools,* Sheffield: Geographical Association.

Graves, N. (1971) *Geography in Secondary Education,* Sheffield: Geographical Association.

Graves, N. (1997) 'Geographical education in the 1990s', in Tilbury, D. and Williams, M. (eds), *Teaching and Learning Geography,* London: Routledge.

Hallam, S. and Ireson, J. (1999) 'Pedagogy in the Secondary School', in Mortimore, P. (ed.), *Understanding Pedagogy and its Impact on Learning,* London: Paul Chapman.

Harris, A., Jamieson, I. and Russ, J. (1995) 'A study of "effective" departments in secondary schools', *School Organisation* 15(3), pp. 283–99.

Harvey, P. (1991) 'The role and value of A-level geography fieldwork: a case study', unpublished PhD thesis, Department of Geography, Durham University.

Job, D. (1999) *New Directions in Geographical Fieldwork,* Cambridge: Cambridge University Press.

Job, D., Day, C. and Smyth, T. (1999) *Beyond the Bicycle Sheds,* Sheffield: Geographical Association.

Lambert, D. and Balderstone, D. (2000) *Learning to Teach Geography in the Secondary School: A Companion to School Experience,* London: Routledge.

Leat, D. (1997) 'Cognitive acceleration in geographical education', in Tilbury, D. and Williams, M. (eds), *Teaching and Learning Geography,* London: Routledge.

Leat, D. (1998) *Thinking through Geography.* Cambridge: Chris Kington Publishing.

Leat, D. and McAleavy, T. (1998) 'Critical thinking in the humanities', *Teaching Geography,* 23(3), pp. 112–14.

Millet, A. (1999) 'Why we need to raise our game', *The Independent,* 11 February.

Mortimore, P. (1994) 'School effectiveness and the management of effective learning and teaching', *School Effectiveness and School Improvement,* 4(4), pp. 290–310.

Mortimore, P. (ed.) (1999) *Understanding Pedagogy and its Impact on Learning,* London: Paul Chapman.

Naish, M., Rawling, E. and Hart, C. (1987) *Geography 16–19: The Contribution of a Curriculum Project to 16–19 Education*, Harlow: Longman.

Ofsted (1998) *Standards in the Secondary Curriculum 1997/98: Geography*, London: HMSO.

Renwick, M. (1985) *The Essentials of GYSL*, Sheffield City Polytechnic, GYSL National Centre.

Roberts, M. (1996) 'Teaching styles and strategies', in Kent, A., Lambert, D., Naish, M. and Slater, F. (eds), *Geography in Education: Viewpoints on Teaching and Learning*. Cambridge: Cambridge University Press.

Romey, W. and Elberty, W., Jr (1984) 'On being a geography teacher in the 1980s and beyond', in Fien, J., Gerber, R. and Wilson, P. (eds), *The Geography Teachers' Guide to the Classroom*, Melbourne: Macmillan.

Rubin, L. (1985) *Artistry and Teaching*, New York: Random House.

Slater, F. (1982) *Learning through Geography*, London: Heinemann.

Slater, F. (1987) 'Steps in planning', in Boardman, D. (ed.), *Handbook for Geography Teachers*, Sheffield: Geographical Association.

Smith, P. (1997) 'Standards achieved: review of geography in secondary schools in England, 1995–96', *Teaching Geography*, 22(3), pp. 123–4.

Tolley, H. and Reynolds, J. (1977) *Geography 14–18: A Handbook for School-based Curriculum Development*, London: Macmillan Education.

TTA (1998) *National Standards for Subject Leaders*, London: Teacher Training Agency.

Watkins, C. and Mortimore, P. (1999) 'Pedagogy: what do we know?', in Mortimore, P. (ed.), *Understanding Pedagogy and its Impact on Learning*, London: Paul Chapman.

Watkins, C., Carnell, E., Lodge, C. and Whalley, C. (1996) *Effective Learning School Improvement Network: Research Matters*, Institute of Education, University of London.

Wragg, E. (1997) *The Cubic Curriculum*, London: Routledge.

8 Differentiation in teaching and learning Geography

Jeff Battersby

Within any class group there will be marked variations in the ways that pupils learn, the speed of their learning and the levels of attainment they achieve as well as the kind of learning difficulties and problems they experience. This would suggest that there is a need for differentiated teaching and learning strategies in all our classrooms, to match learning opportunities to learning needs of pupils.

Differentiation was identified as an equal opportunities issue by the Prime Minister, John Major, when he stated in 1992 that he wanted 'to ensure that we actively recognize pupils' abilities and aptitudes and create the means for this diversity to flourish. That is the way to genuine equality of opportunity' (Major 1992).

Differentiation in the National Curriculum is meant to be an enabling process focused on the development of the curriculum and concerned with creating optimum learning conditions for each child. Previously, differentiation was identified as a tool used to separate and rank the pupils, as a means of organizing them. Differentiation is now equated with good practice in teaching which allows for differences within a teaching group rather than leading to the distribution and allocation of pupils to a supposedly homogeneous group which could be taught as a separate unit.

Differentiation really came onto the curriculum agenda as a result of *Better Schools* (DES 1986a). The acceptable curriculum was identified as broad, balanced, relevant and differentiated. Differentiation has been a key issue in any discussion of curriculum change and planning and is seen as being essential to achieving a curriculum entitlement for all pupils. The Warnock Report (1978) stated that the purpose of education for all children is the same; the goals are the same but the help that individual children need in progressing towards them will be different.

In clearly identifying levels of attainment for each Attainment Target, the National Curriculum assumes that individuals do not progress at a uniform rate. It states that it will help alert teachers to problems experienced by individual children so that they can be given special attention. The National Curriculum encourages teachers and pupils to operate on a more individual basis, to plan programmes of work which take account of pupils' achievements and which allow them to work at different levels to ensure that they each achieve their maximum potential.

Differentiation is based on an understanding of individual difference, and of the worth and value of each pupil's learning. Consequently, teachers need to differentiate in their curriculum planning according to Barthorpe and Visser (1991). However, Dowling (1990) and others feel that differentiation is a means of emphasizing and reinforcing inequalities in curriculum provision. The curriculum has to satisfy two apparently contrary requirements. On the one hand it needs to reflect the broad educational aims which apply to all children, of whatever ability and at whatever school, while on the other hand it needs to accommodate differences in the ability and other characteristics of children, even of the same age.

A number of important questions emerge in relation to pupil entitlement to the Key Stage Programme of Study. The Order for Geography states in its access statement that the Programme of Study for each Key Stage should be taught to all or the great majority of pupils in the Key Stage in ways appropriate to their abilities (DfE 1995). Can differences in pupils' abilities affect their access to the curriculum? Does differentiation imply teaching a different curriculum to pupils of different ability? Can we teach the same curriculum to all pupils by tailoring teaching strategies to the learning needs of the pupils?

Responses to these questions have implications for curriculum planning through schemes of work. Differentiation is not necessarily about creating individual programmes for individual pupils. In some cases this may be a good idea but not in others, as, for example, the pupil who learns more effectively in a group than in isolation. Differentiation is concerned with providing appropriate educational opportunities for all pupils and to match learning opportunities with individual learning needs.

As pupils' learning needs vary it will be necessary to employ a range of teaching styles and methods in the classroom. It calls for skilful teaching, detailed planning and preparation, and perceptive responses to the individual pupils. Detailed knowledge of each pupil's learning needs is essential if they are to be addressed successfully. This involves the careful selection of relevant learning resources, building suitable expectations into pupil's work programmes, and sharing learning objectives with the pupils. Individual pupils will then be enabled and encouraged to take increasing responsibility for their own learning, to measure their successes and achievements, to begin to identify their own learning needs and to help in meeting them.

The following essential elements must be included in course planning if successful teaching and learning for pupils are to occur:

- clear learning objectives and learning outcomes in terms of the pupil's knowledge, understanding and skills;
- a variety of teaching and learning strategies to differentiate the learning experiences of pupils;
- a variety of resources available to support pupils' learning;
- a variety of tasks and activities which provide different opportunities for pupil learning and for different outcomes;
- opportunities to vary in the pace and depth of learning;
- different strategies for assessment of pupil learning;
- effective feedback on the pupils' learning outcomes and target setting for their future learning.

(Battersby 1995: 26)

Furthermore, teachers need to consider the quality of the pupils' learning environment and to promote one which encourages and enables effective learning to take place. The curriculum needs to challenge the pupils, to have high expectations of involvement and attainment, to enable and encourage positive achievement as a realistic goal and engage pupils in active and enjoyable learning. Classrooms need to reflect this philosophy.

There are still important questions to address concerning how judgements are made about the appropriate teaching and learning environments for individual pupils and the expectations of an individual pupil's capabilities. The focus is now centred on differentiation in teaching and learning and how best this might be accomplished. Differentiation in learning can be achieved when pupils are presented with learning opportunities which enable them to learn effectively and to demonstrate what they know, understand and can do. In most learning situations the role of the teacher is as a facilitator of learning, providing structured situations which encourage investigation and enquiry using a variety of resources.

Differentiation is 'simply effective teaching' argues Waters (1995: 82). 'It is the planned process of opening out the curriculum to enable access to all pupils.' He summarizes a number of strategies for differentiation:

Planning

- clear learning objectives, shared with pupils
- the need to plan small achievable steps
- schemes of work that plan for revisiting
- schemes of work which have a full range of structured and open-ended tasks
- develop the model of core tasks with reinforcement and extension activities
- schemes of work with clear progression.

Teaching

- using a wide range of activities and teaching styles
- clear instructions, explanations and expectations
- an awareness that each pupil has unique abilities
- the importance of the pace of a lesson
- the need for a balance of questioning techniques
- the use of open-ended questions and enquiries
- flexibility of approach and response to pupils
- encourage a supportive classroom atmosphere.

Resources

- the importance of clearly designed, uncluttered materials matched to pupils' abilities
- using texts of appropriate readability
- using materials that are free of gender/ethnic bias

Pupil needs

- talking with teachers about their learning
- talking to each other about their learning
- sufficient repetition to consolidate learning

- the ease of access to learning resources
- classroom display that encourages learning and reflects high expectations.

- varied activities to match pupils' attention span
- the use of pupil review to set realistic goals
- positive marking which points to improvement.

Achieving differentiation

Differentiation can be achieved by outcome, by the rate of progress, by task, by the resources available or by a combination of any of these. The summary diagram opposite (Figure 8.1) serves to illustrate these strategies.

Differentiation by outcome

Differentiation by outcome results from pupils being presented with common or neutral tasks built around common resources with differentiated or different positive levels of achievement being identified to measure the pupils' responses to the tasks. The assessment criteria or mark scheme indicates the positive quality anticipated. Pupils might be shown a video extract of the shanty areas of Sao Paulo and be given the task of writing a newspaper report about life in the shanty slums. Some pupils may produce a limited summary of the video, others may outline the positive and negative aspects of living in the shanty, while other pupils may compare the shanties of Sao Paulo with other areas known to them. Thus there are different outcomes from the same resource input and identified task.

Differentiation by resources and by outcome

The same task could be presented to all pupils in a class but with varying resources, perhaps targeted to specific pupils. A range of textbooks and newspaper extracts with different readability measures, different maps, diagrams and photographs may also be provided. The outcomes will be different and will reflect the suitability and accessibility of the resources in support of the task.

Differentiation by graded tasks and outcomes

The stimulus material and resources are common to all pupils, though these may vary in their difficulty and accessibility to different pupils. A series of tasks or questions can be set which become increasingly difficult, demanding and complex. Each of the tasks can be open to all pupils to attempt or some of the tasks may be too difficult or complex for certain pupils. Some pupils will be able to work through some of the tasks quickly while others will fail to go beyond the first one.

Stepped questions which also have an incline of difficulty enable the lower achiever to gain positive achievement in the early parts of each question while

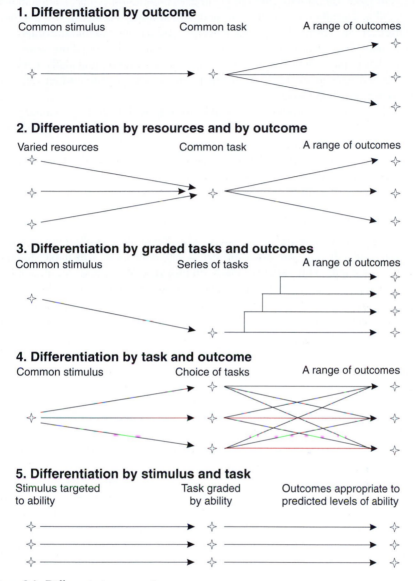

1. Differentiation by outcome

Common stimulus   Common task   A range of outcomes

2. Differentiation by resources and by outcome

Varied resources   Common task   A range of outcomes

3. Differentiation by graded tasks and outcomes

Common stimulus   Series of tasks   A range of outcomes

4. Differentiation by task and outcome

Common stimulus   Choice of tasks   A range of outcomes

5. Differentiation by stimulus and task

Stimulus targeted   Task graded   Outcomes appropriate to
to ability   by ability   predicted levels of ability

Figure 8.1 Differentiation strategies

Source: Davies (1990).

becoming less successful with the later parts; the able pupils will attempt successfully all parts of the question or task.

Consideration should be given to the overall diet presented to the pupils, especially if the same format is used in each lesson, assessment or teaching unit.

Different tasks will present different challenges to different pupils. Data handling tasks will make different demands on pupils than a written report or a decision-making exercise. Those who find one more demanding may not find the other tasks equally difficult. The more appealing the task to the individual pupil the more it will enable that pupil to demonstrate knowledge, understanding and skills. Different learning and assessment styles will enable pupils to demonstrate a wider variety of their competences in Geography.

Teaching and learning strategies should vary as should the tasks presented to the pupils. Initial tasks might involve a card sorting exercise where pupils are asked to categorize and match photographs, information, terminology and given examples to name, define and describe. A second task involving groupwork to research and summarize information from resources might require pupils to name, classify and describe a pattern from data resources which might also require pupils to extract information, interpret and explain it. An enquiry task which seeks to enable pupils to explain causes and effects, reviewing costs and benefits and analysing informa-tion, enables most pupils to engage with it. The examination of alternatives and an assessment of different strategies through a report or essay will make different demands on pupils. This variety of tasks will provide opportunities for all pupils to demonstrate some capability in their knowledge, understanding and skills in Geog-raphy. The tasks themselves present an example of progression in demand and complexity, yet provide opportunities for a wide range of ability and opportunities to demonstrate subject competence.

Differentiation by task and outcome

Differentiation by task is achieved through the designing and setting of specific tasks for particular ability groups of pupils. All pupils are provided with the same stimulus resources and then either with a variety of tasks or with one main task, subdivided into a series of smaller ones. The example of the video input on a shanty slum may lead to pupils being presented with tasks which ask them to produce an annotated sketch map or diagram, to produce a cost-benefit analysis of the provi-sion of new government housing and to write a report for the Brazilian government as to how effective this strategy might be in solving the housing crisis. Different outcomes will result from each of the tasks. Pupils may produce a simple, detailed or complex sketch map, diagram, analysis or report. Those whose ability is lower will be unlikely to manage the whole task, while those of higher ability will accomplish all elements.

Differentiation by stimulus and by task

Stimulus material is targeted to specific ability levels identified by the teacher. The materials might be a simple structured worksheet, one with some structured and some open-ended questions, or, for the most able, an assignment involving the testing of a hypothesis. Tasks which are graded to ability levels range from those which seek description and simple explanation to those which ask pupils to evaluate policies and strategies. Pupils produce outcomes appropriate to their predicted level of ability.

These strategies for differentiation suggest the idea of targeted work and specific strategies targeted to enable successful pupil learning. While these should enable the pupils to achieve positive outcomes to their learning, differentiation should not be so fine-tuned that it does not allow for the unplanned and unexpected outcomes. Pupils should do better than expected sometimes, but at others not quite reach their goal because it has been set just out of reach at that particular moment.

Differentiation in the assessment of a pupil's ability will be achieved through a combination of tasks set and the outcomes to them. Differentiation by task is achieved by targeting a task suitable to a pupil to ensure that the assessment is appropriate and the level of performance is as predicted. Differentiation by outcome is achieved through the nature of the pupil's response to a common task or series of tasks. The assessment criteria, or mark schemes, are critical to the success of this method of differentiation of pupils. Differentiation by a combination of task and outcome will be through the teacher deciding the most relevant strategy for a pupil to demonstrate their achievement. In reality this happens in most situations where a task may start off based on a common resource but develops into a series of differentiated sub-tasks, thereby producing different outcomes.

GCSE is firmly based on the principle of differentiation and the general assess-ment criteria state that all examinations must be designed to ensure proper discrim-ination so that candidates across the ability range are given opportunities to demonstrate their knowledge, abilities and achievements – that is to show what they know, understand and can do. Differentiated papers or differentiated ques-tions within papers will be required accordingly in all subjects, while in the case of coursework differentiation will be achieved by presenting candidates with tasks appropriate to their individual levels of ability.

Differentiation guards against dangers of under-achievement and unsatisfactory assessment experiences. If set tasks are too difficult for some of the candidates, the assessment will be a dispiriting experience for them and the marks that they gain are more likely to register random success with partially understood ideas than to give credit to a coherent set of concepts, skills or abilities. Conversely, if the set tasks are too easy, the assessment may be equally unsatisfying and discrimination among candidates may be the results of small slips rather than the evidence of higher abili-ties required for the award of the higher grades.

Differentiation, according to Stradling *et al.*(1990), is a loaded word associated with long-standing debates about comprehensive schooling and more recent ones concerning the National Curriculum. The common curriculum is at odds with differentiation for it seeks to provide a common entitlement to all pupils irrespec-tive of individual ability or need. Addressing and meeting individual needs legiti-mizes the differences we are trying to accommodate while providing a curriculum which is no longer common to all. The structure and content of the National Curriculum implies that mixed ability teaching is inappropriate and that such groupings do no meet the needs of individual pupils.

Differentiation in the National Curriculum is meant to be an enabling process which focuses on the development of optimum learning conditions for each pupil which can be achieved under a wide variety of organizational structures, including mixed ability teaching groups. This raises other important questions about how judgements are made concerning the optimum and appropriate learning conditions, expectations, strategies and outcomes which are identified for individual pupils. If differentiation results in inequalities the alternative is not a solution, but represents a failure to address the problem.

Pupils who are unable to develop their understanding of new ideas or become more proficient in their skills can be said to have learning difficulties. It is therefore necessary to identify strategies and opportunities which will enable such pupils to develop their competence and proficiency in these areas. It is necessary for teachers to reappraise their teaching methods in order to improve the learning opportunities for each pupil. Questions need to be asked which address the learning difficulties of the pupils as a consequence of the curriculum. Difficulties are all too often identified as relating to the pupil rather than as possibly arising from the curriculum. It is in this area that teachers can acknowledge their responsibility for teaching and learning in their subject and explore alternative strategies, structures and opportunities to enable all pupils to gain access to the curriculum and begin to achieve positively.

Differentiation in teaching and learning in the classroom and in schemes of work requires a fundamental rethinking of curriculum expectations and objectives. In the past, differentiated work for any pupil with learning difficulties has been through minor modification of questions and tasks on worksheets or reduced expectations of positive achievement in relation to the set tasks. The provision of alternative worksheets and resources has tended to marginalize those pupils who are experiencing difficulties in grasping new ideas, concepts or skills, and this in turn has created problems in the integration of these pupils with others in the class.

Hart (1992) argues that schools need to make a significant shift in pedagogy if pupils' learning needs are to be addressed. She feels that there is a need to create 'more opportunities for learning through talk and practical experiences, more emphasis upon co-operative work and self-directed activities'. This is illustrated in her summary diagram of 'curriculum imbalances':

written outcomes	drama, oral presentation, drawing, construction, collage
teacher-led discussion	pupil-led discussion
learning through written word	learning through talk
individual tasks	co-operative tasks
teacher-initiated activities	pupil-initiated activities
closed tasks (i.e. one right answer)	open-ended tasks
whole-class teaching	individual/small group teaching
teacher evaluation, marking, assessment	pupil self-assessment, peer collaboration

Changes to these perceived imbalances would require changes in the organization and planning of teaching and learning strategies and associated learning opportunities to take into consideration ways of improving, extending and enhancing the curriculum in order to use and develop the basic literacy skills of reading and writing.

Other questions arise in relation to our responses to pupil achievements in the tasks presented to them. How far do we evaluate the relevance and the accuracy of the pupils' responses to their tasks if they apparently demonstrate a general understanding of the ideas and seem to gain positive achievement generally? Each pupil's response to each task needs to be evaluated to ensure that a correct range of learning opportunities is being offered to each pupil so that they reach their potential and are able to demonstrate what they know, understand and can do.

Hart makes the telling point that 'by encouraging a focus upon differences, differentiation diverts our attention away from making the crucial connection between individual responses and general questions about curriculum', and that we need to 'be alert to what individual children's responses may have to tell us about the appropriateness of curriculum experiences provided for all children'. We therefore need to shift the 'focus of attention from the abilities and characteristics of the children to the abilities and characteristics of the curriculum' (Hart 1992: 139–40).

We must discover how to create conditions which will enable all our pupils to learn successfully and must feed these into a virtuous circle of improvement in the quality of education for all. Differentiation has a significant part to play in this aim.

In practical terms there is a need to focus attention on classroom procedure, in relation to the learning objectives and any intended outcomes of pupils' knowledge, understanding and skills. These objectives should be shared with the pupils. Geography lends itself to a wide variety of teaching and learning strategies which should feature in all lessons so as to enable pupils to develop their competence in the subject. Equally, wide range of readily available resources suited to a range of pupils' preferred learning styles should be used in each lesson.

Differentiation can be achieved through the use of open-ended questions and tasks designed to enable pupils to demonstrate their knowledge, understanding and skills at a variety of levels. Structured or closed questions can also achieve this objective and provide for a more predictable outcome. Demonstration of achievement is dependent on the skill of the teacher asking appropriate questions while encouraging responses which allow a clear demonstration of a pupil's ability.

An awareness of the individual needs of pupils and the ability to make quick, yet accurate, judgements about them before diagnosing, introducing and implementing remedial action to meet such needs, represents the real art of the teacher. It is through such practices that the individual needs of pupils are addressed and met, highlighting differences in provision and response, differentiation in practice which is enabling equality of access to the entitlement curriculum.

References

Barthorpe, T. and Visser, J. (1991) *Differentiation, Your Responsibility*, National Association of Remedial Education, Nasen Enterprises.

Battersby, J. (1995) *Teaching Geography at Key Stage 3*, Cambridge: Chris Kington Publishing.

Currie, S. and Whittle, R. (1984) *Reducing Under-achievement: Learning to Succeed Development Project*, Cardiff: Welsh Joint Education Committee.

Davies, P. (1990) *Differentiation in the Classroom and in the Examination Room: Achieving the Impossible?* Cardiff: Welsh Joint Education Committee.

Dearing, R. (1994) *The National Curriculum and its Assessment: Final Report*, London: SCAA.

DES (1986a) *Better Schools*, London: HMSO.

DES (1986b) *Geography from 5 to 16, Curriculum Matters 7*, London: HMSO.

DES (1988) *The Education Reform Act 1988*, London: HMSO.

DfE (1995) *Geography in the National Curriculum*, London: HMSO.

Dowling, P. (1990) 'The Shogun's and other curriculum voices', in Dowling, P. and Noss, R. *Mathematics versus the National Curriculum*, Basingstoke: Falmer.

Hart, S. (1992) 'Differentiation: part of the problem or part of the solution?', *Curriculum Journal* 3 (2): 131–42.

Major, J. (1992) in *Times Educational Supplement*, 28 February 1992.

National Curriculum Council (1989) *Curriculum Guidance 2: A Curriculum for all*, York: NCC.

National Curriculum Council (1990) *Curriculum Guidance 3: The Whole Curriculum*, York: NCC.

Ofsted (1993) *Handbook for the Inspection of Schools: Guidance on the Inspection Schedule*, London: HMSO.

Stradling, R., Saunders, L. and Weston, P. (1990) *Differentiation in Action*, London: HMSO.

Warnock, M. (1978) *Meeting Special Educational Needs*, London: HMSO.

Waters, A. (1995) Differentiation and classroom practice, *Teaching Geography*, 20 (2): 81–3.

9 Using assessment to support learning

David Lambert

Introduction: assessment in education

This chapter sets out to examine the potential of 'formative assessment' to promote learning in geography classrooms (Torrance and Pryor 1998). Written by a geographer and for geography educationists, the chapter nevertheless necessarily engages in discussion at a general and often system-wide level. There is a need to experiment with sustained effort in order to translate the general principles discussed here into effective day-to-day classroom practice. The chapter is written in the profound belief that such effort will be richly rewarded, but (to re-emphasise the point) pupils as well as teachers will be at different 'starting points' depending on the range of theoretical debate and developments in practice characterising particular system contexts.

There is not sufficient space in this chapter to consider in any detail the pros and cons of formative assessment in relation to its distant relative, 'summative assessment'. Though writing from an English perspective, a system that has experienced a substantial rise in the use of external summative testing and examinations in recent years, formative assessment tends to be subservient to summative assessment the world over. The latter tends to dominate our thinking about assessment in education (Black 1998; Stobart and Gipps 1997), and it will simply be taken as read that:

- summative assessment his its place in education, mainly in the form of end-of-course tests and external examinations; but that
- it should be kept in its place, because it can exert influence that is not always educational.

In concentrating on formative assessment the chapter does not, therefore, adopt an 'anti-testing' stance, though there are certainly debates to be had over the efficacy of particular forms of external, summative assessment and the purposes to which data thus obtained are put (see Black 1998; Gipps 1994; Davis 1998, 1999). The position that *is* taken up here centres on the question of what balance needs to be struck between different kinds of assessment practice (Lambert and Lines 2000), and the implications for geography teachers who, in accepting the above assertions, also accept the need to raise the specifically educational functions of formative classroom assessment. Allowing assessment in education to be dominated by tests serves to overemphasise the administrative and bureaucratic functions of assembling assessment data at the expense of developing assessment processes serving educational ends.

The closing years of the last century were a turbulent time for those with an interest in the relationship between learning and assessment, that is its educational function. Around the world there have been responses of various kinds to the perceived international pressures of globalisation, often manifest in moves to centralise education infrastructures such as curriculum and assessment (see Naish 1990) and to use, assessment as the measure – and sometimes the means – to raise standards. In England and Wales, the introduction of a National Curriculum following the Education Reform Act of 1988 provided the platform for a quite extraordinary rise in regular testing of children from the age of 5 in the so-called 'core subjects' of English, mathematics and science. Teachers of other subjects, including Geography, were (and are) also expected to provide criterion-referenced summative assessments on the children they have taught, by a process known as 'teacher assessment' based on centrally laid-down Level Descriptions of attainment (see Butt *et al.* 1995; Hopkins *et al.* 2000; Lambert 1996, 1997a).

Furthermore, all subjects in England and Wales, including Geography, are examined at 16 years old and beyond by the vast 'examinations industry' (Lambert and Lines 2000) including GCSE and A level public examinations. These examinations seemed to have acquired ever higher stakes: examination results are now published in the form of league tables, policy-makers are increasingly demanding that schools, and the teachers who work in them, be judged by 'value added' statistics (using predominantly test results) and the present government has introduced 'performance related pay' as an element of its radical policy suite designed to raise expectations and standards among teachers, parents and pupils. Thus, all teachers are increasingly aware of the power exerted through the 'results' they (or more accurately, their pupils) achieve, which is possibly why assessment matters are often discussed generically rather than in a subject-specific way – and why questions concerning summative testing tend to dominate teachers' thinking. Of course, it is not sensible to examine assessment in geography education without recourse to general principles. This chapter will, therefore, attempt to remain clearly focused on geography classrooms while at the same time refer to evidence derived from wider sources. But we are not going to discuss, and therefore contribute to, the mounting material on testing and examinations in Geography or beyond, but concentrate on explicating the potential of teachers using *classroom assessment* to support learning, now widely referred to as 'formative assessment'.

Identifying formative assessment

Possibly in reaction to the dangers of the narrowing, teaching-to-the-test mentality that can begin to mount when high-stakes[1] summative testing begins to dominate the minds of pupils, parents and teachers, there has been a surge of interest in formative assessment. A recent issue of the professional journal *Teaching Geography*

(*TG*) contained three articles discussing in various ways the role of assessment in enhancing learning. While one of these (Hopkins 2000) remained rooted in the traditional context of making sense of, or interpreting for its readership, statutory duties and responsibilities, and another focused on a particular strategy for using assessment information (Hamson and Sutton 2000), a third (Leat and McGrane 2000), took the cue from, but radically reworked, several central government pronouncements concerning the relationship between teaching, learning and the curriculum (see box below). One can conclude from such re-visioning that the statutory documents (reviewed anew for the launch of 'Curriculum 2000', the most recent formulation of the National Curriculum for England and Wales) should be seen more as a facilitating framework than a set of tightly designed curriculum rules to follow. Leat and McGrane showed how the idea of 'level descriptions' could be adapted and form the basis for assessing, but also supporting the development of thinking in Geography lessons.

'Moving onto something better' from the Secretary of State for Education and Employment

We want to develop creativity and high level thinking skills, deepening knowledge and stretching achievement. In short, developing new forms of excellence with diversity …

… I have been very impressed by the growing evidence in this country and abroad of the impact on standards of systematic and disciplined approaches to the teaching of higher order thinking skills …

… It is not about some loosely defined or woolly approach to study skills. It is about the ability to analyse and make connections, to use knowledge effectively, to solve problems individually and to think creatively. It is about developing mental strategies to take on both academic and wider challenges. Above all, the evidence shows that the systematic teaching of thinking skills raises standards.

(Blunkett 2000)

However, notwithstanding the encouraging signs for professionals such as Leat and McGrane from the snippets quoted from the Secretary of State for Education in the box above, and indeed the apparent concern over the present unsatisfactory use of classroom assessment by teachers reported by Ofsted (see box overleaf), it seems that interest in formative assessment among the *policy-makers* may only be skin deep. In David Blunkett's full article, reference to assessment was limited to external test outcomes, the introduction of yet more tests in the core subjects (for every year in Key Stage 3) and GCSE performance. There was at best only tacit acknowledgement of any value attached to low-stakes, day-to-day classroom assessment undertaken by teachers – nor how to understand such processes better and to improve them if they are to be found wanting (and often, they are).

Visions of a formative classroom assessment

A *The limits of assessment competence in geography classrooms according to the Office for Standards in Education (Ofsted)*

day-to-day assessment ... is weak and the use of assessment to help planning of future work is unsatisfactory in one in five schools. What is particularly lacking is marking which clearly informs pupils about the standards they have achieved in a piece of work, and what they need to do to improve; whilst marking needs to be supportive of efforts made, it also needs to be constructively critical, and diagnostic of both strengths and weaknesses.

(DfEE 1998)

B *Extract from the Task Group on Assessment and Testing – the vision of a national assessment system*

Promoting children's learning is a principal aim of schools. Assessment lies at the heart of this process. It can provide a framework in which educational objectives may be set, and pupils' progress charted and expressed. It can yield a basis for planning the next educational steps in response to children's needs ... it should be an integral part of the educational process, continually providing both 'feedback' and 'feedforward'. It therefore needs to be incorporated systematically into teaching strategies and practices at all levels.

(DES/WO 1988, para. 3/4)

If we take a close look at the Ofsted quotation (A, above) we can see that what the inspectorate has in mind in relation to formative assessment is demanding. According to this quotation, Ofsted inspectors look for assessment that:

- helps teachers plan future work;
- informs pupils of the standards they have reached;
- shows pupils what they need to do to improve;
- is diagnostic of strengths and weaknesses;
- is constructively critical.

Interestingly, it is possible to trace the contents of this list, at least in principle, back to the assessment framework devised to underpin the introduction of the 1988 National Curriculum. The hastily convened Task Group on Assessment and Testing (TGAT) produced a ground-breaking report (DES/WO 1988) which encouraged the kinds of ambitious formative assessment practices that subsequently Ofsted inspectors reported they were looking for. Again, close examination of the TGAT quotation in B, above, is useful. It recommended assessment practice which:

- informs planning;
- articulates standards ('feedback');
- shows pupils what to do next in order to improve ('feedforward');
- becomes an organic part of teaching and learning.

The two lists and the quotations opposite are remarkably similar. Arguably, the TGAT quote goes a little further in that it equates assessment with teaching, in effect saying that the two cannot be separated, although it may be that teaching is what Ofsted had in mind with the phrase 'constructively critical'. This is, however, a very significant point to contemplate and helps counter the claim that busy teachers have 'no time' to engage seriously with formative assessment practices: this, the argument runs, would be tantamount to saying they have no time to teach effectively! The shift in thinking represented by the two quotations opposite takes us away from an assumption that assessment is something done after the teaching is finished and towards the notion that it is integral to teaching; you cannot claim to be teaching without undertaking forms of assessment, and by implication, this assessment activity helps ensure the quality of what is taught and learned (and how). It is this point that Leat and McGrane (2000) have explored so imaginatively.

Assessment for learning

From the above discussion we can begin to identify formative assessment in a way that distinguishes it from assessments that (merely) measure performance; remember the popular adage that 'weighing the baby does not make it grow'. What I mean by this in the classroom context is that the 'assessment of learning', though useful in several respects, does not *itself* help teachers teach better or learners learn better. When we consider definitions of formative assessment, therefore, we need to explore the idea of 'assessment for learning' (Sutton 1995).

For example, what are the practical implications of the following theoretical positions? First:

> Formative assessment is concerned with how judgements about the quality of student responses … can be used to shape and improve the student's competence by short-circuiting the randomness and inefficiency of trial and error learning.
>
> (Sadler 1989: 121)

And second:

> … for students to be able to improve, they must develop the capacity to monitor the quality of their own work during actual production. This in turn requires that students possess an appreciation of what high quality work is [and] that they have the evaluative skill necessary for them to compare with some objectivity the quality of what they are producing in relation to the standard.
>
> (ibid.: 119)

Among the many discussion points that can be derived from such statements, three very important realisations stand out, confirming what we noted from our deliberations of the TGAT and the Ofsted reports on p. 126. Each carries significant implications for classroom practice:

- Formative assessment has to take place during a course of study so that the learner has a chance to make a difference; some commentators would urge us to go beyond the preposition 'during' and describe formative assessment as an organic *part of* effective teaching.
- Effective formative assessment is in essence a form of *communication*, a conversation between pupils and teachers consisting of analysis, hints and suggestions in the form of feedback and feedforward. As with most conversations, the bottom line is that the participants are getting to know each other better – their motivations and preferences, and the expectations teachers and students have of each other.
- Genuine formative assessment involves the learners so that they grow to understand that assessment is not just something done to them, but something that is part of their learning action. This means students being involved in *self-assessment*. For this to stand any chance of working successfully students need to be familiar with the success criteria relating to the work and how to apply them.

Despite the persuasiveness of such 'theoretical' positions it remains the case that assessment for learning (that is, formative classroom assessment) is a very poorly developed relation to the assessment of learning. The Assessment Reform Group (ARG) maintains that the former is utterly dominated by the latter, possibly to a damaging degree:

> A clear distinction should be made between assessment of learning for the purposes of grading and reporting, which has its own well-established procedures, and assessment for learning which calls for different priorities, new procedures and a new commitment. In the recent past, policy priorities have arguably resulted in too much attention being given to finding reliable ways of comparing children, teachers and schools.
>
> (Assessment Reform Group 1999: 2)

The importance of the ARG's position is perhaps plain to see, but is one which seems to require enormous courage or ambition on the part of teachers and pupils to act upon, despite the tacit support from Ofsted and others who take a predominantly professional/educational interest in assessment rather than an administrative/ bureaucratic one.

On the other hand, if assessment for learning can be undertaken successfully, as the ARC urges, then surely we do not need to be too worried about the high-stakes summative tests which assess the product of learning. Pupils who have been taught to be deeper, more confident thinkers can surely achieve better test scores than otherwise they would have done. The ARC certainly think so, continuing,

The important message now confronting the educational community is that assessment which is explicitly designed to promote learning is the single most powerful tool we have for both raising standards and empowering lifelong learners.

(ibid.: 2)

The basis for making this statement is the research evidence to which we now should turn, for it helps underpin what we have been arguing here. Evidence helps teachers to nurture that 'act of faith', and enables them to invest the necessary time and energy in developing formative classroom assessment strategies.

Research evidence

Partly in response to the overriding attention paid to testing, especially at the policy level, Black and Wiliam (1998a, 1998b) undertook an extensive review of research conducted internationally on formative assessment. The principal motive was to find whether internationally accumulated research provided convincing evidence that formative assessment 'worked'. The absence of such evidence, in a form that was available and accessible to wider professional and public audiences, was thought to be a major stumbling block to the promotion of formative assessment, allowing politicians especially to rely on exhorting the 'rigour' of external tests as the means of 'raising standards'. The ARG refers to Black and Wiliam's review, stating that assessment research has 'proved without a shadow of doubt that, when carried out effectively, informal classroom assessment with constructive feedback to the student will raise levels of achievement' (1999: 1). This claim is placed in stark contrast to another statement that '[t]here is no evidence that increasing the amount of testing will enhance learning' (ibid.: 2)

It is unusual in the field of education that research can communicate such a clear, unambiguous message. We need to be careful, however, to ensure that we 'hear' this message accurately. Among the findings synthesised and summarised from several hundred research articles and reports, Black and Wiliam showed broadly that effective formative assessment produces significant 'learning gain'. Translated into more familiar terms, understandable to secondary teachers in England and Wales, the authors calculated that formative assessment, incorporating effective feedback strategies, could increase pupils' GCSE performance by one or two grades. Furthermore, research seemed to suggest that resulting raised levels of performance were greater among lower attaining pupils, a particularly resonant finding in the context of the English education system which traditionally has a persistent, long tail of underachievement in comparison with other comparable systems. Developing effective formative assessment practices can help rectify this system failure.

Among the main research findings are the following headlines, all of which deserve some consideration in the context of geography classrooms:

- Although formative assessment has become a familiar term in schools, its implications are not well understood. Marking pupils' work regularly and conscientiously may not always have formative impact. Rather than being formative, marking can appear to be little more than 'serial summative' assessment.
- Neither teachers nor students readily adopt formative assessment processes when they perceive this to mean adding to their existing practice. The break-through occurs when it is understood to be part of teaching and learning. As we have seen, this seems to require a leap of faith by both teachers and pupils.
- Pupils need to be trained in self-assessment so that they can understand learning goals. This may take some time to achieve. The aim would be to
  - break the pattern of passive learning;
  - make learning goals ('the overarching picture') explicit;
  - establish the 'desired goal – present position – way to close the gap' mentality in pupils.
- Feedback should be about the particular qualities of pupils' work, with advice for improvement. This may be one of the most difficult professional skills for teachers to acquire. As Black and Wiliam note, much pupil feedback tends to be 'social and managerial' in purpose and not *subject-specific* in nature. Learning how to engage pupils, sometimes individually, with subject-specific feedback requires deep thinking on the part of the teacher. The content has to be worthwhile, relevant and non-trivial (that is, worth learning!). Further-more, feedback should avoid comparisons with other pupils so that the work is the object of focus, not the class 'pecking order'. It should also encourage
  - creating a culture of success;
  - pupils to take risks, make mistakes and use such occasions as learning opportunities;
  - reconstruction of the teacher–pupil 'contract of contentment' (where neither is challenged by the other.
- Opportunities for pupils to express their understanding have to be built into the teaching – to initiate interaction and allow the teacher to build up know-ledge of the learners. Thus
  - teaching and assessment are indivisible;
  - choice of tasks (chosen teaching strategy) has to be justified in terms of the learning aims they serve;
  - teachers can change what they do in the light of what they learn about the students through listening to them.

It is arguably this final innocuous point that goes to the heart of what is meant by effective formative classroom assessment. Thus assessment is concerned with 'get-ting to know' pupils (see Lambert 1997b; Rowntree 1987), and then being prepared to change what we do with them in geography lessons as a result of what we learn. To be able to respond constructively in this way is one of the 'standards' for the initial training of teachers laid down by the government (DfEE 1998). It is one of the most demanding requirements of initial teacher trainees.

Conclusion: priorities for geography education?

To conclude this discussion, I wish to speculate on how a departmental team of geographers may interpret their developmental priorities in relation to enhancing their day-to-day assessment practice. As was emphasised at the start of this chapter, how this is done needs to take into account other pressing assessment requirements, such as preparing pupils for external examinations or teachers assessing the National Curriculum Levels for pupils at the end of Key Stage 3. What we also noted was that although it is relatively easy to find advice on both these issues, whether from commercially published sources (such as Balderstone and King 1998), the awarding bodies themselves or from government agencies (such as SCAA 1996), assistance for developing practical classroom assessment is usually harder to obtain. Circumstances are further complicated by the self-evident truth that subject teams tend to be at different starting points, and in entirely different educational contexts, making it difficult to generalise about priorities. There could be many small-scale action research projects, or even Masters degree dissertations, hidden away in what Black and Wiliam referred to as the classroom (or departmental) 'black box'.

Nevertheless, it is possible to make one speculation about a particular set of actions likely to repay big dividends on the investment of time and energy. This centres on the establishment and maintenance of National Curriculum 'standards portfolios' of geography attainment. A full discussion of how to do this, and the approach to assessment underpinned by them, can be found elsewhere (Lambert and Balderstone 2000; Lambert and Lines 2000) as there is not the space here to do so in sufficient detail. Fundamentally, standards portfolios are ring binders in which is assembled a selection of pupils' work which, *in toto*, illustrates what the departmental team considers to be the standard at any particular 'level'. In practice, the department requires a portfolio for National Curriculum Levels 3, 5 and 7 – by definition, if colleagues can agree these Levels then they also are probably close to agreeing Levels 2, 4, 6 and 8 as well.

The strength of standards portfolios lies in the selection of pupils' work. The Level descriptions are abstract and general and therefore difficult to gain purchase on, but the pupils' work 'speaks' plainly about pupils' real capacities. Selection is clearly subjective, but 'moderated' by the Level descriptions and other teachers' interpretations of what they mean. Colleagues can expect to argue over what value they are prepared to give to pieces of work (note, the 'work', not the pupils), and it is unlikely that a portfolio for any particular Level will ever finally be settled: judgements will always be contingent. Of course, such contingency is a source of strength not weakness: it forces the teaching team to consider and reconsider the nature of achievement in Geography, and from such work teachers can derive increased clarity of subject-specific feedback in their work with pupils.

All manner of important practical concerns need to be sorted out, including those governing how meaningful feedback can be woven into lessons and how to prepare the pupils, before classroom assessment can begin to achieve its potential. However, the much harder task is to identify what 'meaningful feedback' consists of. Standards portfolios can provide the basis for determining this in relation to the National Curriculum. But being flexible assessment instruments, standards portfolios could also provide alternative versions of 'progress', for example tracing conceptual development or, as in the case of Leat and McGrane (2000) referred to earlier, thinking capacity. There is perhaps some interesting research and development work to be done in this field of geography education.

Note

1 The concept of high-stakes testing probably originates from analysis in the USA. The term is a useful one for all education systems, denoting how some tests *really matter* in a public sense, because job prospects or future educational opportunities depend directly on the test outcome. Research has shown that when testing operates in high-stakes conditions the impact on teaching can be so great as to distort healthy teaching and learning relationships.

References

Assessment Reform Group (1999) *Assessment for Learning: Beyond the Black Box*, Cambridge: University of Cambridge School of Education.

Balderstone, D. and King, S. (1998) *GCSE Bitesize Revision: Geography*, London: BBC.

Black, P. (1998) *Testing: Friend or Foe? Theory and Practice in Assessment and Testing*, London: Falmer Press.

Black, P. and Wiliam, D. (1998a) 'Assessment and classroom learning', *Assessment in Education*, 5(1): 7–74.

Black, P. and Wiliam, D. (1998b) *Inside the Black Box*, University of London, Department of Education, Kings College.

Blunkett, D. (2000) 'Moving on to something better', *Teaching Today: NASUWT Termly Review*, 25(Spring): 6–7.

Butt, G., Lambert, D. and Telfer, S. (eds) (1995) *Assessment Works*, Sheffield: Geographical Association.

Daugherty, R. (1995) *National Curriculum Assessment: A Review of Policy 1987–1994*, London: Falmer Press.

Davis, A. (1998) *The Limits of Educational Assessment*, Oxford: Blackwell.

Davis, A. (1999) 'Educational assessment: a critique of current policy', *Impact No. 1*. Philosophy of Education Society of Great Britain.

DES/WO (1988) *Task Group on Assessment and Testing: A Report*.

DfEE (1998) *Teaching: High Status, High Standards. Requirements for Courses of Initial Teacher Training*, Department for Education and Employment: Circular 4/98.

Gipps, C. (1994) *Beyond Testing: Towards a Theory of Educational Assessment*, Brighton: Falmer Press.

Hamson, R. and Sutton, A. (2000) 'Target setting at Key Stage 3', *Teaching Geography*, 25(1): 8–11.

Hopkins, J. (2000) 'Assessment for learning in geography', *Teaching Geography*, 25(1): 42–3.

Hopkins, J., Telfer, S. and Butt, G. (eds) (2000) *Assessment in Practice*, Sheffield: Geographical Association.

Lambert, D. (1996a) 'Assessing pupils' attainments and supporting learning', in A. Kent *et al.* (eds) *Geography in Education*, 260–87, Cambridge: Cambridge University Press.

Lambert, D. (1997a) 'Teacher assessment in the National Curriculum', in D. Tilbury and M. Williams (eds) *Teaching and Learning Geography*, 255–66, London: Routledge.

Lambert, D. (1997b) 'Assessing, recording and reporting pupils' progress and achievement', in S. Capel, M. Leask and T. Turner (eds) *Starting to Teach in the Secondary School*, 172–92, London: Routledge.

Lambert, D. and Balderstone, D. (2000) *Learning to Teach Geography*, London: Routledge.

Lambert, D. and Lines, D. (2000) *Assessment in Education: Perceptions, Purpose, Practice*, London: Falmer Press.

Leat, D. and McGrane, J. (2000) 'Diagnostic and formative assessment of students' thinking', *Teaching Geography*, 25(1): 4–7.

Naish, M. (ed.) (1990) *Experiences of Centralisation*, British Sub-Committee of Commission for Geographical Education, IGU, University of London Institute of Education.

Rowntree, D. (1987) *Assessing Students: How Shall We Know Them?* London: Kogan Page.

Sadler, D. (1989) 'Formative assessment and the design of instructional systems', in *Instructional Science*, 18: 119–44.

SCAA (1996) *Consistency in Teacher Assessment: Exemplification of Standards (Geography)*, London: School Curriculum and Assessment Authority (now the Qualifications and Curriculum Agency).

Stobart, G. and Gipps, C. (1997) *Assessment: A Teacher's Guide to the Issues*, London: Hodder & Stoughton.

Sutton, R. (1995) *Assessment for Learning*, Salford: R.S. Publications.

Torrance, H. and Pryor, J. (1998) *Investigating Formative Assessment*, Milton Keynes: Open University Press.

10 Raising attainment in Geography

Prospects and problems

David Leat

The history of the National Curriculum Geography Orders in England and Wales[1] provides a depressing commentary on the status of educational research, especially in relation to curriculum development. Rawling (1992) provides a telling account of the political constraints that operated inside the Geography Working Group, set up by the Department of Education and Science (DES) and the Welsh Office, which placed much emphasis on the mastery of knowledge by pupils. She writes of the Interim Report (DES and Welsh Office 1989) 'with many paragraphs drawing attention to pupils' lack of place knowledge and the inadequacy of thematic-based courses (e.g. see para 2.14), (Rawling 1992: 229). She further quotes the Secretary of State for Education calling, in the House of Commons, for young people to learn about places and where they are and not just vague concepts and attitudes. As recorded in the government-prescribed Orders, the Statements of Attainment (SoAs) constitute a deficit model of the curriculum by stating precisely what pupils need to know.

While some members of the working group and many correspondents in the consultation process made cogent arguments for alternative ways of framing the document, the political view prevailed. The imperative was that: 'Children don't seem to know where places are, what they are like, or why they are as they are – so they had better be taught.' There was no irrefutable case that could be made against this deficit model; there was no weight of evidence that could persuade doubting minds that this was the wrong construction.[2] Research into geographical education or attainment had not generated a compelling alternative.

Sadly, therefore, geography teachers had to proceed with a model that looked doomed from the start, particularly because the assessment framework appeared totally impractical. So the profession beavered away, producing schemes of work, manufacturing elaborate assessment frameworks and consuming literally millions of teacher-hours, only for the inevitable climbdown to occur. In January 1995, after much consultation, new orders were distributed to schools removing some, if not all, of the absurdities of the original orders.[2]

However before too much blame is attached to educational researchers, it must be said that where strong evidence did exist to guide the construction of the assessment framework, most notably in science, it did not significantly influence the curriculum orders.

The Piaget stumbling block

It is extraordinary just how tarnished the words 'theory' and 'research' are in education. Medical charities attract millions with the promise that the money will improve the treatment of ailing bodies, but there is virtually no public perception that educational research can improve the learning of disadvantaged minds. Theory has, in certain circles, become almost a term of abuse or ridicule. Politicians are inclined to use it to vilify certain styles of teaching associated with 1960s' progressivism. A false dichotomy is presented in some educational debates between a theoretical stance which is rubbished and a practical approach which is lauded. Practical is good and theoretical is bad.

This trend is perhaps encapsulated by current status of the work of Piaget among teachers. Those trained in the 1960s and 1970s seem to shiver at the mention of the name. They can recount lecture courses which detailed Piagetian experiments and theory, but they cannot trace any practical application of this knowledge to their classroom teaching. Thus, the name 'Piaget' has become a trigger to switch off and discount the possible relevance of educational research. This is not a fair judgement of the value of Piaget's work, more a reflection of the failings of initial teacher-training courses. Teacher education institutions, reacting to the charge of being too theoretical, have tended to remove or reduce inputs about learning theory. There is a strong irony in the fact that one of the major milestones of twentieth-century educational research has helped create a barrier to the assimilation of research findings into the practice of teaching.

Piaget's work does have important implications for teaching, although it is more recent work which has made these implications most tangible. Piaget proposed that children do not think in the same way as adults; rather, they go through a series of neuro-physiological stages of mental development – sensorimotor, pre-operational, concrete operational and formal operational (see Beard 1969 for further detail). Some cognitive scientists would prefer to argue that there are trends rather than stages in the development of individual minds. Flavell (1985) suggests that perhaps the most important difference distinguishable in young minds is that they know less and therefore their concepts are less elaborated and powerful. Nonetheless, whether it is attributable to stages or trends, it is widely accepted that there are differences in the cognitive attributes of children at different ages, and these differences are a powerful organizing framework for considering the purpose of teaching.

Shayer (1992) calculated which stages of Piagetian development were a necessary condition for attaining Levels in the (then) seventeen science Attainment Targets (ATs). He concludes that, on average, concrete operational thinking will not get a pupil past Level 4 and that formal operational thinking is required for Level 5 and upwards. This information is given further significance by results from the Concepts in Secondary Science and Mathematics Programme (Shayer *et al.* 1976), which showed that only about 15 per cent of British 14-year-olds were operating at this cognitive level. No such calculation has been done for Geography, but even without it the implication is clear. A pupil's level of cognitive development places an absolute ceiling on his or her academic achievement as measured by the

National Curriculum Levels or public examinations because, unless he or she employs formal operational thinking, the higher levels are out of reach.

It is as well to remember that, despite the low standing of theory as a concept, we all operate as teachers from a basis of personal theory (e.g. Calderhead 1987). This personal theory may or may not bear much resemblance to more formal theory, but it will inevitably influence the image we have of what constitutes good teaching and suitable learning activities. It is important, therefore, that we operate from good theory, although the judgement of what constitutes good is, of course, problematic.

The limits of concrete thinking

This is not an appropriate place to rehearse descriptions of Piagetian stages, but it may be helpful to give some indication of the significance of formal operational thinking to geographical attainment. One characteristic of concrete thinking is that conversations or stories are reported in detail as blow-by-blow accounts, whereas formal operations are characterized by the ability to analyse speech and reduce it to principles, ideas and generalizations. As Shayer (1972: 342) comments, 'Matters of ethics become discussible on the more complex plane of the reconcilia-tion of interests and responsibilities of people.' In any controversial issue, one prin-ciple, rule or moral stance is the yardstick to measure and judge, ruling out compromise, modification and accommodation of alternative views. There is a rigidity that denies the consideration of an alternative point of view. Having recently studied the work of a Year 7 (11–12 years of age) class on the removal of hedgerows, I was struck by the starkness of their views – this was a black-and-white issue. The common view was that it was bad for farmers to remove hedgerows because it affected wildlife, therefore it was unreasonable for farmers to do this. There was little room for compromise in their plans for the farm that they were studying.

Formal operational thinking allows the world to be considered more flexibly, because situations can be formulated and represented in some symbolic form. For some years, as a schoolteacher, this meant nothing to me; I did not understand its significance. However, my second teaching post was in a field-study centre, where a popular activity with Year 7 classes was measuring aspects of rivers. Over time it became clear that relatively few pupils could grasp the idea that a shallow, fast stretch of river had the same amount of water flowing through it per second as a slow, deep stretch just downstream. Some would latch on to the speed and others on the depth to conclude that one or the other had more water. Life became very confused if the width varied also. I began to appreciate that the majority could not accommodate more than two variables in their thinking at once: either depth and discharge or speed and discharge. This is one of the strongest distinguishing features of concrete thinking – an inability to manipulate more than one variable mentally. However, with experience, I found that I could explain the concept of discharge fairly successfully to most by resorting to variously shaped cardboard boxes and describing discharge as a box of water that goes by you in a second, if you are on the bank. On reflection, I realize that this concrete demonstration had reduced the number of variables.

Typically, concrete thinkers cannot hypothesize. This is rooted in their difficulty in 'playing with' variables. This clearly makes any task requiring a plan, or solution problematic. While concrete thinkers will be able to produce a plan it will tend to lack a considered justification. When I taught near Reading, we took our Year 11 (15–16-year-old) pupils to do an environmental assessment of a stretch of the Kennet Valley, which suffered a range of pressures common in urban fringe areas. Following the fieldwork, the pupils had to produce a plan to deal with the pressures. The less successful pupils produced neat plans, but the explanations betrayed not only the sense of a black-and-white world but also an inability to predict the problems that their plans would create. They were unable to rehearse mentally the interplay of factors such as landscape, land use, conflict, access and environmental quality.

A last illustration of the limits of concrete thinking relates to explanation. Concrete thinkers are characterized by not asking why things happen and certainly not checking the validity and plausibility of explanations. They concentrate on what happens. Again, this is a function of their difficulty in handling variables. In some recent work with Year 9 pupils (13–14 years old) on the Los Angeles riots, with a teacher colleague, the difficulty of explanation became very clear. The causes of the riots were the beating of Rodney King, the subsequent acquittal of his assailants and the public reaction to these events – that is, what happened. The pupils could explain the deeper causes of the riots only if this could be achieved through text comprehension. In other words they scanned text for the words 'the causes were … '. Isolating a variable such as poverty and tracing its effects through to the riots was an uphill task that needed a lot of scaffolding.

Implications for National Curriculum Geography

Piaget's work has been subject to a great deal of criticism and revision in the last twenty years. There has been much adverse discussion of his experiments, particularly in the way that the tasks were explained and framed for the children (e.g. Bryant 1974; Donaldson 1978). It has been argued that concrete and formal operational thinking are not necessarily constant states, and, indeed, pupils can vary between the two depending on the domain, subject or subject matter. However, Piaget's stages are still generally accepted as a reasonable description of cognitive development.

As Key Stage 3 (age 11–14) is the time when many pupils are moving towards the boundary of concrete and formal operational thinking, it is an appropriate section of the National Curriculum to consider. Before the Dearing-proposed revisions in 1994, there were for Geography 114 SoAs spread over Levels 3 to 7. Of these, twenty-five SoAs included the word 'explain' and at least another seven implied it; twelve included the word 'analyse', and seven included 'evaluate'. Furthermore, a large proportion of SoAs directly demanded an understanding of relationships between one variable or set of variables and another variable or set of variables; thirty-one were very explicitly about relationships and a further twenty-three

involved cause or effect (which are essentially about relationships between variables, either over time or in space). A few examples of statements (NCC 1991) will
serve to illustrate these points:

> AT4 L5b Analyse the factors that influence the location and growth of indi-
> vidual settlements, and identify the effects of such growth
> AT3 L6f Describe characteristics of one type of vegetation and relate those
> characteristics to environmental conditions and processes, including climate
> and human actions
> AT5 L7a Analyse the effects of technological developments on the exploita-
> tion of natural resources and the management of environments.

These statements contain multiple factors and demand an understanding of how
they interrelate. They also require explanation, prediction, analysis, synthesis and
evaluation, all processes that require the manipulation of sets of variables, which is
just what concrete thinkers cannot do. The majority of Key Stage 3 pupils are
concrete thinkers, at least most of the time, so one can argue that if statements are
interpreted literally, then most are beyond the target pupils.

Although the revisions are widely welcomed the new orders have not removed
this fundamental issue. The Level 5 description contains the following (Schools
Curriculum and Assessment Authority 1995):

> They (pupils) describe how ... processes can lead to similarities and differences
> between places ... They offer explanations for ways in which human activities
> affect the environment.

At Level 6 it is expected that:

> They describe ways in which processes operating at different scales create
> geographical patterns and lead to changes in places. They describe and offer
> explanations for different approaches to managing environments and appre-
> ciate their different approaches have different effects on people and places.

These descriptions require the use of the schemata of formal operational thinking.

The National Curriculum emerged out of a concern to raise standards, and
better teaching or, more accurately, better instruction and clearer targets were to
be the means to achieve this. The argument presented here offers another view,
namely that better attainment is dependent on teaching pupils to think, or, to be
more accurate, to develop their capacity to think.

The evidence from science and mathematics

There is now very promising evidence from science education to suggest that
attainment can be raised by focusing on meaningful learning and teaching
thinking.

The Cognitive Acceleration in Science Education (CASE) Project was developed at King's College, London, by Shayer and Adey. The CASE activities were developed following a study of research into cognitive acceleration (Adey and Shayer 1994). It is classified as an infusion approach to teaching thinking, because it seeks to achieve this through the medium of teaching a curriculum subject. This contrasts with direct or bolt-on approaches, such as de Bono's (1986) CoRT (Cognitive Research Trust) programme.

The CASE Project research phase involved schools in a cross-section of local education authorities. The procedure was to teach a two-year course, either in Years 7 and 8 or 8 and 9, using CASE materials, which included a problem-solving activity at least once a fortnight. In all schools, control classes were established.

The course team identified central concepts in science, in order that they would be explicitly taught for; for example, variables, relationships, probability and the use of abstract models to explain and predict. There are strong echoes here of some of the central concepts in geography. The authors would describe themselves as post-Piagetians, and they make clear reference to the influence of both Piaget and Vygotsky in their work. So, for example, they start most units with concrete activities, and they explicitly aim to accelerate students from the concrete to the formal operational thinking stage and thereby raise attainment. The activities were built around three important concepts derived from cognitive psychology: *cognitive conflict, metacognition* and *bridging.*

Cognitive conflict is a term used to describe the dissonance that occurs when a child is presented with a situation which challenges his or her existing conceptual framework or understanding. The constructivist view of learning describes how the learner's existing knowledge resides in a series of schemata, which may be viewed as packages of information about related objects, actions or feelings. It is conceived that there are components within each schema and that there are relationships both within and between schemata. If new information is presented which conflicts with the existing schema, it may be rejected because no links can be made with the information already possessed. If the new information accords with the existing information, adjustment and growth can take place in the structure of the schema, altering the understanding of already encoded information, but this may be a slow process (for further detail see Driver *et al.* 1985, 1993). For the dissonance to take effect, the learner needs to be prepared carefully, so that the new experience is not only a shock but also connects with existing understanding, The carefully prepared shock is vital in the accelerated development of important concepts. In the Children's Learning in Science Project (e.g. Driver 1989), this concept has been used as the root approach in getting pupils to expose their existing conceptualizations and then to test them in experiments.

The issue here is that lessons must be demanding but accessible. There is evidence from both Britain and the USA that what happens in many classrooms is routine 'busywork', and that in many instances teachers avoid setting difficult and demanding tasks because it can make classroom management more difficult (Carter and Doyle 1987). Reports from Her Majesty's Inspectors (HMI) frequently point to lack of challenge being a significant problem in many lessons in English and

Welsh schools. This may be exacerbated in many instances by pupils' low self-esteem and a culture of low expectation. Trainee teachers at Newcastle University often complain that pupils will automatically say, 'I can't do it', when faced by a task that requires some thought.

One of the most pertinent illustrations from geography classrooms of what cognitive conflict may look like is provided by the inquiry process. At the beginning of this, one can encourage pupils to identify their existing understandings and attitudes. By judicious presentation of material through the rest of the process, one can lead pupils to question their baseline knowledge. In the case of hedgerow removal mentioned earlier, it is possible to start the unit by asking the question. 'Who is the best farmer?' and using data on costs, output and income to lead pupils to a conclusion that the best farmer is the one who makes the most profit. By following this with photographs and maps which compare the wildlife and landscape on intensive farms with unimproved farms, the pupils are forced to reconsider their earlier understanding of good farming, and they develop more extensive schemata, and with them understanding, relating to farming.

Metacognition is a term first coined by Flavell (1977), and at its simplest means to be aware of one's own thinking. In time, the term has come to take on an extended meaning with increased use. It also carries an implication that, through thinking about thinking, the individual can begin to make conscious choices about the strategies that he or she employs in tackling a problem. Metacognition is a common feature of thinking skills courses (Perkins and Salomon 1989).

Mathematical education has developed a particular interest in metacognition, through the effort to shift the understanding of mathematics from being a body of knowledge to be learned and towards being an active process of inquiry and generalization (Mason 1988). In teaching pupils to be expert modellers, it is proposed that they need to develop 'inner speech' in which they are able to discuss and argue with themselves (Schoenfeld 1987). Inner speech is a representation of metacognition and avoids the pitfall of reducing thinking to a checklist of strategies. Metacognition offers the prospect in maths of teaching pupils to model rather than a model.

Turning to *bridging*: it has long been the cherished ambition of educators to bring pupils to the point where they are able to tackle unfamiliar problems. This is deemed to be increasingly important in an era of rapid technological and economic change. People will rarely do the same jobs throughout their working lives and they will need to be able to transfer skills and knowledge from one context to another. In the CASE project, therefore, a conscious effort was made at the end of lessons to help pupils to recognize other contexts to which the concept or reasoning pattern could be applied, to increase the chances of transfer. The teacher sought to identify similar contexts in science, in other subjects and even in everyday life. In a recent teaching episode with an ex-PGCE student and his Year 7 class, who were investigating the closure of a village shop, the central concepts of the lesson were cause and effect. At the end of the lesson, therefore, the pupils were asked to list all the topics in humanities during the year in which they had studied causes and effects. They did this readily and seemed to register that any issue or event in humanities would have causes and effects. Although this was not explored, it is not a huge leap to consider that, with reinforcement, they could begin to use these concepts as a broad framework for approaching any issue.

Tanner and Jones (1993), reporting on a project to investigate the development of metacognitive skills in Welsh mathematics students, discerned a difference in the debrief questioning skills of some teachers. Some tended to ask questions which were specific to the task, leaving the pupil to generalize and make links. Others asked more general questions which encouraged pupils to transform their experience into internal processes for self-regulation. They reported that in the latter case the pupils were more able to assimilate the processes into their conceptual schema.

I would add to this important list a fourth principle that is implicit in the CASE project, but is worth stating because it may be more readily identifiable for geography teachers – namely the value of groupwork and talk. This is not the place to discuss the importance of language in geography teaching (e.g. Williams 1981; Slater 1989). Suffice it to say that the development of higher-level thinking is inextricably bound up with language. Bruner (1985) regarded groupwork as a form of scaffolding which allows the successful completion by groups of tasks that are too difficult for some individuals in the group. This, of course, can be a very important approach to differentiation. These suggestions have been further elaborated and evidenced in mathematics and science (Forman and Cazdan 1985; Wheatley 1991).

It is pertinent here to refer to the work of Vygotsky (1978). He saw cognitive development as a largely cultural phenomenon, passed on through mediation of the child's experience. The mediator was critical in helping the child learn from experience. Vygotsky developed the concept of the Zone of Proximal Development (ZPD), which he described as, 'the distance between the actual developmental level as determined by independent problem solving and the level of potential development as determined through problem solving under the guidance or in collaboration with more able peers' (Vygotsky 1978, p. 86). This definition encapsulates both the prospect of raising the cognitive performance of pupils, perhaps to formal operational thinking, and the importance of interaction between pupils. Put simply, it is the very process of talking that precipitates learning. The CASE authors do stress, however, the importance of the way in which teachers frame tasks that will be the basis of talk.

Parallel to the 'teaching thinking' movement there is also a growing interest in concept mapping, particularly in science, as a route to encouraging more meaningful learning. Concept mapping has its origins in Ausubel's (1963, 1968) assimilation theory, which proposed that what the learner already knows is the most important determinant of further learning. This is a constructivist viewpoint. Concept mapping was developed from this principle by Novak with colleagues at Cornell University (Novak and Gowin 1984; Novak 1990). Concept maps are drawn representations indicating the relationships between concepts. For any individual concept, the greater the number of links to other concepts the greater will be the elaboration and understanding of that concept. In science, three stages are usual in constructing the map:

1   the concepts pertaining to the topic are listed;
2   the concepts are arranged hierarchically, with arrows connecting them;
3   words or phrases are added to the lines to explain the nature of the relationship.

Some geographical topics are not as tidy as science, and in some instances factor maps might be more appropriate organizers. Thus in seeking to understand the demise of the British coal industry, factors such as mechanization, competition from other fuel sources, government policy, foreign competition, safety standards, the miners' unions and investment could be set out as a set of factors, the interplay between which could be explored on the map. However, the topic of glaciation would be amenable to a traditional concept-map approach.

The extent to which science educators have become interested in concept mapping may be judged by the fact that a whole special issue of the *Journal of Research in Science Teaching* was devoted to it in 1990. One article included in the issue listed one hundred references related to concept mapping (Al-Kunifed and Wandersee 1990). The range of beneficial outcomes proposed for the use of concept mapping includes improved understanding of scientific topics (Gurley 1982), more meaningful learning (Lehman *et al.* 1985), reduced anxiety among students (Jegede *et al.* 1990), and better subject knowledge and a changed view of the curriculum among teachers (Starr and Krajick 1990). While concept mapping is a single tool with a strong pedigree, it also nests within the 'teaching thinking' universe, as successful concept mappers are also better problem solvers (Okebukola 1992). This would imply that concept mapping is one way of developing metacognitive awareness.

Implications for teaching style

The foregoing suggests that different teaching styles are required to implement these approaches to teaching thinking. This is not a simple matter of learning a few new skills, but raises a more fundamental question as to how a teacher conceives her or his subject and therefore how it should be taught. Tanner and Jones (1993) noted the contrast in approach between teachers who regarded mathematics as a static unified body of knowledge and those with a largely constructivist stance, who perceived the subject as actively built up by the pupil in the form of connected schemata. Novak (1990) reports a similar difficulty with science teachers who regard science as a large body of knowledge to be mastered. From my own experience, teachers who are introduced to teaching thinking through geography all have difficulty with the change in teaching demanded, and to some extent are reduced to the status of novices, a finding also reported by Rich (1993).

Debriefing at the end of lessons is one of the keys to metacognition. It is part of the CASE style of teaching to encourage pupils to talk openly about how they have tackled problems. A typical question in a whole-class debrief might be, 'How did you do that?' or, 'Did you have a different approach?' Through this consideration of the lesson as a learning experience, it is hypothesized that pupils develop reasoning patterns. I recently taught a lesson to a group of Year 7 pupils in which groups of four pupils were given twenty-six separate pieces of information relating to possible causes and effects of the closure of a village shop. Many of these items were red herrings. The groups had first to establish which items were relevant and then build them into an explanation. This was the fourth of a series of problem-solving and decision-making activities. In the discussion at the end, some groups outlined how they had tackled the problem. In the written evaluations by the pupils, them were many comments to suggest that a level of metacognitive awareness was beginning to emerge; for example, 'I learnt how to decide what information to use and what information not to use' and, 'I learnt that it is important to consider everything before making conclusions and also to link clues together to make one reason covering everything.' These are emergent reasoning patterns which, given further reinforcement, could substantially alter cognitive functioning.

Does cognitive acceleration work?

Until recently, the claims for thinking skills programmes were not well substanti-ated. Commonly, the programmes have not been evaluated systematically. In a review of the evaluation evidence centred on the most popular intervention programmes, Sternberg and Bhana (1986) concluded that the studies were seri-ously flawed because outcome measures were of a testimonial nature or so closely linked to the programmes that they were biased. Resnick (1987), in a summary of evaluation studies in America, reported findings of some improvement in reading comprehension, grade averages and improved problem solving in mathematics and science, but no evidence of transfer. It is against this background that the results of the CASE project can be seen (Adey and Shayer 1994).

By 1989, CASE pupils had taken their General Certificate of Secondary Educa-tion (GCSEs), having been remixed with control pupils in GCSE classes using normal teaching approaches. Not only did CASE pupils achieve substantially higher grades in science but, more significantly, they achieved higher grades in English and mathematics as well. Thus, in 1989, 41.7 per cent (science), 49.1 per cent (mathematics) and 44.6 per cent (English) of CASE boys got grades C and above, while the figures for the non-CASE counterparts were 12.8 per cent, 16.4 per cent and 16.1 per cent. For 1990 girls (CASE figures first), the results were 50.0 per cent against 33.3 per cent in science, 55.16 per cent against 42.42 per cent in mathematics, and 85.18 per cent against 58.06 per cent in English. It must be pointed out, however, that there was a reverse effect in lower grades, with CASE male pupils scoring a higher percentage of grade G in all three subjects. This transfer lends weight to the notion that reasoning patterns can be developed and applied to other subjects. Unfortunately, there are no results to indicate whether there was any effect on Geography. These findings await replication, but there are some other promising signs.

St Mary's Roman Catholic Comprehensive School in Newcastle has been running a cognitive acceleration programme for more than five years, as a whole-school policy. This involves three 'teaching thinking' approaches. The lower band is given Instrumental Enrichment (IE) (Link 1989), an intervention strategy developed by the Israeli psychologist Feuerstein, during Years 7–9. The rationale here is that these pupils have generally failed to develop the cognitive functions which are the necessary precursors of higher-level thinking, such as the abilities to perceive and compare. Without these functions, pupils tend to be impulsive when faced with problems. The upper band receives both Somerset Thinking Skills (Blagg *et al.* 1988) and CASE teaching. If lower-band pupils make sufficient progress, they graduate to CASE lessons in Year 9. The year 1993 was crucial for the school, as the first cohort who had experienced the cognitive acceleration curriculum from Year 7 took their GCSEs. In recent years, the highest percentage of pupils getting five or more GCSEs at grades A–C had been 27 per cent. In 1993, this rose by approximately 10 per cent.

The prospects for cognitive acceleration in Geography

The argument presented in this chapter has run as follows: the National Curriculum was founded on the notion that it would improve attainment. How this was to be done has never been made clear, except that there would be clearer targets and, somehow, better teaching as a result of the competition induced by market forces unleashed by the publication of league tables of Standard Attainment Tasks.

Despite a history of a very uncertain relationship between educational research and curriculum planning and implementation, there is real evidence to suggest how raising attainment should be tackled. An analysis of pre-Dearing-review KS3 SoAs suggests that attainment in Geography will be limited if pupils cannot engage in formal operational thinking. The great majority of statements required an understanding of interaction between a number of variables, through the need to understand cause and effect or to explain and analyse. The new Level descriptions have not removed this barrier; higher cognitive demand is embedded in the higher levels. Those pupils limited to concrete thinking will not be able to achieve these. There is good evidence from the CASE project, in particular, that cognitive acceleration or teaching pupils to think can substantially improve GCSE results and, one would anticipate, National Curriculum attainment. How can Geography reap the same benefits?

First, groups of teachers can make their own efforts to fuse the successful principles of CASE and IE with the methodology of geographical inquiry and problem solving, with an emphasis on issues. An example was given earlier of the inquiry approach to the issue of 'Who is the best farmer?'. I am currently engaged in the production of KS3 'thinking' units, which are being developed and tried with the assistance of teachers in the Tyneside area. The results are highly encouraging, but it will take many years before hard evidence about their efficacy will be available.

The second approach affects teacher education. Teaching pupils to think does require a paradigm shift in thinking about teaching. Most prospective teachers have been heavily influenced in their conception of what teaching is by the way in which they have been taught; indeed, it could hardly be any different. For most students, however, this experience is still heavily laced with didactic transmission styles. If the gains in achievement generated by the CASE project are to be trans-ferred across the curriculum, then there needs to be developed in geography teachers a new repertoire of skills that can be labelled as intervention skills. This is not to say that instruction skills are unnecessary, but that alone they are not suffi-cient to repair the disadvantage of slow cognitive development. Just how this can be accomplished within the framework of the government reforms of teacher educa-tion remains to be seen.

Notes

1 The National Curriculum for Geography came into force for 5–7-year-olds (Key Stage 1), 7–11-year-olds (Key Stage 2) and 11–14-year-olds (Key Stage 3) in September 1991. Key Stage 4 for 14–16-year-olds should have started in September 1994, by which time the General Certificate of Secondary Education (GCSE) courses would have been brought into line with National Curric-ulum requirements. This change has now been postponed until at least 1996. Each Key Stage had a compulsory content of material to be taught, the Programmes of Study. The assessment framework was provided by 5 Attainment Targets (ATs): Skills, Knowledge and Understanding of Places, Physical Geography, Human Geography and Environmental Geography. Each AT had ten Levels, which described, supposedly, progressive levels of attainment in those areas. Most Levels had several statements. Problematically, nearly all the statements contained command words such as 'describe', 'explain' and 'analyse', and a geographical knowledge component. The framework for the Geography proposals was produced by a working group appointed by the Secretary of State for Education.
2 The new Orders for Geography acknowledge the many weaknesses of the original, notably the difficulty of assessing the Statements of Attainment. The new orders contain one Attainment Target with 8 Level descriptions, which attempt to characterize a range of performance outcomes. Teachers would have to decide which descriptions best fitted each pupil. There have been some reductions in the content coverage required.

References

Adey, P. and Shayer, M. (1994) *Really Raising Standards*, London: Routledge.

Al-Kunifed, A. and Wandersee, J.H. (1990) 'One hundred references related to concept mapping', *Journal of Research in Science Teaching*, 27: 1069–75.

Ausubel, D.P. (1963) *The Psychology of Meaningful Verbal Learning*, New York: Grune and Stratton.

Ausubel, D.P. (1968) *Educational Psychology: A Cognitive View*, New York: Holt, Rinehart and Winston.

Beard, R. (1969) *Piaget's Stages of Development*, London: Routledge and Kegan Paul.

Blagg, N., Ballinger, M. and Gardner, R. (1988) *Somerset Thinking Skills Course*, Oxford: Blackwell.

de Bono, E. (1996) *CoRT Thinking*, Oxford: Pergamon.

Bryant, P. (1974) *Perception and Understanding in Young Children*, London: Methuen.

Calderhead, J. (ed.) (1987) *Exploring Teachers' Thinking*, London: Cassell.

Carter, K. and Doyle, W. (1987) 'Teachers' knowledge structures and comprehension processes', in J. Calderhead (ed.) *Exploring Teachers' Thinking*, London: Cassell.

DES and Welsh Office (1989) National Curriculum Geography Working Group Interim Report. London: DES and Welsh Office.

Donaldson, M. (1978) *Children's Minds*, Glasgow: Fontana.

Driver, R. (1989) 'Changing conceptions', in P. Adey, J. Bliss, J. Head and M. Shayet (eds) *Adolescent Development and School Science,* London: Falmer.

Driver, R., Guesne, E. and Tiberghian, A. (1985) *Children's Ideas in Science,* Milton Keynes: Open University Press.

Driver, R., Squires, A., Rushworth P. and Wood-Robinson, V. (1993) *Making Sense of Secondary Science,* London: Routledge.

Flavell, J. (1977) *Cognitive Development,* 1st edn. Englewood Cliffs, NJ: Prentice-Hall

Flavell, J. (1985) *Cognitive Development,* 2nd edn. Englewood Cliffs, NJ: Prentice-Hall.

Forman, E.A. and Cazden, C.B. (1985) 'Exploring Vygotskyan perspectives in education: the cognitive value of peer interaction', in J.V. Wertsch (ed.) *Culture, Communication and Cognition: Vygotskyan Perspectives,* Cambridge: Cambridge University Press.

Gurley, L.I. (1982) 'Use of Gowin's vee and concept mapping strategies to teach responsibility for learning in high school biological sciences', unpublished doctoral thesis, Cornell University, Ithaca, NY.

Jegede, O.J., Alaiyemola, F.F. and Okebukola, P.A.O. (1990) 'The effect of concept mapping on students' anxiety and achievement in biology', *Journal of Research in Science Teaching,* 27: 951–60.

Lehman, J.D., Carter, C. and Kahle, J.B. (1985) 'Concept mapping, vee mapping and achievement: results of a field study with black high school students', *Journal of Research in Science Teaching,* 22: 663–73.

Link, F.R. (1989) 'Instrumental enrichment: a strategy for cognitive and academic improvement', in F.R. Link (ed.) *Essays On The Intellect,* Alexandria, VA: Association for Supervision and Curriculum Development.

Mason, J. (1988) 'Modelling: what do we really want pupils to learn?', in D. Pimm (ed.) *Mathematics, Teachers and Children.* London: Hodder and Stoughton.

Novak, J. D. (1990) 'A useful tool for science education', *Journal of Research in Science Teaching,* 27: 937–49.

Novak, J.D. and Gowin, D.B. (1984) *Learning How to Learn,* New York: Cambridge University Press.

Okebukola, P.A. (1992) 'Can good concept mappers be good problem solvers in science?' *Research in Science and Technological Education,* 10: 153–70.

Perkins, D.N., and Salomon, G. (1989) 'Are cognitive skills context bound?', *Educational Researchers,* 18: 16–25.

Rawling, E. (1992) 'The making of a national geography curriculum', *Geography,* 77: 292–309.

Resnick, L.B. (1987) *Education and Learning to Think,* Washington, DC: National Academic Press.

Rich, Y. (1993) 'Stability and change in teacher expertise', *Teacher and Teacher Education,* 9: 137–46.

Schoenfeld, A.H. (1987) 'What's all this fuss about metacognition?', in A.H. Schoenfeld (ed.), *Cognitive Science and Maths Education,* Hillsdale, NJ: Erlbaum.

Schools Curriculum and Assessment Authority (1995) *The National Curriculum Orders,* London: Schools Curriculum and Assessment Authority.

Shayer, M. (1972) 'Conceptual demands in the Nuffield O-level physics', *School Science Review,* 54: 26–42.

Shayer, M. (1992) 'Improving standards and the National Curriculum', *School Science Review,* 72: 17–29.

Shayer, M., Kuchemann D.E. and Wylam, H. (1976) 'The distribution of Piagetian stages of thinking in British middle and secondary school children', *British Journal of Educational Psychology*, 46: 164–73.

Slater, F. (ed.) (1989) *Language and Learning in the Teaching of Geography*, London: Routledge.

Starr, M.L. and Krajcik, J.S. (1990) 'Concept maps as a heuristic for science curriculum development: Towards improvement in processes and product', *Journal of Research in Science Teaching*, 27: 987–1000.

Sternberg, R.J. and Bhana K. (1986) 'Synthesis of research on the effectiveness of intellectual skills programmes: Snake oil remedies or miracle cures?', *Educational Leadership*, 44: 60–7.

Tanner, H. and Jones, S. (1993) 'Developing Metacognitive Skills in Secondary School Students', in *Proceedings of the Second International Colloquium on Education: British and American Perspectives*, Swansea: Department of Education, University College of Swansea.

Vygotsky, L. (1978) *Mind in Society*, Cambridge, MA: Harvard University Press.

Wheatley, G.H. (1991) 'Constructivist perspectives on science and mathematics learning', *Science Education*, 75: 9–12.

Williams, M. (ed.) (1981) *Language Teaching and Learning – Geography*, London: Ward Lock.

11 Issues in ICT and Geography

David Hassell

Introduction

Information and Communications Technology (ICT) may be a term that has only become popular in the past few years, but the notion of ICT has a long history within the teaching and learning of geography. The use of ICT as a tool for teachers and learners has never had such prominence and is something that must be addressed by all phases of education, reaching across formal and informal education. Despite the importance of the technology, there are many issues for all geographers, ranging from access to the technology, to identifying its effective use and application. More importantly it could be claimed that ICT is changing geography continually, be it in the patterns of work that geographers study or the formal understanding of how the subject can and should be taught. Another key issue is that 'half-life' of change within the technology, which means that new teaching and learning opportunities appear at an ever increasing rate and this has considerable implications for the initial training and continuing professional development of teachers.

There is a huge range of opportunities for enhancing the teaching and learning of geography and discussion often concentrates on these benefits. However, there are also many ways that ICT can support teachers in the execution of their professional duty, which can improve the teaching and learning process, the teachers' efficiency or their activity behind the scenes. The big questions for all involved in geography is how can the issues which restrict the use of ICT be overcome and when they are, how can ICT be integrated effectively to enhance geography? Finally, will ICT have any fundamental impact on the subject itself?

Why ICT?

Many teachers have managed to teach effectively for years without using ICT, so why bother? This is a question that has been asked many times and for which there is a range of answers. There is a considerable body of research (NCET 1994) which has looked at a wide range of factors, which can be divided into intrinsic and extrinsic reasons. Research has shown that the learning process can be improved in a number of ways:

- ICT can provide a safe and non-threatening environment for learning with the flexibility to meet individual needs and abilities of each student;
- ICT gives students immediate access to richer source materials;
- difficult ideas are made more understandable when information technology makes them visible;
- ICT can affect the power to try out different ideas and take risks, encouraging analytical and divergent thinking.

However, it is not only the hardware and software that enhance the process, for as many commentators have explained, it is not the technology but what it is used for that is most important. Students must have well-designed, meaningful tasks and activities and they will make the most effective use of computers only if teachers know how and when to intervene (NCET 1994; NCET and GA 1996). Extrinsically, ICT is already pervasive in society and many feel there is a duty to ensure that pupils leave school prepared for life in the technological world of the twenty-first century.

In 1993 the Department of Education (as it was then) brought together a conference of geographers to debate the issue. Two questions that emerged were: Can Geography lessons be enriched with information technology? Are there some IT skills and capabilities which pupils should expect to be taught in school Geography? Having looked at how ICT might enhance the subject as well as the role of ICT in the world at large, the answer to the questions was undoubtedly yes! It was proposed that a statement was needed to crystallize the essence of what ICT might offer the subject, and the document *Geography – a pupil's entitlement to IT* (NCET and GA 1994) was the result. This was jointly published by the Geographical Association (GA) and the National Council for Educational Technology (NCET, now BECTa) and two versions, one for primary and one for secondary, were distributed to all maintained English schools. The idea of entitlement is valid for all ages and the documents propose that pupils studying Geography are entitled to use ICT:

- to enhance their skills of geographical enquiry;
- to gain access to a wide range of geographical knowledge and information sources;
- to deepen their understanding of environmental and spatial relationships;
- to experience alternative images of people, place and environment; and
- to consider the wider impact of IT on people, place and environment.

The term 'pupil entitlement' focuses on those uses of ICT in which pupils should expect to gain competence during their school Geography course and although there may be an overlap they do not have to match core IT skills.

The changing climate for ICT

The role of ICT in Geography has been recognized for many years with a wide range of activity supported by evangelists promoting its use. However, the adoption of

ICT has been restricted by the lack of access to equipment, training and other issues, many of which are beyond the gift of the average geography teacher. Though governments have spent considerable funds on the use of ICT there has never been a systematic strategy to make the most of technology. Since 1997 the government has realized the need to have a strategic approach to developing ICT use in schools, and has put in place a range of initiatives which aim to improve the situation whilst providing a number of issues for teachers.

Prior to 1997, the Labour Party commissioned an investigation and report (The Independent ICT in Schools Commission 1997), under the chairmanship of Denis Stevenson, which identified that ICT was a key issue for the future and put forward a range of proposals, including that the government should:

- announce that addressing the issue of ICT is a top priority;
- construct an overall strategy, and appoint a departmental minister to drive it;
- make national agencies key players in this strategy;
- enable all organizations to participate in a coherent and productive way;
- encourage every school to formulate, implement whole-school ICT policies;
- sustain and give coherence to the many small and low-key initiatives to be undertaken over a five–ten-year period required to achieve the long-term objective.

After the general election the government adopted a number of Stevenson's proposals in a consultation paper 'Connecting the Learning Society' (DfEE 1998a) which set out its targets for the following five years. These included:

- by 1998 plans for a National Grid for Learning (NGfL) should be in process of implementation;
- by 1999 all Newly Qualified Teachers would need to become ICT literate;
- by 2002 serving teachers should feel confident, and be competent to teach, using ICT;
- by 2002 all schools, colleges, universities and libraries should be connected to the NGfL;
- by 2002 most school leavers should have a good understanding of ICT;
- by 2002 the UK should be a centre for excellence in software content for education;
- from 2002 the majority of administrative communications in schools should be electronic.

There are a number of executive government activities that together form the National Grid for Learning (NGfL) initiative which is designed to ensure the targets are achieved. There are four key elements to the initiative.

Training   There are two major initiatives, the first being a new ICT National Curriculum for initial teacher education, which is expected to ensure that all NQTs are trained in the use of ICT to enhance their curriculum teaching. Second, £230 million is being spent between 1999 and 2003 on providing the opportunity for every teacher to have training in the use of ICT to support the teaching and learning in the curriculum (Hassell 1999). This money comes from the National Lottery via the New Opportunities Fund and is managed by the Teacher Training Agency. The scheme aims both to bring teachers up to a minimum standard (as described in *The Use of ICT in Subject Teaching – Expected Outcomes for Teachers in England and Wales* (TTA 1999a)) and also to ensure that teachers finish the programme with improved competence and confidence and with an action plan for future continuing professional development. However, the funding only amounts to approximately £450 per teacher, which cannot be spent on teacher cover or travel to any centres, so the training will mainly be based on distance learning techniques and on teachers contributing some of their own time. The Green Paper on the teaching profession, *Teachers – meeting the challenge of change* (DfEE 1998a), also provides an indicator of the future with the notion that all teachers will have to ensure they keep their ICT skills up to date. Many heads are already looking carefully at applicants' ICT skills as they appoint new staff.

Infrastructure Many schools do not have the computers or the external network connections to satisfy the government's target. Between 1998 and 2002 an element of central government funding (Standards Fund), with match funding from LEAs (over £760 million) is being spent on enhancing school infrastructure. LEAs have a wide range of approaches to dealing with their Standards Fund grants. These include devolving the grant to schools to make their own decisions, working in partnership with all schools to achieve better purchasing deals, and providing an integrated system with on-line LEA support. However, there will always be inconsistencies in the effectiveness of approaches, which could see some schools working on their own with little support and having to 'reinvent' the wheel. Another strand to the larger initiative is that of Managed Services which was introduced in 1999. This initiative (*Open for Business, Open for Learning*, DfEE 1998b) aims to provide schools with more effective purchasing by accrediting a number of providers and setting up national framework contracts for the purchase of equipment and services along with training and technical support. Any school can take advantage of the service that should provide better value for money and greater confidence in developing a school's ICT infrastructure.

The National Grid for Learning (NGfL) web sites As part of the government's initiative there are a number of web sites to support schools' education. The British Educational Communications and Technology Agency (BECTa) has a central role to provide a web infrastructure that supports all learners, and in particular schools. The NGfL web site (http://www.ngfl.gov.uk/) has been established to provide an architecture into which a wide range of providers can deliver material that will support learners. BECTa also has responsibility for the Virtual Teacher Centre (http://vtc.ngfl.gov.uk/) and there are similar sites for Scotland (http://www.svtc.org.uk/), Northern Ireland (http://www.nine.org.uk/) and Wales (http://vtccymru.ngfl.wales.gov.uk/) supported by other agencies. These aim to provide access to a range of materials, guidance and services for teachers. The materials range from official documents such as the National Curriculum and schemes of work, through support for the use of ICT in every subject, to conferencing facilities and links to a wide range of other providers. The sites will develop over coming years and, whilst there is an enormous potential for geographers, in the short term there are going to be issues about access and teacher and pupil skills.

Other initiatives There are a range of other initiatives that are designed to reduce the teacher's bureaucratic burden through the use of ICT, to encourage inter-agency activity and to improve software and content provision. Geographers have problems with effective access to data and suitable software and equipment to support the subject, and over coming years the software initiative may improve the situation.

The NGfL is providing over £1 billion of new funding, which seems a lot of money, but it will not solve all the problems for geographers trying to make the most of ICT in their teaching. Everybody should be aware of the initiatives to ensure that they make the most of them, but there will be limits to their effects. However, changes in the ICT industry and patterns in home and personal ownership of computers will also have a large influence. Some analysts predict the cost of personal computer ownership dropping dramatically over the next fifteen years to the price for a basic machine reaching the cost of a video player, which could influence accessibility enormously, for example every pupil could have a suitable portable in their bag.

The range of ICT

If teachers should be using ICT and there are improving opportunities for geographers to use the technologies, where does one start? In a short chapter such as this it is difficult to describe the range of opportunities in detail, but Table 11.1 provides an overview of the scope and some of the applications of ICT. For a more detailed treatment of the use of ICT, the IT pages of *Teaching Geography* and the references at the end of the chapter will provide a source of further ideas. Technology is advancing at an ever-increasing speed and whether this reflects new opportunities or delivers existing ones more effectively, it confronts teachers with an ever-changing panorama of issues. The table of examples is neither static nor is it mutually exclusive, because one of the major changes in ICT is the notion of converging technologies. In the recent past you needed a different software tool for every job, for example a word processor was only for drafting and redrafting text and then laying it out in a rudimentary fashion. With the latest word-processing software you can combine multimedia, write collaboratively on-line, calculate and display information in variety of ways – the software is becoming more integrated as well as gaining new features. Also, a number of the ideas could be integrated in a single geographical activity. Finally, the table is not comprehensive. There is a lot of specific software which could be used effectively in Geography, but hopefully the examples provide an overview of the range of opportunities that exist.

Table 11.1 Examples of the ICT opportunities to support Geography

Technology	Sample geographical application
Presentation packages (word processing, DTP and presentation software, e.g. Powerpoint)	when researching information for an investigation use a word processor to analyse and manipulate a text, e.g. to edit and extract useful information from an article copied from a CD-ROM or the Internet;
	as one of the products from an investigation to use a desktop publishing package to produce a leaflet promoting the case for or against a local by-pass;
	to support decision-making on sustainable use of rainforests, use a word processor to present a coursework report (combining text, maps and graphics);
	use a presentation package to combine various types of information to argue the case to the class on the new superstore location.
Data logging	in an investigation into depressions to record hourly weather information with an automatic weather station to investigate the passage of a depression;
	use data-logging equipment to record and compare river flow along a river's length;
	use a weather satellite system to collect, record and investigate the daily timing of equatorial rain cells (this could also be completed as an Internet activity).
Data handling (databases and spreadsheets)	to analyse the environmental impact of housing developments on a number of sites by using a spreadsheet to analyse and present fieldwork scores;
	use a data-handling package to analyse information collected from a land use survey in an urban area;
	as part of a locality study to compare and contrast climatic data using a spreadsheet to present data graphically;
	use a database with graphing facilities to display information about global economic development in graph/chart form.
Simulations and modelling software	use a simulation package to investigate the effects of migration on population change in a region;
	as part of course work use a modelling package to investigate the length of time it takes for a drainage system, e.g. the Aral sea, to find equilibrium;
	use a spreadsheet to calculate the costs of alternative development proposals for a derelict site.
Mapping and geographic information systems (GIS)	use a mapping package to present comparative socio-economic data about the European region;
	to investigate the changing traffic pressure in a locality using a mapping package to present flow rates over time from a series of observations of major roads;
	use a GIS as a tool to support decision-making in a local issue such as the location of a new retail park.

(*continued on next page*)

Table 11.1 (cont.)

Digital images (from the Internet, digital cameras, or scanned images from film cameras, Photo CD, or other sources)	to record information on fieldwork either to exemplify what has been seen or to use in presentations, such as views of the buildings, areas to be assessed for environmental quality or physical features; to provide materials, either for class or individual work, these can be used to stimulate discussion and the images can also be used in pupils' work or annotated to develop and illustrate understanding.
Electronic communication (e-mail and web links)	as part of an exercise to compare contrasting localities pupils can exchange information with other schools on agreed topics or by asking questions; to investigate contrasting climate or to investigate the movement of weather systems, schools can set up a partnership to exchange weather data by e-mail.
Multimedia authoring (on machines or via the Internet)	as part of a class activity on tourism the class cooperate to produce a multimedia package to present information on a number of holiday destinations to help other students; developing web pages on the school site to display the arguments on a local issue and to collect views from others.
Information-rich sources (CD-ROM and the World Wide Web)	to provide up-to-date information such as weather satellite images or weather information on any country of the world; to investigate leisure and tourism through access to information on localities, services and travel in this country and abroad; as part of an investigation into employment use a CD-ROM of UK census data to find and display information on patterns in chosen areas; use the Internet to find information on recent tectonic activity before exploring the impact, causes and effects of a specific earthquake somewhere in the world.

Looking at the examples in Table 11.1 from a geographical standpoint there is a range of processes which ICT can support, including to:

- collect, keep and use individual or class collected data;
- monitor the environment;
- explore and extract relevant information;
- create, edit, manipulate and use appropriate maps, diagrams and graphs;
- investigate, develop and present geographical ideas;
- predict and solve problems; and
- help make decisions.

Linking this back to the entitlement document, how many of these opportunities are provided in schools at the moment? Although all schools should provide opportunities to address these issues using traditional methods, they can all have value added through the use of ICT.

The challenge for Geography

Discounting the subject of IT, geography could be the place in the curriculum where the range of ICT technologies has the greatest impact. The discussion so far in this chapter has concentrated on the role of ICT to enhance the teaching and learning of the subject. However, the impact of ICT is much more pervasive and is an issue which Geography as a subject must come to terms with. This impact can be seen in the changing patterns in society, the tools that exist to support decision-making in the real world and the way ICT could alter what we teach, when we teach it, and how we teach it.

Changes in the types of jobs, the distribution of workers across industry sectors and the types of work and skills are having a growing influence on work patterns and the location of industry. Examples of these changes include the concentration of transatlantic companies in Ireland, the development of computer programming and printing in widely distributed locations, such as India and Hong Kong. Some of these changes affect the local business community, for example the closure of local insurance and other services due to the vast increase in remote service activity such as call centres. These changes, combined with aspects such as the ability to telecommute are changing the face of travel requirements as an increasing proportion of economic activity is based on e-commerce and less is based on traditional industries and in particular manufacturing.

Throughout a huge range of human activity, including commerce and the public sector, ICT is playing an increasing role in decision-making, ranging from locating a road or superstore to the identification of flood or weather hazards. ICT can enable better decision-making as it is possible to take into consideration a wider range of variables, as well as supporting the monitoring of natural hazards and systems to provide greater warning and providing the opportunity to take action to reduce impact. As a result, ICT can provide better and faster tools for decision-making. These changes have an impact in two ways; first, they change the Geography we teach, but second, they change the decision-making skills and processes that we should be developing in children. The key issue in this area is how can the subject community ensure that the Geography of formal curriculums that is taught and examined keeps up with these changes?

A second issue is how the technology has the power to change what goes on in the geography classroom. Geography is a complex subject which relies on the development of spatial awareness and skills, and an understanding of a wide range of abstract concepts. Many of these concepts cannot be illustrated 'live' whilst providing opportunities for developing enquiry and decision-making skills. All teachers would expect that as pupils progress through school they should be able to complete increasingly complex geographical enquiries more effectively and make more appropriate decisions based on the evidence. Most people would agree that for pupils to become more autonomous in this work they have to have a good grounding in a wide range of geographical concepts, and this often determines what and in which order things are taught. However, if you have ever watched young children play a computer game such as *SIMCITY* (Electronic Arts 1990) the city planning game, and then questioned them to find out how and why they made certain decisions, the answers can be very revealing. Once children have used the software for a while they start to make complex decisions based on their understanding of how the underlying 'model' works. The software has the benefits of explicit interaction where there is instant feedback. The children also have an environment where they can discover relationships themselves and where abstract concepts can be illustrated in a simplified form (Bliss 1994). Of course, pupils using this sort of software are motivated by the game element and spend a long time on the computer developing their understanding. But, normally would we try and teach 9- or 10-year-olds about settlement planning (whatever one thinks of the *SIMCITY* model) at the level of detail in this software? This is only an anecdote, but it illustrates that with the right tools where students have access to methods of demonstrating, exploring, posing questions and decision-making with effective feedback, the need for a detailed knowledge may no longer be a barrier to the development of higher-order skills. For example, if one were teaching about the change in agricultural land use, a map-based package with data on different areas over time could be a valuable tool. Students would be able to investigate and identify patterns and explore how patterns changed, by displaying data for a specific year, whilst the system would be able to demonstrate visually any dynamic changes. A more sophisticated system could allow students to model changes and ask 'what if … ?' questions, which would enable them to investigate the relationship between the variables involved. Finally, it would be possible to predict future change in different scenarios and evaluate the predictions. As a result of having such systems, we could see different teaching approaches, with a change in the emphasis in learning outcomes, from product to process, and in the content that is taught. The challenge for Geography in the future will be to build on these opportunities whilst providing a curriculum which is viable and supportable by the teaching force.

The challenge for developers and providers

Whilst the technology moves on in leaps and bounds, school still suffer from the lack of access to effective software, data and other information. Software is a particular problem, for example the majority of mapping software or GIS available for schools is either not suitable or priced at a level which is prohibitive. There are a few exceptions and the development of software technologies will mean that GIS which runs over the Intranet or Internet may start to solve some of the problems. Another of the considerable concerns is the lack of modelling or simulation software which enables students to gain better understanding of the hidden processes which geographers need to study. However, even if the software were available, a key problem for schools is the access to data, in particular cartographic and statistical data. It is worth comparing the UK situation with that in the USA. In the US the freedom of information legislation and government policy to make data available mean that it can be easier to visit a US web site to find information about our own country. Digital map data are technically available, but for most schools they are just not accessible. The challenge here seems to be for developers and providers of data, but it is even more important for teachers to communicate what they need and to take any opportunities that arise to guide developers.

The challenge for teachers and schools

As a geography teacher of children with a range of ages and abilities to be taught and the pressure of local and national imperatives on standards and many other issues, ICT provides considerable challenges. Despite the hype and the range of articles imploring teachers to use the technology, it is vital that ICT be used only where it really does add value to the geography. The first issue is to ensure that ICT will make a difference. It is possible to ask the following questions (from the BECTa/GA Geography project) when reviewing whether the use of ICT is adding value:

- Is it a non-trivial use of ICT which enhances good geography?
  For example, typing climate figures into a spreadsheet and graphing them, without any consideration of the reasons for graphing and the type of graph selected, might be considered a trivial use.
- Is it an effective way of delivering the defined learning outcomes in Geography?
  For example, students may have a better understanding of an abstract concept because the ICT application has given them the opportunity to investigate it more fully.
- Is it efficient use of classroom time?
  For example, some IT applications free the students from mechanical and repetitive tasks, enabling them to spend longer on the analysis or investigational aspects of their work. A lot of time may be taken up initially when implementing something new, but this may 'pay off' in the longer term through benefits in learning.
- Do students have opportunities to evaluate and reflect on their use of ICT?

A key issue for geography departments will be to map what resources they have access to, the skills the teachers have and then to try to develop a plan to provide the entitlement for students. It is important to remember that teachers have an entitlement as well to ensure they have the confidence and competence to make the most of ICT. This does not just concern what is used with the students in class, but how the ICT can help the teacher carry out his or her professional duties. ICT can:

- support the development of materials, making it easier to produce differentiated worksheets and reduce preparation;
- provide access to resources, statistics and other information;
- enable teachers to exchange good ideas and obtain peer support;
- aid the assessment, reporting and recording of student progress including supporting target setting;
- provide access to research and inspection evidence as well as professional development.

Obviously, the NOF training initiative will have an impact on teacher confidence and competence, but establishing a departmental development plan is an ongoing issue for all.

Another issue to think about is the range of facilities which a department should have to ensure that students can be provided with their entitlement to Geography and ICT and to identify an action plan to help the department work towards this goal. Although the list of facilities a department should have will change as new technologies appear, a good starting point for a department to aim for would be the list below:

1   Generic ICT facilities which include multimedia computers (with printing facilities) with
    - word processing; database; spreadsheet; desk-top publishing and multi-media authoring tools;
    - an Internet browser for access to resources on the World Wide Web, and associated e-mail and on-line services.
2   A digital camera.
3   Geography-specific facilities
    - quality CD-ROM electronic atlas and encyclopaedia;
    - modelling software suitable for geographical models;
    - Geographic Information System (GIS) with digital map data;
    - automatic data-logging weather station;
    - map and statistical data for local and place studies.

In addition, departments will also build up a selection of content-rich resources, which will include specific geography software, CD-ROMs, Internet sites, and so on.

The challenge for us all

It is easy to look at the use of ICT and say there are so many problems and issues that ICT just cannot be integrated successfully. This approach is not viable, since our students deserve to have a geographical education which reflects the world in which they live, where ICT is completely pervasive and more importantly changing the nature and processes involved in the subject.

Obviously, there is not enough money in the system, but there are a number of key initiatives that geographers must make the most of. What is important is for geographers to work together and for there to be some strategy for the future. The Geographical Association has produced a position statement, *Geography in the Curriculum* (GA 1999) which might provide the starting point for this strategy. The statement includes an understanding of ICT, but may not have made explicit the underlying changes in geography that ICT brings about. Geographers can play a vital role for placing ICT in context, to provide the perspective for technologies in decision-making, taking into account values and attitudes and at the same time strengthening the subject. What is required is for all the participants to work together to find a strategy and solutions which are appropriate and effective. If this chapter stimulates the reader to think further about ICT, here are some questions that might provide some starting points for your thoughts.

- How will ICT continue to change Geography?
- What role does the use of ICT in society (e.g. in planning or hazard management) have for the school curriculum?

- What opportunities does ICT provide to enrich the teaching and learning experience?
- How can we train and support geography teachers to use ICT effectively?
- Do I make the most of ICT for myself and my students?
- What do I need to make a difference?

The challenge for all of us is not necessarily to answer these questions today, but to think about how we might evolve solutions and manage the change which comes about from the impact of ICT.

References

Bliss, J. (1994) 'From mental models to modelling', in H. Mellar, J. Bliss, R. Boohan, J. Ogborn and C. Tompsett, (eds) *Learning with Artificial Worlds: Computer Based Modelling in the Curriculum*, London: Falmer Press.

Department for Education and Employment (1998a) *Teachers – meeting the challenge of change*, London: HMSO, http://www.dfee.gov.uk/teachers/greenpaper/index.htm.

Department for Education and Employment (1998b) *Open for Business, Open for Learning*, London: HMSO, http://www.dfee.gov.uk/grid/challenge/index.htm

Electronic Arts (various dates for different versions from 1990) *SIMCITY*, San Mateo: Electronic Arts.

The Geographical Association (1999) *Geography in the Curriculum*, Sheffield: The Geographical Association.

Hassell, D. (1999) 'Will you get some training?', *Teaching Geography*, 24, 2: 92–3.

National Council for Educational Technology (1994) *IT Works*, Coventry: NCET.

NCET and The Geographical Association (1994) *Geography: A Pupil's Entitlement to IT*, Coventry: NCET.

NCET and The Geographical Association (1996) *Investigating Patterns in Human Geography*, Coventry: NCET.

Teacher Training Agency (1999a) *The Use of ICT in Subject Teaching – Expected Outcomes for Teachers in England and Wales*, London: TTA.

Teacher Training Agency (1999b) *The Use of Information and Communications Technology in Subject Teaching, Identification of Training Needs – Secondary Geography*, London: TTA.

Web sites

National Grid for Learning	http://www.ngfl.gov.uk/
Virtual Teacher Centre	http://vtc.ngfl.gov.uk/
Scottish VTC	http//www.svtc/org.uk/
Northern Ireland Network for Education	http://www.nine.org.uk/
Welsh VTC	http://vtccymru.ngfl.wales.gov.uk/
BECTa	http://www.becta.org.uk/
Department for Education and Employment	http://www.dfee.gov.uk/
The Geographical Association	http://www.geography.org.uk/
The Geography and ICT web site	http://vtc.ngfl.gov.uk/resource/cits/geog/
Qualifications and Curriculum Authority	http://www.qca.org.uk/
Teacher Training Agency	http://www.teach-tta.gov.uk/

12 Fieldwork in the school Geography curriculum

Pedagogical issues and development

Ashley Kent and Nick Foskett

The development of fieldwork in school Geography

In the English literature it is not hard to find eulogistic references to the benefits of school Geography. For instance:

> Fieldwork is the best and most immediate means of bringing the two aspects of the subject (i.e. a body of knowledge and a distinctive method of study) together in the experience of the pupil. Therefore, fieldwork is a necessary part of geographical education; it is not an optional extra.
>
> (Bailey 1974: 184)

> Fieldwork is not a separate teaching style to be adopted in geographical education, but a sine qua non of all good education through geography.
>
> (Lidstone 1988: 59)

> Geography without fieldwork is like science without experiments; the 'field' is the geographic laboratory where young people experience at first hand landscapes, places, people and issues, and where they can learn and practice geographical skills in a real environment. Above all, fieldwork is enjoyable.
>
> (Bland, Chambers, Donert and Thomas 1996: 165).

Then? Well not quite, since in several parts of the world the tradition of school fieldwork is far from established. For instance, in the USA 'fieldwork is not a common part of the geography education in the United States' (Bednarz 1999: 164). This is arguably also true of college level fieldwork in the USA where according to Allender (1999), fieldwork is an elective in most courses because of other reasons: it is expensive, there are legal liability worries, virtual reality fieldwork seems more cost-effective and there is a lack of skilled instructors. A similar story is told from China, where 'it seems unlikely that fieldwork will assume a key position in geography in China' (Zhang 1999: 175), and from the Netherlands, where 'class-based study of secondary sources has become more important than enquiry outside the classroom' (Swaan and Wijnsteekers 1999: 171).

Some have argued that in England the battle to secure a place for fieldwork in the Geography curriculum has been won. 'The struggle to get fieldwork accepted as an integral and essential element of secondary school geography examination syllabuses has long passed' (GA Sixth Form – University Working Group 1984: 209). Even more confident was Everson (1969) in suggesting that: 'It is a truism to state that the campaign to put fieldwork into the mainstream of school geography is now over.' Geography educators in England in 1999, however, would be wary of making such claims since there are a number of challenges to be faced if the fieldwork tradition is to be maintained. Since the two authors of this chapter are English, most of its content concerns fieldwork undertaken by English schools. Little had been written about fieldwork in higher education until the most helpful overview from Kent, Gilbertson and Hunt (1997).

Although fieldwork was undertaken by a number of teachers in the inter-war years, 'it was not until after the Second World. War that fieldwork seriously began to intrude itself into teaching – and, incidentally, into external examinations' (Ministry of Education 1960: 13). Much of the early post-war growth was due to the provision of courses for A level students, particularly laid on by the Field Studies Council (FSC). 'During the 1950s and 1960s thousands of A level students were introduced to fieldwork in the one-week residential courses at FSC centres such as Flatford Mill, Juniper Hall, Malham Tarn and Preston Montford' (Boardman and McPartland 1993: 67). However, it was the establishment of the Certificate of Secondary Education (CSE) in 1965 and its successor (the GCSE) in 1988 which provided an official boost for fieldwork for pupils below the age of 16 years. This legitimation continued with the establishment of a National Curriculum in 1988. For instance, the 1995 Geography National Curriculum required that all pupils 'undertake fieldwork' (DFE 1995: 2) making it a statutory obligation for all schools in the state sector. Reports of Ofsted (Office for Standards in Education) inspections of secondary schools reinforced that requirement:

> The use of practical and field based activities make a fundamental contribution to good teaching in all Key Stages. A well planned programme, with activity in all years, from local studies to more distant residential courses, stimulates students' curiosity and develops skills, knowledge and understanding through personal experiences.
>
> (Smith 1997: 126)

Since such comments came from the senior geography HMI (Her Majesty's Inspectorate) and were based on 7400 lesson observations, they carry a certain weight!

In addition to the commitment of many geography teachers, two other developments have reinforced the value and importance of fieldwork in England. Firstly, three major national land use surveys have been undertaken in which pupils were the main data collectors. These were Dudley Stamp's land utilisation survey of the 1930s; Alice Coleman's land use survey of the 1960s; and the Geographical Association's 'Land Use UK' survey in 1997. Coastline 2000 is planned for the near future! Secondly, and probably most influential in England, has been that individual study investigations and enquiry have been built into GCSE and A level syllabuses, so that most students experience the joys and challenges of undertaking personal geographical research.

The most lasting and arguably most common justification for organising field-work comes from former students whose memories of such activities are generally positive! 'For most geographers field work is a key component of their enthusiasm for the subject and one of the strongest elements of their own personal biography' (Foskett 1997: 189). A recent study entitled 'The experiences of higher education (HE): the case of geography teachers in England' (Kent 1999), reported that most teachers found difficulty in recollecting the detail of their HE geography courses, but not so for the fieldwork they undertook! Teachers recalled, for instance, 'a heavy emphasis on residential, practical fieldwork … this was a strength of the course' and 'this course inspired me, in particular with fieldwork and enthusiasm for getting out there!'

But what is the place and role of fieldwork today? Kent *et al.* (1997) summarise the key issues facing fieldwork in Geography in the late 1990s, and although this list refers to HE there is considerable significance here for school Geography. The key issues identified are:

- The importance of the evaluation of the various different modes of field teaching and their effectiveness;
- The need for and value of planning progression in fieldwork teaching;
- The problems of maintaining small-group teaching in fieldwork;
- The problems of fieldwork financing and the question of 'value for money' in fieldwork teaching;
- Gender issues in fieldwork planning and operation;
- The conflict between specialised 'option-based' fieldwork and the role of field-work in integration within geography as a whole;
- The establishment of links between project-based fieldwork and student projects or dissertations;
- The relative effectiveness of different forms of fieldwork assessment;
- The potential of virtual reality fieldwork.

Smith (1992) in his research into Geography fieldwork planning has raised similar issues which he sees as needing to be addressed in the near future since he argues that 'fieldwork, in its present form, is under threat and yet it still has a major role to play' (Smith 1992: 397). The questions (and related issues) he asked were:

- Are the aims and objectives well known and clear enough to be accepted not just by the geography department but by pupils, parents, other staff, the head-teacher, governors and industrialists for example?
- Has the fieldwork planner got the motivation, time and the right attitude to overcome all the constraints so as to achieve these aims and objectives and to take advantage of the improved and widened range of opportunities available to him or her?

- Do the benefits for pupils and staff outweigh the costs at the present time?
- How much of these 'costs' are environmental, economic or organisational?
- With increasing complexity is there sufficient time to plan and implement fieldwork programmes properly and if not where is the time going to come from?
- How much of the success or failure of putting an ideal fieldwork programme into practice is due to external (to the school) rather than internal factors?
- To what extent is the provision of Geography fieldwork now influenced by economic and administrative rather than educational preconditions? If this extent is significant how much of a threat does it present?

These issues are of importance to all teachers at the start of the twenty-first century. In the sections that follow, we seek to explore and develop responses to some of the key pedagogic issues in fieldwork.

The aims of school fieldwork

The questioning and review of curriculum at all levels from national scale to specific planning for the classroom is inherent within most educational systems. Geography has been in the vanguard of such review in many countries, partly as a result of the innovation of curriculum developers in the subject, and partly as a result of the continuing threat to its existence within school curriculums where the core fields of mathematics, science and languages have been given increasingly greater emphasis. Geography has been both the site and stake of many macro and micro political battles in the curriculum war. Joseph (1985: 8) challenged the geography establishment in Britain to demonstrate 'what ... is necessary to enable geography to make its distinctive contribution to the breadth and balance of the whole curriculum'. Essential within that process is the clarification of the aims of each element of the Geography curriculum, and the frequent cry that fieldwork is an essential component of the Geography curriculum requires explicit demonstration and justification.

The aims of fieldwork have traditionally been implicit within the dominant methodologies of fieldwork practice, as outlined by Foskett (1997: 195). The traditional approaches, for example, of what Job (1996) terms the 'fieldwork excursion' had aims rooted in the development of content knowledge. Within this broad observational paradigm, the expedition approach focused primarily on the exemplification of classroom-based work in the field, while adding some element of physical challenge to the process. In contrast the Cook's tour had the same aims but without the physical challenge. The data collection/hypothesis testing and field enquiry approaches (e.g. Hart and Thomas 1986: 205) extended the learning opportunities available through fieldwork, and promoted the application of learning objectives to the planning of fieldwork. Learning in the field became as rigorous as learning in the classroom from a planning perspective, and the fieldwork training for teachers described in many recent books has prioritised the clarification of learning objectives (e.g. Richardson 1998). But what are the objectives of fieldwork that make it distinctive from classroom-based work, for without such clarification the case for the inclusion of fieldwork even in a strong geography curriculum is hard to argue?

Fieldwork may have aims related to knowledge, understanding, skills or attitudes and values in relation to 'learning' in Geography specifically or in relation to wider educational goals such as enhancing environmental awareness or equipping pupils with generic practical and intellectual skills. Boardman's (1974) study of the objectives of fieldwork as perceived by secondary school teachers in the West Midlands in the UK, provides some useful insights into early perspectives on fieldwork aims. Of the 30 objectives identified by the teachers, the majority are related to cognitive aims of learning and the enhancement/application of skills initially developed in the classroom. Of those seen as most important by teachers, a focus on mapping interpretation skills – e.g. 'to relate landforms to contour patterns' – ranked as the most important objective, and on the recognition and exemplification of features and processes learned in the classroom – e.g. 'to comprehend in the field concepts learnt in the classroom' – ranked as the sixth most important objective, is clear. Affective domain objectives also appear within Boardman's results, but are given less emphasis by the teachers. The objective 'to enjoy the study of geography and acquire a deeper interest in the subject' ranks fifth in the priority list of objectives, but other affective aims, for example, 'to show an aesthetic awareness of and respect for the countryside', and 'to cooperate with the teacher and other pupils outside the classroom', are seen to be much less important. Beyond subject-specific cognitive and affective aims, Boardman's study shows only limited evidence of wider fieldwork aims. Contribution to pupils' physical development is limited to Geography-specific skills, and there is no substantive reference to transferability in the skills and knowledge acquired – Geography fieldwork has, from Boardman's research, aims which are quite specific to the subject. Graham Smith (1999) has repeated Boardman's research in a contemporary context, and identified an increased emphasis on the practice of classroom-acquired skills in the field, particularly in relation to data collection and field measurement. Smith identifies, too, the increasing importance of affective objectives, although they still play a secondary role in relation to cognitive objectives, and there is still little evidence of wider aims for fieldwork in Geography.

The importance of including both affective and cognitive aims in fieldwork planning has been emphasised by many writers (e.g. Job 1996; Foskett 1997; Nundy 1999). Peter Smith (1987), writing in the context of Geography, but also of outdoor education and environmental education, identifies the aims of fieldwork in relation to three broad categories of experience – outdoor studies, outdoor pursuits, and personal and social development. 'Outdoor studies' is predominantly the field of cognitive development, with an emphasis on acquiring new knowledge, applying classroom-generated ideas in the field, and generating questions and hypotheses for testing by empirical methods. A key focus here is on the development and practice of skills, including subject-specific skills such as field sketching, generic skills such as data collection, and intellectual skills such as problem solving. The integration of affective development within outdoor studies is also drawn out by Smith, though, through the enhancement of an affinity for the human or natural environment, and the development of a sense of place and personal environmental responsibility. This affective arena is central, though, to Smith's second category of 'personal and social development', which stresses the development of personal awareness and growth and the enhancement of skills of co-operation, teamwork and understanding of other pupils and teachers. The third of Smith's categories is that of 'outdoor pursuits' in which the emphasis is strongly in the field of psychomotor development. Experiencing personal physical challenge and enhancing practical skills contributes to such development, but also links strongly to affective development in terms of personal development.

Smith's (1987) view of the aims of fieldwork is comprehensive, but leaves as implicit, however, the processes of reinforcement that link the three categories of aims synergistically. Furthermore, it is based primarily not on empirical evidence of the processes at work but on the evidence of experience – the observations of individual teachers' planned intentions, rather than measured outcomes, and the accumulated evidence from inspection systems. While this may be important in providing classroom credibility to the ideas, it is important to consider whether research evidence can provide a contribution to exploring the ideas further or identifying the processes of synergy. Two research directions provide this evidence to:

- justify the inclusion of fieldwork in the curriculum by providing outcomes (or aims) that contribute distinctively to both geographical and wider learning;
- refine the identification of fieldwork aims to optimise the achievable outcomes from specific fieldwork activities.

The first of these directions is the research within the field of educational psychology which suggests that there is a strong link between experiential learning and improved pupil learning outcomes. The concept of 'meaningful learning' (Ausubel 1968) emphasises the gains that derive from 'discovery' learning rather than rote learning, while the principles underpinning constructivist views of learning (e.g. Driver and Easley 1978) emphasise hypothesising, active enquiry and the testing of ideas in unfamiliar environments as promoting enhanced learning. The idea that many aims for geographical learning for pupils can be accelerated or enhanced by the experience of fieldwork may be important in having curriculum or lesson aims that incorporate fieldwork approaches.

The second direction is research into the fieldwork process itself, which draws out the importance of affective domain gains for pupils of all ages and has also begun to examine the relationship between affective and cognitive gain. Mackenzie and White's (1982) work with pupils in Australia identified the overall cognitive gain from fieldwork, and they note the enhanced gain from 'active' as opposed to 'passive' fieldwork. They suggest that 'memorable episodes' (such as getting wet through working in a river) enhance learning and improve long-term knowledge retention, and that explicit planning of such episodes into the fieldwork and their linkage to specific knowledge outcomes can be a deliberate strategy linked to specific learning aims.

The suggested link between affective and cognitive gain has been supported by the work of Kern and Carpenter (1986) with US college students. Using an experimental method in which one group of students undertook transect work in the field while another did so theoretically in the classroom, Kern and Carpenter showed that while there was no difference in gain between the two groups with 'low order' cognitive fields such as knowledge recall, there was substantial gain in relation to higher order skills such as understanding, analysis and evaluation in the group that had undertaken the fieldwork. This progress they attribute to the catalytic effect of affective learning.

More recent studies have also highlighted the importance of affective gain, both in itself and in terms of enhancing cognitive gain, which suggests the importance of integrating aims in the planning of fieldwork that draw on, and link, both areas of operation. Harvey (1991), for example, working with A-level students at a field study centre in the UK, suggests that the affective gains outweigh cognitive gains from residential fieldwork in the long term by 'motivation ... through novelty of milieu, self concept enhancement, productive role modelling and changing students' scripts for learning' (Harvey 1991: ii). Harvey concedes that this may reflect the observation that much of the fieldwork he observed was focused on testing and demonstrating ideas already learned in the A-level classroom, rather than on *ab initio* field enquiry, which may also reflect the limitations of fieldwork couched in aims that relate only to reinforcement of existing knowledge in the interests of public examination achievement.

Nundy (1998; 1999) supports the idea of the impact of affective gain on cognitive development very strongly through his work on the gains to primary age pupils of fieldwork on river processes. His experimentally based methodology shows that there is enhanced learning for pupils in terms of constructing learning frameworks and the development of meaningful learning for those pupils studying by fieldwork rather than classwork, and emphasises this is the result of the interaction of affective and cognitive development. Enhanced cognitive gain is greatest where the development of self-image through the fieldwork experience is also strongest. In an echo of Mackenzie and White's view of the need to plan key episodes and their use within the learning, Nundy suggests that

> ... residential field course frameworks can [...] lead to enhanced levels of learning outcome. [...] Subjects have to be presented with 'challenges', be involved with group work and 'talk' and have the opportunity to control and re-construct their learning and thinking.
>
> (Nundy 1999:197)

Within this cognitive/affective interaction lie the roots of fieldwork aims that will meet the joint challenges of enhancing geographical learning and making a contribution to the pupil or student's wider personal and intellectual development. That fieldwork contributes to geographical learning is evidenced by the fact that in the UK the

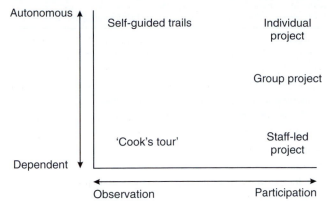

Figure 12.1 The continuums of autonomy and participation in fieldwork

Source: Kent *et al.* (1997).

observations of the government inspectors of Ofsted (Office for Standards in Education) have indicated clearly that high achievement in Geography in schools is linked to a high profile for fieldwork in the curriculum (Smith 1997). This chapter examines some of the wider opportunities in fieldwork in relation to the development of thinking skills, ICT development and environmental education.

Teaching and learning strategies

Various attempts have been made to categorise broad approaches and strategies used in fieldwork, e.g. (Job 1996a; Foskett 1997). Field teaching/field excursion; hypothesis testing; and framework fieldwork are the models discussed in Kent (1996). Foster's (1997) categorization into: observational; investigative; and enquiry-based fieldwork is very similar. Kent *et al.* (1997) identify two continuums of fieldwork activity from the student viewpoint: first between observation and participation; and second between dependency and autonomy (Figure 12.1). These authors group field courses into broad domains of activities, such as observational fieldwork and participatory fieldwork.

Many authors attempting to make sense of the emerging paradigms of fieldwork have identified a chronological order to the popularity of the approaches. Kent *et al.* (1997) have attempted to plot the changing approaches to fieldwork in higher education (Table 12.1) and most recently Job (1999) has graphically represented fieldwork approaches (Figure 7.2). In that diagram one axis concerns the extent to which a fieldwork approach relies on measurement and data collection and the degree to which it draws on more qualitative forms of experience. The other axis concerns the starting point and forms of investigations. Did they arise from experience in the field or were they predetermined by someone else or by geographical theory? Job's view is that there is a trend towards the more sensory (x axis) and open ended (y axis) approach to fieldwork. Many of these changes, he and others argue,

Table 12.1 Changes in approaches to fieldwork in HE Geography, 1950–97

Date	Approach		
1950	*Traditional 'look-see' or 'Cook's tour' field courses* • observational and descriptive		
1960	• 'landscape'-based or centred on 'sight-seeing' visits to specific sites of interest in geography • passive student participation		
1970	*'New' Geography – 1960s 'revolution'* Problem-orientated, project-based fieldwork • inductive and deductive approaches (positivist) hypothesis generation and testing, data collection and statistical analysis, interpretation and report writing		
1980	• detailed scales, often carried out in a small area • active student participation although often staff-led		
1985	*Enterprise in Higher Education – transferable skills* Problem-orientated fieldwork still dominant but introduction of transferable skills element • project design skills • organizational skills • leadership skills • group skills • active student participation but emphasis switches from staff-led to student-led projects	Thematic and guided trails • individual student initiative • group initiatives	
1990	*Massive growth in student numbers – teaching large classes* • field courses incorporate elements of all previous modes of fieldwork • may commence with 'look-see' perhaps combined with thematic guided walks/trails • followed by staff-directed, problem-orientated projects • then student-initiated problem-centred work with added dimension of transferable skills		
1997	*Serious problems of cost of fieldwork to both departments and students combined with even larger classes* • the future? • 'virtual reality' to assist with field courses • but will 'virtual reality' be any cheaper or ever be as satisfactory?		Cumulative

Source: Kent *et al.* (1997).

come from dissatisfaction with the quantitative approaches which fail to engage children with environments, for 'overemphasis on quantification may be limiting our natural inclination to explore, interpret and draw meaning from the places we visit, in our own way' (Job 1999: 2).

A seminal source of dissatisfaction with fieldwork arises from Harvey's research (1991) in which he identified a number of tensions emerging between the cognitive and affective dimensions of fieldwork activities undertaken by 16–19-year-old students, suggesting a need for greater balance between the two elements. Equally important was Hawkins' (1987) development of a 'process model' for fieldwork in which the:

> students should, and could, experience a learning process, beginning with techniques designed to heighten their awareness, and going on to equip them with the relevant knowledge and understanding, develop in them a feeling of personal concern and responsibility, and lead them ultimately to participate in social and environmental decision-making ... an awareness-to-participation process model is more dynamic and participatory.
>
> (Hawkins 1987: 218)

Progression in fieldwork has not been much discussed nor, arguably, implemented in many instances. Bland *et al.* (1996) argue that progression must be a key consideration when framing departmental field policies. In particular, progression should be in relation to the skills and techniques used, the level of difficulty of tasks performed; the level of supervision needed; the place and theme studies undertaken; the geographical ideas and concepts studied; and the issues and problems investigated. Helpful guidelines for teachers of 4–19-year-olds were produced jointly by the Field Studies Council and the Geographical Association (1999) which show examples and strands for progression in fieldwork (Figure 12.2), and the idea of progression in enquiry skills and thinking skills is also addressed later in this chapter.

Finally, a key future requirement for successful teaching and learning strategies is engaging geography teachers in discussions about, and practical examples of, the latest thinking. In particular, the future lies with recently trained teachers, so the model for residential fieldwork planning, teaching and evaluation discussed by Kent 'has been a highlight of the Geography initial teacher training course at the London Institute of Education for several years' (Kent 1996a). A particular benefit for the beginning teachers has been that they have contributed to a subsequent publication. See for example, Kent (1996b). Elsewhere Lidstone reinforces that view (Lidstone 1988). Unfortunately there do not seem to be many similar in-service opportunities for geography teachers to consider and evaluate emerging fieldwork strategies although a successful course entitled 'Fieldwork Strategies for A level Geography' was held at the Yorkshire Dales Field Centre in 1995.

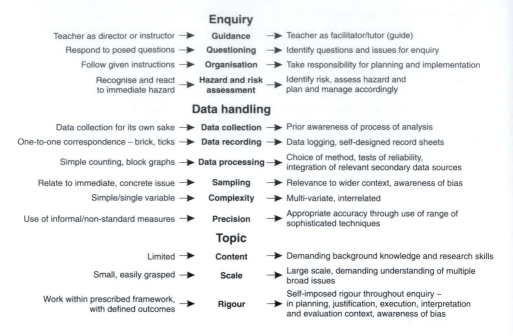

Enquiry

Teacher as director or instructor → **Guidance** → Teacher as facilitator/tutor (guide)

Respond to posed questions → **Questioning** → Identify questions and issues for enquiry

Follow given instructions → **Organisation** → Take responsibility for planning and implementation

Recognise and react to immediate hazard → **Hazard and risk assessment** → Identify risk, assess hazard and plan and manage accordingly

Data handling

Data collection for its own sake → **Data collection** → Prior awareness of process of analysis

One-to-one correspondence – brick, ticks → **Data recording** → Data logging, self-designed record sheets

Simple counting, block graphs → **Data processing** → Choice of method, tests of reliability, integration of relevant secondary data sources

Relate to immediate, concrete issue → **Sampling** → Relevance to wider context, awareness of bias

Simple/single variable → **Complexity** → Multi-variate, interrelated

Use of informal/non-standard measures → **Precision** → Appropriate accuracy through use of range of sophisticated techniques

Topic

Limited → **Content** → Demanding background knowledge and research skills

Small, easily grasped → **Scale** → Large scale, demanding understanding of multiple broad issues

Work within prescribed framework, with defined outcomes → **Rigour** → Self-imposed rigour throughout enquiry – in planning, justification, execution, interpretation and evaluation context, awareness of bias

Figure 12.2 Strands for progression in fieldwork

Source: Field Studies Council and the Geographical Association (1999).

Developing pedagogical themes in fieldwork

Of the many aspects of fieldwork into important pedagogical issues within them, we believe that five are of particular significance in ensuring the contribution of field-work to both Geography and wider generic fields. These are the domains of enquiry skills; ICT development; thinking skills; values enquiry; and environmental educa-tion. Each of these is considered here.

1   Enquiry skills and fieldwork

The development of an enquiry-based approach to learning across the Geography curriculum through the 1980s stimulated its adoption in the context of fieldwork. Hart and Thomas (1986: 205) believed that the adoption of such an approach 'strengthens and enhances the value of fieldwork … and makes it an essential, natural ingredient of all work in geography'. In particular they suggested that 'meaningful fieldwork … seeks to find answers to pertinent questions about the many ways in which people interact with the various environments in which they live and work' (ibid.: 205).

The concept of enquiry-based learning is that pupils and students learn most effec-tively by structuring that learning around key questions (Slater 1982). The approach has been formalised in a number of designated sequences of enquiry, as for example in the 'Route for Geographical Enquiry' developed by the 'Geography 16–19' Project in the UK in the 1980s (see Naish *et al.* 1987). Roberts (1996), however, has stressed that a number of different approaches to the design of teaching and learning can be adopted which conform to the idea of enquiry-based learning. In particular she distinguishes 'closed', 'framed' and 'negotiated' styles which represent progressively a move away from teacher-controlled learning. A 'closed' approach to learning involves the enquiry questions and the enquiry methodology being generated by the teacher with the 'findings' and knowledge outcomes tightly under the teacher's control. A 'framed approach' involves the teacher providing 'limits' on the nature and format of the investigation, but negotiating some components with pupils. A 'negotiated' approach involves pupils deciding what questions they want to investigate that are of concern and interest to themselves, under guidance from the teacher, whose role is to provide guidance and support as the pupil identifies appropriate data and analytical approaches and reaches his or her own interpretations.

The adoption and encouragement of 'enquiry' within fieldwork is now widespread in the UK, Australia and New Zealand (Foskett 1997; Richardson 1998), and is beginning to emerge as an important approach elsewhere, for example in the USA, South Africa, China and Hong Kong (Bednarz 1999; Wilmot 1999; Zhang 1999; Lai 1999). The use of fieldwork-based enquiry by individual students as part of formal summative assessment has also developed strongly, indicating that such individual enquiries provide an appropriate indicator of a student's geographical understanding and skills. To support this latter development the importance of building progression into the use of such enquiry skills as a pupil is underlined by Foskett (1997) and by Bland *et al.* (1996). Such progression might develop from closed enquiry with younger pupils, through framed enquiry, to negotiated enquiry with pupils in the upper part of secondary school. Roberts (1996: 91–102) provides examples of each type of enquiry, which indicate how progression in the development of enquiry skills might be structured through the Geography curriculum:

Closed enquiry   Teaching shopping hierarchies through fieldwork. The teacher chooses the focus of the fieldwork, and devises a list of hypotheses to be tested and questions to be investigated, which are given to the pupils. The teacher chooses the shopping centres in which the work will be undertaken, designs the pupils' questionnaire and chooses the sample structure and size. The teacher collects in the data, collates it, selects appropriate graphing methods, and gives the pupils instructions on drawing the graphs. The conclusions are devised by the pupils in response to directed questions from the teacher.

Framed enquiry   Choosing a development site for a computer component company. Pupils are divided into groups charged with choosing the best location for a new factory in an urban area. The initial enquiry question is posed by the teacher, and background information on the sites and the company is also provided by the teacher, but the pupils must decide what other questions to ask and what information they must obtain during site visits through fieldwork. The teacher has decided that pupils must use ratings of different criteria to make their decision, but pupils must choose the criteria and the rating scale. Pupils present their findings to the whole class, who decide as a whole which site to choose.

Negotiated enquiry   Choosing an Individual Enquiry at A level. An individual student must choose a topic for study, generate questions and a methodology, then analyse and interpret the data. The teacher, in discussion, listens to the range of possible ideas and, by questioning, helps the student frame appropriate enquiry questions. The student chooses to consider the issue of the construction of a new supermarket near to his home.

The development from closed to negotiated enquiry may also, of course, encompass increasing challenge in relation to the types of fieldwork techniques that can be applied. Furthermore, the skills being developed are generic, and may be applied across the Geography curriculum and be transferred to other curriculum areas.

2   Fieldwork and ICT development

Although still highly variable in its use in schools, the growing centrality of Information and Communications Technology (ICT) in schools is inevitable and its place in fieldwork will be very important.

Probably the first published and specific advice to teachers of geography keen to incorporate ICT in their fieldwork, was the work of Bilham-Boult (1988). In his introduction, he pointed out that 'the application of computers to fieldwork is still very much in its infancy. Its full potential has yet to be explored, and there exists an enormous variation in practice'. This comment is probably still true today!

More recently (Table 12.2), David Hassell (1996) has written about the opportunities for using ICT to support coursework which often equates with fieldwork. As he argues, 'coursework provides an ideal place to enable pupils to use the IT skills they will be building through their school career to improve their geography work' (Hassell 1996). Not only is Geography enhanced by such technology, but so too are the ICT skills required by National Curriculum ICT, GCSE and Post-16 courses (see Nowicki 1999).

Further research, such as that by Lawler (1986) who focused on ways in which the use of computers helped a group of GCSE children to analyse their fieldwork data, is clearly needed. Such research may well confirm that effectively deployed, such technology 'provides for rapid handling of data which enables the emphasis to be on the enquiry process, the in-field skills and the interpretation of findings, and not on mechanical data processing' (Foskett 1997).

3   Fieldwork and the development of thinking skills

Recent research in science education has emphasised the role of teaching using tasks that challenge children to think and problem solve in enhancing pupils' 'cognitive gain'. The Cognitive Acceleration in Science Education (CASE) Project (Adey and Shayer 1994) has developed activities which challenge pupils

Table 12.2 Opportunities for using IT to support coursework

Software/hardware	One potential application
Word processing	In any enquiry to support pupils' intended writing where they can draft and redraft reports.
Drawing, painting and DTP packages	Tools for illustration in any type of material, e.g. combining text and images to provide a high-quality method for designing survey sheets.
Spreadsheets	To provide a tool for evaluating and modelling a range of decisions, e.g. evaluating routes in an enquiry on the location of a new bypass. Using a weighting scheme, the spreadsheet provides opportunities to evaluate many different options effectively.
Databases	To provide access to data, explore patterns and relationships and display results effectively. For instance, in an enquiry on tourism a database of questionnaire results would enable the pupils to explore links between gender, age and holiday location.
CD-ROM	To provide access to a wide range of information and deepen understanding of spatial relationships; e.g. a census CD-ROM can support an enquiry into the contention that quality of life can be low in urban and rural areas.
Mapping and geographic information systems (GIS) software	To explore spatial relationships by querying a database and displaying the results spatially. For instance, a GIS can support investigations into the link between the economic and social factors and regional inequalities in India.
Portables in the field	Using portables in the field enables direct entry of information from a questionnaire or observations. This enables initial analysis to determine whether further measurements or questionnaires need to be carried out, e.g. checking that mistakes have not been made in the collection of river data.
Data logging	To record data accurately over a period which could not be achieved manually, e.g. to explore the link between local facility use and daily weather. Data from automatic weather stations can be exported to a spreadsheet or database for comparison and analysis.
Remote sensing	To provide access to richer images of an area which can illustrate change over time and be manipulated. For instance imagery of the local area can be used to support an enquiry into the actual and potential loss of urban green space.
Internet	The Internet can provide access to a wealth of resources. For example, people's views and information on issues related to the Kobe earthquake can be obtained when investigating the impact of physical processes.

Source: Hassell, D. (1996).

to question, theorise and hypothesize, to work beyond simple 'knowing' and 'understanding' in areas of thinking that include analysis, evaluation and problem solving. Adey and Shayer suggest that such thinking skills enhance achievement in science, but also raise standards more broadly by equipping children with transferable skills.

'Thinking skills' include a wide range of 'skills' such as 'choosing', 'deducing' and 'applying logical thinking'. At a simple level we can distinguish 'creative skills', which are constructive and involve drawing information and ideas and imagination together to generate a new perspective, and 'critical skills', which are deconstructive and involve reducing ideas to their component parts. Sternberg's (1985) 'triarchic classification' of thinking skills distinguishes three components of thinking skills. Knowledge components involve inputs to the mind – 'seeing', 'hearing', 'scanning', 'analysing'. Performance components involve outputs from the mind following intellectual processing that the child has undertaken, and include 'remembering', 'reflecting' and 'decision-making'. Metacomponents relate to the control of thinking and the notion of 'metacognition' – in simple terms, 'thinking about thinking', and include skills such as 'planning' and 'evaluating'.

Important within the development of thinking skills is the idea of 'transfer'. Transfer is essentially the extent to which current learning enhances subsequent learning, and can be seen in two ways – as 'lateral transfer' in which the ideas and skills are used in a different but no more challenging situation, and 'vertical transfer' in which they are used in a more challenging or complex situation. Leat (1998) describes this process of transfer as 'bridging' and emphasises that it provides a 'multiplier effect' in the pupils' learning.

The development of thinking skills has also been applied in geographical education by the 'Thinking Through Geography' Project (Leat 1998). This has developed approaches using a wide range of strategies, each focusing on a generic concept important within Geography but having great utility for transfer to other arenas, such as 'classification', 'cause and effect', and 'systems', using teaching strategies that are innovative and varied. By using such 'thinking activities' pupils start to develop analytical and reasoning skills which support 'transfer', metacognition, and increasingly independent learning through questioning and thinking.

Foskett (1999) has suggested that the potential benefits of a thinking skills approach can be subject to a further multiplier effect if conducted through fieldwork. Much of the empirical research into fieldwork in schools and colleges has emphasised the cognitive and affective gain that it generates for students. Mackenzie and White (1982), Kern and Carpenter (1986), Harvey (1991) and Nundy (1998;1999) all suggest that fieldwork stimulates the enhancement of higher-order thinking skills, and that this gain is further enhanced by the interaction of affective and cognitive development processes. Foskett (1999) shows how such developments might contribute to each area of Sternberg's triarchic classification.

Firstly, all fieldwork is based on observation, recording and data collection and the process of 'monitoring' and evaluating that data. The thinking skills involved in this process exemplify Sternberg's 'knowledge' components. Secondly, although 'performance' has traditionally been restricted in fieldwork to data presentation, recent growth in the use of problem-solving and decision-making in relation to issue-based fieldwork has emphasised the role of performance. The role of 'talk' in developing such 'performance thinking skills' is stressed by Adey and Shayer (1994), Nundy (1999) and Leat (1998). Thirdly, the notion of building in progression in fieldwork experience for pupils such that they develop the skills of 'independent enquiry' requires the development of metacognition skills through the planning, reviewing, evaluating and reflection skills which such enquiry necessitates.

Beyond Sternberg's three components thinking skills lies the notion of transfer, which is evidence of high-level thinking skills. In fieldwork the opportunity for classroom to field to classroom transfer of knowledge and ideas is large, whether through testing theories from classwork by hypothesis testing or by generating theories from field observation. Both vertical and lateral transfer can be integrated into planning fieldwork enquiry by emphasising 'transfer' issues in the objectives for the work.

The potential of fieldwork for enhancing thinking skills is clearly considerable – and indeed, it has always done so, albeit without the explicit intent of teachers. Table 12. 3 exemplifies the ways in which thinking skills can be planned into fieldwork. This represents a starting point for planning, for each stage will require careful management to optimise the learning processes that enhance cognitive gain, such as groupwork or pupil talk, while ensuring appropriate affective domain aims are integrated to reinforce cognitive gain.

Table 12.3 Integrating thinking skills development into fieldwork planning

Stage	Thinking skills processes	Fieldwork planning process	Example
1	Lateral transfer from classwork	Developing enquiry questions or setting up hypotheses	Set up 'enquiry' into impact of tourism on e.g. a local beauty spot
2	Knowledge components	Reflective and critical data collection	Consider litter survey, erosion of footpath measures, visitor interviews as data methods; monitor data as collected
3	Performance components	Decision-making, problem-solving, hypothesising	Present alternative models for managing tourism
4	Metacomponents	Evaluating group/individual knowledge/performance components	Evaluate data collection and evaluate group/individual role
5	Transfer – lateral	Integration of findings and principles into classwork or other subject areas	Re-visit environmental management topic and apply findings to different cases
6	Transfer – vertical	Construction of higher levels of model	Draw out big concepts of 'cause and refinement'. Linkage to 'big concepts', 'effect', 'planning', 'decision-making', etc.

4   *Fieldwork and values enquiry*

Wondering at and experiencing the environment through fieldwork is an established tradition which has been somewhat neglected of late. This perhaps explains a good deal of the criticism by Hawkins (1987), Harvey (1991) and Job (1996 and 1999). The specific suggestions that have been made to offset this 'affective-deficit' include an awareness-to-participation process model (Hawkins 1987), raising sensory awareness; Haiku poetry; making connections through literature and the use of stimulus cards (Job 1999). Owen-Jones' (1987) research work specifically brought together affective and cognitive learning in a strategy which successfully involved values education through fieldwork set in Kew Gardens.

The Earth Education movement in the USA has informed such recent UK work. For instance,

> We hoped to establish this sense of place forever in their understandings, or perhaps more accurately in their feelings, for we wanted it to become embedded inside them, where it would be a continuous source of awareness about who and where they were. Second, like a friendly wizard, we wanted to convey to them a feeling for life's wondrous mysteries in which they are bound up with every other living thing on earth. And we hoped that this recognition of miraculous inter-relationships would become a mental touchstone against which they could forever check their actions.
>
> (Van Matre 1989: 47)

De facto most values education through fieldwork has recently taken place through issues-based enquiries at KS3 and KS4 and particularly in A level fieldwork influenced by the Geography 16–19 Project Route for Enquiry which has a clear 'values enquiry' strand and ends up with students making personal evaluations, judgements and responses.

5   *Fieldwork and environmental education through geography*

The contribution of fieldwork to environmental education has been recognised by both education policy-makers (NCC 1990) and researchers (Fien 1993; Job 1996). The Belgrade Charter of 1976, promoting environmental education in its signatory countries, contains the origins of the notion that environmental education comprises education *about* the environment, education *through* the environment, and education *for* the environment. Despite this distinction, Fien (1993) believes that the purpose of all environmental education is education *for* the environment, with a primary aim of developing in individuals a critical, analytical perspective on the environment and environmental issues with a view to the stimulation of fundamental change in people's interactions with the environment. Hence, a key aim in fieldwork will be the raising of awareness about environmental issues and conflicts and the encouragement of discussion and exploration of environmental attitudes and values.

Environmental education is essentially a politically and ideologically framed process reflecting the views of curriculum planners. While all environmental education can be underpinned by fieldwork in school and college, all approaches and strategies require careful reflection on the nature and purpose of the environmental education which is being promoted. Fieldwork that involves the choosing of least-environmental-impact developments, for example, or which emphasises rational, scientific interpretations of environmental processes, may be interpreted as promoting a strongly technocentric perspective, while fieldwork based on perceptions and values of environment, such as the Earth Education approach of Van Matre (1989), may be interpreted as promoting strongly ecocentric views.

It is also clear that all fieldwork is environmental education, whether the primary and explicit aims of the work express this or not. The importance of the hidden curriculum within the school is often explicitly recognised, yet its existence in the curriculum outside the school buildings is just as significant. It is in the attitudes and values of the implicit environmental curriculum that much of the real learning *for* the environment occurs, and the existence of fieldwork (or not), the approaches adopted and the ideologies these represent convey much of the learning pupils make in this arena. Where the first-hand environmental experience of pupils is only delivered through Geography fieldwork, auditing this experience against the explicit and implicit aims of environmental education would seem to be an essential part of fieldwork planning.

Teaching through fieldwork – a perspective on the future

As a resource-intensive element of the curriculum, fieldwork will always need to be justified by those committed to its importance in Geography. Perceptions from outside Geography that fieldwork is simply an affective experience, or worse still, just a mere amusement, need continuous challenge. This process requires geography educators to reflect on the value of fieldwork and rethink the strategies we use in the field, as Job (1999) has begun to do. At the political level, we need also to lobby strongly for the inclusion of fieldwork as a required element in centrally-dictated Geography curriculums, and for fieldwork skills to be recognised as an important component of the features of geographical literacy at all levels. In this respect, the inclusion of fieldwork as a higher profile component of a revised International Charter on Geographical Education (IGU 1992) would give a strong lead in this direction. We also need to ensure that fieldwork has a 'futures perspective' looking to brighter, more just, sustainable and equitable futures. See Hicks (1993).

Reflection and research on the nature of learning through fieldwork and the ways of optimising its impact is essential, too, for 'effective learning cannot be expected just because we take students into the field' (Lonergan and Anderson 1988: 70). Little objective research has been undertaken on fieldwork as a learning process, either in schools or in higher education, and we often struggle to provide evidence to support our beliefs about the benefits of fieldwork. The research that has been undertaken (for example, Mackenzie and White 1982; Nundy 1998) provides strong supporting evidence, but leaves many research questions completely unaddressed. Though piecemeal, there is the beginnings of a research literature and agenda as witnessed by a number of recent MA dissertations, completed for the MA Geography in Education course at the Institute of Education. See for example those by Crouch (1991); Wu (1992); Rynne (1995); and Macintosh (1998).

A significant threat to real fieldwork that is emerging rapidly in higher education is the development of 'virtual fieldwork', and the explosion of ICT means that such notions will soon emerge beyond their current limited development in schools. The advantages of virtual fieldwork in organisational, logistical, cost and safety terms are obvious, and such approaches enable highly-focused learning to occur – examples and proposals may be found on the web at www.geog.le.ac.uk/vfc/about/background.html. At best, though we believe such approaches can only support real fieldwork rather than replacing it, for the affective dimensions that contribute so strongly to learning in this domain are largely absent from the virtual field scene.

The place of fieldwork in the school of the future is not assured, and the case needs to be remade with each curriculum review from school to national scales. Its potential contribution to geographical understanding, and its generic contribution to the development of enquiry skills, ICT, values enquiry and environmental education support the argument very strongly. We believe that:

> With effective planning and management and a commitment to the educational and personal benefits of fieldwork, geography teachers can ensure that it remains as one of the most significant learning experiences that pupils have during their school careers.
>
> (Foskett 1997: 200)

References

Adey, P. and Shayer, M. (1994) *Really Raising Standards*, London: Routledge.

Archer, J.E. and Dalton, T.H. (1968) *Fieldwork in Geography*, London: Batsford.

Ausubel, D.P. (1968) *Educational Psychology: A Cognitive View*, New York: Holt, Rhinehart and Winston.

Bailey, P. (1974) *Teaching Geography*, Newton Abbott: David and Charles.

Bednarz, S.W. (1999) 'Fieldwork in K-12 geography in the United States', *International Research in Geographical and Environmental Education*, Vol. 8, No. 2.

Bilham-Boult, A. (ed.) (1988) *Using Computers in Fieldwork*, Coventry Microelectronics Education Support Unit.

Bland. K., Chambers, B., Donert, K. and Thomas, T. (1996) 'Fieldwork', *Geography Teachers' Handbook*, P. Bailey and P. Fox (eds), Geographical Association, pp. 165–76.

Boardman, D. (1974) 'Objectives and constraints on geographical fieldwork', *Journal of Curriculum Studies*, 6(1), pp. 158–66.

Boardman, D. and McPartland, M. (1993) 'A Hundred Years of Geography Teaching. From Regions to Models: 1944–1969', *Teaching Geography*, April, pp. 159–63.

Crouch, N. (1991) 'An evaluation of fieldwork-based GCSE geography coursework in some Essex schools'. Unpublished MA dissertation, University of London, Institute of Education.

Department for Education (1995) *Geography in the National Curriculum*, London: HMSO.

Driver, R. and Easley, J. (1978) 'Pupils and paradigms: a review of literature related to concept development in adolescent science students', *Studies in Science*, 5: 61–84.

Driver, R., Squires, A., Rushworth, P. and Wood-Robinson, J. (1994) *Making Sense of Secondary Science*, London: Routledge.

Everson, J. (1969) 'Some aspects of teaching geography through fieldwork', *Geography*, January, 54(1): 64–74.

Field Studies Council with Geographical Association (1999), *Progression in fieldwork: 4–19*.

Fien, J. (1993) *Education for the Environment: Critical Curriculum Theorising and Environmental Education*, Geelong: Deakin University Press.

Foskett, N. (1999) Forum: fieldwork in the geography curriculum – international perspectives and research issues, *International Research in Geographical and Environmental Education*, 8(2).

Foskett, N.H. (1997) 'Teaching and learning through fieldwork', in D. Tilbury and M. Williams (eds), *Teaching and Learning Geography*, London: Routledge.

Foskett, N.H. (1999) Fieldwork and the development of thinking skills in geography and environmental education. Proceedings of the IGUCGE Geography and Environmental Education: International Perspectives Conference, London, April 1999.

GA Sixth Form – University Working Group (1984) 'The enduring purpose of fieldwork', *Teaching Geography*, June.

Hart, C. and Thomas, T. (1986) 'Framework fieldwork', in D. Boardman (ed.), *Handbook for Geography Teachers*, Sheffield: The Geographical Association.

Harvey, P.K. (1991) 'The role and value of A-level geography fieldwork: A case study', unpublished PhD thesis, University of Durham.

Hassell, D. (1996) 'Using IT in coursework', *Teaching Geography*, April, 21(2): 77–80.

Hawkins, G. (1987) 'From awareness to participation: new directions in the outdoor experience', *Geography*, 72 (1): 217–22.

Hicks, D. (1993) 'Mapping the future: a geographical contribution', *Teaching Geography*, October:146–9.

IGU (1992) International Charter for Geography Education, Brisbane: IGU.CGE.

Job, D. (1996) 'Geography and environmental education: an exploration of perspectives and strategies', in W.A. Kent *et al.* (eds), *Geography in Education*, Cambridge: Cambridge University Press.

Job, D. (1999) *New Directions in Geographical Fieldwork*, Cambridge: Cambridge University Press.

Joseph, K. (1985) 'Geography in the School Curriculum', paper delivered to The Geographical Association, 19 June 1985.

Kent, W.A. (1996a) 'A strategy for geography fieldwork', in J. van der Schee, *et al.* (eds), *Innovation in Geographical Education*, Centrum voor Educatieve Geograpfie Vrije Universiteit, Amsterdam.

Kent, W.A. (ed.) (1996b) *Fieldwork Strategies for Geography 16–19 – Examples from Devon*, London: Institute of Education, University of London.

Kent, W.A. (1999) 'Experiences of geography in higher education: the case of geography teachers in England', paper presented at the IGU Conference on Geographical Education, San Marcos, Texas, May 1999.

Kent, M., Gilbertson, D. and Hunt, C. (1997), 'Fieldwork in geography teaching: a critical review of the literature and approaches', *Journal of Geography in Higher Education*, 21(3): 313–32.

Kern, E.L. and Carpenter, J.R. (1986) 'Effect of field activities on student learning', *Journal of Geological Education*, 34: 180–3.

Lai, K.C. (1999) 'Caves and Waves – What do adventurous experiences during field trips mean to pupils?' proceedings of the IGUCGE Geography and Environmental Education: International Perspectives Conference, London, April 1999.

Lawler, C.D. (1986) 'CAL and physical-based fieldwork in geography', unpublished MA dissertation, University of London, Institute of Education.

Leat, D. (1998) *Thinking Through Geography*, Cambridge: Chris Kington Publishing.

Lidstone, J. (1988) 'Teaching and learning geography through fieldwork', in R. Gerber and J. Lidstone (eds), *Developing Skills in Geographical Education*, Brisbane: IGUCGE

Lonergan, N. and Andersen, L.W. (1988) 'Field-based education: some theoretical considerations', *Higher Education Research and Development*, 7: 63–77.

Macintosh, A. (1998) 'Should there be a fieldwork entitlement in geography education?' unpublished MA dissertation, University of London, Institute of Education.

Mackenzie, A.A. and White, R.T. (1982) 'Fieldwork in geography and long-term memory structures', *American Educational Research Journal*, 19(4): 623–32.

Ministry of Education (1960) *Geography and Education*, London: HMSO.

Naish, M., Rawling, E. and Hart. C. (1986) *Geography 16–19 – The contribution of a curriculum project to 16–19 education*, Harlow: Longman.

National Curriculum Council (NCC) (1990) *Curriculum Guidance 7: Environmental Education*. London: NCC.

Nundy, S. (1998) 'The fieldwork effect: an explanation of the role and impact of fieldwork at Key Stage two'. Unpublished PhD thesis, University of Southampton.

Nundy, S. (1999 – in press) 'The fieldwork effect: the role and impact of fieldwork in the upper primary school', *International Research in Geographical and Environmental Education*, 8(2).

Owen-Jones, G. (1987) 'Values education through fieldwork', unpublished MA dissertation, University of London, Institute of Education.

Richardson, P. (1998) 'Fieldwork', in R. Carter (ed.), *Handbook of Primary Geography*, Sheffield: The Geographical Association.

Roberts, M. (1996) 'Teaching styles and strategies', in A. Kent, D. Lambert, M. Naish and F.A. Slater (eds), *Geography in Education: Viewpoints on teaching and learning*, Cambridge: Cambridge University, Press.

Rynne, E. (1995) '"A" level geography student as researcher', unpublished MA dissertation, University of London, Institute of Education.

Smith, G. (1999) 'Changing fieldwork objectives and constraints in secondary schools', *International Research in Geographical and Environmental Education*, 8(2)..

Smith, P.L. (1992) 'Geography fieldwork planning in a period of change 1985–1990', unpublished PhD thesis, University of London, Institute of Education.

Smith, P.R. (1987) 'Outdoor education and its educational objectives', *Geography*, 72(2): 209–16.

Smith, P.R. (1997) 'Standards achieved: a review of geography in secondary schools in England, 1995–96', *Teaching Geography*, 22(3): 25–6.

Sternberg, R.J. (1985) *Beyond IQ: A Triarchic Theory of Human Intelligence*. Cambridge: Cambridge University Press.

Swaan, M. and Wijnsteekers, E. (1999) 'Fieldwork in the Dutch Mountains – a bridge too far', *Research in Geographical and Environmental Education*, 8(2).

Van Matre, S. (1989) *Earth Education – A new beginning*, West Virginia: Institute for Earth Education.

Wilmot, D. (1999) 'Making issues-based enquiry a reality in South African classrooms through cooperative fieldwork', Proceedings of the IGUCGE Geography and Environmental Education: International Perspectives Conference, London, April 1999.

Wu, C. (1992) 'Fieldwork in geography education: an analytical review of the case in Hong Kong', unpublished MA dissertation, University of London, Institute of Education.

Zhang, H. (1999) 'Contemporary Chinese concepts of fieldwork in geographical education', *International Research in Geographical and Environmental Education*, 8(2).

13 Inclusion in Geography

Maggie Smith

The focus on inclusion in recent years runs through many different aspects of education – it is a feature throughout the new standards for initial teacher education that are being developed by the Teacher Training Agency for 2002; the planning for and monitoring of inclusion is a focus in the inspection of schools by the Office for Standards in Education (Ofsted); and inclusion has been the subject of a number of publications from Ofsted, the Qualifications and Curriculum Authority (QCA) and the Department for Education and Employment (DfEE) in the last two years. Although these developments are, at least in part, a reaction to the recommendations of the report of the Stephen Lawrence Inquiry (the Macpherson Report) in 1999 (see the box opposite) the focus on inclusion in education goes further than looking at the issues related only to minority ethnic groups. This chapter therefore will firstly investigate the different ways in which the term 'inclusion' is defined in the education field, and then examines some of the implications for teaching and learning Geography in (and out of) the classroom.

What is meant by inclusion?

The relatively recent nature of the discussions and concerns about inclusion means that there is not yet a great deal of literature on this subject, and that which exists deals with generic issues rather than those which are subject specific. The Secondary Education Section Committee (SESC) of the Geographical Association is, however, carrying out a substantial project collating research, individual expertise and experience, and case studies on inclusion in Geography. This chapter has been based on much of that work and the author wishes to express her gratitude to Linda Thompson, the Chair of the Section Committee, and to the members of the Committee, for allowing her access to their work. A full account of the work of the SESC can be found on the Geographical Association's website, which is listed at the end of this chapter.

There are a number of different reference points that might be used when trying to unravel exactly what is meant by inclusion in education. This chapter will be examining three of these – firstly, the statutory statements as set out in the National Curriculums of England, Wales and Northern Ireland which provide details of how inclusion can be incorporated across the curriculum so that all pupils have a chance

---

Recommendations of the Macpherson Report relating to education

67 That consideration be given to amendment of the National Curriculum aimed at valuing cultural diversity and preventing racism, in order better to reflect the needs of a diverse society.

68 That local education authorities and school governors have the duty to create and implement strategies in their schools to prevent and address racism. Such strategies to include:

- that schools record all racist incidents; that all recorded incidents are reported to the pupils' parents/guardians, school governors and LEAs;
- that the numbers of racist incidents are published annually, on a school-by-school basis;
- that the numbers and self-defined ethnic identity of 'excluded' pupils are published annually on a school-by-school basis.

69 That Ofsted inspections include examination of the implementation of such strategies.

70 That in creating strategies under the provisions of the Crime and Disorder Act or otherwise police services, local government and relevant agencies should specifically consider implementing community and local initiatives aimed at promoting cultural diversity and addressing racism and the need for focused, consistent support for such initiatives.

(HMSO 1999)

---

to succeed. The second reference point is the Ofsted definition of 'inclusion' and 'inclusive schools' in their framework for the inspection of schools in England. This definition links inclusion to the ethos of the school and its willingness to offer new opportunities to pupils who may have experienced difficulties in the past, and it looks at how a school might take account of the varied life experiences of all pupils. The third concept of inclusion is expressed in the Index of Inclusion, which is a guide produced by the Centre for Studies on Inclusive Education (CSIE), an independent educational charitable organization, which gives advice and information on inclusive education. Its guide sets out ways in which schools can foster high achievement for all children.

Inclusion in the National Curriculums

Perhaps one of the most succinct accounts of inclusion can be found in the National Curriculum in Wales published by the Qualifications, Curriculum and Assessment Authority for Wales (ACCAC). The statement on 'Access for all pupils' which is part of the Common Requirements of the curriculum for all subjects, while acknowledging that the large majority of pupils will be taught the Key Stage Programmes of Study that are appropriate for their age, suggests that, when necessary, students can be taught material from earlier Key Stages if this enables them to make progress and 'demonstrate achievement' (ACCAC 2000). In a similar way, material from later Key Stages may be used with gifted and talented pupils so that they are encouraged to make further progress. The National Curriculum for Wales also notes that specific provision must be made for pupils who need to use:

1   means of communication other than speech;
2   non-sighted methods of reading;
3   technological aids in practical and written work;
4   aids or adapted equipment to allow access to practical activities.

It also requires that provision must be made for pupils whose first language is not English or Welsh.

The inclusion statement here therefore has two aspects; one is the flexibility given to teachers to tailor their subject content so that it best meets the individual levels of progress and achievement that can be sustained by each pupil, and secondly it recognizes the need to make particular provision for certain types of disability or special need that individual pupils might have.

A similar concept of inclusion can be seen in the National Curriculum for Northern Ireland. This states that:

> The Northern Ireland Curriculum does not constitute the whole curriculum for schools. Schools can develop the whole curriculum to express their particular ethos and meet their pupils' individual needs and circumstances.
>
> (The Northern Ireland Council for the
> Curriculum, Examinations and Assessment [CCEA] 1996)

As in the National Curriculum for Wales therefore, there is a notion of flexibility for teachers to adapt the curriculum to suit the pupils in their classes. The Northern Ireland Curriculum is currently (2001) being revised – the new curriculum being planned to have a phased implementation from September 2003. It is interesting to see that in the consultation process 90 per cent of respondents supported a proposal by the curriculum authority to broaden the access statement so that it emphasizes equality of opportunity for all pupils (CCEA 2001).

The access statement in the National Curriculum for England follows a similar pattern to those of Wales and Northern Ireland:

> Schools have a responsibility to provide a broad and balanced curriculum for all pupils. The National Curriculum is the starting point for planning a school curriculum that meets the specific needs of individuals and groups of pupils.
>
> (DfEE/QCA 1999)

This statutory inclusion statement requires schools to provide 'effective learning opportunities for all pupils'. It indicates that teachers can make adaptations to the Programmes of Study in the National Curriculum so that the work given to the children is relevant to them as individuals and challenges them in a way that is most suited to their personal needs.

This general statement however goes on to explore in detail three principles that schools must follow in order to ensure that its teaching enables every pupils to have the best 'chance to succeed'. These principles are:

A   setting suitable learning challenges;
B   responding to pupils' diverse learning needs;
C   overcoming potential barriers to learning and assessment for individuals or groups of pupils.

The Inclusion Statement in the National Curriculum for England expands on each of these principles in considerable detail and provides exemplars and some subjec- based information. Below is a summary of the main points relating to each of the principles and outlines of how each might impact on teaching and learning.

A   Setting suitable learning challenges

This principle reflects similar statements in the curriculums for Wales and Northern Ireland. It states that the large majority of pupils will be taught the Key Stage Programmes of Study that are appropriate for their age, but it suggests that, when necessary, a flexible approach should be taken so that students can be taught material from earlier, or later, Key Stages if this enables them to make progress and show what they can achieve.

B   Responding to pupils' diverse learning needs

The term 'diverse' here is taken to encompass:

- girls and boys;
- pupils with SEN;
- pupils with disabilities;
- pupils from all and any social, cultural and ethnic backgrounds.

Teachers should 'respond' to this by actions such as:

- creating effective learning environments;
- securing pupils' motivation;
- making sure that the teaching approaches used provide equality of opportunity for all;
- planning appropriate assessment opportunities;
- setting targets for the pupils' learning.

C   Overcoming potential barriers to learning and assessment for individuals and groups of pupils

Barriers that might stand in the way of pupils' learning and achievement are most likely to be the result of a pupil's special educational need(s) or disability. Teachers therefore need to take account of this in their planning, and make any appropriate provision so that the pupils concerned can participate fully in the curriculum and in assessment. This principle details some of the particular circumstances that teachers may need to make provision for and it suggests some actions that could be taken. The particular circumstances may include children with special educational needs (SEN), such as behavioural or emotional difficulties, language or communication difficulties; children with disabilities such as visual or hearing impairments; and children for whom English is a second language (ESL).

These three principles impact on geography teaching in the same way as they impact on the teaching of all the subject areas of the National Curriculum. There are however some aspects of Geography in which there are particular strengths for teaching inclusively and teaching about inclusion. Here are also, however, some areas, due to the nature of the subject, where Geography is presented with particular problems that need careful thought and planning in order to be fully inclusive. These aspects will be explored later in this chapter.

Inclusion as defined by Ofsted

The Ofsted framework for inclusion defines an educationally inclusive school as one 'in which the teaching and learning, achievements, attitudes and well being of every young person matter' (Ofsted). It notes that inclusive schools are effective schools, and ones in which there is a 'willingness to offer new opportunities to pupils who have experienced previous difficulties'. It makes the important distinction that inclusion does not mean treating all pupils the same nor does it necessarily mean that some pupils need to be doing different work from the rest of the class. What it does mean is that due regard is taken of the varied life experiences and needs of each pupil so that each pupil has an equal opportunity to make progress in his or her own way whatever their age, gender, ethnicity, attainment or background.

Interestingly, the Ofsted definition of inclusion presents a more comprehensive listing of the 'different' groups of children, for whom particular provision should be made. These are:

- boys and girls;
- minority ethnic and faith groups, travellers, asylum seekers;
- pupils who need support to learn English as an additional language (EAL);
- pupils with special educational needs;
- gifted and talented pupils;
- children 'looked after' by the local authority;
- sick children, young carers, children from families under stress, pregnant schoolgirls, teenage mothers;
- any pupils at risk of disaffection and exclusion.

The Index of Inclusion

The Centre for Studies on Inclusive Education (CSIE) is an organization that is committed to promoting inclusive education in schools. It defines inclusion generally as 'young people and adults with disabilities being included in mainstream society' (CSIE 2001) and inclusion in schools as being about the 'development of communities where all people are equally valued and have the same opportunities for participation'(ibid.). To this end the centre has produced the Index of Inclusion which is a guide to the building of such communities in schools. The guide sets out a cycle of activities through which schools can review their existing approach to inclusion, decide on areas that need change, formulate whole-school policies and evaluate their effectiveness. Throughout these guidelines however, CSIE makes it quite clear that inclusion should not be regarded as another name for 'special needs education' but is concerned with the learning and participation of all pupils who are or may be suffering pressures that might cause them to be excluded from the cultures, curriculums and communities that operate in schools. To counteract this sort of exclusion, schools need to restructure their policies and practices so that they can respond to the particular diversity of pupils in their locality. The diversity of pupils' backgrounds should therefore be regarded as a resource, not as a problem.

Although there are differences in emphases between the three broad definitions of inclusion that have been explored here, it is clear that there is consensus that inclusion should mean that *all* young people have equal access to the opportunities provided in schools – both within and outside the curriculum, and that the backgrounds and experiences of *all* pupils are valued and taken into account when the teaching programme is planned.

What actions can be taken to increase inclusion within Geography?

The response of geography teachers and geography departments in ensuring that inclusion is an integral part of their planned programmes of teaching and learning will obviously vary in detail according to the particular local circumstances of their school.

The following ideas have been adapted from a scheme created by Ian Selmes, a member of the SESC of the Geographical Association. They are presented here as starting points to stimulate thought and discussion about inclusion in geography lessons and within geography departments.

1   *What can the geography department do to ensure that its practices are inclusive?*

- Do all pupils have full access to their National Curriculum entitlement?
- Are all aspects of a student's potential developed through their experience of Geography?
- Are positive attitudes developed towards diversity in both teachers and pupils?

- Does the nature of the geographical education that is provided reflect the diversity of pupils' backgrounds?
- Is the participation of pupils in geographical activities increased (and correspondingly is pupil exclusion from activities reduced)?
- Does planning cater sensitively for the learning of all – but particularly those who are vulnerable to exclusionary pressures for any reason – not just those with disabilities or special needs?
- Are departmental practices inclusive for staff as well as pupils?

2   What strategies can be taken to ensure that the curriculum is accessible to all pupils?

- Is attention paid to the understanding and use of written and spoken language?
- Do the materials used reflect the backgrounds and experiences of all learners?
- Does the range of activities reflect the interests of boys and girls?
- Are alternative means of giving experience or activity provided for those who cannot engage in an activity?

3   What teaching and learning strategies can be used to foster inclusion?

- Does classroom management allow for pupils to work individually, in pairs and in groups?
- Is there a variety of teaching and learning activities?
- Is work able to be presented in a variety of ways?
- Are pupils encouraged to take responsibility for their own learning?
- Do pupils share their knowledge, understanding and skills?
- Do pupils offer support to one another?
- Are pupils consulted in the materials used, the activities undertaken and/or the support they need?
- Are field trips (including residential trips) and visits made accessible to all pupils?

4   What can be done to enable pupils to understand differences?

- Do pupils explore views, lifestyle and cultures that are different from their own?
- Is all language treated as equally valuable?
- Are stereotyping and bias questioned in materials and discussions?

5   How can assessment be inclusive?

- Do the pupils understand the aims and expectations in a lesson or sequence of lessons?
- Do pupils understand why and how they are being assessed?
- Are assessments used formatively to develop the learning of pupils?
- Is there a range of assessments used so that all students an display their skills?

- Are pupils given feedback that recognises what they have learnt and what they might do next?
- Are pupils involved in assessing and commenting on their own learning?
- Can pupils set clear goals for their own learning?
- Does the teacher check on the progress of all pupils during lessons?
- Do the pupils feel that they are being treated fairly?

6   *How can the effectiveness of inclusion policies be monitored and evaluated?*

- Is there liaison with other concerned parties e.g. the SENCO?
- Is inclusion a regular agenda item at departmental meetings?
- Is there regular feedback on inclusion to senior manager and governors?
- Are data for different groups of pupils examined in relation to areas of under-achievement and 'value-added'?

These discussion points can be turned into a full audit of inclusion within a school geography department, and in turn can facilitate the production of an indi-vidualized action plan for the geography department. A detailed example of an audit can be seen in Table 13.1 on the following pages.

What specific areas of the Geography curriculum might be considered in relation to inclusion?

As mentioned earlier in this chapter, the National Curriculum for England contains three principles for inclusion that teachers should consider in their plan-ning and teaching to ensure that an inclusive curriculum is provided for pupils. The text box on pp. 196–7. lists those aspects of the inclusion statement that could readily be considered when planning the teaching of Geography.

The nature of Geography means that there are many opportunities for the subject to play a full role in teaching inclusively and teaching about inclusion. Geography is well placed to challenge stereotypical views and develop in pupils an appreciation of the views of others. Likewise the teaching of Geography provides opportunities for the study of social and cultural diversity; it provides sensory and experiential learning though the use of a range of resources and through work in environments outside the classroom. There are, however, challenges. Activities such as fieldwork may have to be adapted in order to enable all children to partici-pate actively and safely; and the extensive use of visual material may pose problems in terms of planning and of locating appropriate resources and equipment so that visually impaired pupils can develop the full range of skills outlined in the National Curriculum Programmes of Study.

There is a range of helpful information and guidance on accommodating specific needs produced by the organizations such as the Geographical Association and the Field Studies Council. A listing of some of these can be found at the end of this chapter.

Table 13.1 Geography Department Inclusion Audit

The inclusion audit comprises a series of questions under 17 headings. The questions invite departmental or individual teacher self evaluation – some are phrased in positive and some in negative terms. For each question decide whether:

• your current practice is good and should be maintained – tick box M
• your current practice is appropriate but could be developed, so you feel you could improve it – tick box I
• your current practice is not effective enough and you therefore need to change it – tick box C

Once completed, the distribution of ticks can support you in prioritising a departmental action plan for inclusion.

Creating inclusive cultures, policies and practices	M	I	C	*Comments*
1 Everyone is made to feel welcome in the department	☐	☐	☐	
	☐	☐	☐	
2 Students help each other i Do displays celebrate collaborative work by students as well as individual achievements?	☐	☐	☐	
ii Do students avoid racist, sexist, homophobic, disabilities, physical and other forms of discriminatory name-calling (including those who want to achieve)?	☐	☐	☐	
iii Do students understand that different attainments may be expected from different students?	☐	☐	☐	
iv Do students understand that different degrees of conformity to school rules may be expected from different students?	☐	☐	☐	
v Do students appreciate the achievements of others whose starting points may be different from their own?	☐	☐	☐	
3 Staff collaborate with each other i Do all teachers attend departmental meetings?	☐	☐	☐	
ii Is there wide participation of meetings?	☐	☐	☐	
iii Are all teachers and classroom assistants involved in curriculum planning and review?	☐	☐	☐	
iv Is teamwork between staff a model for the collaboration of students?	☐	☐	☐	
v Do staff feel comfortable about discussing their problems in their work?	☐	☐	☐	

Table 13.1(cont.)

Creating inclusive cultures, policies and practices		M	I	C	Comments
	vi Are all staff involved in drawing up priorities for school development?	☐	☐	☐	
	vii Do all staff feel ownership of the school development plan?	☐	☐	☐	
4 Staff and students treat one another with respect	i Do staff address all students respectfully, by the name they wish to be called, with the correct pronunciation?	☐	☐	☐	
	ii Do students treat all staff with respect irrespective of their status?	☐	☐	☐	
	iii Do the views of students make a difference to what happens in the department?	☐	☐	☐	
	iv Do staff and students look after the physical environment of the department?	☐	☐	☐	
5 There is a partnership between staff and parents/ carers	i Do staff encourage the involvement of all parents/carers in their children's learning?	☐	☐	☐	
	ii Are parents/carers clear about what they can do to support their children's learning at home?	☐	☐	☐	
6 There are high expectations for all students	i Does every student feel that they attend lessons in which the highest achievements are possible?	☐	☐	☐	
	ii Are all students encouraged to have high aspirations about their learning?	☐	☐	☐	
	iii Are all students treated as if there is no ceiling to their achievements?	☐	☐	☐	
	iv Is the achievement of students valued in relation to their own possibilities rather than the achievement of others?	☐	☐	☐	
	v Do staff avoid viewing students as having a fixed ability based on their current achievement?	☐	☐	☐	
	vi Are students entered for public examinations when they are ready rather than at a particular age?	☐	☐	☐	
	vii Are all students encouraged to take pride in their own achievements?	☐	☐	☐	
	viii Are all students encouraged to appreciate the achievement of others?	☐	☐	☐	

(continued on next page)

Table 13.1 (cont.)

Creating inclusive cultures, policies and practices		M	I	C	Comments
	ix Do staff attempt to counter negative views of students who are keen and enthusiastic or attain highly in lessons?	☐	☐	☐	
	x Do staff attempt to counter negative views of students who find lessons difficult?	☐	☐	☐	
	xi Do staff attempt to counter the derogatory use of labels of low achievement?	☐	☐	☐	
	xii Do staff avoid gender bias in their teaching and have equal expectations for both?	☐	☐	☐	
7 Students are equally valued	i Are differences in family structure acknowledged?	☐	☐	☐	
	ii Are students who attain less according to National Curriculum norms as valued as high-attaining students?	☐	☐	☐	
	iii Is the work of all students displayed within the classroom?	☐	☐	☐	
	iv Are the achievements of boys and girls given equal support and prominence?	☐	☐	☐	
8 Staff seek to remove all barriers to learning and participation in school	i Do staff understand their potential for preventing student difficulties?	☐	☐	☐	
	ii Are the barriers that arise through differences between school and home culture recognized and countered?	☐	☐	☐	
	iii Do staff avoid using negative labels for students, who have been categorized as 'having special educational needs'?	☐	☐	☐	
9 The department arranges teaching groups so that all students are valued	i Are teaching groups treated fairly in the use of facilities, location of teaching rooms, allocation of teaching staff and staff cover?	☐	☐	☐	
	ii Where setting occurs are their plans to prevent disaffection in lower sets?	☐	☐	☐	
	iii Where setting occurs do the arrangements give students an equal opportunity to move between sets?	☐	☐	☐	
	iv Is the department mindful of the legal requirement to educate together students who do and do not experience difficulties in learning?	☐	☐	☐	

Table 13.1(cont)

Creating inclusive cultures, policies and practices		M	I	C	Comments
10 'Special needs' policies are inclusion policies	i Is there an attempt to minimize the categorization of students as 'having special education needs'?	☐	☐	☐	
	ii Are the attempts to remove barriers to learning and participation of one student seen as opportunities for improving the classroom experience of all students?	☐	☐	☐	
	iii Is support seen as an entitlement for those students who need it rather than as a special addition to their education?	☐	☐	☐	
	iv Is there an attempt to minimize the withdrawal of students for support outside their lessons?	☐	☐	☐	
11 IEPs are used to reduce the barriers to learning and participation of all students	i Are Individual Education Plans about providing access to and supporting participation within the curriculum?	☐	☐	☐	
	ii Do Individual Education Plans improve the teaching and learning arrangements for all students?	☐	☐	☐	
12 Lessons are responsive to student diversity	i Do lessons extend the learning of all students?	☐	☐	☐	
	ii Do lessons build on the diversity of student experience?	☐	☐	☐	
	iii Do lessons reflect differences in student knowledge?	☐	☐	☐	
	iv Do lessons reflect the different rates at which students complete tasks?	☐	☐	☐	
	v Do lessons allow for differences in learning styles?	☐	☐	☐	
	vi Are the learning aims of activities clear?	☐	☐	☐	
	vii Are mechanical copying activities avoided?	☐	☐	☐	
	viii Do lessons sometimes start from a shared experience that can be developed in a variety of ways?	☐	☐	☐	
	ix Do lessons involve work to be done by individuals, pairs, groups and the whole class?	☐	☐	☐	
	x Is there a variety of activities, including discussion, oral presentation, writing, drawing, problem solving, use of library, audio-visual materials, practical tasks and information technology?	☐	☐	☐	

(continued on next page)

Table 13.1(cont)

Creating inclusive cultures, policies and practices		M	I	C	Comments
13 Lessons are made accessible to all students	i Is particular attention paid to the accessibility of spoken and written language?	☐	☐	☐	
	ii Is technical vocabulary explained and practised during lessons?	☐	☐	☐	
	iii Do curriculum materials reflect the backgrounds and experience of all learners?	☐	☐	☐	
	iv Are all lessons made equally accessible to all boys and all girls by including a range of activities which reflect the range of interests within both genders?	☐	☐	☐	
	v Do staff recognize the additional time required by some students with impairments to use equipment in practical work?	☐	☐	☐	
14 Assessment encourages the achievements of all students	i Do records of achievement reflect all the skills and knowledge of students such as additional languages, other communication systems, hobbies and interests and work experience?	☐	☐	☐	
	ii Are assessments (including national assessments) always used formatively so that they develop the learning of students?	☐	☐	☐	
	iii Are a range of assessments used that allow all students to display their skills?	☐	☐	☐	
	iv Do students understand why they are being assessed?	☐	☐	☐	
	v Are students given feedback that indicates recognition of what they have learnt and what they might do next?	☐	☐	☐	
	vi Are students involved in assessing and commenting on their own learning?	☐	☐	☐	
	vii Can students set clear goals for their future learning?	☐	☐	☐	
15 Classroom discipline is based on mutual respect	i Does the approach to discipline encourage self-discipline?	☐	☐	☐	
	ii Do staff share their concerns and pool their knowledge and skills in overcoming disaffection and disruption?	☐	☐	☐	

Table 13.1 (cont)

Creating inclusive cultures, policies and practices	M	I	C	Comments
iii Are classroom routines consistent and explicit?	☐	☐	☐	
iv Are students consulted on how to improve attention to learning?	☐	☐	☐	
v Are there clear procedures, understood by students and teachers, for responding to extremes of challenging behaviour?	☐	☐	☐	
vi Is it recognised by all staff and students that it is unfair for boys to take up more of a teacher's attention than girls?	☐	☐	☐	
16 Homework contributes to the learning of all — i Does homework always have a clear teaching aim?	☐	☐	☐	
ii Is homework related to the skills and knowledge of all students?	☐	☐	☐	
iii Are there opportunities for recording homework in a variety of ways?	☐	☐	☐	
iv Does homework extend the skills and knowledge of all students?	☐	☐	☐	
v Do teachers support each other on how to set useful homework?	☐	☐	☐	
vi Are students given sufficient opportunity to clarify the requirements of homework before the end of lessons?	☐	☐	☐	
vii Is homework integrated into curriculum planning for the term/year?	☐	☐	☐	
viii Does homework encourage students to take responsibility for their own learning?	☐	☐	☐	
17 All students take part in activities outside the classroom — i Are field trips, including overseas visits, made accessible to all students in the school, irrespective of attainment or impairment?	☐	☐	☐	
ii Are all students given opportunities to take part in activities outside the school?	☐	☐	☐	

Source: SESC (2001).

Aspects of the National Curriculum (England) Inclusion Statement which link to geographical education

Principle B   Responding to pupils' diverse learning needs

Examples for B/3a – creating effective learning environments

Teachers create effective learning environments in which:

- stereotypical views are challenged and pupils learn to appreciate and view positively differences in others, whether arising from race, gender, ability or disability
- pupils are enabled to participate safely in clothing appropriate to their religious beliefs, particularly in subjects such as science, design and technology and physical education *and geography field trips*

Examples for B/3b – securing motivation and concentration

Teachers secure pupils' motivation and concentration by:

- planning work which builds on their interests and cultural experiences
- using materials which reflect social and cultural diversity and provide positive images of race, gender and disability

Examples for B/3c – providing equality of opportunity

Teaching approaches that provide equality of opportunity include:

- enabling the fullest possible participation of pupils with disabilities or particular medical needs in all subjects, offering positive role models and making provision, where necessary, to facilitate access to activities with appropriate support, aids or adaptations, *e.g. fieldwork*

Examples for B/3d – using appropriate assessment approaches

Teachers use appropriate assessment approaches that:

- use materials which are free from discrimination and stereotyping in any form

Principle C   *Overcoming potential barriers to learning and assessment for individuals and groups of pupils*

Examples for C/3a – helping with communication, language and literacy

Teachers provide for pupils who need help with communication, language and literacy through:

- using visual and written materials in different formats, including large print, symbol text and Braille
- using ICT, other technological aids and taped materials

Examples for C/3b – developing understanding

Teachers develop pupils' understanding through the use of all available senses and experiences by:

- using ICT, visual and other materials to increase pupils' knowledge of the wider world, encouraging pupils to take part in everyday activities such as play, drama, class visits and exploring the environment

Examples for C/3c – planning for full participation

Teachers plan for pupils' full participation in learning and in physical and practical activities (e.g. fieldwork) through:

- using specialist aids and equipment
- providing support from adults or peers when needed
- adapting tasks or environments
- providing alternative activities, where necessary

Pupils with disabilities

4   Not all pupils with disabilities will necessarily have special educational needs. Many pupils with disabilities learn alongside their peers with little need for additional resources beyond the aids which they use as part of their daily life, such as a wheelchair, a hearing aid or equipment to aid vision. Teachers must take action, however, in their planning to ensure that these pupils are enabled to participate as fully and effectively as possible within the National Curriculum and the statutory assessment arrangements. Potential areas of difficulty should be identified and addressed at the outset of work, without recourse to the formal provisions for disapplication.

5   Teachers should take specific action to enable the effective participation of pupils with disabilities by:

  c   identifying aspects of Programmes of Study and attainment targets that may present specific difficulties for individuals.

Examples for C/5b – developing skills in practical aspects

Teachers create opportunities for the development of skills in practical aspects of the curriculum through:

- ensuring that all pupils can be included and participate safely in geography fieldwork, local studies and visits to museums, historic buildings and sites

Examples for C/5c – overcoming specific difficulties

Teachers overcome specific difficulties for individuals presented by aspects of the Programmes of Study and attainment targets through:

- helping visually impaired pupils to learn about light in science, to access maps and visual resources in Geography and to evaluate different products in design and technology and images in art and design

Examples for C/8a – developing spoken and written English

Teachers develop pupils' spoken and written English through:

- providing a variety of reading material [for example, pupils' own work, the media, ICT, literature, reference books] that highlight the different ways English is used, especially those that help pupils to understand society and culture

NOTES

Words in italics do not appear in the National Curriculum Orders but give aspects of geographical education to which the statement applies.

Conclusion

'Inclusion is good for everyone' was the headline in an article on inclusion in the *Times Educational Supplement* in July 2001. The article continued by commenting that schools that cater effectively for a diverse range of children do best by all their pupils. Inclusion is undoubtedly a high priority and important issue in teaching today. It depends on effective communication throughout all sectors of the school; and it requires careful thought, planning, monitoring and evaluation on the part of teachers in order to be effective. For geography teachers it involves a raising of the awareness of the opportunities presented by the subject to teach for and about inclusion, but it also involves careful consideration of aspects of the subject that can act as a barrier to full pupil inclusion. It almost goes without saying that training and support is a vital in order for teachers to be confident in working with inclusion policies. Finally it must be recognized that effective inclusion is a gradual process – both attitudes and practice need to change in order for inclusion to work.

References

ACCAC (2000) *The National Curriculum for Wales*, The National Assembly for Wales.
CCEA (1996) *Northern Ireland Curriculum*.
CCEA (2001) *Curriculum Review Update*.
CSIE (2001) *School change through inclusion*, http://inclusion.uwe.ac.uk/csie/
DfEE *Removing the barriers*, http:/www.dfee.gov.uk/
DfEE/QCA (1999) *The National Curriculum for England*, London: DfEE/QCA.
HMSO (1999) *The Stephen Lawrence Inquiry (The Macpherson Report)*, London: HMSO.
Ofsted *Evaluating Educational Inclusion – Guidance for Inspectors and Schools*.
   www.ofsted.gov.uk/
QCA Inclusion website: http://www.qca.org.uk/ca/inclusion/
Wilce, H. (2001) 'Amazing mainstream', *Times Educational Supplement*, 6 July 2001.

Further resources

The Geographical Association, 160 Solly Street, Sheffield Sl 4BF, website: http://www. geography.org.uk/ The Geographical Association publishes guidance material (see its publications list) and produces the journal *Teaching Geography* which contains articles on inclusion. See especially: Desforges H. (1999) 'Inclusive geography fieldwork', *Teaching Geography*, 24(1), and Kitchin, R. (2001) 'Investigating disability and inclusive land-scapes', *Teaching Geography*, 26(2).

The webpages on the GA site contain further information on incluson:
- visual impairment in geography;
- a departmental inclusion audit;
- a departmental inclusion policy template;
- lesson observation template and prompts;
- the Ofsted Inspection framework for inclusion;
- guidance on inclusive fieldwork in geography
- case studies exemplifying good practice;
- links to related resources.

BECTA (British Educational Communications and Technology Agency), Millburn Hill Road, Science Park, Coventry, West Midlands CV4 7JJ.

http://inclusion.ngl.gov.uk/ This inclusion site has a free catalogue of resources for teachers.

The Field Studies Council, Preston Montford, Montford Bridge, Shrewsbury, Shropshire SY4 1HW publishes a range of guidance material on fieldwork.

14 Language and learning in Geography

Graham Butt

Introduction

The importance of geography teachers gaining an understanding of how the use of language can affect the learning of their subject is undeniable. Language provides the medium for learning Geography in every classroom and should therefore be a major consideration in the planning and preparation of lessons.

The term 'language' is perhaps deceptively straightforward at first glance. However, it encompasses a huge variety of talk, reading and writing that children undertake; the relationship between these activities and the process of learning; and the nature of communication between the teacher and the learner. The action of learning is closely associated with that of comprehending and using different forms of language. All teaching methods and materials used by the geography teacher therefore have import implications for language and understanding.

Research into the use of language specifically within the geography classroom is somewhat piecemeal, although valuable contributions have been made by Williams (1981), Hull (1985), Slater (1989) and Carter (1991). Nonetheless there is a considerable amount of literature exploring the relationship between language and learning (Piaget 1959; Vygotsky 1962; Chomsky 1968, etc.) as well as a major report – the Bullock Report (DES 1975) – which for a time stimulated a variety of subject specialists to explore the ways in which both teachers and children used language in the classroom. The inter-relatedness of language and learning, and the effects of the use of language on both conceptual development and the learning process, were major considerations of much of the work carried out. Unfortunately the impetus for these 'Language Across the Curriculum' studies did not continue after the late 1970s, leaving many of the issues surrounding talking, writing, reading and learning in geography largely unexplored. The role of language in the process of learning in Geography is therefore widely acknowledged, but not fully investigated.

Recently the Language in the National Curriculum (LINC) report produced materials based on existing good practice in the use of language, but was suppressed by the government for not fully emphasizing the importance of grammar in pupils' work.

Geography teachers must be aware of the importance of their role in guiding the form and function of language used within the classroom and the impact this has on children's learning. Slater (1989: 109) carefully outlines the two distinct functions of language use in Geography lessons as being 'to communicate what has been learned and is known', as well as being 'part of the *activity* of learning'. The distinction between the two functions is important, although often confused or conflated. Recently there has been a greater focus on the latter, i.e. 'talking and writing to learn'.

Talk within the geography classroom

Casual observation soon confirms the way in which teacher talk dominates the geography classroom. Teachers tend to talk much more than pupils during each lesson and closely control the amount of talking in which pupils are allowed to engage. Most children become quickly aware of the times which the teacher considers to be appropriate for talking, the acceptable content for discussions and the length of time they are permitted to talk. Very rarely are pupils able to negotiate what is talked about: the teacher controls the process and creates the rules by which communication takes place.

The teacher is in a very powerful position to direct how talking is used to help children learn. This 'gatekeeping' role can either be performed to the benefit of children's learning – if the teacher encourages a wide range of different types of talk – or to its detriment – if the teacher totally dominates what is said in the classroom. It is important that children are enthused and encouraged by what the teacher says, but this is only one part of the language and learning process. Evidence suggests that children must themselves engage in talking about Geography, as well as listening, if they are to understand fully the subject's concepts and terminology.

Additionally, pupils often associate language forms used by the teacher with 'assessment', rather than as a part of the process of facilitating learning. Many geography classrooms exist where closed oral 'question and answer' sessions directed by the teacher are merely:

> guessing game(s) whereby the teacher has the knowledge, and tries through questioning to extract the right answers from the pupil. They in turn reach towards the preferred response, the correct answer. Alternatively, they adopt a variety of strategies to keep their heads below the parapet.
>
> (Carter 1991: 1)

Here, talk, in the form of question and answer, can actually restrict much of the learning process. Such activities probably do not involve the majority of children in the class and those that do participate are often not learning in the most profitable ways. Guessing the right answer represents only a very limited representation of how talking can enhance learning!

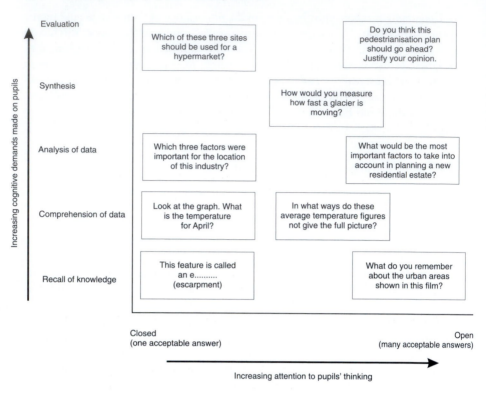

Figure 14.1 Two dimensions of questioning

Source: Roberts (1986: 69).

Roberts (1986) refers to these two dimensions of questioning by highlighting the type of thinking that different questions entail, and considering whether the questions posed are either open or closed. This is clarified by the above diagram (Figure 14. 1).

A number of important points are raised by this diagram. The 'y' axis shows the increasing cognitive demands made upon pupils – most questions that teachers ask actually fall into the lowest categories on this axis, consisting of recalling knowledge or comprehending data. Few of the questions that teachers ask tend to 'stretch' pupils into higher orders of thinking involving synthesis and evaluation. The implicit message this may give to children is that being able to remember facts in geography lessons is more important than working things out.

The 'x' axis represents the extent to which pupils consider a range of possible answers in their attempts to respond 'successfully' to the teacher's question. If the question is closed there is probably only one right answer, but if it is open a greater degree of thinking about a range of possible answers should occur. Most questions asked by teachers are of the closed recall type, essentially asking children to tell the teacher what is already known, rather than attempting to work towards new understandings.

Table 14.1 Analyses of questions

Question type	Explanation
1 A data recall question	Requires the pupil to remember facts or information, without putting the information to use. 'What are the main crops in this country?'
2 A naming question	Asks the pupil simply to name an event, process or phenomenon without showing insight into how it is linked to other factors. 'What do we call this process of coastal deposition?'
3 An observation question	Asks pupils to describe what they see without attempting to explain it. 'What happened when the soil dried?'
4 A control question	Involves the use of questions to modify pupils' behaviour rather than their learning. 'Will you sit down, John?'
5 A pseudo-question	Is constructed to appear that the teacher will accept more than one response, but in fact s/he has clearly made up his/her mind that this is not so. 'Is this an integrated railway network, then?'
6 A speculative question	Asks pupils to speculate about the outcome of an hypothetical situation. 'Imagine a world without trees; how would this affect our lives?'
7 A reasoning question	Asks pupils to give reasons why certain things do or do not happen. 'What motivates these people to live so near a volcano?'
8 An evaluation question	Is one which makes a pupil weigh up the pros and cons of a situation or argument. 'How strong is the case for a bypass round this village?'
9 A problem-solving question	Asks pupils to construct ways of finding out answers to questions. 'How can we measure the speed of the river here and compare it with lower down?'

Source: Carter (1991: 4).

This idea is taken further by Carter (1991) who lists a variety of question types starting with closed recall questions and ending with more open evaluative and problem-solving ones (Table 14.1).

The more open the questions become the more likely it is that the answers given by pupils will be tentative and exploratory, in itself evidence that new learning is occurring. Some teachers may feel threatened by this as these responses often deviate from the 'known' and 'expected' and possibly create a potential loss of academic control.

An important element of all oral question and answer within the classroom is the teacher's intention. Is it to explore concepts, ideas and thoughts and engage in supported, but often tentative, thinking to create new learning (often by using open questions)? Or is it to repeat what the teacher already knows along a rigidly determined pathway? The former approach may liberate pupils' thinking, the latter restricts it to the teacher's predetermined route. I would suggest that a balance of both is required within the geography classroom.

Marsden (1995: 94) helpfully lists a variety of factors which he considers illustrate good questioning:

- asking questions fluently and precisely;
- gearing questions to the student's state of readiness;
- involving a wide range of students in the question and answer process;
- focusing questions on a wide range of intellectual skills, and not just on recall;
- asking probing questions;
- not accepting each answer as of equal validity, though sensitively;
- redirecting questioning to allow accurate and relevant answers to emerge;
- using open-ended as well as closed questions so that creative thought and value judgements are invited.

Even when the teacher receives the 'right' answer to a recall question, this should not simply be taken as evidence that a pupil (or indeed the whole class) fully understands the concepts surrounding the response. For example, many pupils may know that the central area of large cities in the developed world is referred to as the 'CBD', but fewer may appreciate that this actually stands for 'central business district', and fewer still may be capable of providing an acceptable definition of its land uses, activities and *raison d'être*.

Group work and language

Giving children the opportunities to discus their own ideas in geography lessons is therefore important if effective learning is to take place. Whole-class teaching rarely gives each child the chance to talk. In many schools there is now a realization that active and pupil-centred styles of teaching and learning are often the best ways of promoting such talk, either as a part of group work, or in role-plays, simulations or decision-making exercises.

Many geography teachers are understandably nervous about allowing pupils too many opportunities to talk. They may fear a potential loss of control, or may simply be unsure about whether pupils will actually discuss what they have been asked to. These are natural concerns, for handing over learning activities to children is not always easy. However, unless such a transference occurs children will not learn for themselves. Establishing effective discussion in groups takes time. Some children find it difficult to take responsibility for their own learning and initially their work may be hesitant and uncertain. Time pressure is a constant concern for teachers and there may be a temptation not to pursue group work, especially if the initial results appear to be both messy and complex.

Research evidence suggests that pupils actually engage in higher-order thinking when discussing questions or problems in groups. As Slater confirms, 'Through talk, children clarify their ideas, come to realize what they do not understand and yet work through what they do know to make new connections' (1989: 111). If the discussion tasks are clearly set, the duration of the group work firmly established, reporting back procedures clarified, and teacher interventions timed correctly, the results can be impressive.

Group work has the added advantage of giving all children the chance of saying something in class. It also helps them to develop their social skills and to take greater control of their own learning. Handling group work requires a deft, supportive and sensitive touch from the teacher, who must appreciate when to intervene and when to stand back. Over-enthusiastic interventions often take the initiative away from the pupils, who should be developing an understanding of their roles and responsibilities in maintaining discussions and completing set tasks.

What has become clear is that teachers who have a restrictive and dominant teaching style, often involving a lot of traditional 'chalk and talk', impair their pupils' learning and concept development through restricting pupil talk. The importance of teacher control is not denied, but there must be opportunities for pupils to advance their learning through discussion.

Writing

In examining the learning associated with writing it is first necessary to understand the different forms that both talking and writing can take – namely transactional, expressive and poetic. The transactional form is the one most commonly evident in geography lessons, being used to convey factual information, express ideas and concepts, and record facts in an ordered and logical sequence. Expressive forms of writing (or talking) are more personal and exploratory, what Slater refers to as 'thinking aloud on paper' (1989: 112). They reveal what the writer feels or believes, and are not inhibited by the more formal and structured patterns regularly seen in the transactional mode. Importantly, expressive language often represents the first stages of exploring new ideas and concepts that have not yet been fully clarified in the writer's mind. Poetic forms are similar to expressive, with words being arranged to provide a pleasing format for writer and reader, often involving metaphorical or figurative use of language.

Transactional language dominates the geography classroom. Teachers regularly engage in transactional writing and talking in a form that is clearly structured, ordered and professional. The purpose of using this type of language is clear – it is efficient in conveying information and 'getting things done'. Teachers also expect children to use transactional language when addressing them both orally and in writing, but often do not appreciate the steps that children must go through to produce such language successfully. The insistence upon transactional language can actually restrict the learning process:

> The demand for impersonal, unexpressive writing can actively inhibit learning because it isolates that which is to be learned from the vital learning process – that of making links between what is already known and the new information.

> It is through the tentative, inarticulate, hesitant, backward- and forward-moving, expressive mode that connections and links between old and new knowledge can be made. Then a student may be ready to set the understanding down in a formal transactional mode.
>
> (Slater 1983: 113)

Or:

> The demand for transactional writing in schools is ceaseless, but expressive language with all its vitality and richness is the only possible soil from which it can grow.
>
> (Rosen 1975: 190)

Geography demands transactional writing because of the very nature of the subject, but it must be realized that children have problems in producing such writing. Merely copying notes from the teacher, or filling missing words into gaps in a worksheet, does produce a form of transactional writing but may not help the pupil learn from the writing experience.

Research has recently moved our thinking forward to consider more closely the audiences which should receive these forms of writing, and the purposes for which they were written. Closely associated with this is the concept of genres which have been debated among certain English teachers in Australia and England.

Audience

Expressive language can be encouraged by getting children to write for (or talk to) different audiences from those which they normally encounter in their classroom-based work (Martin *et al.* 1976; Williams 1981; Slater 1983; Carter 1991). The theory is that by getting pupils to write for realistic audiences (often other than the teacher) the immediacy of the teacher's assessing role will be downplayed, and the pupils will engage in more exploratory forms of writing.

The variety of audiences that pupils could write for are recorded by Britton *et al.* (1975), and later by Slater (1983), and can be summarized as follows:

- pupil to self;
- pupil to trusted adult;
- pupil to teacher, as partner in a dialogue;
- pupil to teacher, as examiner or assessor;
- pupil to pupil, or peer group;
- pupil to younger child.

The list can be extended by considerations of other audiences such as 'teacher as peer', 'teacher as layperson', 'teacher as working group member', and 'adult other than teacher' either within or outside school (Carter 1991).

The task for the teacher of creating both an original audience for children to write for, and establishing an understanding that this audience (rather than the 'teacher as assessor') is the main focus for their work, is difficult but not impossible. In classroom-based research carried out by Butt (1993), such audiences were created with the intention of helping children's writing in geography lessons to become more original, individual and creative. It was postulated that changing the audiences that pupils wrote for might change their thought, learning and under-standing processes and ultimately improve their writing and talking in geography lessons.

Through pupil-centred discussion and the use of varied teaching resources, followed by writing for different audiences (such as an aid agency, a wood-gatherer, shanty-town dweller, hospital consultant, television audience, MP, etc.), the children often displayed a deeper understanding of the geography being studied and a greater appreciation of values and attitudes. Butt (1993) devised a matrix for analysing the 'levels of geographical attainment children achieved' against their 'sense of audience', concluding that in many cases changing the audience has some effect on the learning process. Also of interest was a range of secondary effects such as the increase in work-related discussion, pupil questioning, perception of the audience's viewpoints, clarification of personal values, and use of the teacher as a 'geographical consultant'.

However, there were certain preconditions to audience-centred learning, namely:

- that a sense of trust and purpose needs to be established before good audi-ence-centred writing will appear – boys did not reveal this sense of trust as readily as girls;
- that removing the idea of teacher as assessor in pupils' minds is important, but also extremely difficult;
- that audience-centred writing should be integrated into schemes of work, but not over-used;
- that audiences should be realistic and plausible;
- that if levels of pupil involvement, discussion and enquiry are allowed to increase through audience-centred work geographical attainment may also rise.

(Butt 1993: 22)

Genres

Genre theory has moved the debate about language forms into considerations of the 'kinds and types' of language used in everyday life (Andrews 1992). The term 'genre' is regularly used in a wide variety of contexts, from descriptions of films and paintings to types of speech and literature. Within its narrower educational context genre theorists have used the term with reference to investigations into the styles of children's writing and textual forms and for debating the significance of the origins of writing processes (Kress 1989). They conclude that the genre and style of writing is closely related to the audience for whom one is writing and to the social context in which the writing takes place.

By extension genre theorists believe that children will not produce different forms of written language if they do not have access to various genres, or the chances to experiment with them. As Butt concludes:

> Thus genres have a fundamental role in language use, because they are closely linked to the audience one is communicating with and the ways in which information is received and understood by that audience. When teachers give children a writing task they must therefore be fully aware of its implied purpose and function, and the audience for which it is being prepared ... If the genre the teacher expects from the child is one that he or she has little or no experience of, then the writing task will most probably not be completed satisfactorily.
>
> (Butt 1993: 16)

Genre theory has its critics though. Rosen (1988), Stratta and Dixon (1992) and others believe that such writing can flourish only if children are placed into realistic contexts with believable audiences. They also need to have the necessary language resources to complete their tasks: two not inconsiderable assumptions!

Before moving on from any discussion about pupil writing it is important to mention briefly the marking of such work. Without becoming too embroiled in deliberations about assessment within the National Curriculum, it is essential that teachers realize the impact that their style of marking has on the motivation of pupils. Teachers who tend to mark as 'examiners', where brief comments are often accompanied by a grade or mark, may have the effect on some pupils of forcing them to try to conceal their lack of understanding. Instead of 'learning through writing', where they will express their own thoughts and feelings, these children attempt to present writing which (in their experience) the teacher values.

In addition, over-enthusiastic correction of every mistake of grammar, spelling and punctuation can be extremely disheartening to some pupils and may dissuade them from writing at all. In general, the use of praise and positive teacher comments, where appropriate, may help to encourage the reluctant writer and start a discussion between the teacher and learner about the geography being studied.

Reading

In geography lessons pupils have to be proficient in a wide range of reading skills. We expect them to acquire the ability to read worksheets, texts, instructions and technical information, as well as carry out specialized non-linguistic reading such as 'reading' maps (graphicacy), satellite images and systems diagrams. Nevertheless, pupils actually spend comparatively small amounts of time reading the written word in most geography classes.

Children often encounter difficulties when reading because texts rarely give clues to their meaning in quite the same ways that spoken words can. There is no intonation, inflection, questioning, gesture or stress in written geography (unless it is read out loud), especially when compared to the oral, visual and body language clues given by most teachers when speaking in class. However, the reader has the advantage that he or she can go back and forward over a text at the speed most appropriate to learning and understanding it, a process that cannot be achieved with the spoken word without the aid of a tape recording or unrestricted questioning. This does not always guarantee comprehension though, since some texts are simply too difficult for the reader to understand.

The length and complexity of sentences in texts and worksheets, together with unfamiliar and technical words, density of text, font size and abstraction of concepts can also make pupil understanding a problem. Indeed, sometimes it is possible to understand all the words in a sentence individually, but not as a whole sentence.

Robson's research (1983) has shown how pupils approach the task of reading and comprehending texts, and what kind of reading/reader is implied by the way in which the text is written. She finds that readability tests related to sentence lengths, syllable numbers and word counts are only partly of use in understanding children's reading difficulties as they do not see the central importance of the reader in the process. Interviews with teachers and sixth formers discovered that few of the students had the competence expected of the 'implied reader', that they were often frustrated by texts, and could not easily link together text, maps, tables, photographs and diagrams to benefit from the whole. Some understanding was gained by pupils, but this was usually localized or merely re-confirmed impressions about geography that had been gained from other sources. Reading therefore becomes selective and incomplete. In some cases teachers are unaware of their pupil's difficulties because they themselves can easily engage with, and understand, the text in a variety of ways.

DARTS

DARTS (or Directed Activities Related to Texts) are designed to help children develop their reading skills and understand texts more fully. The teacher chooses the aspect of the text upon which they want the pupils to concentrate and issues instructions to enable them to focus on the text's structure and meaning. This may involve underlining key words, deleting parts of a text for pupils to replace (using either their own words, or words supplied by the teacher), re-forming a text under given headings, hypothesizing about the ending to a piece of text, or comparing more than one text and looking for similarities and differences.

In many DARTS pupils are asked either to re-create or re-organize text in a more easily understood form. In Geography these activities might usefully be supplemented by the pupils creating a diagram or a table from the written information already provided. Alternatively, according to the nature of the text being analysed, the teacher may wish the pupils to underline aspects of content, arguments, opinions, advantages, disadvantages, or even create classifications. Often pupils can be encouraged to talk through their findings with a partner or in small groups, or even present a more formal version of the text's content to the rest of the class.

Some DARTS require pupils to sequence text that has been disarranged by the teacher. This helps pupils to concentrate on the structure of a text in relation to its meaning and flow of ideas (Table. 14.2).

Table 14.2 Example of a sequencing DART: tea

1	Fermentation in a cool, damp room to make black tea
2	The plants are pruned so they becomes bushes not trees
3	Two leaves and a bud are picked from each plant
4	Tea is sold in an auction, e.g. London
5	Into our teapots
6	The land is cleared and the soil broken up and fertilized, ready for planting
7	For green tea the process stops here
8	Different types of tea are blended together
9	Tea is packed into chests ready for export
10	The harvested tea is taken to a special building for withering
11	Young tea plants are grown in nurseries
12	Plants are covered by bamboo frames to shade them from the sun
13	The tea is taken to a factory to be packeted
14	Tea is taken by van to the shops and supermarkets
15	Firing – to produce the black tea we drink
16	The leaves are rolled to remove any remaining juices
17	The plants are transplanted to fields on the hillsides
18	Plants are sprayed to prevent disease

Source: Simons and Plackett (1984).

Geographical terminology

Geography has its own specialist language and terminology which can create problems for pupils. However, the use of technical language is necessary to help advance the development of pupils' understanding of geographical concepts. Many of the terms geographers use are homonyms, words which are similar to those with everyday meanings but which have a special significance in geography. For example pupils will be aware of words such as 'space', 'city', 'communications', 'market', 'labour', 'environment' and 'energy', but may be unaware of their particular and specialist meanings in geography. Learning the terms used in geography is important as a precursor to geographical concept development, but merely rote learning these terms does not imply that concepts are being understood (Milburn 1972). Therefore the teacher needs to set oral or written exercises to probe the pupils' understanding of these concepts.

Conclusions

As Carter (1991: 2) implies, children should be encouraged to use language in geography lessons for a wide range of audiences and purposes. It should be a vehicle to help them engage more closely with the geography they are learning, rather than hindering or frustrating their understanding. They may have to restructure or transform the written or spoken word to appreciate its meaning, as well as being given opportunities to reflect upon their own use of language. All of these tasks will occur only with the support and guidance of the teacher. They are central to achieving new learning.

If geography teachers constantly emphasize the use of language solely as a tool to control, discipline and assess pupils they will fail to achieve its potential in promoting learning. A variety of pupil-centred talking, writing and reading activities in Geography provides the basis for the larger development referred to in this chapter.

References

Andrews, R. (1992) 'Editorial' in *English in Education*, 26(2): 1–3.
Britton, J. *et al.* (1975) *The Development of Writing Abilities (11–18)*, London: Macmillan.
Butt, G. (1993) 'The effects of audience centred teaching on children's writing in Geography', *International Research in Geographical and Environmental Education* 2(1): 11–24.
Carter, R. (ed.) (1991) *Talking about Geography*, Sheffield: Geographical Association.
Chomsky, N. (1968) *Language and Mind*, New York: Harcourt Brace Jovanovich.
DES (1975) *A Language for Life: The Bullock Report*, London: HMSO.
Hull, R. (1985) *The Language Gap*, London: Methuen.
Kress, G.R. (1989) 'Texture and meaning', in Andrews, R. (ed.) *Narrative and Argument*, Milton Keynes: Open University Press.
Marsden, W.E. (1995) *Geography 11–16: Rekindling Good Practice*, London: David Fulton Publishers.
Martin, N. *et al.* (1976) *Writing and Learning Across the Curriculum*, London: Ward Lock.
Milburn, D. (1972) 'Children's vocabulary', in N.J. Graves (ed.) *New Movements in the Study and Teaching of Geography*, London: Heinemann.
Piaget, J. (1959) *Language and Thought of the Child*, London: Routledge.
Roberts, M. (1986) 'Talking, reading and writing', in D. Boardman (ed.) *Handbook for Geography Teachers*, Sheffield: Geographical Association.
Robson, C. (1983) 'Making sense of discourse', unpublished MA thesis, University of London, Institute of Education.
Rosen, H. (1975) in *A Language for Life: The Bullock Report*, London: HMSO.
Rosen, M. (1988) 'Will genre theory change the world?', *English in Australia* 88: 18–23.
Simons, M. and Plackett, E. (eds) *The English Curriculum: Reading and Comprehension*, London: English and Media Centre.
Slater, F. (1983) *Learning Through Geography*, London: Heinemann.
Slater, F. (ed.) (1989) *Language and Learning in the Teaching of Geography*, London: Routledge.
Stratta, L. and Dixon, J. (1992) 'The National Curriculum in English: does genre theory have anything to offer?', *English in Education*, 26(2): 16–27.
Vygotsky, L.S. (9162) *Thought and Language*, Cambridge, MA: MIT Press.
Williams, M. (ed.) (1981) *Language Teaching and Learning: Geography*, London: Ward Lock.

Section 3

Geography for the twenty-first century

The six chapters in Section 3 raise questions that need to be answered in order to ensure the well-being of Geography in the future. As in the previous section there were more questions than space available to explore them. These chapters therefore represent just some of the diversity of challenges that Geography faces in the twenty-first century.

The newly established Geo Visions project outlined in Chapter 15 takes a fresh look at what young people today want from geographical education, and from that explores some of the ways in which we might meet those aspirations. In the following chapter, Alan Reid looks at the new requirement in the latest revision to the National Curriculum (2000) for Geography that requires the teaching of 'environmental changes and sustainable development' rather than 'environmental relationships and issues' as given in the previous National Curriculum for Geography. He examines the relationship between environmental education and education for sustainable development and discusses some of the issues relating to teaching effectively about environmental change and sustainable development. Paul Machon's review of citizenship and its links to Geography is the theme of Chapter 17. He links his ideas to the statement produced by the Geographical Association on Geography's role in contributing to citizenship education. Following on from that, John Huckle sets out a strong argument for the need to promote a deeper understanding of the relationship between geography and society. He argues for a revival of the critical tradition in geography education in order to meet the needs of a changing society. In Chapter 19, Doreen Massey outlines a case for the development of a new 'geographical imagination' in order to meet the challenges posed by globalization.

On a rather different note in the final chapter in this section we are presented with worrying trends in the numbers of students currently taking Geography at all levels from middle school through to initial teacher education. The negative feedback that this might create presents a threat to the future of Geography and perhaps adds an impetus to the need for geography educators to ensure that the subject remains relevant to the needs of the twenty-first century.

15 The Geo Visions project

Roger Carter, Roger Robinson, Scott Sinclair and project members

Introduction

This era of massive change means that the world and the conditions in it provide new horizons, structures and processes almost every day. It is vital, therefore, that education is constantly re-appraised to provide what is needed by young people to equip them as far as possible for the future. This need is brought home when you consider that in the year 2020 today's Year 2 pupils will be 30 years old.

There is a need to step back and make time for a fresh look at the future and its needs and possibilities, and to consider them in the context of justice and equality. The potential role of geography in young people's education, and especially its relationship with environmental sustainability, development education and global citizenship, is part of these debates.

The Geo Visions Project is an initiative that brings together educators and people outside formal education to:

- reflect and raise debate about the future needs of 5- to 19-year-olds, and
- consider how school Geography can contribute to the development of capabilities in young people and in the education system to satisfy these needs.

It is about the future beyond the year 2000, rather than modifications of the current curriculum in the immediate future. The Geo Visions Project builds on work undertaken over the last twenty years by the Development Education Centre (Birmingham) in partnership with geography teachers, which contributes locally and nationally to curriculum developments for 5- to 19-year-olds.

The focus for debate

Geo Visions starts from the question 'What kind of geographical education is needed for the twenty-first century?'. Within the aims listed overleaf Geo Visions raises debates about:

Methods in geography teaching

The move to keep school and lessons interesting is well-served by developments in enquiry learning. However, there needs to be frequent reassessment of the balance of methods being used, and of developments in learning/teaching and their application to school Geography.

The many theories, models and concepts in school Geography, their changing validity, appropriateness and value for understanding

For example, a few years ago 'core/periphery' concepts were a vital key for understanding economic development at all scales – from local to global. Each year the value of this model is further challenged by changes in technology, in organization, in relationships between place and economic development. School Geography can too easily become fossilized in an irrelevant world of the past. Educators must look at how they encourage the next generation to constantly explore reality and critique their past and present learning.

The themes and places chosen for study in school Geography

For example, at present the theme of 'globalization' is particularly important because inter-relationships constantly change. Again, without constant reappraisal, school Geography can become cluttered with outdated information and effectively ignore those places that have become very important and relevant to the students' lives.

The role of school Geography

Geography effectively bridges the humanities and the sciences which means its role in schools can change with circumstances. Moreover, it is often necessary to stand back from practical involvement in the curriculum in order to see the potential for a subject. Much of the value of geography is beyond basic skills acquisition.

Potential for change

The potential for change already exists within the education system: the revision of the National Curriculum is now seen as an ongoing process. What is needed is a thoughtful and creative broad view of school Geography, its role in the education of the whole human being and their needs in the future. The movement from concepts to capabilities is one major strand in education.

The need for wider views, openness and a longer-term vision is becoming increasingly accepted. More and more people see the rapid changes in the world leaving established structures either shattered and irrelevant or unable to accommodate new processes.

Geo Visions – aims

The aims of Geo Visions are listed below with specific points about what the project hopes to achieve.

Geo Visions will explore and raise debate about:

- The capabilities people will need in the twenty-first century to:
  - lead a fulfilled life, and
  - help create a better world.
- The key concepts and learning appropriate for school Geography so that it makes a contribution to the development of these capabilities.
- The relationships between school Geography and changes in the real world.
- The alternative roles of school Geography in education.

Geo Visions aims to create a time-tabled process that will lead to:

- Wider debate and consultation about the issues raised and their implications for geography curriculum planning and teaching.
- The integration of findings, where appropriate, into curriculum initiatives and planning new curriculums.
- The integration of findings into the content and methods of school Geography.

At the first meeting of Geo Visions in July 1998, Chris Durbin, John Huckle, Jeff Serf and Frances Slater provided four visions for school Geography. Summaries of these visions are included below; the full text and references for each are available on the DEC (Birmingham) website. The presentations of these four personal visions were followed by an open debate. This led to a series of group visions: the building blocks for these visions were then expressed as ideas during an extended workshop activity.

> Each generation perceives itself as justifiably different from its predecessor but plans as if its successor generation will be the same as them; this time it needs to be different.
>
> (Extract from Charles Handy, *The Empty Raincoat*, from Chris Durbin's Geo Vision)

Chris Durbin introduced his ideas with poetry and clips from BBC environmental teaching programmes (above and overleaf). He developed themes of uncertainty and confusion as he worked towards his personal Geo Vision, which Chris intended would develop *essential freedoms* – freedoms of movement, speech and information. This was set in a context of *trends on planet earth* that he summarized as uncertainty, complexity, transformation, paradox and chaos. Chris is aware that such trends contrasted with *trends in education* which he sees in the short term as:

- certainty
- simplicity
- progress
- causation
- organisation.

and, in the long term as:

- lifelong learning
- learning anywhere and everywhere
- blurred phases and stages
- digital, multimedia and on-line.

What the teacher said when asked 'what er we avin for geography miss?'

This morning I've got too much energy much too much for geography
I'm in a high mood
so class don't think me crude
but you can stuff latitude and longitude

I've had enough of the earth's crust today I want to touch the clouds
Today I want to sing out loud
and tear all maps to shreds
I'm not settling for river beds
I want the sky and nothing less

Today I couldn't care if east turns west
Today I've got so much energy
I could do press-ups on the desk
but that won't take much out of me

Today I'll dance on the globe in a rainbow robe
while you class remain seated
on your natural zone
with your pens and things
watching my contours grow wings

All right class, see you later.
If the headmaster asks for me
say I'm a million dreaming degrees beyond the equator
a million dreaming degrees beyond the equator

(Extract from a poem by John Agard, a Caribbean poet
(from Chris Durbin's Geo Vision)

Chris Durbin's Geo Vision is

If this group can produce a geography which enquires into

- emotions and moments, partial truth and perception
- the celebration of diversity
- uncertainty and complexity
- relationships with other cultures
- successes and failures
- now and the future

then the students of the future will be delighted!

John Huckle has a vision of a future critical school Geography which seeks to recover a radical tradition in geographical education. John provided three background papers: 'The objectives of global citizenship education', 'Manuel Castells on the network society' and 'Geography to change the world', and an outline for a series of Key Stage 3 geography textbooks.

John urged group members to acknowledge that the creation of Geo Visions involves political as well as philosophical choices. He reminded us that reality is process as well as form, and that this reality is experienced through senses and culture. He considered the nature of 'network' societies. John then focused on young people, recognising the growing significance of a cultural economy for them. He acknowledged the potential of Geography to develop young peoples' sense of identity as well as the knowledge, skills and values that contribute to global citizenship. John maps the tasks ahead for Geo Visions under five headings:

1   Philosophy and/or how school Geography should represent the world.
2   Culture and/or how to reflect the social construction of reality.
3   Post-modernity and/or how to account for a fast-changing world.
4   Young people and/or how to educate in ways that develop their sense of identity.
5   Global citizenship and/or how to find a new rationale for school Geography.

John's papers reflect a preference for a future school Geography based on dialectical materialism, critical pedagogy and democratic socialism. For instance, through the paper 'Geography to change the world' he hints at what such a school Geography might include.

Jeff Serf identified important factors that will influence the shape of things to come whether we like it or not. He developed a 'vision' of possibilities in the light of each. First, Jeff considered the 'movers and shakers' who monitor the curriculum, he then contrasted some of their ways with what he hopes for in the future:

... there will be open and honest debate about teaching and learning, about objectives and outcomes, processes and means. There will be meaningful discussion about issues relating to the new professionalism, what teachers need to teach, learners need to learn, and how best to achieve these goals.

Second, he considered *technology* and its potential use for both empowerment and oppression:

> In the future ... technology will support and empower teacher and learner in the education process. It will not be, to misquote Freire (1972), the technology of the oppressed.

Turning his attention to the National Curriculum and Geography Jeff quoted recent critiques that suggested that young people can be robbed of their culture and rights by the exclusion of their experience from the curriculum and its language. He hopes to see a geographical education that is valued by all, and a Geography that reflects and stimulates intellectual development:

> In the future ... teaching and learning will occur in an environment that reflects and simulates intellectual development. All teachers and learners will be included in all aspects of the education process so they can, in turn, be included in all aspects of their communities; local to global.

Frances Slater used research as a starting point for her Geo Vision. She recounted the stories of five research projects in geographical education to show how assumed 'truths' and single viewpoints are often found embedded and unchallenged in school Geography. As links between language and learning are of particular concern to Frances, she explained some ideas and concepts from this field in order to emphasise the *subjectivity of all texts*. Frances asserts that these all include viewpoints and bias and the possibility of *alternative meanings* which can be ascribed to them. In other words, texts are not a mirror of the world.

Frances suggested that if the word 'texts' be used to replace 'resources' in the classroom it might help to change perceptions and shed a new light on teaching and learning processes.

The Geo Vision that Frances presented is of teachers who understand the process of constructing and re-constructing reality in the classroom. It is of a Geography that encourages learners to be more sceptical of texts, emphasises argumentation and helps to create critical questioning people. To quote Frances:

> The delight of their research for me was that they made me think and think again, as they asked their questions and developed conversations with others through 'the literature' and in classrooms. Geography teaching and environmental education benefits from the searching and re-searching of people/society/culture/environment relations as taught and constructed and re-constructed in classrooms. It makes us think again about its complexity and embeddedness, about the delicacies of understanding needed to teach it.

A shared vision

At the second Geo Visions meeting in October 1998, Tony Thomas (Field Studies Council) and Eleanor Rawling (Consultant in Geographical Education) offered overviews of the ideas arising from the July meeting.

Tony used the analogy of marketing a product for consumers to remind us how important consultation, dissemination and influence are if the ideas are to take effect.

Eleanor suggested that a group as diverse as Geo Visions should look for 'Highest common factors' (HCFs) rather than feeling that consensus would mean descent to the 'Lowest common denominator' (LCD). She identified several HCFs in Geo Visions from the work so far:

- focus on children/young people as learners;
- re-emphasize professionalism of teachers;
- emphasis on 'deep learning' not content coverage;
- move to a school Geography which is relevant to young people's lives;
- use technology imaginatively.

Besides these beginnings of consensus several issues have arisen within the group. Among these are discussions around the importance or otherwise of teachers' understanding of modern social and political theory, and debates about the balance between an all-out subject-based struggle for curriculum time and emphasis on Geography's contribution to citizenship, sustainable environment and social education.

Beyond these areas of difference a shared vision is emerging. In the October meeting the group somewhat hesitantly moved away from the current conventional curriculum planning model (content, skills, values) to debate within themes that emerged from work on Geo Visions.

The 'cards' in Figure 15.1 were amongst those written and agreed by groups in response to the question:

> What are the most important 'things' (themes, issues, concepts, areas, ideas) … that the Geo Visions Project should address if we are to help geographical education to play its part in meeting the needs of young people and enable them to live fulfilled lives and contribute to the making of a better world?

These led to four headings for enquiry: 'Knowledge and understanding', 'Children and young people', 'Society and change' and 'Dissemination and influence'. Further work has been agreed and is being pursued by members of the group, for example, as part of the inquiry under 'Knowledge and understanding', group members are:

- exploring and widening 'texts' in the sense explained by Frances Slater in her 'Geo Vision', and using these in classroom work;

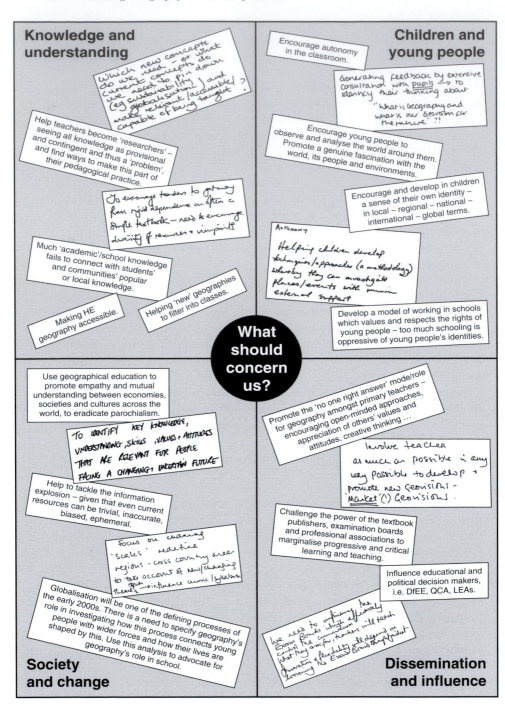

Knowledge and understanding

Which new concepts or what current concepts do we need to pin down (eg sustainability / globalisation) and make relevant /accessible / capable of being taught ?

Help teachers become 'researchers' – seeing all knowledge as provisional and contingent and thus a 'problem', and find ways to make this part of their pedagogical practice.

To encourage teachers to get away from rigid dependence on often a single textbook – need to encourage diversity of resources & viewpoints

Much 'academic'/school knowledge fails to connect with students' and communities' popular or local knowledge.

Making HE geography accessible.

Helping 'new' geographies to filter into classes.

Children and young people

Encourage autonomy in the classroom.

Generating feedback by extensive consultation with pupils → to identify their thinking about "what is Geography and what is our Geovision for the future "?

Encourage young people to observe and analyse the world around them. Promote a genuine fascination with the world, its people and environments.

Encourage and develop in children a sense of their own identity – in local – regional – national – international – global terms.

AUTONOMY

Helping children develop techniques / approaches (a methodology) whereby they can investigate places / events with minimum external support

Develop a model of working in schools which values and respects the rights of young people – too much schooling is oppressive of young people's identities.

What should concern us?

Use geographical education to promote empathy and mutual understanding between economies, societies and cultures across the world, to eradicate parochialism.

TO IDENTIFY KEY KNOWLEDGE, UNDERSTANDING, SKILLS, VALUES & ATTITUDES THAT ARE RELEVANT FOR PEOPLE FACING A CHANGING & UNCERTAIN FUTURE

Help to tackle the information explosion – given that even current resources can be trivial, inaccurate, biased, ephemeral.

Focus on changing 'scales' relative regions - cross country area to take account of new/changing themes influence ethnic / globalism

Globalisation will be one of the defining processes of the early 2000s. There is a need to specify geography's role in investigating how this process connects young people with wider forces and how their lives are shaped by this. Use this analysis to advocate for geography's role in school.

Promote the 'no one right answer' mode/role for geography amongst primary teachers – encouraging open-minded approaches, appreciation of others' values and attitudes, creative thinking ...

Involve teachers as much as possible in any way possible to develop + promote new Geovisions - Market (?) Geovisions.

Challenge the power of the textbook publishers, examination boards and professional associations to marginalise progressive and critical learning and teaching.

Influence educational and political decision makers, i.e. DfEE, QCA, LEAs.

We need to influence the Exam Boards which effectively control the curriculum – what they ask for, teachers will teach. Innovation & flexibility will depend on loosening the Exam Board stranglehold

Society and change

Dissemination and influence

Figure 15.1　A creative process: what should concern us?

- exploring concepts, especially globalization, global citizenship and sustainable development and the part they should play in school Geography;
- opening a dialogue between teachers, academics, examiners, students and parents for published debate about geographical education; and
- establishing contacts with other groups.

Geo Visions posed the following questions for geography educators:

- What do you think is important for the future of Geography and its contribution to education?
- What do your pupils/students want from Geography?
- What should geography be offering them?
- In what direction should geography educators be encouraging school Geography to develop?
- How can geography educators influence the educators influence the education system, share their visions and move towards them?

Acknowledgement

This article was prepared in association with the Geo Visions Project members: Nicola Arber, Elisabeth Barratt Hacking, Susan Bermingham, Tony Binns, Steve Brace, Roger Carter (Chair, co-ordinator), Claire Dabner, Chris Durbin, Roger Firth, John Hopkin, John Huckle, Lisa James, Lucy Kirkham, David Lambert, Margaret Mackintosh, John Morgan, John Morris, Eleanor Rawling, Roger Robinson (co-ordinator), Jeff Serf, Scott Sinclair (co-ordinator), Frances Slater, Diane Swift, Steve Thomas, Linda Thompson, Roger Wassell-Smith, Sophie Yangopoulo.

Further information about Geo Visions and its aims can be found on the Tide/DEC website: www.tidec.org

Reference

Freire, P. (1972) *Pedagogy of the Oppressed*, Harmondsworth: Penguin.

16 Environmental change and sustainable development

Alan Reid

The purpose of this chapter is to provide guidance for geography teachers about environmental change and sustainable development at Key Stage 3 in the new National Curriculum for England (DfEE/QCA 1999). Education for sustainable development is inextricably linked with values and attitudes. It is vital, therefore, to reflect on and analyse your own practice, experience and ideas in ways which make sense of them and clarify your own views, so as to identify effective teaching strategies which will facilitate and support pupils' learning. As such, this chapter is intended to encourage discussion, analysis and reflection about:

- frameworks to assist analysis and evaluation of current practice;
- challenges about practice and/or underlying assumptions in 'environmental change and sustainable development';
- priorities for the next phase of curricular implementation, including approaches to these priorities, opportunities needed to address them, and how progress in relation to these priorities is monitored, i.e. action planning.

What is 'environmental change and sustainable development'?

In the new National Curriculum (DfEE/QCA 1999), the introductory statements about Geography at Key Stage 3 link 'environmental change and sustainable development' with the overall teaching objectives for geographical knowledge, skills and understanding:

> Teaching should ensure that geographical enquiry and skills are used when developing knowledge and understanding of places, patterns and processes, and environmental change and sustainable development.

Their importance to the Programme of Study is reinforced through their integration within statements about geographical enquiry and skills, including:

> In undertaking geographical enquiry, pupils should be taught to:
> 1e appreciate how people's values and attitudes, *for example, about overseas*

aid, including their own, affect contemporary social, environmental, economic and political issues, and (taught) to clarify and develop their own values and attitudes about such issues.

(The statements in italics indicate the non-statutory examples in the Orders.)

In terms of breadth of study, the new Order requires that geographical enquiry and fieldwork about environmental change and sustainable development are not treated as separate topics, but should combine with studies of place, physical and human patterns and processes, across the required countries, maps and themes, as typified by statements 6i–6k:

6i   development, including
   i   ways of identifying differences in development within and between countries;
   ii effects of differences in development on the quality of life of different groups of people;
   iii factors, including the interdependence of countries, that influence development.

6j   environmental issues, including
   i   how conflicting demands on an environment arise;
   ii how and why attempts are made to plan and manage environments;
   iii effects of environmental planning and management on people, places and environments, *for example, managing coastal retreat, building a reservoir.*

6k   resource issues, including
   i   the sources and supply of a resource;
   ii the effects on the environment of the use of a resource;
   iii resource planning and management *for example, reducing energy use, developing alternative energy sources.*

Specifically, at Key Stage 3 'knowledge and understanding of environmental change and sustainable development' requires that pupils should be taught to:

5a   describe and explain environmental change, *for example, deforestation, soil erosion,* and recognise different ways of managing it;
5b   explore the idea of sustainable development and recognise its implication for people, places and environments and for their own lives.

Such statements reinforce the distinctive contribution of geography to environmental understanding through emphasising the spatial dimension to environmental change, management and protection, coupled with the investigation of the interaction of people and environments (GA 1999a). At Key Stage 3 of course, this follows on from work at Key Stage 2, where in relation to environmental change and sustainable development pupils have been taught to:

5a   recognise how people can improve the environment, *for example, by reclaiming derelict land*, or damage it, *for example, by polluting a river*, and how decisions about places and environments affect the future quality of people's lives;

5b   recognise how and why people may seek to manage environments sustainably, and to identify opportunities for their own involvement, *for example, taking part in a local conservation project*.

While as part of the breadth of study at Key Stage 2, this will have included enquiries about:

6e   an environmental issue, caused by change in an environment for example, increasing traffic congestion, hedgerow loss, drought, and attempts to manage the environment sustainably, *for example, by improving public transport, creating a new nature reserve, reducing water use.*

How does 'environmental change and sustainable development' measure up?

Teachers will discuss, analyse and evaluate what is expected in the new Order. One approach is to compare the various statements with those in a range of similar initiatives. First and foremost, a comparison with previous versions of the National Curriculum shows a refocusing of the terminology for environment-related matters which echoes broader shifts in thinking about the environment (Barry 1999; Macnaughten and Urry 1998). Within geographical and environmental studies as well as school Geography and environmental education, key environmental concepts have been steadily moving away from meanings exclusively associated with natural environments, countryside/gardens, wilderness, and non-human nature. As within wider society, environmental concepts now embrace notions of urban and 'artificial' environments, along with sustainability and its relation to cultural, moral, spiritual, economic, social and political considerations, as the primary organising ideas for environmental learning (Huckle and Sterling 1996; Palmer 1998).

Is it still geography education?

The effective development of 'environmental change and sustainable development' in geography education requires a clear understanding of geography's purpose and its distinctive and wider contribution to the school's curriculum (GA, 1999b). The aims of geography education, as typified by the position statement from the GA (1999a), include:

•   to develop in young people a knowledge and understanding of where they live, of other people and places, and of how people and places interrelate and interconnect; of the significance of location; of human and physical environments; of people–environment relationships; and of the causes and consequences of change;

- to develop the skills needed to carry out geographical study, e.g. geographical enquiry, mapwork and fieldwork;
- to stimulate an interest in, and to encourage an appreciation of, the world around us;
- to develop an informed concern for the world around us, and an ability and willingness to take positive action both locally and globally.

Distinctive and wider contributions of Geography to the curriculum and environmental learning include investigating the links between people and physical environments and people–environment relationships, and environmental education and education for sustainable development, respectively (GA 1999a). By way of example, Geography in the National Curriculum was preceded by the publication of *Curriculum Guidance 7* on environmental education as a cross-curricular theme (NCC 1990) and was seen as a 'principal vehicle' for its 'delivery'. However, even from its inception with an attainment target across Key Stages 1–4 dedicated to environmental Geography (AT5) (DES 1991), links with environmental learning, and in particular, environmental education, have not always been as clear, strong and coherent as might have been expected (Chambers 1991; Tilbury 1997; Reid 1998).

Environmental Geography as an Attainment Target focused on: (i) the use and misuse of natural resources; (ii) the quality and vulnerability of different environments; and (iii) the possibilities for protecting and managing environments. Following the Dearing Review, a substantially slimmer version of Geography in the National Curriculum (DfE 1995) used the study of environmental change at Key Stage 2 to precede the investigation of environmental issues at Key Stage 3 (Thematic Studies 15):

In investigating environmental issues, pupils should be taught

a why some areas are viewed as being of great scenic attraction, and how conflicting demands on the areas can arise;

b how attempts are made to plan and manage such environments and how these can have unintended effects;

c how consideration of sustainable development, stewardship and conservation affect environmental planning and management;

and either

d about provision of a reliable supply of fresh water and the causes, effects and prevention of water pollution;

or

e about provision of a reliable supply of energy and the effect on the environment of the development of *two* different energy sources.

Although content phrases such as conflicting demands, natural resources and (non-)renewable resources, pollution, restoration, prevention, unintended effects, solutions to problems, stewardship and conservation, environmental planning and management are less prominent in the new Order, the priority given to curricular continuity, and the 'light touch' during the revision process, suggests that these ideas are still intended to interpret and embellish the statements in the National Curriculum. There may have been a semantic shift, but the new statements do not represent as radical a break with the past in geography education as has previously happened with the 're-visioning' of environmental education and environmental matters across the curriculum (Scott and Reid 1998).

Is it still environmental education or is it education for sustainable development, or ... ?

In addition to the content listed above, environmental change and sustainable development overlap with environmental education in terms of teaching and learning methodology. Tilbury (1997, p. 108), in listing the positive contributions to environmental education within school Geography, notes that 'geography education places emphasis on problem-solving and enquiry-learning, role-play, simulations and field-work which encourage pupils to carry out practical investigations and become actively involved in environmental management', or as the GA (1999a) puts it:

> Through geography, young people develop a knowledge and understanding of the concept of sustainable development, and the skills to act upon their understanding as part of, for example, Local Agenda 21 initiatives.

In the past, the statutory statements on these topics have been identified with Geography's contribution to pupils' environmental education (SCAA 1996). Thus we might also compare the statements about environmental change and sustainable development with those of environmental education and its heir apparent, education for sustainable development (SDEP 1999). The text box opposite illustrates some of the trends and themes in the aims and objectives of environmental education, while the text box on p. 231 sets out principles and definitions of education for sustainable development as developed by the Government's Sustainable Development Education Panel (SDEP).

Planning issues and involvement

A number of planning issues require more detailed consideration:

1   The broad aims for pupils being taught about environmental change and sustainable development tend to correspond with attempts to increase awareness through knowledge and understanding in environmental education and education for sustainable development. Attitudes and personal lifestyle decisions can be investigated (implicitly or explicitly), and unlike the previous

Aims and objectives in environmental learning

Environmental education is the process of recognising values and clarifying concepts in order to develop skills and attitudes necessary to understand and appreciate the inter-relatedness among man, his culture and his biophysical surroundings [sic]. Environmental education also entails practice in decision making and self-formulation of a code of behaviour about issues concerning environmental quality.

World Conservation Union (IUCN 1970)

Objectives for environmental education, as set out in the Belgrade Charter:

1   To foster clear awareness of and concern about economic, social, political and ecological interdependence in urban and rural areas.
2   To provide every person with opportunities to acquire knowledge, values, attitudes, commitment and skills to protect and improve the environment.
3   To create new patterns of behaviour of individuals, groups and society as a whole towards the environment.

(UNESCO 1976)

A liberal interpretation of the prepositional model of environmental education, based on the Tbilisi recommendations (Palmer 1998):

* education *about* the environment (that is, basic knowledge and understanding of the environment and human interactions, through studying the local or wider environment);
* education *in* or *through* the environment (that is, using the environment as a resource for learning, especially skills and competencies, with an emphasis on enquiry and investigation and pupils' first-hand experiences); and
* education *for* the environment (nurturing caring values, attitudes and positive action for the environment, through personal responsibility and empathy).

A socially critical interpretation of the prepositional model of environmental education (Fien 1993):

Education *about* the environment is the most common form of environmental education. Its objectives emphasise knowledge about natural systems and processes and the ecological, economic and political factors that influence decisions about how people use the environment.

(continued on next page)

Education *through* the environment uses pupils' experiences in the environment as a medium for education. The aims of this learner-centred approach to environmental education are to add reality, relevance and practical experience to learning and to provide pupils with an appreciation of the environment through direct contact with it … it may also foster environmental concern if pupils become captivated by the importance and fragility of ecosystems … or immersed in the values conflict over an environmental issue.

Education *for* the environment has an overt agenda of values education and social change. It aims to engage pupils in the exploration and resolution of environmental issues in order to … promote lifestyle changes that are compatible with the sustainable and equitable use of resources. In doing so it builds on education about and through the environment to help develop an informed concern for the environment, a sensitive environmental ethic, and the skills for participating in environmental protection and improvement.'

Order, the investigation and clarification of attitudes and values towards the environment (part of an 'education for the environment') are now required. However, despite considering how actions affect the environment, the statements do not advocate action for a better environment, nor do they explicitly encourage pupils' 'commitment to sustainable development', as set out in the aims introducing the new National Curriculum (DfEE/QCA 1999). Geography may be the lead subject, it may make discrete contributions or be used to support or enrich the wider curriculum. Through environmental change and sustainable development though, the requirements and opportunities will need to be interpreted creatively and effectively to balance and complete contributions to the environmental dimensions of citizenship as promoted in the text box aabove and by the SDEP (1999).

2   Achieving the goals of environmental education through knowledge and understanding of environmental change and sustainable development is more likely to favour the cognitive dimensions to learning at the expense of the affective, ethical and action-orientated dimensions. The emphasis is on understanding sustainable development and the uses, abuses and threats to the environment, rather than admiring, respecting and experiencing the environment, and participating in the promotion and evaluation of local and wider forms of sustainable development (see text boxes on pp. 233 and 241). Omitted from 'education for sustainable development' but encouraged by 'education in the environment', the role of emotions in learning – like excitement, admiration, awe and bewilderment – may be underplayed; although if a more prominent role is given to fieldwork and out-of-school learning in environmental change and sustainable development, this

Education for sustainable development

> Education is critical for promoting sustainable development and improving the capacity of the people to address environment and development issues ... It is critical for achieving environmental and ethical awareness, values and attitudes, skills and behaviour consistent with sustainable development and for effective public participation in decision making.
>
> (UNCED 1992)

Definitions

Two definitions of education for sustainable development are offered by the Sustainable Development Education Panel (SDEP 1999, p. 30). The first is aimed at policy makers.

> Education for sustainable development is about the learning needed to maintain and improve our quality of life and the quality of life of generations to come. It is about equipping individuals, communities, groups, businesses and government to live and act sustainably; as well as giving them an understanding of the environmental, social and economic issues involved. It is about preparing for the world in which we will live in the next century, and making sure that we are not found wanting.

The second is aimed at the schools sector:

> Education for sustainable development enables people to develop the knowledge, values and skills to participate in decisions about the way we do things individually and collectively, both locally and globally, that will improve the quality of life now without damaging the planet for the future.

Key concepts of sustainable development

Sustainable development concerns a wide range of interrelated issues which may be approached through the following seven principles or dimensions. The first concerns the interdependent nature of the world. This gives rise to the need for a participative response through the exercise of citizenship and stewardship, which is the theme of second concept.

The third through to sixth concepts cover further key dimensions of sustainable development, leading to the seventh which, as a logical

(*continued on next page*)

consequence of those that precede, is concerned with the limits of knowledge and exercise of the precautionary principle.

1   Interdependence – of society, economy and the natural environ-
     ment, from local to global.
2   Citizenship and stewardship – rights and responsibilities, participa-
     tion and cooperation.
3   Needs and rights of future generations.
4   Diversity – cultural, social, economic and biological.
5   Quality of life, equity and justice.
6   Sustainable change – development and carrying capacity.
7   Uncertainty, and precaution in action.

(SDEP 1999: 31).

The principles are exemplified with guidance statements in the *SDEPs First
Annual Report* (SDEP 1999). General learning outcomes and specific
learning outcomes at each Key Stage associated with the seven key concepts
are also listed there, and at:

   http://www.environment.detr.gov.uk/sustainable/educpanel/1998ar/ann4.htm

might be avoided. Such unevenness to the contributions favours an additive
rather than holistic approach to environmental learning (Sterling and Cooper
1992). It does not explicitly 'join up' these dimensions of an 'education for sustainable development' with other new agenda areas, like citizenship and PSHE. With
limited evidence of 'joined-up thinking' at a policy level, making the links to
develop environmental responsibility and environmental competence will require
careful planning and attention within and across departments, particularly if it is
not to be left to the pupils alone, as has happened previously.

3   In being grounded in the topic of *environmental change,* with pupils being
     taught how people affect the environment, and how and why people seek to
     manage and sustain their environment, contributions to environmental
     learning may become associated primarily with environmental problems
     and their solutions, rather than with environmental appreciation. This
     state of affairs fits quite readily with an issues-based, people-environment
     tradition of enquiry in geography, but less so with other traditions which
     draw on regional, cultural and critical geographies (Marsden 1995). The
     value of these other traditions is that they may be employed by teachers to
     challenge the continued dichotomy between 'people and the environment',
     recognising people as being *a part of*, as well as *apart from*, their own and
     others' environments. A shift in emphasis away from nature, experience
     and interpretation and towards sustainable development may risk
     marginalising these traditions in geography education.

Making use of Local Agenda 21

In 1992, 178 countries attending the United Nations Conference on Environment and Development (UNCED: the Rio 'Earth Summit') signed Agenda 21. Agenda 21 is a non-binding treaty that sets out a framework of political recommendations designed to protect the environment and move towards sustainable development. One chapter of the Agenda is devoted to educational issues in the broader sense. It is here that specific mention of the role of education in promoting Agenda 21 is made. Section 36.5 recognises that, to be effective, environmental and development education should be included in all disciplines at all levels of education.

Bullard (1998) describes an activity for undergraduates where seminar discussions and Internet resources are used to stimulate debate and enhance pupils' understanding of Local Agenda 21 as part of a series of learning activities on resource management. Emphasis is placed on exploring local authorities' Local Agenda 21 strategies and examining how these are being implemented and monitored. This technique can be adapted to Key Stage 3 schemes of work that seek to investigate the methods and motives for local environmental management, and the ways in which global-scale policy decisions are filtered down to the level of the individual. The following enquiry questions might be used to structure the learning, with teachers and pupils working in conjunction with Local Agenda 21 officers to investigate local solutions to wider problems:

- Which aspects of sustainability are being concentrated upon in Local Agenda 21 action plans?
- To what extent is your local authority's strategy a 'wish list'?
- Exactly how is sustainability going to be achieved?
- How will the effects of the Local Agenda 21 strategy be monitored?
- How is public participation in Local Agenda 21 being encouraged?
- On which environmental resources does the Local Agenda 21 strategy focus? Why do you think this might be?

As suggested by Bullard's exercise, teachers, pupils and the wider community might also ask:

- What do you consider to be the role of the school in Local Agenda 21? How is the school and its members already involved?
- How do the actions and proposals in the Local Agenda 21 strategies relate to other geographical themes in your schemes of work?
- Is Local Agenda 21 likely to be an effective route to environmental management in the school and community?

(continued on next page)

The exercise can make extensive use of the Internet to provide high-volume information from a diversity of sources and at low cost to the institution. Bullard's case studies use links to Tagish's *Directory of UK Local Authority websites* and the UK Government's list of organizations which list all UK local authority websites. Web addresses for these are, respectively: http://www.tagish.co.uk/tagish/links/localgov.htm and http://www.open.gov.uk/index/filclgov.htm

The full text of Agenda 21 is available from a number of sources including a United Nations supported website at gopher://gopher.un.org:70/11/conf/unced/English.

In general, the most detailed information is available by county councils and city councils rather than borough councils, with very comprehensive coverage of LA21 strategies from Surrey County Council (http://www.surreycc.gov.uk/scc/environment/country.html), Cheshire County Council (http://www.cheshire.gov.uk:80/cheshpln/la2l/eb.htm) and Newcastle-upon-Tyne City Council: http://www.newcastle-city-council.gov.uk/ag2lb.htm

(adapted from Bullard 1998)

4   The command phrase 'taught to', with its didactic and instructional overtones, has become commonplace throughout the programme of study. 'Taught why' – as with statement 15a in the previous Order – does not appear, but of course, that does not mean it will not happen. Being 'taught why' can facilitate the study of values and attitudes, as in the statements about the breadth of study. This presents teachers with opportunities to develop a more critical and evaluative approach to teaching and learning in geography, and hence about the environment.

5   Despite the welcome, flexibility and room for interpretation that the new Order represents, the flip side is that the distinct lack of elaboration may fail to challenge misconceptions, inaccurate knowledge, and received wisdom regarding environmental change and sustainable development. The difficulty of applying the level descriptions to accredit learning across the breadth of the Key Stage is a case in point. The level descriptions remain indirectly related to the statements, requiring the judgement of teachers in deciding which description best fits the pupil's performance. The levels exhibit examples of progression, but they do not always apply to environmental change and sustainable development equally. For example, only levels 7 and 8 and 'exceptional performance' make direct reference to sustainable development, accrediting only a minority of pupils for their understanding of 'how considerations of sustainable development can affect their own lives as well as the planning and management of environments and resources'.

So what might be done?

Guidance about environmental change and sustainable development is inadequate if it dwells on the 'why' questions without addressing the 'how' and the 'who', or if it fails to acknowledge the difficulties sometimes associated with bringing about curricular change. Despite what was presented in text boxes on pages 229 and 231, geography education, environmental education and education for sustainable development are not uncontentious, and we cannot simply presume a shared professional understanding of them in terms of what they are each setting out to achieve. Scott, in discussing disagreements regarding the goals for education on themes like environmental change, environmental citizenship and sustainable development, highlights its implications for curriculum planning and change:

> The lack of consensus within schools about how environmental education should or might be experienced by pupils, and to what end, compounds this difficulty, as it makes creating an implementation strategy problematic.
>
> (Scott 1999: 108)

Scott's recommendation is to begin locally with where children, teachers and communities are, and work from there in an inclusive way. This involves developing a shared recognition of differing ideas about and priorities for the aims and outcomes of education, approaches to teaching and learning in these aspects of the curriculum, and the professional competences needed by teachers for their work in schools (Scott 1999: 110).

Making 'environmental change and sustainable development' happen

Following a wide-ranging survey of environmental learning across Europe, Sterling and Cooper (1992) argued that its effectiveness at any level, from children to policy makers, depended on a number of conditions, in that it needs to:

- be planned, and preferably long term;
- be holistic in conception and practice, rather than narrowly based;
- be inclusive of action skills, rather than just aiming at raising awareness and understanding;
- be resourced and supported;
- have free access to environmental information;
- use a variety of approaches and methodologies;
- be participative;
- use means of communication appropriate to local circumstances and cultures; and
- encourage two-way communication between teachers and learners, and between all levels of society.

The following sections and the resource list in the text box on p. 239 illustrate these points further.

Planning for inclusion and effectiveness in the department and school

Teachers' planning for schemes of work often starts from the Programmes of Study and the needs and abilities of their pupils. Although level descriptions can help to determine the degree of challenge, differentiation and progression for work across each year of a Key Stage, the integration of environmental learning throughout the curriculum means that professional issues are not reduced to those of the single subject alone. Wider issues regarding whole-school approaches and policies, school planning and the design and management of the curriculum, departmental schemes of work, range of learning experiences, and comparable assessment, monitoring and reporting, are all part of supporting learning and achievement in environmental change and sustainable development.

To illustrate, the recommendations made by the SDEP about 'education for sustainable development' (ESD) did not find their way as fully into the requirements of the Order as other 'new agenda' areas like citizenship. However, ESD is now included in the new rationale for the school curriculum (non-statutory), and is featured most heavily in science and design and technology (both statutory) in addition to Geography, with 'environmental change and sustainable development' being seen as part of this contribution. ESD is also contained within the new area of citizenship (statutory at Key Stages 3 and 4).

Other opportunities where teachers might expect environmental learning to inform activities include provision within the stated aims of the school, tutor periods and assemblies. Members of the school may have links with external initiatives, source of expertise and financial support on environmental matters, whether in the local area, nationally or internationally. Pupils may be exchanging information and comparing attitudes and values about environmental change and sustainable development with pupils with different nationalities and cultural backgrounds. Schools may have policies and co-ordinators for environmental management and environmental education which staff and/or pupils are involved in. Environmental change and sustainable development may be raised in meetings involving departments, staff, parents and liaison; it might also be part of non-National Curriculum work and special curricular events, and community work and extra-curricular activities. Accordingly, the wider life, physical environment and ethos of the school, and colleagues' interests, may each affect the priority given to these areas.

The Council for Environmental Education (1998) (see text box on p. 241) argues that clear and effective leadership, management, support and involvement in this work across the school may contribute to:

- enriching lives and lifelong learning;
- raising standards of achievement;
- developing active and responsible citizenship;
- commitment to sustainable development.

In terms of effectiveness in planning for teaching and learning, these are

Table 16.1 A framework of geography 'styles' of teaching and learning

Stage of teaching and learning	Closed	Framed	Negotiated
Questions	Questions not explicit or questions remain the teacher's questions.	Questions explicit, activities planned to make pupils ask questions.	Pupils decide what they want to investigate under guidance from teacher.
Data	Data selected by teacher, presented as authoritative, not to be challenged.	Variety of data selected by teacher, presented as evidence to be interpreted.	Pupils are helped to find their own data from sources in and out of school.
Interpretation	Teacher decides what is to be done with data, pupils follow instructions.	Methods of interpretation are open to discussion and choice.	Pupils choose methods of analysis and interpretation in consultation with teacher.
Conclusions	Key ideas presented, generalisations are predicted, not open to debate.	Pupils reach conclusions from data, different interpretations are expected.	Pupils reach own conclusions and evaluate them.
Summary	The teacher controls the knowledge by making all decisions about data, activities, conclusions. Pupils are not expected to challenge what is presented.	The teacher inducts pupils into ways in which geographical knowledge is constructed, so that they are enabled to use these ways to construct knowledge themselves. Pupils are made aware of choices and are encouraged to be critical.	Pupils are enabled by the teacher to investigate questions of concern and interest to themselves.

Source: Roberts (1996: 240).

associated with *coverage, continuity, progression, teaching objectives, assessment, recording and reporting* (GA 1999b). *Coverage* will involve linking environmental learning in Geography to the wider curriculum, e.g. citizenship, sustainable development education, and other subjects including those mentioned above. Positive outcomes for assessing provision in terms of attitudes, behaviour and personal development may include those features of effective teaching and learning that are also of interest to Ofsted:

- pupils reacting positively to, and showing respect for, their surroundings;
- pupils' behaviour being consistent within and beyond the classroom;
- pupils showing initiative and taking responsibility for environmental matters;
- pupils being aware of and acting on the environmental policies of the school;
- pupils showing empathy with others and debating issues openly

(CEE 1998)

Continuity involves building on prior knowledge, understanding and skills from Key Stage 2, as does ensuring that pupils make successful transitions from one school or Key Stage to another and from year to year (Jones 1999). For example, cross-phase liaison may reveal pupils' previous involvement at primary school in environmental award schemes like Eco-Schools, which tend to focus on reducing consumption of energy, water or other materials, and recycling and cutting waste.

A planned approach to work and *assessment* across schemes of work is required to reinforce and strengthen environmental understanding, awareness, responsibility and achievement. With regard to progression and access to environmental information, pupils need to do more than use best-selling textbooks (Kent 1996, Table 16.1 and text boxes on p. 233 and p. 239). Securing breadth of knowledge, depth of geographical understanding, and the use of geographical skills, attitudes and values involves attention to a range of teaching and learning strategies and styles.

Teaching and learning strategies and styles

Margaret Roberts (1996: 240, see Table 16.1) highlights the distinction between teaching strategies and teaching styles by suggesting that the former are found in a particular set of practices used by teachers in their teaching (e.g. for a particular part of a lesson), while the latter are the consistent set of practices used by teachers throughout their teaching (e.g. over a whole course). Planning opportunities for a variety of teaching and learning strategies and styles for environmental change and sustainable development is necessary because:

- pupils learn in different ways;
- pupils have different learning needs;
- some topics lend themselves to particular approaches;
- preparation for lifelong learning requires flexibility of approach;
- styles of assessment dictate styles of learning;
- some approaches are characteristic of, or distinctive to, geography (e.g. fieldwork).

(GA 1999b: 8)

Teaching strategies, outcomes and resources

Teaching strategies

Which of these strategies do you use in teaching and learning about 'environmental change and sustainable development'?

Didactic approaches	lecturing from teacher, presentation from pupil
Reading	fiction/non-fiction
Fieldwork	individual investigation, group investigation, interviewing, questionnaire, surveys, field sketching/recording
Problem solving	resolving a problem set
Assignment	resolving a problem set with multiple objectives or criteria
Experiential	visual, auditory, kinaesthetic, intrapersonal, interpersonal, scientific, logical
Creative	responding to specific stimuli, responding to varied stimuli
Discussion	classroom discussion led by the teacher, group discussion, dialogue in pairs, discussion and recording of ideas for future action
Action drama	role-playing situations, simulation of situations
Games	playing games relating to learning, devising games relating to learning
Experimental work	structured experiments, unstructured experiments
Observation	observing an activity, observing an event, observing the environment.

Which strategies lend themselves to environmental learning? Are there others you (might) use? How do they link with styles of assessment?

What constraints might there be to developing new strategies? How might you overcome these constraints?

Pupil activities

Which of the following pupil activities are most frequently used in teaching and learning about 'environmental change and sustainable development'?

(continued on next page)

Play, modelling, listening, reading, planning, calculating, word-processing, physical activity, assessing, recalling, designing, map reading, collecting, problem solving, illustrating, map drawing, investigation, watching, copying, interviewing, drawing, writing, observing, talking, measuring, composing, evaluating, researching, questioning, reviewing, singing, experimenting, performing, selecting, translating, discussing, computing, answering, asking, surveying.

Which are most appropriate?

Which are planned for, and which happen incidentally?

How do they relate to the work that pupils tend to produce in learning about environmental change and sustainable development, for example:

Written	report, diary, log, essay, story, questionnaire, letter, notes/draft, newspaper, magazine, storyboard, display
Visual	picture, poster, diagram, cross-section, transect, film, video, photograph, decoration, graph, chart, table, printout, demonstration, cartoon, speech bubbles, map
Oral	performance, role play, recorded discussions, recorded conversations, interview, debate, radio programme
3-D	model, sculpture, artefact, weather equipment, experiment.

What else might you look for as outcomes of learning about environmental change and sustainable development (see text boxes on pp. 229 and 231)?

Resource use

Which of the following resources are used in your department in teaching and learning about 'environmental change and sustainable development'?

Textbooks, videotapes, audiotapes, newspapers and magazines, field-work, photographs, maps, ICT, fiction, members of the local community.

How often are they used? How can you make these accessible to all (noting, for example, gender, ethnicity, ability)?

How might you plan to introduce a new resource?

(Based on GA 1999b: 8–9)

Taking action – pupils and teachers

Environmental change and sustainable development

Actions to implement Local Agenda 21 strategies in schools and communities might include individualistic measures such as reducing consumption, increasing recycling and developing environmental awareness, or wider plans for sustainable transport policies and reductions in energy use. These activities vary considerably in terms of the amount and quality of time and resources needed. Staff and pupil involvement may be influenced by general advertising, general media (newspapers, television, radio, etc.), local authority awareness campaigns or other educational activities. Pupils might evaluate their effectiveness, and of 'doing your bit' through posters and information sent out with electoral cards or council tax notification, awareness campaigns in the workplace, exhibitions and resources in local libraries, and leaflets and notices in local newspapers or local authority news sheets.

Schemes, initiatives and campaigns about environmental awareness, environmental management, and promoting sustainable development are supported by groups ranging from local wildlife groups to national bodies like Going for Green and Eco-Schools, Friends of the Earth, and the Council for Environmental Education. A website for teachers, that provides links to environmental organisations, libraries of information and resources, discussion forums, professional development and teaching and learning materials, has been prepared by members of the GA's Environmental and Sustainable Development Education Working Group, and is available at http://www.bath.ac.uk/Departments/Education/geogee.htm.

Examples include the ECOHOT line at Griffith University in Queensland, which provides links to materials and resources for teachers and pupils on environmental topics, lessons, and assignments: http://www.gu.edeu.au/centre/ecohotline/frameset5.html

It also has links to professional development packs like *Learning for a Sustainable Environment*: http://www.ens.gu.edu.au/ciree/LSE/main.htm and *Teaching for a Sustainable World*: http://www.environment.gov.au/education/aeen/pd/tsw/intros/index.html

(*continued on next page*)

The Geographical Association

An extensive list of professional and academic sources on environmental education and geography education can be found in the GA's *Bibliography of Geographical Education*, pp. 160–5 (Foskett and Marsden 1998).

Tel: 0114 296 0088
E-mail: ga@geography.org.uk
Website: http://www.geography.org.uk

Council for Environmental Education

The CEE provides a national umbrella for its member organisations to promote environmental education and education for sustainable development in England.

Tel: 0118 950 2550
E-mail: info@cee.i-way.co.uk
Website: www.cee.org.uk

Simply observing the frequencies of particular teaching strategies and styles in Geography suggests that teachers adapt their practice to a variety of factors (pp. 239–40). This includes the learning culture in a school; the department, pupils and resources; the content of a theme being taught; and meeting the needs of coping with and managing the daily demands of being a teacher. Roberts bases her classification of approaches to Geography teaching in the National Curriculum on the amount of control teachers maintain over subject content and activities (Table 16.1). Styles of geography teaching are differentiated using four indicators for where control is exercised: (a) questions, (b) data, (c) interpretation, (d) conclusions. At one end of the spectrum, i.e. the 'closed' style, teachers maintain tight control over all aspects of the subject knowledge, while at the other extreme, i.e. the 'negotiated' style, the construction of knowledge is maximised by the learners themselves (see also box text on page). The distinctions between the categories are illustrated in Table 16.1, where the side headings relate to a simplified teaching and learning sequence appropriate for geography lessons.

References

Barry, J. (1999) *Environment and Social Theory*, London: Routledge.
Bullard, J.E. (1998) 'Raising Awareness of Local Agenda 21: the use of Internet resources', *Journal of Geography in Higher Education*, 22(2): 201–10.
CEE (Council for Environmental Education) (1998) *Inspecting the Environmental Dimension of Schools*, Reading: CEE.

Chambers, B. (1991) 'Approaches to environmental education: A review of two new publications by the Chair of the GA Environmental Education Working Group', *Teaching Geography*, 16(2): 80–2.

DES (1991) *Geography in the National Curriculum (England)*, London: HMSO.

DfE (1995) *Geography. The National Curriculum for England*, London: HMSO.

DfEE/QCA (1999) *Geography. The National Curriculum for England. Key Stages 1–3*, London: DfEE/QCA.

Fien, J. (1993) *Environmental Education: A Pathway to Sustainability?*, Geelong: Deakin University Press.

Foskett, N. and Marsden, W. (1998) *A Bibliography of Geographical Education*, Sheffield: GA.

GA (Geographical Association) (1999a) *Geography in the Curriculum: A Position Statement from the Geographical Association*, Sheffield: GA.

GA (1999b) *Leading Geography: National Standards for Geography Leaders in Secondary Schools*, Sheffield: GA.

Huckle, J. and Sterling, S. (eds) (1996) *Education for Sustainability*, London: Earthscan.

IUCN (World Conservation Union) (1970) *International Working Meeting on Environmental Education in the School Curriculum, Final Report*, USA: IUCN.

Jones, B. (1999) 'Continuity in the Key Stage 2–3 geography curriculum', *Teaching Geography*, 24(1): 5–9.

Kent, A. (1996) 'Evaluating the geography curriculum' in Kent, A., Lambert, D., Naish, M. and Slater, F. (eds) *Geography in Education: Viewpoints on Teaching and Learning*, Cambridge: Cambridge University Press.

Macnaughten, P. and Urry, J. (1998) *Contested Natures*, London: Sage.

Marsden, W. (1995) *Geography 11–16: Rekindling Good Practice*, London: David Fulton.

NCC (1990) *Curriculum Guidance 7: Environmental Education*, York: NCC.

Palmer, J. (1998) *Environmental Education in the 21st century: Theory, Practice, Progress and Promise*, London: Routledge.

QCA/DfEE (2000) *A Scheme of Work for Key Stage 3 Geography: Update*. London: QCA/DfEE.

Reid, A. (1998) 'How does the geography teacher contribute to pupils' environmental education?', unpublished doctoral thesis, University of Bath.

Roberts, M. (1996) 'Teaching styles and strategies' in A. Kent, D. Lambert, M. Naish and F. Slater (eds) *Geography in Education: Viewpoints on Teaching and Learning*, Cambridge: Cambridge University Press.

SCAA (1996) *Teaching Environmental Matters Through the National Curriculum*, London: HMSO.

Scott, W. (1999) 'Teacher education for sustainability: critiquing assumptions about purposes and the primacy of action', *Environmental Education and Information*, 18(2): 105–16.

Scott, W. and Reid, A. (1998) 'The revisioning of environmental education: a critical analysis of recent policy shifts in England and Wales', *Educational Review*, 50(3): 213–23.

Sterling, S. and Cooper, G. (1992) *In Touch: Environmental Education for Europe*, Godalming: WWF UK.

SDEP (Sustainable Development Education Panel) (1999) *First Annual Report, 1998*. London: DETR.

Tilbury, D. (1997) 'Environmental education and development education: teaching geography for a sustainable world', in D. Tilbury and M. Williams (eds) *Teaching and Learning Geography*, London: Routledge.

UNCED (1992) *UN Conference on Environment and Development: Agenda 21 Rio Declaration*, Paris: UNESCO.

UNESCO (1976) The Belgrade Charter, *Connect*, 1(1): 1–3.

17 Citizenship and geographical education

Edited by John Morgan,
based on work by Paul Machon

Geography!

In Britain's schools, but interestingly not its universities, geography teaching is largely apolitical, working instead within long-established traditions that have underpinned the status quo. Contentious issues, if they are dealt with at all, are located in narrowly defined areas that inhibit the active involvement of pupils in the events themselves. There are exceptions to this, particularly in development education, environmental geography and the continuing debate about 'values' in geography. But such work is always limited by the choices teachers make within their own schools and the structural limits to choice such as examination syllabuses and specifications. But these exceptions remind us that geography does have the potential to convey the contentious and political. Its content, after all, describes distributions, locating and accounting for differences (in short is relational) with profound political implications – Dicken and Lloyd's 'access to goods and proximity to bads' (1980: 281–361). Finally there is also geography's distinctive claim that here is a discipline that locks the use of natural worlds into the beliefs and actions of our social worlds.

The lack of experience that many geography teachers have in dealing with the political and contentious is a concern for citizenship education. One cause of this lack of experience is the way that disciplines are constituted – what is legitimate subject matter and what is not – and in school Geography politics is so often excluded. Subjects build boundaries around themselves within which an orthodox body of work develops and significant transformations occur to new concepts that cross those borders to become absorbed in another discipline. This, we argue here, now has to happen to the political concept of citizenship in geography.

This chapter

This chapter's concern is to reflect upon citizenship, a concept with the capacity (and now the opportunity) to 'cross those borders' and then to consider how citizenship may be taught through geography. The opening section provides a theoretical account of citizenship, locating the National Curriculum proposals in a particular liberal and democratic tradition, before turning to a brief critique of such assumptions. An understanding of the formal political concept of citizenship is crucial to the development of critically reflective practitioners and we hope that some geographers will explore one of the many excellent introductions to political theory such as McClelland's *A History of Western Political Thought* (1998). However, at this point we think that it is important to note that political theory is properly a branch of moral philosophy, that is here we are primarily concerned with values. The second part of this chapter explores the contribution that Geography, as a subject taught in schools, can contribute to education for citizenship. In both sections our aim is to begin a process of reflection amongst geography teachers in ways that we hope, will allow the subject of Geography to acquire this new material while maintaining its descriptive and explanatory power.

Citizenship

Citizenship is not a static concept but has evolved as social settings change. However, at its core, is the concept's concern with the iterative relationship between an individual's duties to the state within which they live and the rights they can expect to receive in return. Here the classical literature usually starts by describing the politics of the early Greek city-states – but our focus is the modern state.

One account of the development of the modern state is the story of the democratization of social power (Mann 1993) and the construction of systems to institutionalize and regulate that power. Some argue that modern states are defined by the possession of a single source of authority, deriving legitimacy from the people and operating through an efficient bureaucracy. What results must meet two demands: protecting the population from danger (both from within and without) and ensuring its own long-term future by doing this effectively. Here education plays a fundamental, and geography a particular, role in establishing parts of such hegemony. In the nineteenth century, for example, British geography was concerned with empire, informing and preparing the population to participate in an economy that enjoyed inexpensive supplies of raw materials, protected markets and frequently service overseas in the army and navy. None of this means that modern states become alike – quite the opposite, for as different state forms develop their varied history, the choice of political strategies and the ideologies employed in the search to find legitimacy ensure difference as well as similarity.

In much of Europe, North America and wherever a similar state form evolved, what developed can be described as liberal and representatively democratic. In these states the dominant economic system is capitalist (hence liberal), with the political system electing party-based representatives, often working in oppositional ways reflecting capitalism's tensions. These representatives are subject to periodic change by mass voting. Marshall (1950) offered a taxonomy of citizenship in such states as possessing three components, civil, political and social. The first permits individual freedom, most clearly expressed in terms of ownership and property. The second ensures the right to participate in mass voting and the right to hold political office.

CE LIVRE EST DÉDIÉ AVX ENFANTS DE CEVX
QVI ONT DONNÉ LEVR VIE POVR LE
SALVT DE LA FRANCE ET LA LIBÉRATION
DE L'ALSACE ET DE LA LORRAINE.

Figure 17.1   Cartoon by Jean-Jaques Waltz

The last ensures the citizen's right to be part of society, usually expressed in terms of its standard of living. As a consequence of this last component the provision of welfare and education becomes a state's concern, for such provision ensures a continuing legitimacy with a citizenry who come to expect that their welfare and education will be protected. This is not to say that the state has to do the providing, but it is to say that it must assure that provision is made, even if that is through market processes. Presented in this way Marshall's description of citizenship is plain and desirable enough. However, in practice progress to this point has been slow, especially where citizenship was defined in exclusive terms, that is by defining a citizenry by excluding 'outsiders'. This approach was and is, at least initially, an easier political balance to maintain (Birnbaum and Katnelson 1995), especially in states that developed strongly nationalist politics. In such states populist politics, mass culture and shared sentiment (see Figure 17.1) can combine to produce a polity that is united across other social distinctions like social class. It is also significant that no established power ever willingly relinquished its advantages to others on such a journey. It would be straightforward to present a history of the last centuries as the confrontational expansion of citizenship and there are echoes of this in much school Geography.

At one level the symbolism of Jean-Jaques Waltz's cartoon in Figure 17.1 is clear enough even without its accompanying text. The sense of loss and sacrifice is accompanied by the sentimental image of the young girl dressed in the folk costume of a better time that has already passed. But the picture's resonance is far greater for those in the Alsace who have taken Waltz's work as somehow defining who they are, so much so that he has become *l'oncle Hansi.*

Proceeding from such accounts 'active citizenship' (Bendix 1996) urges vigilance against the loss of rights or the expansion of duties without a concomitant increase in rights. Equally dangerous would be the development of an apathetic citizenry (or 'passive', Bendix again) because this threatens to relinquish power to the state by neglect. Rights can be eroded by the state itself – importantly liberal formulations of citizenship do not conceive of the state as intrinsically good but much more as a necessary evil upon which the cautious citizen keeps a suspicious eye.

The desire to include citizenship in the National Curriculum is driven by a concern about political apathy or disengagement and the threat that this poses to social inclusivity. This is detailed in the Final Report in terms of falling voting figures among the young, although it is acknowledged that the figures themselves are disputed. It is therefore no surprise that the Report is firmly located within the liberal and democratic tradition that has been described. As the Final Report notes:

> The benefits of citizenship education will be: for pupils – an entitlement in schools that will empower them to participate effectively as active informed, critical and responsible citizens; ... for society – an active and politically-literate citizenry convinced that they can influence government and community affairs at all levels.
>
> (QCA 1998: 9)

Liberal for whom?

The liberal democratic account of citizenship has critics, however unproblematic the account may seem to have been so far. Some of the criticisms, we suggest here, are of particular importance to those now charged with teaching citizenship within the Natioanl Curriculum and are also relevant where civics is already taught.

Citizenship – at least the classical liberal formulation of it – is an abstract political concept. It tends to be presented as a series of opposites: state and individual, market and consumer, rights and duties. It has also been noted that classical liberalism is suspicious of the state and this locates three critical themes that we now touch upon: the location of social power, the state's desire to protect itself and the risk that liberalism poses to an individual's rights.

Because the concept is an abstract one, liberal citizenship is rather poor at describing the material and unequal distribution of social power. An individual's power is always likely to be limited by the greater power of others. This can be seen in structured ways in social differentiation based on socio-economic class, ethnicity, gender and age. Many of the 'limits' are market-based and so appear to operate through inviolable and natural laws. Market forces, it is frequently argued, remove jobs from parts of the world where labour is expensive and relocate them where it is cheaper, so underpinning, 'globalisation'. Other inequalities, for example in the quality of publicly provided education, are tacitly authorised by the state (Goodin and LeGrand 1987).

The impact of all these inequalities is seen in differences in the provision of goods, access to finance and the standard of services provided. These combine to produce distinctive spatial patterns of production and consumption. Among the key services is education, where differentiated provision threatens any formation of meritocracy. The spatial inequalities that result could be an important focus of school Geography – but raise a thorny issue. Presenting the evidence of such spatial inequalities is relatively straightforward, but teachers would be hard-pressed to provide students who recognised themselves as victims of these inequalities with the ability and the optimism of spirit to respond to the challenges positively – which we may term *empowerment*. Indeed, providing an authentic and credible account of an individual's weak position without empowerment would be doubly alienating and so even more likely to disenfranchise.

Earlier in the chapter much was made of the 'state's management of its own authority'. This is effected in part by ensuring an appropriate standard of living for people, meeting Marshall's 'social' element of citizenship. This is not easy in capitalist states where losers outnumber winners and the taxation of the latter may be a disincentive to their enterprise. The state's task is approached by endeavouring to establish inequality as both legitimate and 'natural' so that its presence remains unremarkable and unchallenged – even by the losers. It is a conventional criticism of education that schools play a part in constructing this ideology and operate as both agents and microcosms of the state. Certainly they can be concerned with their own authority and at times even against the interests of pupils as classic studies like Willis (1977) showed. This locates a key difficulty, for teaching citizenship is the search for reflection, participation and action – but within structures that are often profoundly authoritarian.

Again the material difficulty remains that rights to citizenship are linked to one's social power and social power is directly related to the inequalities that people experience. Classical liberalism portrays the state as some sort of neutral referee, managing the inevitable tensions and arbitrating between those in dispute on the worth of the case. This neutrality is challenged if the state's relationship with business and the effect of insider pressure groups, the media and others with power are examined. This also happens at a global scale, where the role of multinationals is an important part of any account of why development has been so hard to effect in much of the world. This reminder of the relative power of some states and some companies may cause the neutral-liberal model of the state to be replaced with one that sees the state behaving with both bias and independence. As a result, at times, the state will ally itself with the powerful, and then on other occasions will act against them in pursuit of its own legitimacy – precisely the sort of arbitrary behaviour that so alarms classical liberals about the state.

Finally, classical liberalism, being suspicious of politics, sees 'being a citizen' as only one aspect of life and not central to it, for, it follows, privileging 'the private' must reduce citizenship's importance. Placing the individual first also makes it harder to encourage them to take courses of action that are for others, or universal, and far easier to create individuated, or particular, decision-makers even when it can be demonstrated that those decisions are against the common good. In practice people live between these two states – perhaps this is a description of a modern citizen – without either category being fully distinct. As important, no one is able to be entirely private because the aggregated results of all those individual and self-serving decisions will eventually damage the common good so extensively that its impact will re-enter and put at risk the private realm. This would threaten the sustainability of social system, and any state.

'Deep' citizenship

The challenge posed by this critique is whether it is possible to form another view of citizenship, one that establishes links between public and private actions so that personal or particular decision-making takes into account universal concerns – indeed they become one. If it is possible to form such a view the real challenge is to prepare students for this, rather than the more passive, shallow or narrowly liberal citizenship.

To be a citizen in the neutral-liberal sense is to describe a very limited form of citizenship, one that elevates self-interest, reduces political activity to infrequent voting and so reduces universalistic decision-making. An alternative, sometimes called 'deep citizenship', argues that the particular and the universal must not be separated, that political reflection is central to doing this and that politics is more central to life than classical liberalism maintains (Clarke 1996). Such an approach would require students to reflect upon the consequences of all their actions, and here knowledge of the natural and social worlds would be crucial. It would also be important because such an approach could reduce the penetration into students' thinking of the 'Eichmann prinzip', the abdication of moral decision-making to others: 'I'm not responsible, I'm only a technician; I'm only following orders.'

To what extent can geography take responsibility for citizenship education?

The second part of this chapter is a response to the Advisory Group on *Education for Citizenship and the Teaching of Democracy in Schools* (QCA 1998). The response emphasises geography's ability to deal with the major components of the political concept of citizenship, both inside and out of the classroom.

Geographical education is a particularly effective way to teach for an 'effective citizenry'. This is based on three assumptions:

- The *first* is that the decision to teach citizenship is essentially an ethical one.
- The *second* is that although citizenship is a political concept this does not privilege political science when it comes to educating for citizenship. Instead the

criteria must be the ability of a discipline to 'carry' the concept in substantive terms and within a teaching tradition that questions and enquires.

• From the second assumption, the *third* is clear, that geographical education can be such a vehicle.

Citizenship is not an elusive concept but one that is usually formulated in terms of an individual's duties and rights in a social context; that is to say that citizenship is the foundation of civic order. The ethical imperative here is the obligation on effective citizens that they work towards the improvement and the maintenance of the health of that civic order. It is necessary to do this because civic order is always hard to create and even harder to preserve with other forces and processes finding conditions easier if civic order is weak or partial. The pairing of duties and rights, noted earlier, is so usual a form of words that we may fail to note that in the discussions which normally follow it is rights that dominate. It is the preoccupation with rights, which are usually expressed in terms of the individual's rights, that the threat of crisis, in civic society, in economic activity and the use to which the natural world is put originates. Educating for citizenship must seek to redress this imbalance by helping the learner to identify the collective consequences of their individual action. In order to do this the learner must be able to seek out information, be able to distinguish the worth of that information on ethical grounds and so make judgements that are both conscious and rational. These are not skills that are easy to learn, not least because the forces and processes that act against a robust civic order can make their case in persuasive and alluring ways.

The part geographical education plays

Citizenship may be a political concept but the outcome of most political processes is spatially differentiated. Within towns socially distinct groups are segregated with huge differences in well-being being separated by small distances. Nationally, quite familiar indices have variations region to region that we should not be prepared to accept (for example, infant mortality varies from 10.5 per thousand to 8.3 per thousand across the UK). Internationally, differentials of money and power allow waste from some states to be endured by others. But space is not just a blank sheet upon such processes write a particular form. Rather it is something that is intimately bound up in the maintenance of the differences, that is, space and distance are used to reinforce and maintain those inequalities. This is geography's province, for geography is concerned to describe such differences, to account for the processes that underpin them and to provide a critique of both form and process. As important, geographical education involves the learner in practical ways both inside and outside the classroom, has approached these tasks at a variety of scales and, finally, is a discipline that has a tradition of bridging the social and the natural worlds. It is to these three aspects of geographical education that this article now turns.

Skills

Geography's concern with the skills of its learners is central to the work done with them. Some of these skills are technical, e.g. mapwork – but here information is being interpreted and evidence evaluated, practising the same skills that the effective citizen must have. Other skills may look more ephemeral, e.g. working with others in a collaborative project in the field – but again this is good practice beyond the geography because it rehearses collective action in pursuit of a defined goal. Even when students work autonomously, both inside and outside the classroom, the experience helps them to develop an independence of thought and concern with the quality of evidence. Working in this manner means students in their geography classes are pursuing answers to problems which are near-universal, but which perhaps are being articulated in a clear way, for the first time, for that learner.

Scale

Scale is at the core of the organisation of geography's material. This familiar observation should not hide a more important fact that this allows the discipline to match its substantive work with the learner's age and level of development. Equally, having a choice over the scale of one's subject matter can also promote a sense of relevance that comes from a study of 'the local'. Geography's appeal is that it allows the imagination to make huge jumps to other places and so begins to portray the world as both the same and different. For example, a study of a local pond, particularly one under the threat of development, can readily be done by primary schools. Subsequently, equivalent processes in the world's rainforests, although on a different scale with evidence which must be approached differently, will become more accessible later. Both examples become 'my world' – the same but different. The use of examples at different scales also reveals the impossibility of seeing processes in isolation. This is obvious as far as environmental issues are concerned. Airborne pollutants, for example, do not recognise or respect national boundaries and moves to contain the risks cannot be constructed on local, or even national, action alone. This understanding draws out still further the boundaries within which I am a 'good citizen'. These boundaries move away from me and my local community, to others in 'my nation' and then to larger supranational units, such as Europe, and finally globally.

The social and natural worlds

Conventionally, citizenship's focus has been on the social world, that is, on the reciprocal relations between the individual and the collective. Very largely because of the time in which these arguments were being developed these relationships were framed by national units. Within these nation-states individual loyalty to others, and the state, was based on criteria such as ethnicity, religion, language and culture; which we now begin to question on ethical grounds referred to above. That is, civic order also matters between nations because they can no longer be autonomous. However, even though the scale of the relationship may be changing it remains narrow in the sense that it retains its exclusively human focus. Environmental concerns now press in on this narrow view and seek to widen the concerns of citizenship to include talking for those things that otherwise have no voice, such as cherished landscapes and endangered animals. Geography is especially well placed to contribute to this widening view as its traditional focus has been the bridge between the social and the natural worlds. As a result there is a wealth of established practice in geographical education which describes the outcome of the relationships between humans and the natural world and which seeks to reveal the processes behind those phenomena (sometimes by a grasp of the technicalities so great that geographers make a journey into other disciplines) and finally, to offer alternative views based on a critique of what has been seen. This is as true in early Key Stage work that uses an empathetic viewpoint to look at differing human responses to earthquakes, as it is in the modelling of the El Niño effect by computers in universities.

Where next?

The advisory group's initial report sketched out an ambitious but realisable approach to the teaching of citizenship. The publication of the orders for teaching citizenship in the National Curriculum from September 2002 offers geography teachers an important agenda, which is:

- To consider our role as teachers in the promotion of courses that contribute to 'good citizenship'. This may well involve a discourse within the discipline, particularly in schools and college Geography, with regard to this and other political concepts.
- Although much of our existing subject content is directly relevant to this enterprise, it would certainly benefit from being scrutinised to sharpen that focus. At present much that we do is curiously apolitical; curious on two counts perhaps because (i) political factors are often too important for work in geography to omit them or to deal with them superficially, and (ii) in higher education political geography is so well established.
- There will need to be additions to what is taught in terms of 'knowledge', but as important will be the need to provide students with the opportunity to develop their critical thinking when it comes to making choices in social and environmental settings.
- Finally, practical work in geography, particularly in the field, presents an opportunity for students to work 'as citizens' and this too needs to be considered afresh.

References

Bendix, R. (1996) *Nation-Building and Citizenship*, 3rd edn., New Brunswick, NJ: Transaction Publishers.

Birnbaum, P. and Katnelson, I. (1995) *Paths of Emancipation: Jews, States and Citizenship*, Princeton, NJ: University of Princeton Press.

Clarke, P.B. (1996) *Deep Citizenship*, London: Pluto Press.

Crick, B. (1964) *In Defence of Politics*, London: Penguin.

Dicken, P. and Lloyd, P.E. (1980) *Modern Western Society: A Geographical Perspective on Work, Home and Well-Being*, London: Harper Row.

Goodin, R.E. and LeGrand, J. (1987) *Not Only the Poor*, London: Allen & Unwin.

McClelland, J.S. (1998) *A History of Western Political Thought*, London: Routledge/Taylor & Francis.

Mann, M. (1993) *The Sources of Social Power, Volume II. The Rise of Classes and Nation-States, 1760–1914*, Cambridge: Cambridge University Press.

Marshall, T.H. (1950) 'Citizenship and social class', in *Sociology at the Cross-Roads* (1963), London: Heinemann.

Oxfam (1997) *A Curriculum for Global Citizenship*, London: Oxfam.

QCA (1988) *Education for the Citizenship and the Teaching of Democracy in Schools*, London: QCA.

Qualifications and Curriculum Authority (1998) *Education of Citizenship and the Teaching of Democracy in Schools*, London: QCA.

Qualifications and Curriculum Authority (1999) *Citizenship: The National Curriculum for England Key Stages 3–4*, London: DfEE/QCA.

Willis, P. (1977) *Learning to Labour: How Working Class Kids get Working Class Jobs*, Farnborough: Saxon House.

18 Towards a critical school Geography

John Huckle

In our working lives as geography teachers we should never forget or abandon those ideals which draw so many of us to the job in the first place. School Geography has the potential to develop young people's understanding of their 'place' in the world and so help form their identity. It can enable them to perceive the structures and processes which help and hinder their development, and can also foster the commitment to social justice and democracy, and the conserving, participatory and critical forms of citizenship, whereby they can seek to conserve or change those structures and processes and thereby help to create a better world. The International Charter on Geographical Education (IGU 1995) provides a comprehensive statement of such ideals and they are reflected in the aims, for Geography in the National Curriculum for England and Wales (DES 1990).

The reality is that such ideals are increasingly neglected or put to one side as geography teachers' work, along with that of other teachers, is deprofessionalized or proletarianized. Teachers are increasingly required to adopt the role of technicians who deliver prescribed and pre-packaged content, assess and stratify pupils by reference to standard norms, spend more and more time serving an educational bureaucracy, and cope with a growing minority of alienated and disruptive pupils. New working conditions and forms of accountability increase teachers' workloads and erode their professional, economic and political status (Harris 1994). Young geography teachers are therefore more likely to work with disillusioned and cynical older colleagues than they were ten or twenty years ago. They are more likely to be affected by the high levels of stress and low levels of morale which pervade some staffrooms and they are more likely to have inadequate resources, facilities or encouragement to teach Geography in an enlightened way. Schools and teachers are variously affected by recent attempts to redefine, restructure and repoliticize schooling, but in general it is becoming harder for geography teachers to work in ways which reflect progressive and radical ideals.

Nevertheless, this chapter urges geography teachers to cling to such ideals and seeks to introduce them to the theory and practice whereby they find contemporary expression. It traces the history of the radical or critical tradition in geographical education and suggests how it can be revived and updated using advances in academic geography and curriculum studies. It outlines the aims, content and pedagogy of a critical geography for a society undergoing profound change and hints at the political skills and alliances which geography teachers will need to develop if they are to gain greater control of their work and develop a true professionalism.

Developing an historical perspective

What counts as school Geography (its content, teaching methods and assessment) is largely, but not wholly, determined by dominant groups and interests in society. The links between powerful economic, political and cultural interests and the everyday realities of geography classrooms are complex and are mediated by such agencies as National Curriculum working parties, textbook publishers, examination boards and PGCE courses, but school Geography is socially constructed and continues to play a role in the economic and cultural reproduction of our advanced capitalist society. It helps to produce young workers and citizens with 'appropriate' knowledge, skills and values and so contributes to changing forms of social regulation whereby the state, and other institutions, maintain social order and ensure the reproduction of both the means and conditions of production.

Our society's need for a school subject which would foster nationalism, imperialism and a positive view of the world of work, while teaching useful knowledge and skills to future clerks, merchants and soldiers, largely explains the entry of Geography into the school curriculum in the late nineteenth century and its subsequent revival and growth in the universities to meet the demand for qualified teachers (Capel 1981). Old geography textbooks reflect the racism, ethnocentrism, sexism and paternalism which pervaded the early teaching of the subject (Marsden 1989), and it was not until the 1970s and 1980s that this legacy was thoroughly exposed and real efforts made to counter stereotyping. Geography and history were favoured as social subjects for inclusion in the curriculum at the end of the last century and they have sustained their privileged position despite periodic challenges (Goodson 1983). The majority of pupils continue to be deprived of sufficient economics, politics, sociology and cultural studies to develop a real understanding of geography, and the provision for social or citizenship education in our state schools is inadequate to sustain, let alone improve, our current deteriorating level of democracy.

While school Geography's legacy of stereotyping has been exposed there has been less attention to the changing ideologies, or ideas which contribute to social regulation, which have pervaded the Geography curriculum. Existing studies (Gilbert 1984) suggest that changing ideological emphases have left generations of pupils largely impotent as agents of social change. Nationalistic and imperialistic ideology taught them an unquestioning respect for nation and empire. Environmental determinism and natural regions taught them to accept a society shaped and limited by nature, while economic determinism taught them to accept the social relations of capitalism as normal and inevitable. The separation of the physical and human geography taught them a false separation of nature and society, while the subject's view of progress reinforced the modern faith in science, technology and bureaucracy. Too much school Geography continues to draw solely on empiricist and positivist philosophies and so describes rather than explains the world. It fails to recognize power, conflict and agency, or to consider social alternatives, and can be seen to suggest to pupils that there are no real alternatives other than to accept the world largely as it is. Anyone doubting this assertion might try asking students who have recently passed A level Geography, what they understand by capitalism, green politics, or the state.

Enough of such pessimism. Capitalist schooling, and an essentially capitalist school Geography, were opposed from the outset. Elementary education for the working class was only conceded when people's popular efforts at self-education proved too threatening to the establishment and when its need for a more literate citizenry and technically competent workforce proved overwhelming (Shotton 1993). In 1885 the anarchist geographer Peter Kropotkin advocated an anti-militarist, anti-imperialist and anti-capitalist education through geography which would examine issues from the point of view of the working class, foster social harmony and mutual aid, and involve pupils in the everyday life of the community (Kropotkin 1885). Such messages have since been periodically applied, revived and updated by a minority of geography teachers who, like other radical educators, have drawn on Marxism, anarchism, progressivism, humanistic psychology and liberation pedagogy (Wright 1989). Radical education 'flowered' briefly in the late 1960s and early 1970s, along with the new Left and the new social movements, and some predict that it will resurface again in the late 1990s or early 2000s as the political pendulum swings back towards democracy, social justice and the empowerment of the individual through collective action.

Current educational reform and the National Curriculum

The conditions of sustained economic growth and social democracy which gave expression to radical ideas in the late 1960s were not to last.. The onset of an economic crisis and the need to restore levels of capital accumulation resulted in the rise of the New Right and the onset of a long period of economic, social and educational restructuring which continues to have profound effects on teachers' lives. The transition from an organized to a disorganized regime of capital accumulation, and from Fordist to post-Fordist labour processes, required changes in the mode of regulation together with new forms of schooling (Flude and Hammer 1990; Whitty 1992). The state's expenditure on education for the majority of pupils would continue to fall in real terms and market forces would play a greater role in allocating pupils to more diverse kinds of school. While opting out, local management of schools, and open enrolment were designed to restratify schools and pupils, National Curriculum testing, examination league tables and Ofsted inspection reports were designed to provide indicators to guide the decisions of those parents who have real choice. The National Curriculum is essentially a minimal provision or entitlement. It does not have to be taught in private schools, but its similarity to earlier academic curriculums hints at its social control function and suggests that it is not suitable for advancing a liberal interpretation of the 1988 Education Reform Act's curriculum objectives: that education should promote the spiritual, moral, cultural, mental and physical development of pupils at school and of society.

The rise of the New Right owed much to its ability to sense people's disillusion-ment with those forms of social regulation which accompanied organized capitalism and to promote an alternative social vision to that associated with the welfare state. Thatcherism developed a mode of regulation and ideology in tune with disorga-nized capitalism and its economic, political and cultural imperatives were to shape the content of the National Curriculum. Too much education was once more seen as a dangerous thing and the curriculum again pressed into service to tighten social regulation and control. There were tensions between those who emphasized tradi-tional, economic and progressive values (Ball 1990), but the outcome was a curric-ulum which seeks to rekindle nationalism, individualism and moral certainty, and prevent a coherent and critical understanding of society and social change. The cross-curricular elements do seek to address the Act's curriculum objectives, but they are non-statutory, not related to one another, not free from ideology (Ahier and Ross 1995), and are likely, following the Dearing Review, to disappear yet further from the perceptions and priorities of most schools and teachers.

After a brief romance with positivism and the 'new' geography in the 1970s, school Geography was challenged in the early 1980s to assess post-positivist philos-ophies (behavioural, humanistic, welfare and radical geographies) and incorporate these into the curriculum so that it would better meet pupils' and society's needs (Cook and Gill 1983; Huckle 1983; Johnston 1986). The response was somewhat limited, for the government's educational agenda soon threatened the very survival of school Geography and its status as a foundation subject could be assured only by promoting its more conservative characteristics. At a time when academic geog-raphy engaged with diverse philosophies and social and cultural theories in order to explain the contribution of space, place and geography to the profound social changes which were taking place (Cloke *et al.* 1991; Thrift 1992), the school subject's professional establishment turned its attention to a reinterpretation of the school subject which seemed to be little informed by these developments and parallel developments in social education (Bailey 1991; Wise 1993). The construc-tion of the Geography National Curriculum was not without its critics and dissenters but the final product gives little indication of the relationship between geography and society and does little to advance teachers' and pupils' under-standing of the threats and promises presented by disorganized capitalism (Morris 1992). It fails to indicate what 'enquiry' really entails or what 'understanding' the themes really involves, and while some teachers and textbook writers have inter-preted it in progressive and radical ways (Hopkin 1994), it has generally been a conservative influence (Roberts 1991).

Such reforming of school Geography between 1985 and 1995 drove an increasing number of radical geography teachers to seek support from the 'adjecti-val' educations which had grown alongside the new social movements from the late 1960s (Dufour 1989). Environmental development, peace, human rights, and futures education, seemed more prepared than school Geography to draw eclectically on the natural and social sciences so that pupils could explore how the world works and how it might be changed. They were more prepared to examine social structures and processes and adopt a genuinely democratic and empowering pedagogy, and seemed more in touch with the realities which confronted and interested pupils from day to day. Supported by development and environmental non-governmental organizations, and by other agencies seeking to promote equality through education, the adjectival educations have developed a wide variety of curriculum material (Hicks and Fisher 1985; Huckle 1988; Pike and Selby 1988) which has influenced geography teaching (Fien and Gerber 1988; Serf and Sinclair 1992). Many radical teachers continue to promote integrated humanities as a vehicle for linking these educations to cross-curricular themes, but it can be argued that a proliferation of adjectival educations, often embracing competing liberal, radical and utopian agendas, has slowed the emergence of a genuinely radical social (and socialist) education which integrates all their concerns (Lauder and Brown 1988; Chitty *et al.* 1991). Like a radical geographical education, such education should now be based on an understanding and application of critical theory.

Critical theory

In the 1980s, when structural Marxism and socialism lost some of their authority and appeal, radical educators increasingly turned their attention to critical theory and the ideas of the German philosopher Jurgen Habermas (Gibson 1986; Young 1989). Such theory draws on both Weber and Marx and shifts the focus from labour and the social relations of production to social interaction and the nature of language and morals. Habermas' principal claim is that interaction has become distorted by the rise of positivism and instrumental reason which promotes science as universal and value-free knowledge and so fosters a distorted and incomplete understanding of our relations with one another and the rest of nature. His critical theories seek to reveal this distorted or incomplete rationality and empower people to think and act in genuinely rational and autonomous ways. They deal with legitimation crisis, knowledge constitutive interests, and communicative action, and can be applied to the development of a critical theory of geographical education.

Habermas argues that the modern state must manage the economy while maintaining the support of the majority of the electorate. It attempts to do this through technocratic systems which are pervaded by instrumental rationality, but economic problems are thereby displaced first to the political and then to the socio-cultural sphere. An inability to maintain simultaneously capital accumulation, full employment, social welfare, and a safe and healthy environment, contributes to a legitimation crisis along with a motivational crisis as people lose faith in state institutions and liberal democracy. The state then develops new kinds of regulation and consultation in an attempt to restore legitimacy and motivation, but opposition parties and movements in civil society may use such innovations to reveal the limits of technocracy and the continuing need for decision-making and problem-solving governed by genuine rationality, democracy and moral principles. Legitimation crisis provides some explanation for many young people's disillusionment with society and politics and hints at the foundations of a relevant citizenship education through geography which would enable them to consider the diverse beliefs, values and strategies of those groups seeking more radical and participatory forms of democracy.

In deciding what kinds of knowledge and geography might best contribute to a new radical agenda, teachers should be guided by Habermas' notion of knowledge constitutive interests. He suggests that human beings have three distinct categories of interest which shape their social construction of knowledge. While their technical interest in the control and management of their physical environment leads to empirical and positivist knowledge, their practical interest in understanding and participating in society through communication with others leads to interpretive or hermeneutic knowledge. Both are of value in relevant contexts but both can act as ideology, for positivism treats the social world as if it were part of the physical world (with given structures and processes), while hermeneutics recognizes the difference but is also too inclined to accept the social world as it is. Both encourage people to overlook the true form of their relations with the rest of human and non-human nature (their state of alienation) which can only be revealed through critical theory.

Critical theory serves people's emancipatory interest in being free from alienation and the constraints of ideology and distorted communication. It recognizes the difference between the physical and social worlds but, unlike hermeneutics, it critiques and seeks to improve the latter by, for instance, making it more egalitarian, democratic and sustainable. Such theory should inform all geographical education which seeks to develop autonomous and self-determining individuals, yet school Geography has been slow to consider and incorporate critical theory as Unwin (1992) reminds us in his comprehensive account of the history of geography in terms of Habermas' knowledge constitutive interests.

The theory of communicative action provides the means whereby we can test the validity of critical theory and develop a critical pedagogy. It maintains that all speech presumes an ideal speech situation in which participants are required to sustain and defend four kinds of validity claim and in which only the force of better argument decides the issue. What they say should be meaningful, true, justified and sincere, and in a truly democratic society it will be possible to redeem all such claims and so arrive at a consensus in ways free from distortion, manipulation and domination. The process of actively constructing and reconstructing theory and practice through rational discussion and democratic politics leads to communicative action based on shared understanding rather than to strategic action based on instrumental reason. It leads to universal knowledge and values, serves to validate critical theory, and may be described as praxis or participative action research. Such enquiry provides geography teachers with a form of socially critical pedagogy, or democratic problem-solving, in which they and pupils employ different kinds of practical and theoretical knowledge to decide what people can, might and should do. It is through such pedagogy that empirical, hermeneutic and critical knowledge is combined and pupils come to recognize their true interests and identities.

Critical approaches to education based on Habermas' work have been criticized by those who claim that he clings too strongly to a modern notion of a universal rationality, knowledge and values, and can be seen to reduce politics solely to a matter of communication. His theory is essentially modernist in clinging to a single grand theory or narrative of emancipation, and idealist in locating the causes and solutions to our current crisis in modes of discourse. He assumes that undistorted communication necessarily corresponds to universal needs and knowledge claims, gives too little attention to the power which sustains technocracy and instrumental reason, and puts too much faith in the new politics of social movements rather than the old politics of class. The recent work of Giroux and others (Aronowitz and Giroux 1991; Giroux 1992) on border pedagogies suggests that it is possible to develop a critical pedagogy between modernism and post-modernism which is anchored in political economy. This would be more sensitive to notions of power, language, context and difference and would be far more modest in its claims to be able to empower others.

Priorities for a critical school Geography

Returning to our ideals as geography teachers it would seem important to make more use of critical theory and pedagogy to help young people find their identity and place in the world – to find out how, why, with what, and where they belong, and to develop their sense of longing and belonging within a range of communities or collectives. This requires us to develop curriculums which help pupils answer the following types of questions:

- How are people and geography (places, spaces, and people–environment relations) being constituted by society?
- What roles can people and geography play in constituting society?
- How should people understand and connect with history, the economy, the state, civil society, and the rest of nature, as they affect their lives and local and distant geographies?
- What provides people with their identity, longings, sense of belonging and meaning in life?
- What social and cultural resources can people use to extend their imaginations, to construct places and communities where they can live sustainably with each other and the rest of nature, and to develop their identities and sense of belonging and meaning in life?
- What longings and belongings should I develop, and what kinds of society, geography and community allow me to express my identity and desires?

Addressing such questions through socially critical pedagogy requires inputs of critical knowledge concerning the economy, the state and civil society, contemporary culture, and people–environment relations. Pupils should develop a basic understanding of the nature of organized and disorganized capitalism (modernity and post-modernity) and the manner in which they shape, and are shaped by, geography. They should understand the processes of economic restructuring and globalization, should assess their impact on workers and communities in diverse locations, and should evaluate the roles of appropriate technologies, labour relations, the market, regulation and planning, in moving Britain, Europe and the global community towards more equitable and sustainable levels of economic welfare.

As far as the state is concerned, school Geography should develop a multidimensional and multilayered form of citizenship which prompts a critical engagement with economic, political, social and cultural rights and responsibilities at local, national, regional and international scales (Lynch 1992). Pupils should explore how governments can protect and extend people's rights and responsibilities but should recognize that post-modernity puts strains on the nation state and conventional forms of politics and prompts greater attention to civil society and social movements based around race, gender, the environment, community and identity. Classroom activities should explore the complementary nature of the old emancipatory politics and the new life politics and help pupils to understand how their search for meaning and identity is made more urgent, challenging and exciting in a post-modern world.

It is the realm of culture and cultural studies which presents critical school Geography with its greatest challenge and potential. Disorganized capitalism is increasingly a cultural economy of signs and spaces in which the information and communication structures of consumer society replace social structures in shaping people's lives (Lash and Urry 1994). Young people increasingly form their identities from the raw material of media and consumer culture and adopt a post-modern attitude which is sceptical of all authority, revels in artificiality, accepts a fragmented and placeless existence, regards security and identity as purely transitory, and welcomes an aestheticization of everyday life in which politics becomes the politics of style, presentation and gesture. Post-modernism threatens fragmentation, relativism and the erosion of community, but it also offers the possibility of using new cultural technologies, products and attitudes to redefine identity, community and pleasure, as a means towards radical democracy. School Geography should acknowledge that young people face a world with few secure signposts yet display much commitment and imagination in using popular culture to construct meanings and identities. Our lessons should educate their sensibilities and interests by exploring how texts of all kinds represent places and environments and shape the geographical imagination, how the meaning of texts can be constructed and reconstructed to serve different interests, and how different senses of longing and belonging are produced in different place, among different groups, at different times (Gilbert 1995; Morgan 1995).

Our relations with the rest of living nature, in a world increasingly pervaded by manufactured risks, are the focus of such phenomena as green consumerism and protest over live animal exports. These reveal the increased significance of identity and cultural politics for young people, and suggest that a relevant school Geography should merge physical and human geography under the umbrella of political ecology, should develop citizenship within the context of the old and new politics of the environment, and so allow pupils to explore the kinds of technology and social organization which may allow us to live more sustainably (Huckle 1993).

A return to professionalism

School Geography is in urgent need of reform. After a decade or more of largely pragmatic development at the bidding of politicians and dominant interests within the subject community, it is now time to acknowledge that the subject has distanced itself from change in society and from those developments in academic geography and curriculum theory which could be used to enable us better to meet our ideals. We need to return to professionalism in geographical education and debate the new social, theoretical and pedagogical challenges with rediscovered energy and enthusiasm (Marsden 1995). New times have brought much de-skilling and de-professionalization, but they also offer the prospect of developing more flexible and responsive curriculums for schools with more empowering structures and cultures (Hargreaves 1994).

New technologies provide a means of transforming modern institutions for schooling into post-modern institutions for education. The open geography classroom with real and virtual links to the community and wider world, in which computer-assisted learning frees teachers to teach and pupils to learn, is an exciting prospect. How soon it arrives, and in what form it arrives, largely depends on wider political struggles over the future of disorganized capitalism and the nature and funding of schooling. Establishing a critical school Geography requires radical teachers to continue to turn existing curriculum frameworks in more empowering directions and to argue their case, by example, in such settings as department meetings, Ofsted inspections, Geographical Association and union branches, and meetings organized by community groups and political parties. They should form alliances with those elements of the new Left and cultural industries which are using critical theory and pedagogy to promote radical democracy and should seek to popularize their subject and its potential for social education within the local community. A strand of critical school Geography has continued to develop in recent difficult times and its fortunes in coming decades partly depend on a minority of geography teachers winning more of the arguments, gaining more support, and so helping to secure the conditions in which their ideals can become reality.

References

Ahier, J. and Ross, A. (eds) (1995) *The Social Subjects within the Curriculum, Children's Social Learning in the National Curriculum*, London: Falmer Press.

Aronowitz, S. and Giroux, H. (1991) *Postmodern Education, Politics, Culture and Social Criticism*, Minneapolis: University of Minneapolis Press.

Ball, S. (1990) *Politics and Policy Making in Education*, London: Routledge.

Bailey, P. (1991) *Securing the Place of Geography in the National Curriculum of English and Welsh Schools: A Study in the Politics and Practicalities of Curriculum Reform*, Sheffield: Geographical Association.

Capel, H. (1981) 'Institutionalization of geography and strategies of change', in D.R. Stoddart (ed.) *Geography, Ideology and Social Concern*, Oxford: Basil Blackwell.

Chitty, C., Jakubowska, T. and Jones, K. (1991) 'The National Curriculum and assessment: changing course', in C. Chitty (ed.) *Changing the Future, Redprint for Education*, London: Tufnell Press.

Cloke, P., Philo, C. and Sadler, D. (1991) *Approaching Human Geography, An Introduction to Contemporary Theoretical Debates*, London: Paul Chapman.

Cook, I. and Gill, D. (1983) 'An introduction to "Contemporary Issues in Geography and Education"', *Contemporary Issues in Geography and Education*, 1(1): 1–4.

DES (Department of Education and Science and the Welsh Office) (1990) *Geography for Ages 5 to 16, Proposals of the Secretary of State for Education and Science and the Secretary of State for Wales*, London: HMSO.

Dufour, B. (ed.) (1989) *The New Social Curriculum*, Cambridge: Cambridge University Press.

Fien, J. and Gerber, R. (eds) (1988) *Teaching Geography for a Better World*, Edinburgh: Oliver and Boyd.

Flude, M. and Hammer, M. (eds) (1990) *The Education Reform Act 1988: Its Origins and Implications*, London: Falmer Press.

Gibson, R. (1986) *Critical Theory and Education*, London: Hodder and Stoughton.

Gilbert, R. (1984) *The Impotent Image, Reflections of Ideology in the Secondary School Curriculum*, Lewes: Falmer Press.

Gilbert, R. (1995) 'Education for citizenship and the problem of identity in postmodern political culture', in J. Ahier and A. Ross (eds) 1995.

Giroux, H. (1992) *Border Crossings, Cultural Workers and the Politics of Education*, London: Routledge.

Goodson, I. (1983) *School Subjects and Curriculum Change*, London: Croom Helm.

Harris, K. (1994) *Teachers: Constructing the Future*, London: Falmer Press.

Hargreaves, A. (1994) *Changing Teachers, Changing Times, Teachers' Work and Culture in the Postmodern Age*, London: Cassell.

Hicks, D. and Fisher, S. (1985) *World Studies 8–13: A Teacher's Handbook*, Edinburgh: Oliver and Boyd.

Hopkin, J. (1994) 'Geography and development education', in A. Osler (ed.) *Development Education, Global Perspectives in the Curriculum*, London: Cassell.

Huckle, J. (ed.) (1983) *Geographical Education, Reflection and Action*, Oxford: Oxford University Press.

Huckle, J. (1988) *What We Consume, The Teachers Handbook*, Richmond: WWF/Richmond Publishing Company.

Huckle, J. (1993) Our Consumer Society (*What We Consume, Unit 3*), Richmond: WWF/Richmond Publishing Company.

IGU (International Geographical Union) (1995) 'International Charter on Geographical Education', *Teaching Geography*, 20(2): 95–9.

Johnston, R. (1986) *On Human Geography*, Oxford: Basil Blackwell.

Kropotkin, P. (1885) 'What geography ought to be', *Nineteenth Century*, 18: 940–56.

Lash, S. and Urry, J. (1994) *Economies of Signs and Space*, London: Sage.

Lauder, H. and Brown, P. (eds) (1988) *Education in, Search of a Future*, London: Falmer Press.

Lynch, J. (1992) *Education for Citizenship in a Multi-cultural Society*, London: Cassell.

Marsden, W. (1989) '"All in a good cause": geography, history and the politicization of the curriculum in nineteenth and twentieth century England', *Journal of Curriculum Studies*, 21(6): 509–26.

Marsden, W. (1995) *Geography 11–16, Rekindling Good Practice*, London: David Fulton Publishers.

Morgan, J. (1995) 'Citizenship, geography education and postmodernity', paper presented to the conference *Geographical Education and Citizenship*, organized by the History and Philosophy Study Group of the IBG-RGS, Oxford University, 21 October.

Morris, J. (1992) '"Back to the future": the impact of political ideology on the design and implementation of geography in the National Curriculum', *The Curriculum Journal*, 3(1): 75–85.

Pike, G. and Selby, D. (1988) *Global Teacher, Global Learner*, London: Hodder and Stoughton.

Roberts, M. (1991) 'On the eve of the Geography National Curriculum: the implications for secondary schools', *Geography* 76(4): 331–42.

Serf, J. and Sinclair, S. (1992) *Developing Geography, a Development Education Approach at Key Stage 3*, Birmingham: Birmingham Development Education Centre.

Shotton, J. (1993) *No Master High or Low, Libertarian Education and Schooling in Britain 1890–1990*, Bristol: Libertarian Education.

Thrift, N. (1992) 'Light out of darkness? critical social theory in 1980s Britain', in P. Cloke (ed.) *Policy and Change in Thatcher's Britain*, Oxford: Pergamon Press.

Unwin, T. (1992) *The Place of Geography*, Harlow: Longman.

Whitty, G. (1992) 'Education, economy and national culture', in R. Bocock and K. Thompson (eds) *Social and Cultural Forms of Modernity*, Cambridge: Polity Press.

Wise, M. (1993) 'The campaign for geography education: the work of the Geographical Association 1893–1993', *Geography*, 78(2): 101–9.

Wright, N. (1989) *Assessing Radical Education*, Milton Keynes: Open University Press.

Young, R. (1989) *A Critical Theory of Education*, London: Harvester Wheatsheaf.

19 Geography Matters in a globalized world

Doreen Massey

'Geography Matters' was the title we gave to an Open University reader for a course which we produced in the early 1980s (Massey and Allen 1985). In that context we had in mind specifically human geography and the message which we wanted to get across was this: that the spatial organization of society matters; it makes a difference to how society works, to how we think about society and ourselves and to what forms of social organisation are possible.

This was an important argument to advance at that point in the history of geography's self-reflection. We were emerging from a period – highly productive and necessary – in which the dominant emphasis had been on the social construction of the spatial. Our theme-tune then was that 'the spatial' (human geography, the geography of society) was socially constructed. There was no separate realm of 'the spatial', as some had previously been inclined to argue; rather, in order to analyse the geographies which we saw around us it was necessary to understand the social processes which had produced them. Geographers must be versed in sociology, in economics, in cultural theory. And we set about that task with a vengeance.

It was an important move, and it opened up geography to a much greater richness of thought and theorizing (a breadth and richness which it retains to this day). However, our intense focus on the social processes producing geographies led us implicitly to see those geographies (of regional inequality, or cultural variation for instance) as *results*, as *outcomes*. They were not part of the processes; they were what those processes produced. And yet it was soon evident, from both theoretical and empirical work, that this simple formula was inadequate. 'Geography', in the sense of the spatial organization of society, is *not* merely a result of social processes; it also influences – sometimes quite decisively – the very way in which those processes operate. And so our theme-tune had to be amended. Not only were we now concerned to argue that the spatial is socially constructed; we also insisted upon the fact that the social is spatially constructed too. That 'geography' is more than an outcome; it 'matters' in the very processes of the working of society.

An example

One of the ways in which I personally came most forcefully to appreciate the need to expand our arguments in this way emerged from my studies of regional inequality in the UK. The 1980s was a decade of significant increases in inequality between the regions of the UK. It was a decade of 'two Britains' in many ways, and geography was one of the dimensions along which that inequality was most pronounced. For those who cared to look it was also easy to see that this regional inequality was an outcome of the form of the dominant social/economic processes (Thatcherism, neo-liberalism, call it what you will). It was evident, in other words, that that element of 'the spatial' was socially constructed. The earlier element of our argument about the relation between the social and the spatial was plain to see.

As the decade drew on, however, it became equally evident that that 'resultant' regional inequality was also crucial in influencing the very operation of the processes which had brought it about: the exacerbated regional inequality was also a significant component in that constellation of causes which brought the neo-liberal boom to a shuddering halt.

For while Surrey, for instance, was, we were told, over-heating, the likes of Liverpool had barely made it to lukewarm. And that geographical unevenness became a constraint on growth. It began to cause rigidities in the labour market – unemployed northerners found it impossible to move south to fill the vacancies that existed there. In consequence national levels of unemployment were higher than they would have been had the 'national average' levels of growth been more evenly distributed across the country. And with wage-pressure in the south and national bargaining systems, so was wage-inflation.

The national economy, in other words, got itself into a position where it was paying (or *we* were paying) both the social and economic costs of congestion (in the south and east) and (in some other parts of the country) the social and economic costs of decline. Macro-economic statistics (i.e. at the national level) could not explain the situation: you had to understand the geography of things to be able to interpret what was going on.

The *coup de grâce* came when the Chancellor of the Exchequer was forced by the inflationary overheating of the south east to put the brakes on – to restrain the rate of economic growth – even though over vast swathes of the country the idea of too much growth was simply laughable. Had the growth been spread less unequally between regions he would not have had to reign it in, or certainly not until much later.[1]

Now, I am not arguing that 'geography' (in this case, regional inequality) was the only cause of the end of the 1980s boom; but I am arguing that it was important – that geography mattered. It is, moreover, a salutary period to reflect upon today, in the uncomfortable awareness that the current government's labour-market strategies – though differing in many ways from those of the Thatcher period – are nevertheless similarly innocent (to put it at its gentlest) of that basic element of absolutely necessary geographical understanding.

Globalization

So 'geography mattered' then, in the 1980s, and that was one – small, local – example of how it mattered, and one which holds out prescient warnings to us today. And it still matters. Indeed it could be argued that, as a matter of empirical urgent fact rather than solely theoretical principle, geography matters even more now, as we approach the new millennium. There are countless ways in which I could exemplify this but I shall focus on just one.

If there is a single word which frames the political agenda, and also the political, social and economic sciences, at the moment it is *globalization*. It is a huge topic, on which I can touch briefly here (see, e.g. King 1995; Hirst and Thompson 1996; Massey 1997), but one thing can be said for certain: it is a thoroughly, essentially, geographical phenomenon. It is also a so-called 'global' phenomenon which has effects right down to the level of daily life; and it is a phenomenon much used as both explanation and excuse by governments and politicians of many stripes. What is at issue in globalisation is a major re-working of the spaces and places through which the human (and indeed natural) world is organized.

And yet, I would argue, in spite of the fact of its frequent (probably over-frequent) use, 'globalization' is a lamentably unexamined concept. All too often it is reduced to a simplified picture: an imagined world geography of universal 24-hour financial trading and instantaneous communication; of unimpeded cultural mixings; of the collapse everywhere of the spatial barriers which used to keep nations and cultures in place, which used to regulate the levels of currencies and the flows of trade. There is much talk of the annihilation of space by time. And there is reference to an iconic economics, where citing a few well-known names (CNN, Sony, McDonald's) is made to conjure up a world in which all companies are trans-national and everywhere. The impression given by all this excited talk is of the emergence of a borderless world, a world of total inconnection.

It is not so. This is an inaccurate geographical imagination, though one which is useful to some. In fact what is going on is far more complex. To give some examples of this greater complexity; first at the same time as some barriers are falling we are also building a newly regionalized world – of Europe, of the Far East, and of the countries of NAFTA. Second, and rather differently, it seems to me that at the same time as in some fora we increasingly speak the language of globalization there has also been a retreat into defensive (and sometimes aggressive) localisms, nationalisms, and parochialisms of all sorts. Third, and yet another contrariety, at the very same time as 'free trade' has once again been installed as the overwhelmingly dominant orthodoxy, the free movement of people in the form of international migration has in fact been increasingly hedged-about and controlled. As trade, and finance, and an economically privileged and skilled elite move ever more easily around the planet, we train sniffer dogs to detect unwanted migrants in the holds of boats, other boats go down in the Mediterranean with human cargoes which had been attempting to flee a future of seemingly inevitable poverty for the tempting possibilities in Europe, and Latin Americans die trying to escape to the promise of a better life in the USA. What is going on in this reality of the immensely complex process of globalization is an intricate renegotiation of the spaces and places of this world, of how we organize a new, planetary, human geography.

Some issues

Such a complex reorganization raises huge issues – issues which, as responsible members of the human species we need to face up to, and each of which is intrinsically geographical. I shall point briefly to just four.

First, we are faced with huge issues which are quite simply ethical and political. This re-making of human geography is taking place in a context of already unequal wealth and power. And in a manner reminiscent of Britain's neo-liberal 1980s inequality, including its specifically geographical dimensions, is increasing. Both within individual countries and between them divides are growing. In 1960 the wealthiest 20 per cent of the world's population was 30 times as rich as the least wealthy 20 per cent. By 1990, after a sustained application of the current form of neo-liberal globalization, they are 60 times as rich. To have on the one hand increasing global geographical inequality and on the other policies which refuse to countenance as in any way legitimate those who are classified as 'merely economic migrants' is surely to head for disaster. It may not be a contradiction of the type the UK experienced in the 1980s (there is no equivalent, for instance, of a World Chancellor of the Exchequer) and it may be that the impoverished countries and peoples of the world have insufficient voice to turn it into a formally *political* crisis. But it is surely an ethical and humanitarian one.

Second, in the midst of the complexities of current globalization there is indeed a greater degree of geographical inter-relatedness. And this, I would argue, is a shift in the geography of human relations which demands that we find (and I already see geographers being at the forefront in this) new ways of conceptualizing places, regions and nations. The whole relationship between 'places' and 'cultures' is being challenged, and we need a new geographical imagination in order to be able not just to survive it, but constructively to make the most of it. Philosophically, we have to imagine how we can 'belong' without being parochial, how – in the face of Kosovo and Rwanda – we can work out ways of loving and appreciating 'the local place' in all its uniqueness and specificity and yet remain informed and committed internationalists. It is to that end that as geographers we can contribute to the recognition of what I have elsewhere called 'a global sense of place' (see Massey 1994). An important message of much recent research in human geography here has been that we must learn to think in terms of relational identities. To imagine 'regions', for instance, in their inter-relatedness and not as separate, bounded entities (Allen *et al.* 1998).[2] To recognize that 'Englishness', for instance, the character of England, does not result from an internalized history, does not somehow grow out of the soil, but rather is importantly in part the product of connections with elsewhere, of a long internationally-connected history (which is a part of what is meant by a global sense of place). Rethinking national identities could hardly be more important at this moment; and to do so successfully we need a rich and reworked geographical imagination of the relation between society and space.

And how, too, shall we think of the new 'Europe'? How shall we characterize its identity? Shall we be able to do so in a manner which includes a full recognition of our continent's utter embeddedness in the influences and impacts of a wider world?

The fundamental point here is that places – regions – nations do not somehow first exist in themselves and then interact, Rather, their very identities are formed in interaction. And, I would argue, recognising this means also, at least potentially, beginning to take a greater responsibility for those relations. In the end, all cultures and places are hybrid, mixed. We are *all*, somewhere in the past, migrants. And it is a deep understanding of that, of the intricate geographies from which we all arrive, and of our relative power within them, which is fundamental to my next point.

Third, then, such reworkings of the human geography of the planet raise crucial issues of democracy and citizenship. It is an area in which geographers have much to contribute.[3] But two immediate points come to mind. I find it one of the bitter ironies of an age of globalisation that it coincides with a closing-in in some ways of our geographical imaginations, with an impoverishment at some level of popular geographical knowledge. I shall return to this point later but it seems to me to be deeply dangerous. For knowledge is a pre-requisite for democracy and citizenship, and the kind of reworked geographical imagination I have just evoked will be crucial for rethinking citizenship in a globalizing world. Moreover, and precisely in the context of the complexities of globalization, what one might call a new geography of democracy is emerging. Within the national stage there is devolution, and attempts to revitalize local democracy. There are proposals for regional government in England. Beyond the national there is the European Union: debates about such things as subsidiarity raise issues of the scales of organization of economic and social life which geographers have been analysing for years.

Fourth, at the turn of this millennium, and for the first time in human history, over half of the world's population will be living in cities, and major cities at that: cities of many millions of people. It is a new population geography which establishes huge challenges both environmentally in the broadest sense (can the planet survive such urbanisation?) and for society. The very size and intensity and heterogeneity of cities can lead to the creativity which has so often made cities the crucibles of the new. It can also lead to conflict, segregation, violence and intolerance. It will be up to us.

So what can we conclude so far? That yes, surely and perhaps now more than ever, geography does matter. That if we are going to be able to cope with the world of the new millennium we have to build for ourselves new geographical imaginations, and geographical research has much to contribute here. And that, unfortunately, we seem to be facing these challenges with popular geographical imaginations (in society at large, in the media, among politicians) which are relatively impoverished.

In the academy

One measure to me of this impoverishment is the paucity of serious international programmes in media such as television and the thinness of our newspapers' foreign coverage. Moreover, the contrast between this and what is going on in universities and in research in geography is startling. In this regard I should like to mention just two very broad developments which have taken place on the frontiers of research in recent years.

First, there is an increasing recognition, across disciplines of the *essential spatiality of life today*. Just read the following:

> It is space rather than time which is the distinctively significant dimension of contemporary capitalism.
>
> > John Urry (leading British sociologist)

> All the social sciences must make room for an increasingly geographical conception of mankind.
>
> > Fernand Braudel (major French historian of Europe)

> The anxiety of our era has to do fundamentally with space, no doubt a great deal more than with time.
>
> > Michel Foucault (philosopher and social theorist)

> That new spatiality implicit in the postmodern.
>
> > Fredric Jameson (American literary theorist)

> It is space not time that hides consequences from us.
>
> > John Berger (writer and cultural theorist)

That last quote in particular perhaps, is worth pondering some more. For what it conjures up is an acknowledgement that each of our lives, places and societies is constituted through wider geographies, and yet that in itself can hide the inter-relations on which we depend: the other peoples and societies whose lives are inextricably linked to our own, whose actions have consequences for us and who are themselves affected by decisions of our own. One point which that perhaps particularly underlines is that not only does 'geography' matter, but a wide-ranging international geography matters. Doing local studies of one's home base is good and necessary but alone it is not enough. It may be a place to start but from that local base we need also to be able to trace out and understand its intricate connections to the wider world. We need to develop a global understanding of the local. Quite apart from anything else, if we do not have that we shall never even understand how 'the local place' comes to be as it is.

The second point I want to make is that *geography as an intellectual discipline* is today central to advanced research in social sciences, cultural studies, and a range of the humanities. In other words, that understanding of the essentially spatial nature of society (my first point) has been reflected in a significant intellectual shift. It has been called 'the spatial turn'. We have moved from a framing of our studies around single Big Histories (of Westernization, or Modernization, or Progress) and have developed a greater understanding of the complexities and multiplicities of social and cultural variation. Now, a crucial characteristic of human geography's focus on spatiality is that it allows in, and forces recognition and analysis of, plurality. This is not an anti-history point. Rather, indeed, the argument is that there is more than one history going on in the world, and that only by thinking rigorously geographically can we get at that.

One example of the impact of this growing recognition of the complex and changing spatialities of life, and its constructive contribution to other disciplines, is our new relationship with the arts, with design, and with the cultural industries (and, as we know, cultural industries are both central to the attentions of young people and an important focus of government policy; they are also a significant and burgeoning sector of the economy). Human geographers are regularly invited to contribute to debates in these fields, on subjects ranging from the spaces of multi-culturalism, to the rethinking of spatiality, to refashioning our notions of community, to the changing city in a globalized age. It is a measure of the interest in current geographical research; and it contributes in turn to enriching the discipline itself.

So, at the frontiers of social and cultural research, there is an increasing recognition both of spatiality as an issue and of geography as a discipline. We must build on that.

A final point is this; the UK is at the moment very good at research in geography but undoubtedly a leader internationally. Geographical research is one of our 'local strengths', a rich vein of work which we must continue.

Notes

1 It is possible to argue that the very form of 'free market' growth in the 1980s necessarily entailed the regional inequality to which it in fact gave rise – i.e. it was intrinsic to it. In other words, and on this reading, growing geographical inequality is an inevitable contradiction at the heart of neo-liberalism in practice. Currently increasing levels of inequality at the world level give support to this argument, though it is perhaps less clear in what form the contradiction may be expressed (see later).
2 The issue of the inter-related nature of regions was discussed further in a workshop at the COBRIG conference.
3 The COBRIG conference included a workshop on global citizenship and for that reason the issue is treated briefly here.

References

Allen, J., Massey, D. and Cochrane, A. (1998) *Rethinking the Region*, London: Routledge.
Hirst, P. and Thompson, G. (1996) *Globalisation in Question*, Oxford: Polity Press.
King, A.D. (1995) 'The lines and spaces of modernity (or who needs postmodernism?)', in M. Featherstone, S. Lash and R. Robertson (eds) *Global Modernities*, London: Sage.
Massey, D. (1994) 'A global sense of space', in D. Massey, (ed.) *Space, Place and Gender*, Oxford: Polity Press.
Massey, D. (1997) 'Problems with globalisation', *Soundings*, 7: 7–12.
Massey, D. and Allen, J. (eds) (1985) *Geography Matters*, Cambridge: Cambridge University Press.

20 Is Geography history?

Rita Gardner and Lorraine Craig

The past few years have seen worrying trends in the numbers of pupils studying Geography in the United Kingdom. Between 1999 and 2000 the numbers taking the upper school assessment in Geography have dropped by 12 per cent, and the subject has fallen from being the fourth most popular in 1996 to eighth place in 1999. At the middle school assessment, Geography has retained its seventh position, the highest-ranking subject that is not part of the National Curriculum for 14- to 16-year-olds, but the total number of candidates is also down.[1]

Comparisons with History in particular are a matter for concern, for both are in the same position as optional subjects in the middle school and, increasingly, owing to pressure on option time in the curriculum and the increasing number of options, pupils are required to choose between these two subjects. While Geography has shown a continuing trend of decline over the past five years, History has held its numbers better.

The picture for geography graduates entering the teaching profession tells a similar story, in terms of both numbers and quality. Geography was declared an official 'shortage' subject last year for the first time, and it now joins the ranks of most of the other National Curriculum subjects in this respect. Reports from the national educational standards watchdog (Ofsted) indicate that the quality of geography teaching in the critical 11–14 age range is not as strong as it ought to be.

The cumulative effect on numbers entering higher education (HE) is now beginning to bite, with more departments having to top up numbers or even substantially recruit through clearing[2] this year, and with entrance grades falling as some institutions strive to attain targets. Coordinated action is required at all levels to reverse this trend. This editorial seeks to document and explain recent trends, and identify possible implications and courses of action.

Decoding the evidence

Middle school

Although Geography has maintained its peak position in the subject 'league table', there has been a steady decline in the numbers taking the middle school (14–16) assessment: from 302 298 in 1996 to 251 605 in 2000. The reasons for the decline in numbers since the mid-1990s of candidates taking subjects that are no longer in the National Curriculum in the middle school years is well documented. It is augmented by general demographic trends. But why is Geography declining disproportionately when compared with subjects such as History, Art and Design, Drama and a second modern language such as Spanish?

A number of possible reasons have been put forward to account for this, although in the absence of targeted research, these remain untested.

- The quality of teaching in Geography in the lower school: recent Ofsted reports have indicated that teaching in Geography is not to the same standard overall as in other humanities subjects. The lower school is critical as pupils make their middle school subject choices at the end of this stage.
- The subject is not always taught by subject specialists in the lower school: hence one reason why the quality of teaching may not be so high.
- Geography students can be submitted for middle school examinations at one of two levels – foundation or higher level – but it is generally taught in a mixed-ability class for the two-year period. When students ask those who have recently completed their middle school studies: 'Should I study Geography?', they may get a negative reply from the less able student, along the lines of 'the examination was easy [foundation] but don't do Geography as the coursework is hard'. This is not the case in History where students are taught throughout in mixed-ability classes and the final examination is one of open-ended questions with an incline of difficulty. The history student does not therefore feel so disadvantaged throughout the course, or in the examination. This change in coursework has been in the system for four years. Could this be one cause for dropping numbers?
- Geography is often taught in the humanities faculty in maintained schools, and limited evidence from advertisements in the *Times Education Supplement* indicates that the Head of Humanities may often be a historian.

The results obtained at the middle-school assessment (GCSE) in Geography bear out some of the comments above. The national average for attainment of grades A to C in 1998 was 54.7 per cent, which increased to 56.6 per cent in 2000. Geography A–C grades, although above the national average, have increased less than History. Geography in 1998 had 56.2 per cent grade A–C, and 58.2 per cent in 2000, in comparison with History which had 59.4 per cent in 1998 and 62.2 per cent A–C grade in 2000.

Teachers currently teaching Geography at lower-school level have to make sure that the curriculum they deliver is exciting, stimulating and as relevant as possible. It is hoped that the schemes of work recently produced by the Qualifications and Curriculum Authority (QCA) will help to address this issue and help to enthuse pupils and their teachers about the subject. Existing teachers and those interested or concerned about the teaching of Geography in schools must continue to campaign for greater flexibility in the curriculum, especially at the middle-school assessment stage. The opportunity for flexibility exists in the form of 'disapplication';[3] steps are being taken now to ensure that these opportunities are made known to teachers and school governors.

Upper school

The number of candidates taking upper-school Geography (A level) declined from 42 181 in 1999 to 37 112 in 2000, a drop of approximately 12 per cent, which follows a drop of 6 per cent between 1998 and 1999. This decline directly reflects the drop in middle-school numbers of 8.5 per cent in 1998, when this year's upper-school group (2000) would have taken these examinations. The subjects that have overtaken Geography in the number rankings this year are Chemistry, History, Business Studies and Art and Design. The last two have never been higher than Geography in the rankings before now, and this possibly reflects a combination of the increased emphasis in the National Curriculum on both Design & Technology and Information Technology, together with a trend towards vocationally oriented courses.

These figures must be considered with the drop in the total number of upper-school assessment candidates from a peak of 794,262 in 1998 to 771,809 in 2000 – a reduction of 2.8 per cent overall. However, there is also the longer-term trend. During the mid-1990s, while Geography numbers rose History declined, and although the drop in numbers has accelerated this year, it comes after a period of growth and stability during the mid-1990s when other subjects such as French and Economics declined dramatically. In addition to the vocational courses, such as Business Studies, marked increases have been seen in Media Studies and Psychology, both of which seem to be considered 'trendy' among the younger generation. Without more detailed information, it remains to be seen whether it is the candidates who might have chosen Geography as a third option subject at upper school who are now choosing elsewhere. The trend in declining applications to university might suggest it is more deep-seated than a simple decline in 'third choice' option. It should be recognised that geographers have attained well above the national average of 58.2 per cent, achieving A grades at upper-school assessment, with 63.8 per cent of Geography candidates attaining these grades.

One possible light at the end of the tunnel is the introduction of the new structure to upper school education commencing in September 2000, in which most pupils study up to five subjects to Advanced Studies (AS) level in the first year of their two-year, upper-school studies (the 'sixth form'), and then specialize in three subjects in the second year. These three subjects are taken as A level examinations at the end of the second year of study. This change in the National Qualification framework may increase the numbers attracted to Geography at AS level. However, the AS level interest in the first place still relies on attracting candidates to the subject for the middle-school assessment. And it is a matter of the course content and teaching that will convert AS level interest to upper school candidates. More universities will have to face the difficult decision of whether to accept candidates with only AS level Geography onto single-honours degree courses.

The second possibly hopeful sign is the current review of 14–19 education that is aiming to develop a more coherent 14–19 curriculum and which may reduce the numbers of compulsory subjects.

Teacher recruitment numbers

Most people would agree that the quality and enthusiasm of teaching at school is one (if not the most) important element in maintaining the health of the subject in HE. Sadly – but not altogether surprisingly given the skills portfolio of Geography graduates and the challenges of teaching in recent years – graduates are not being attracted into teaching. There has been a year-on-year drop in applications for postgraduate certificate of education (PGCE) courses, and in recent years the national target for Geography places set by the government department responsible for education (DfEE) has consistently failed to be reached. In 1999, Geography applications to initial teacher training exceeded the target by 20 per cent but when converted into actual acceptances by students of places offered this reduced to 89 per cent of the target. Similarly, in 2000, applications exceeded the target by 14 per cent, but when converted into acceptances by students of places offered this reduced to 82 per cent of the target.

On 30 March 2000, in recognition of the general problem in teacher recruitment, the Secretary of State for Education announced that training salaries of £6000 would be paid to all students entering secondary PGCE initial teacher training courses in England, as from September 2000. The salary would also be available to all primary PGCE trainees from the same date as a one-year pilot. The full effect of these salaries has yet to be seen.

Teaching vacancies

Vacancies for geography teachers in the maintained secondary sector hover around the 0.6 per cent mark (0.6 in 1998, 0.5 in 1999, and 0.7 in 2000), but this still remains 50 per cent under the rate of 1.5 per cent seen in 1990. However, there continue to be marked regional differences, with notable high percentages of vacancies in inner London (2.4 per cent) and outer London (1.3 per cent).

Anecdotal evidence indicates that the postgraduate students leaving in summer 2000 are having difficulty in finding jobs. This is because geography teachers who are leaving are not being replaced owing to the contracting numbers of middle school and upper school candidates. What this means is that more Geography teaching in schools is likely to be done by the non-specialist, filling in the surplus periods on the timetable after the specialist has left. The non-specialist is likely to be more involved at the earlier (lower school) stage, and thus there is the story of a reinforced downward spiral.

Assessing the implications

What effect will this have on the higher education numbers?

There is no sign at the moment of a new equilibrium level in middle and upper school numbers being reached in Geography. There have been, and continue to be, so many changes to the secondary education system that it is difficult to see when a new equilibrium will be reached.

As yet, there seems to have been little impact on the total number of undergraduate students entering single-honours geography degree courses in the UK. (In 1997 this was recorded as 5,052; in 1998 the figure was 5,159; in 1999 it was 5,496.) There have been fluctuations in the number of higher education institutions (HEIs) offering single-honours geography degree courses – there were 118 courses in 1997, 121 courses in 1998 and 116 courses in 1999 – but a decrease in the number of higher education geography departments offering degrees. In 1997 there were 99 departments; two years later the number had reduced to 95; and in the most recent publication due out in October 2000 the number has reduced to 92. By the time the academic year starts in 2001, this will have reduced by at least two more as institutions have notified the Royal Geographical Society (with the Institute of British Geographers) of the forthcoming closure of their geography departments.

It was perhaps inevitable that consolidations would take place in both departments and institutions in all subjects following the recent shifts in university structure in the UK. With funds currently available from the national funding body for higher education (HEFCE) to support such initiatives, more closures are likely over the coming years. Furthermore the cessation of the control of maximum student number intakes in 2000 is likely to exacerbate the situation. While such changes are inevitably difficult for individuals and institutions, what is important for the discipline is to maintain a strong number of viable departments offering a breadth of courses and benefiting from buoyant student numbers.

Geography in the wider context of earth and environmental science

There is every indication that the interest in environmental courses has passed its peak. Starting from lower bases, both environmental science/studies and earth science degree intakes have dropped. (Environmental and other physical sciences took 2810 students in 1997, 2524 in 1998, 2259 in 1999; earth sciences, recorded as geology in the official statistics, dropped from 1486 in 1997 to 1429 in 1998, though showed a minor increase in 1999 with 1436 students.) It would seem that there is not a drift from potential geography students towards either earth or environmental science courses as might be portrayed in some university circles.

What is being done?

In April 1999 the Royal Geographical Society (with the IBG) and the Teacher Training Agency (TTA) hosted a conference to consider and make recommendations about issues affecting teacher shortage in Geography. In particular, the conference focused on identifying the factors responsible for the decline in numbers of geography graduates entering initial teacher training. Issues explored included the quality of initial teacher training (ITT) courses, the links between schools and higher education Geography, the public perceptions of geography teaching and the wider labour market. A report was published in summer 2000 with eight recommendations for action.

A Steering Group has been convened (by the RGS-IBG and the TTA) to take forward the recommendations from the report. The Steering Group has representation from several sectors (HE, ITT, schools and careers), and includes a recently qualified teacher of Geography, a head teacher, and representatives from the RGS-IBG and the UK's Geographical Association. One full-time member of staff has been appointed to implement the recommendations. This post of Project Development Officer, funded by the TTA, commenced in the RGS-IBG in mid-September 2000.

In the short term there is a programme of work planned to ensure that HEIs are aware of downward trends in students studying Geography at middle and upper school levels and in the numbers of geographers entering ITT. Fliers are to be produced to encourage students to consider teaching as a career, and posters will promote teaching Geography. The RGS-IBG/GA liaison is also focusing on the issue of falling numbers of school students in Geography as its key item.

In the medium term and at the local level there are a number of practical possibilities that are being investigated. Some of them revolve around strengthening existing links between universities and their local schools, and developing new ones. Others might encourage students to join a mentoring scheme in their local school, or undertake a third-year dissertation on a subject related to geographical education. A focus group of HE departments will assist in assessing these and other options, and all departments will be encouraged to undertake activities. Good ideas are always welcomed.

At a national level, broader reforms in teaching are designed to create a more attractive environment for today's graduates: recognition for performance, opportunities for continuing professional development, better administrative support and improved working conditions. Modernising the teaching profession is central to the ambitions laid out by the government in its recent Green Paper, *Teachers, Meeting the Challenge of Change.* For those whose first experience of teaching is in a gap year, often with no formal preparation, are there ways to encourage a positive experience of teaching through such activities?

Conclusion

It is clear from the facts and figures presented above that UK Geography has a potential problem, though the seriousness of the problem is not at all clear at the moment. Geography is not alone, though it appears in better heart than Environmental Science or Earth Science. Nevertheless, the subject, its practitioners and its professional bodies need to act swiftly and effectively to stem a decline that seems to be affecting all levels in the educational system. There is a damaging potential for serious negative feedback between these different levels. The weakest points in the system at present seem to be the relatively poor quality and, in some cases, the non-specialist teaching at lower-school levels, and the attraction of insufficient numbers of high-quality graduates into teaching as a career. The TTA at least has recognised the problem, and Geography is the first discipline that it has supported directly with an initiative to promote teaching.

Notes

1 In order to minimize the use of UK-specific terms in this editorial, general phrases are used in place of more specific phrases referring to learning stages in the UK National Curriculum, which is the standard framework for all school educational provision between the ages of 5 and 16 in the UK. Here 'lower school' will be used to refer to Key Stage 3 in the National Curriculum, where 14-year-old students sit national tests and tasks (the 'lower school assessment'); 'middle school' refers to Key Stage 4 in the National Curriculum, when 16-year-old school students sit the GCSE or General Certificate in Secondary Education examinations (the 'middle school assessment'); and 'upper school' refers to the final two years of secondary school education (the so-called 'sixth form'), when 18-year-old students take the A level (Advanced level) examinations (the 'upper school assessment'). Further explanation of the UK National Curriculum can be found at the following website: http://www.nc.uk.net/.

2 Clearing is the eleventh-hour process whereby potential students in the UK apply directly to higher education institutions for places on their courses.

3 Disapplication refers to the recently introduced process whereby certain pupils may, in certain circumstances (e.g. to maximize their learning performance), be permitted to take fewer than the prescribed number of National Curriculum subjects.

Section 4

Research, geography and continuing professional development

There is a wealth of research in the broad field of geography education: much of which has been mentioned in the preceding chapters and their accompanying reference lists. In this section however, the intention has been to concentrate on research that will be of direct relevance to beginning teachers as they commence and work through their PGCE course, and then start to think about the direction and nature of their future career in teaching. The three chapters that make up the section focus particularly on this aim.

Firstly, in Chapter 21, Margaret Roberts explores the role of research in the teaching and learning of Geography from an angle that focuses on the 'actors' and on the 'contexts'. She outlines a model of the teaching and learning situation and shows how research fits into the model – pointing out those areas where research is lacking as well as those areas where research is more plentiful.

In Chapter 22, Rod Gerber encourages beginning teachers to see themselves as learners. He notes that teachers of Geography continue to learn and develop their practice and ideas in a number of ways throughout their professional lives and he put forward an argument for this fact to be better recognized and researched so that it can form a platform from which programmes of continuing professional development can be formulated.

In the final chapter, Michael Naish explores the nature and history of action research. He uses case studies which, although they relate in subject matter to themes that were of particular concern in geography education in the early 1990s, nevertheless demonstrate clearly the methodology involved in action research, and show how geography teachers can use action research not only to enhance their own professionalism, but also to contribute to moving forward the frontiers of geography education.

Section 4

Research, geography and continuing professional development

21 The role of research in supporting teaching and learning

Margaret Roberts

Introduction

During the past decade, the role of educational research in the UK has been the subject of considerable debate. Discussion has centred on issues such as: priorities for educational research; how 'user groups' of research should be involved; the extent to which research should lead to 'applied outcomes'; and the 'relevance' of research (Rudduck and McIntyre 1998). Underpinning this debate is the notion accepted by most educational researchers that there should be some sort of connection between educational research on the one hand and the policy and practice of education on the other. How this connection is conceptualised varies, however, particularly in relation to teaching. Hargreaves has argued that teaching should be a 'research-based' profession and that it should be 'evidence-based' (Hargreaves 1998). These phrases suggest a direct relationship between applied research and application in the classroom. Hannon (1998), however, sees the role of research somewhat differently when he states, 'Teachers do not use research as a cookbook but as a resource in constructing their view of what is worth aiming for and likely ways to get it' (p. 151).

The general debate about educational research has raised questions that are important for geographical education. What is worth researching? Can research provide evidence for a basis for teaching geography? How can it help teachers to construct their views of what is worth aiming for? These questions provide a context for this chapter which sets out to explore the role of research in supporting the teaching and learning of Geography in schools. The approach I have adopted is different from others who have written about geography education research. Other approaches have given emphasis to what has been researched and how. Foskett and Marsden (1999) have compiled a useful bibliography, categorising what has been written on geographical and environmental education into themes. Williams (1996) and Slater (1996) were both concerned with how research into geographical education has been carried out and have illustrated different 'approaches', 'methods' and 'ideologies' with examples. The starting point for these writers was the research itself.

I have approached the question about the role of research in supporting teaching and learning from the other end of the research/practice debate. I want to focus more on the 'actors' involved in the process of teaching and learning, the teachers and the learners, and the contexts within which the teaching and learning of Geography takes place.

A model of the teaching and learning situation

I have represented the teaching and learning situation diagrammatically in the model shown in Figure 21.1 on which I have identified three components of the teaching and learning situation in schools: learners, teachers and the context. They are represented by three overlapping circles, A, B and C. I have used the term 'learner' to mean the children, pupils or students learning Geography, although I recognise that the teacher is also a learner in the classroom. I have used the term 'teacher' to mean the adult in the teaching and learning situation although I recognise that pupils can teach their peers. By the 'context' I mean everything in the school and organised by the school which can support learning. Together, these three overlapping inner circles represent the world of formal school education. They are situated on the diagram in the wider context of the world outside the school. I have labelled this outer circle, marked H, as 'culture' by which I mean the complex processes through which groups and individuals make sense of their world. Within the cultural circle I have identified four interrelated aspects of culture as being particularly relevant to the teaching and learning of Geography: experience, cultural change, policy and values. I have drawn the boundaries between the inner circles and the wider context as broken lines, to emphasize the fact that the formal world of schooling and the cultural context are not distinct. Much learning takes place beyond the confines of formal schooling and this is significant to what takes place in school.

Beyond the circle representing the cultural context I have placed the 'real world'. This is the world that is mediated to us through culture experienced individually and in groups. The 'real' world that geographers investigate in schools is mediated particularly through what is currently accepted as appropriate for geographical education, influenced to some extent by what constitutes and has constituted 'geography' in higher education, and by national and school policies.

Mapping geography education research onto the model

I would now like to use this model to explore how research in geographical education can support the teaching and learning of Geography in schools. For each section, marked A–H on the model, I will discuss the type of research that can be mapped into the section, giving examples.

A   *Learners*

The research I have mapped into section A is concerned with how learners construct their own meanings of the world, i.e. how they make sense of what they know and experience. Researchers have investigated children's understanding of concepts in physical geography, for example the greenhouse effect, ozone depletion

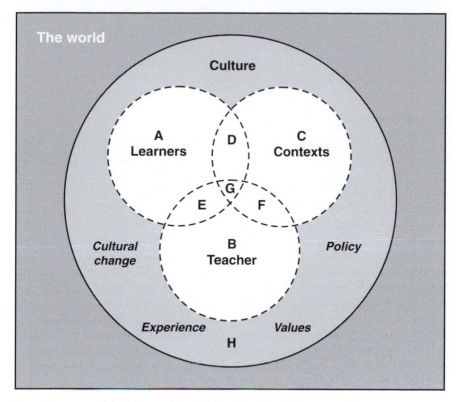

Figure 21.1 A model of the teaching and learning situations: actors and contexts

Note
See text for discussion of A–H.

and acid rain (Dove 1996). Others have researched childrens understandings of place, e.g. Matthews (1992). Robertson (2000) has investigated the affective rather than the cognitive domain in her study of the hopes and visions young people expressed for an area in which they carried out a land-use survey of England and Wales in 1987.

   The research mapped onto this sector is underpinned by a constructivist theory of learning. According to this theory, which is currently widely accepted, knowledge is not 'out there' for learners to receive. It has to be actively constructed by the learner and made sense of in terms of existing ways of thinking. Sometimes, the prior concepts of learners gained from experience in the wider context can be a barrier to learning in school. Research into learners' prior conceptions can inform the teacher of the potential difficulties of teaching specific geographical concepts and can suggest ways of tackling them. It is important for teachers to know individual starting points so that they can cater for different needs.

   Research in this sector generates a particular way of thinking about teaching and

learning. Such a view can inform and transform curriculum development and practice, as Driver (1994) has shown in relation to the science curriculum.

In Geography there has been more research into children's ideas of concepts in
physical geography than in human geography. There has been more research on the
cognitive domain than on the affective domain.

B   Teachers

The research I have mapped into this section recognises that teachers, in the same
way as learners, bring prior conceptions to the teaching and learning situation. They
bring geography subject knowledge, constructed during their own schooling, during
different higher education courses and through continuing professional study of the
subject. They also bring pedagogic knowledge, knowledge of how they understand
and practice teaching Geography, and this is influenced by their own experiences as a
teacher and as a learner. Examples of research on teachers include work on their
perceptions of environmental education (Corney 1997) and on their interpretations
of the Geography National Curriculum (Roberts 1995). Investigating teacher
perspectives was a major part of the research by Parsons (1988) on the implementation of the Schools Council's Geography for the Young School Leaver Project.

Research in this sector increases knowledge and understanding of different ways
of conceptualising the subject, ways of teaching it and different ways of interpreting
policy. It indicates how influential teachers' prior conceptions can be on the way
they work in the classroom. This research can enhance professional understanding
by raising important questions about taken for granted views and practices that are
taken for granted. It can probe the values underpinning practice.

C   The school context and resources

Research in category C focuses on resources as objects of research in themselves.
Most of the geography education research that can be mapped into this section is
related to textbooks. There have been many studies of geography textbooks investigating, for example, changes (Marsden 1988) and bias (Hicks 1980).

Most of the research in this area seems to be concerned with making teachers
and publishers more aware of how textbooks represent the world. Lester and Slater
(1996), however, researched and constructed a text on South Africa designed to make
the learner aware of different representations in text. I would suggest that the role of
research into resources is of growing significance for two reasons. First, developments in
Geography in higher education emphasise different views and representations of the
world. One authoritative text cannot represent it. Second, the increasing availability of
a large amount of information through the Internet gives access to far more viewpoints
and voices than are available in schools. Future research into resources needs to take
account of new perspectives in Geography in higher education and the easy access of
learners to knowledge not controlled by a teacher. It needs to investigate how learners
can be made aware of issues of representation for themselves and how they can be
supported to help them make sense of different viewpoints and voices.

D   Learners using resources

Research in section D, at the interface of learners and resources, is investigating the learners' use and understanding of resources. Research in this section is dominated by research into learners' understanding of maps. Examples of research into map use include the use by young children of maps in their physical environment (Spencer *et al.* 1989) and children's understanding of thematic maps in atlases (Wiegand 1996).

There has been some research on other resources used in geographical education. Blades and Spencer (1987) have studied young children's understanding of aerial photographs. As part of research into thinking skills, Leat and Nichols (1999) have investigated how secondary school pupils manipulate and make sense of text in 'mysteries' activities in Geography.

Research in this section is important because the teaching and learning of Geography at the beginning of the twenty-first century in the UK is very dependent on the use of resources. Geography examinations at GCSE and A level present data which candidates are expected to use and interpret. The Geography National Curriculum for England requires that pupils learn to use both primary and secondary sources of data. Yet, with the exception of research into understanding of maps, there is relatively little research into how learners use and make sense of data in the resources presented to them.

E   Teacher/learner interactions

Research in this overlapping section of the model focuses on ways in which teachers and learners interact with each other. This interaction involves the use of language, spoken or written. Much of the research into classroom talk in geography lessons has been carried out as part of research into language across the curriculum, (Mercer 1995). Carter's research (1991) was specifically focused on Geography and contributed to the National Oracy Project.

Teachers and learners also interact through written work. Again, much of the research has been carried out across the curriculum and has referred to geographical examples. This work has focused on, for example, how learners interpret what teachers expect from written work (Sheeran and Barnes 1991) and how pupils responded to written activities set up by teachers to explore audience-centred writing in Geography (Butt 1993).

Research in this area is crucially important because language is the medium through which most learning takes place in Geography. What learners learn, how they learn and what they think is important to learn are strongly influenced by written and spoken dialogues between teacher and learner and between learner and learner. Research into this area can probe familiar habitual classroom practices. It helps us to see them differently and to understand them more fully. It can indicate what helps and what hinders learning. Research can suggest strategies for teachers to use to promote learning.

F   Teachers and the resources they use

Little research has been carried out on the way teachers use different resources and the thinking underpinning such different use. An example which could be included in this section is Job's (1996) investigation of how teachers thought about the use of the environment. He revealed the different ideologies underpinning practice, and produced a framework that helps clarify understanding.

G   Learners, teachers and resources

Research in this sector, at the overlapping centre of the model, is concerned with teachers, learners and resources, when all three elements are present in the research. It includes curriculum development research, research on assessment and research into classroom practices.

The Geography curriculum development projects of the 1970s and 1980s were all developed through research.

Research that focuses on the whole process of assessment can also be mapped onto this sector. Daugherty (1996) provides a useful overview of research on assessment, in which he comments that 'the professional discourse about assessment has only infrequently been informed by research studies seeking to gather evidence from empirical investigation' (p. 242). This would suggest that policy decisions that have a profound effect on teaching and learning are made at national and school level without the benefit of evidence from research. It seems vitally important at a time when so much importance is placed on the results of summative assessments that more is understood about how different forms of assessment help and/or hinder learning. It is also important to know how the official assessment structures influence the teaching and learning of Geography. Such research should inform policy which in turn influences teaching and learning.

Classroom research that takes place in a 'real-life' rather than experimental setting with a teacher, a class of learners and resources, can be mapped onto this section. Some of this work is on a small scale, for example, Rickinson (1999) has investigated the teaching and learning of people–environment issues in the classroom. An example of developmental research in this area is Leat's (Leat and Nichols 1999) work with teachers in their classrooms in the north east of England. The focus of this work is on 'thinking skills', and the work has included development and research of resources, close observation and recording of classroom practices and interviews with teachers and learners. Much of the research is carried out by the teachers as action researchers with the aim of changing and improving teaching and learning in their own classrooms. Action research has the potential to improve understanding of classroom processes, to change and improve classroom practices, to improve the quality of learning and to promote professional development.

H   The wider context

I have selected three aspects of the cultural context to examine the role of research in this sector: cultural change, policy and values.

Research on the history of geographical education provides an overview of changes in teaching and learning practices and of underpinning rationales. Research into the history of geographical education helps us understand the present. It reveals that what has been accepted as good practice in teaching and learning is subject to change and is therefore open to question. Furthermore, accounts of geographical education in the past help to ensure that valuable lessons learnt from the curriculum research and development projects of the 1970s and 1980s are not lost.

The teaching and learning of Geography in England and Wales is taking place in the context of nationally produced policy frameworks. Research into policy asks critical questions about how policy has been constructed (Rawling 1992), about its underpinning ideologies (Lambert 1994) and about its reconstruction by teachers in schools (Roberts 1995). As policy undoubtedly influences the teaching and learning of Geography in schools, it is essential that critical questions continue to be asked about policy. Policy research does not have a direct impact but it does have a role in informing future policy decisions, with possible profound effects on the teaching and learning of Geography.

All the research into geographical education mentioned so far is underpinned by views about the purposes of geographical education. What sort of geography and what sort of educational practices are valued in the research and why? Whose interests do they serve? It is important that these bigger questions about what is valued and why are not ignored in research directly focused on teaching and learning. In this section I would include research which maps other research onto different ideologies, revealing underpinning values (e.g. Slater 1996). The role of this research, like the other research referred to in this section, is more diffuse, but has the power to change the way we think about teaching and learning.

Conclusions

I would now like to return to the questions raised at the beginning of this chapter: What is worth researching? What evidence is provided by research to support the teaching and learning of Geography? Can it help teachers construct their views on what is worth aiming for?

The model in Figure 21.1 has provided a framework for revealing areas of attention and neglect in geography education research. There is undoubtedly scope for more sustained detailed research in every sector of the model, including areas which have received most attention such as textbook research and children's understanding of maps. I would, however, highlight some areas of neglect:

- children's prior understanding of concepts in human geography;
- resources other than textbooks, with attention to the implications of accessibility of new and varied sources of data;
- learners' uses and understanding of resources other than maps;
- processes of teaching and learning in real-life classroom situations.

There is also a need for research that investigates issues through a range of scales, from the individual learner to the social and cultural context, and from national policy to how it impacts on learning in the classroom.

Some geography education research provides evidence that would seem to be of direct relevance to teaching and learning in the classroom. For example, research on misunderstandings of geographical concepts, on how children understand maps, how writing frames can support learning, and curriculum development projects all provide ideas and strategies to improve teaching and learning. Action research, involving classroom teachers, has direct implications for improving practice.

However, the application of the 'evidence' from research entails more than copying the strategies that others have developed. It often demands significant changes in thinking about teaching and learning. Educational research aimed at increasing knowledge and understanding of the processes of teaching, learning and assessment can lead to insights that can be profoundly influential.

I would not value research that has the potential to be applied directly to teaching and learning more than I would value research which is more diffuse in its influence. The role of research in supporting teaching and learning in Geography is greater than providing information on what works in the classroom. It also has a role in challenging assumptions, in identifying underpinning values and in asking critical questions about purposes. Research into geographical education can help us see things differently and freshly. It can empower teachers to construct their own understandings, to clarify their own values and to have professional confidence to make changes in classroom practices.

References

Blades, M. and Spencer, C. (1987) 'Young children's recognition of environmental features from aerial photographs and maps', *Environmental Education and Information*, 6(3): pp. 189–98.

Butt, G. (1993) 'The effects of audience-centred teaching on children's writing in geography', *International Research in Geographical and Environmental Education (IRGEE)*, 2(1): pp. 11–25.

Carter, R. (1991) *Talking about Geography: The Work of Geography Teachers*, Sheffield: Geographical Association.

Corney, G. (1997) 'Conceptions of environmental education', in Slater, F., Lambert, D. and Lines D. (eds) *Education, Environment and Economy: Reporting Research in a New Academic Grouping*, (Bedford Way Papers), London: University of London Institute of Education.

Daugherty, R. (1996) 'Assessment in geographical education', in M. Williams (ed.) *Understanding Geographical and Environmental Education: The Role of Research*, London: Cassell.

Dove, J. (1996) 'Student misconceptions on the greenhouse effect, ozone layer depletion and acid rain', *Environmental Education Research*, 2(1): 89–100.

Driver, R. (1994) *Making Sense of Secondary Science: Research into Children's Ideas*, London: Routledge.

Foskett, N. and Marsden, B. (eds) (1998) A *Bibliography of Geographical Education 1970–1997*, Sheffield: Geographical Association.

Hannon, P. (1998) 'An ecological perspective on educational research', in R. Rudduck and D. McIntyre (eds), *Challenges for Educational Research*, London: Paul Chapman.

Hargreaves, D. (1998) 'A new partnership of stakeholders and a national strategy of research in education', in J. Rudduck and D. McIntyre (eds), *Challenges for Educational Research*, London: Paul Chapman.

Hicks, D. (1980) 'Bias in books', *World Studies Journal*, 1(3): 14–22.

Job, D. (1996) 'Geography and environmental education: an exploration of perspectives and strategies', in A. Kent, D. Lambert, M. Naish and Slater, F. (eds) *Geography in Education: Viewpoints on Teaching and Learning*, Cambridge: Cambridge University Press.

Lambert, D. (1994) 'Geography in the National Curriculum: a cultural analysis', in R. Walford and P. Machon(eds), *Challenging Times: Implementing the National Curriculum in Geography*, Cambridge: Cambridge Publishing Services.

Leat, D. and Nichols, A. (1999) *Mysteries Make You Think*, Sheffield: Geographical Association.

Lester, A. and Slater, F. (1996) 'Reader, text, metadiscourse and argument, in J. van der Schee, G. Schoenmaker, H. Trimp and H. van Westrhenen (eds) *Innovation in Geographical Education*, Utrecht/Amsterdam: Centrum voor Educatieve Geografie Vrije Universiteit.

Marsden, W. (1988) 'Continuity and change in geography textbooks: perspectives from the 1930s to the 1960s', *Geography*, 73(4): 327–43.

Matthews, M.H. (1992) *Making Sense of Place: Children's Understanding of Large-Scale Environments*, Hemel Hempstead: Harvester Wheatsheaf.

Mercer, N. (1995) *The Guided Construction of Knowledge: Talk amongst Teachers and Learners*, Clevedon: Multilingual Matters.

Parsons, C. (1988) *The Curriculum Change Game: A Longitudinal Study of the Schools Council GYSL Project*, London: Falmer Press.

Rawling, E. (1992) 'The making of a national geography curriculum', *Geography*, 77(4): 292–309.

Rickinson, M. (1999) 'People–environment issues in the geography classroom: towards an understanding of students' experiences', *International Research in Geographical and Environmental Education (IRGEE)*, 8(2).

Roberts, M. (1995) 'Interpretations of the geography National Curriculum: a common curriculum for all?', *Journal of Curriculum Studies*, 27(2): 187–205.

Robertson, M. (2000) 'Young people speak about the landscape', *Geography*, 85(1): 24–36.

Rudduck, J. and McIntyre, D. (eds) (1998) *Challenges for Educational Research*, London: Paul Chapman.

Sheeran, Y. and Barnes, D. (1991) *School Writing*, Milton Keynes: Open University Press.

Slater, F. (1996) 'Illustrating research in geographical education, in A. Kent *et al.* (eds), *Geography in Education: Viewpoints on Teaching and Learning*, Cambridge: Cambridge University Press.

Spencer, C., Blades, M. and Morsley, K. (1989) *The Child in the Physical Environment*, Chichester: John Wiley.

Wiegand, P. (1996) 'A constructivist approach to children's understanding of thematic maps', in J. van der Schee, G. Schoenmaker *et al.* (eds), *Innovation in Geographical Education*, Utrecht/Amsterdam: Centrum voor Educatieve Geografie Vrije Universiteit.

Williams, M. (ed.) (1996) *Understanding Geographical and Environmental Education: The Role of Research*, London: Cassell.

22 Understanding how geographical educators learn in their work

An important basis for their professional development

Rod Gerber

Adult learning from the basis of experience

Geographical educators, like all other adults, should be conscious that they continue to learn throughout their lives through professional and everyday experiences that are situated in different formal and informal contexts. This lifelong process can be explained by understanding the interrelatedness of the concepts of lifelong learning, everyday learning, situated learning and experience-based learning. Previous wisdom has concluded that learning:

- occurs incidentally in the early years of life;
- is cultivated formally during the schooling years;
- is acquired and refined in one's work;
- is largely non-existent during one's later years.

Often, these foci were considered in isolation and were unrelated. Nowadays, it is held that learning is a lifelong process – something which individuals do naturally and often with different forms of assistance. Theorists such as Brookfield (1986), Cafferella and O'Donnell (1991), Candy (1991) and Hammond and Collins (1991) have recognized this in their considerations of adolescent and adult learning. Their recognition that learning is a process which pervades our lives is strong. Consideration is offered for the nature of this learning in terms of the extent to which it is directed or self-directed. Geographical educators may undertake formal study at a university to obtain a higher degree. This is a directed form of learning. Alternatively, they may investigate a different teaching strategy by exploring, in a self-directed manner, various sources and people to learn more about it with a view to using it in their classes. By so doing, geographical educators are engaging in adult education. Foley (1995: xiv) states that adult education can take one of four forms:

1   Formal education that is organized by professional educators, where there is a defined curriculum, and which often leads to a qualification, e g. completing a PGCE course to become a geography teacher.

2   Non-formal education in which some sort of systematic instruction is provided on an infrequent basis, e.g. attending an INSET workshop or writing assessment items for a new geography curriculum.
3   Informal education in which people learn from their experiences, e.g. learning how to improve teaching fieldwork through the experiences of several field trips.
4   Incidental learning that occurs as the result of everyday learning in situations unrelated to a person's professional activities, e.g. extending one's understanding of the concept of spatial association through watching the behaviours of two football teams in a weekend fixture.

Larsson (1996) states that adult learning has to do with 'changing the patterns adults are caught in' (p. 9). It relates closely to the situation in which adults find themselves and the learning needs that they have in these situations. He suggests that adults enter educational situations with a set of existing interpretations and skills which will be changed if adult education occurs. He suggests that such changes may include: learning new knowledge and developing new skills; developing new interests; learning a new kind of working life that is more challenging and provides access to more of one's talents as a geographical educator; enhancing one's self-confidence; and acquiring knowledge that is not available in one's everyday world (Larsson 1996). Such learning should be judged according to its capacity to change the conditions for learning in everyday contexts. Larsson declares:

> A good adult education must not only have the qualities of challenging everyday interpretations, be relevant and have a genuine meaning for the students – it must be aware that all those interpretations that are communicated in the educational discourse must be subordinated to the judgement of specific cases in everyday life.
>
> (Larsson 1996: 16)

Everyday learning is a process that occurs throughout people's lives. Throughout our lives we become conscious of the content of the world around us. We interpret it, i.e. we develop personal knowledge, and learn as we change our interpretations of things in our life-world. The importance of the situations in which everyday learning occurs is emphasized by Larsson (1996) as follows:

> Our individual experiences form us also. In principle, everyone is on different ground. Our interpretations are thus formed by the place we are at and have been at geographically and socially. We interpret the world differently according to the place we are at and the person we accordingly have become. Where we are in space and time is fundamental for our experiences and interpretations and thus for our learning.
>
> (Larsson 1996: 4)

Geographical educators are often people who have a strong affinity for environments and other cultures. The range of personal, everyday environmental experiences that they have certainly has an impact on their enthusiasm to facilitate similar experiences amongst their students and to extend their own experiences by travelling to other environments during their vacations.

The role of experience in learning that has just been mentioned has been formalized in the concept of experience-based learning. It is based on the following set of assumptions: experience is the foundation of, and the stimulus for, learning; learners actively construct their own experience; learning is a holistic process; learning is socially and culturally constructed; and learning is influenced by the socio-emotional context in which it occurs (Boud *et al.* 1993). As such, experience-based learning cannot be reduced to a set of prescriptions. As Andresen, Boud and Cohen (1995) summarize, all experience-based learning is characterized by the involvement of the whole person through his or her intellect, feelings and sense, recognition and active use of all the learner's relevant life experiences and learning experience, and continued reflection upon earlier experiences in order to add to and transform them into deeper understanding. Additionally, experience-based learning may involve decisions as to whether the activity that leads to learning has been intentionally designed for that purpose, whether the learner's engagement in the experience has been facilitated by some other person (e.g. a teacher), and whether the outcomes of the learning are to be assessed.

Geographical educators have long recognized the need for experience-based learning through the widespread use of field studies as an integral component of school Geography curriculums. Their belief that direct observational experiences are essential to understanding our world better continues to be promoted. Journals such as *Teaching Geography* abound with examples or case studies of the merits of field-based experiences for students. However, the merits of experience-based learning for geographical educators has been much less explored. For example, in the recently published *Geography Teachers' Handbook* (Bailey and Fox 1996) the chapter on teacher education and training (Chapter 30) introduces the concept of professional development for geographical educators, but it stops short of promoting experience-based learning as an important basis for such development of geographical educators throughout their careers.

This section may be concluded by reflecting that the above-mentioned aspects of lifelong, adult, everyday and experience-based learning necessarily occur in a context, i.e. they occur as situated learning. Billet (1996), in a recent synthesis of the literature on situated learning, proposes a framework which bridges the contributions of socio-cultural theories, e.g. Vygotsky and Leontiev, and cognitive theories, e.g. Ericsson and Simon, and Glaser. In it, the conditions for maximizing the development of propositional knowledge include exposing learners to different views, clarifying initial understandings, developing models as a part of everyday activity which will pattern propositional knowledge and engagement in joint problem-solving. Its constructivist nature highlights that the construction of knowledge must be situated in a specific context if it is to be meaningful and useful in living. As Larsson notes:

We cannot imagine either thought or action without presupposing both the individual and the surrounding world. This 'life-world' is formed by its existence in space and time, simply because its concept is a world that is situated in time and space. Thus, we are formed by the situation that we are living in, since it is the content of our lives.

(Larsson 1996: 6)

Consequently, geographical educators as adults who are consciously engaging in lifelong, experience-based, everyday learning need to reflect on themselves as learners just as much as they focus on their students as learners. How this can be understood and promoted will be demonstrated in the following sections.

How do adults learn in their work?

Concern about the ways in which adults learn in their work is a recent phenomenon when considered from an experiential perspective. One earlier example of such an approach was Steffan Larsson's (1986) study of teachers' conception of changes in their professional practice. The results of this study were that when the teacher had taught for some time there is:

- a change in his or her focus of attention from him or herself to the learners;
- a collection of knowledge about the way different pieces of teaching work;
- a change in what kind of knowledge he or she wants to transmit (from facts to principle or ways of reasoning);

and work becomes routinized leading to a decreased interest in the work. Unfortunately, none of these outcomes reported how teachers learned in their work.

Steffan Larsson (1993) offered one of the earliest statements on the need to investigate how people learned in their work. He recognized that people in different work situations and types of work have the potential to learn differently. Following this statement, the topic of how people learn in their work, based on their own experiences, is being explored in different situations in the Australian context. An investigation of how white-collar workers in the insurance industry, a government department, a library and a private education institution learned in their job (Gerber *et al.* 1995) revealed learning occurred through:

1   Self-managed observation and from mistakes, e.g. through trial-and-error and a commitment not to make the same mistake again.
2   Interaction with other people, e.g. fellow workers and local experts.
3   Formal training, e.g. training modules and formal seminars organized by workplace trainers or staff development officers.
4   Offering leadership, e.g. mentoring less experienced workers and teaching other workers.
5   Open lateral planning, e.g. planning training modules and adopting innovative approaches to learning.

6   Quality assurance, e.g. performance evaluation and attainment of incentives offered by the organization, or the achievement of public acclaim for one's level of performance.

The above study may be termed a horizontal one in that it focused on generally experienced workers at a similar level in their workplaces. It is matched by another (Gerber 1996) which selected workers within an organization across a range of technical and managerial jobs, e.g. a vertical slice of the occupations in the organization. The workers in this study in a single industrial company revealed that they learned their jobs through:

1   Making mistakes, e.g. through taking calculated risks and correcting mistakes.
2   Self-education on and off the job, e.g. reading books and technical reports and formal training in company-organized seminars.
3   Practising one's personal values and attitudes, e.g. using one's initiative, questioning what one is doing and being willing to stand up for one's beliefs.
4   Applying theory and practising skills, e.g. using theory learned in pre-service training/education in one's work and conscious practice of skills to improve work performance.
5   Being an advocate for colleagues, e.g. negotiating for colleagues in enterprise agreements and maintaining health and safety standards for the workforce.
6   Problem-solving, e.g. deciding on the best solution to a work problem.
7   Preparation for a task, e.g. understanding the elements of the work task and choosing suitable equipment for the task.
8   Teamwork, e.g. working as a member of a work team and observing other team members at work.
9   As a part of a lifelong process, e.g. keeping an open mind about the work and adopting an optimistic approach to learning one's job.

What these results indicate is that workers learn on the job in a number of ways, some of which are grounded in individual choice and decision making, while others are developed and made available to workers for their consumption. What was particularly noticeable in these results was the highly personalized nature of the learning process for on-the-job training and learning. It was grounded in the personal development of the individual workers, their strategies for informal training, their learning of intuitive means and, for some, their willingness to think laterally and act as an advocate for their colleagues. Individual workers displayed reasonable control over their learning despite the different levels of status for their substantive jobs in the organization. Generally, the learning occurred when it was required and when the workers were motivated to seek it, i.e. it was an intentional act on the part of the worker.

Solving problems and addressing challenges were prime motivations for workers to learn in their work. They were not usually able to do so through formal training because of the rate of occurrence of these problems and challenges. If key people were available then their help was used to address the problem. If they weren't then the tendency was for the worker to intuit a response and to use a trial-and-error approach to see what happened. The process was repeated until success was achieved.

The extent to which the workers were able to reflect on their actions varied according to their decisions. In the use of trial-and-error approaches, the workers were able to reflect after each decision whether correct or incorrect. When incorrect decisions were made, the workers considered what they had done, made another choice and reflected on the extent to which it was successful. The importance of the learning associated with these decisions is that the workers remembered not to make the same mistake twice. Reflections were usually built into formal learning activities through group discussion and tasks that required some thought about decision, e.g. reacting to different scenarios. Similarly, any kind of evaluation of performance required workers to reflect on the quality of their performance.

To what extent do geographical educators learn professionally, using the approaches that have been derived from more general research into workplace learning?

How do geographical educators learn in their professional work?

Geographical educators are generally employed in schools, universities, field study centres and government ministries. These different contexts merely reflect different workplace settings in which learning on the job is done. While the demands on the educators do vary there will be a reasonable amount of common ground in the ways that they learn. In fact, geographical educators do use most of the ways that have been expressed by other workers to learn in their jobs. What is likely to differ are the types of examples of learning, because they will be related directly to the different professional contexts in which these educators operate. The main ways in which geographical educators learn are through:

- making mistakes;
- self-education on and off the job;
- practising personal values;
- applying theory and practising skills;
- problem-solving;
- interacting with others;
- offering leadership to others;
- open lateral planning;
- being an advocate for colleagues;
- formal training;
- quality assurance.

The following synopses will elaborate the above.

i   Learning through making mistakes

The concept of making and correcting mistakes as a way of learning is never highlighted in any written documents for geographical educators. Therefore, anecdotal
evidence will be offered to justify its inclusion in this list. How many beginning
geographical educators have made errors in geographical facts, concept or generalizations, demonstrations of skills, lost their way on a fieldtrip, offered an inaccurate
explanation in solving a geographical problem or become disoriented in an unfamiliar environment? All or some of these misadventures have occurred to beginning and to some experienced geographical educators in their professional work.
For the thinking geographical educator, the fact that they have occurred is not that
important. What is more important is that the geographical educators recognized
them as mistakes and did not repeat them in the future. Some would argue that this
is the most powerful way to learn.

ii   Learning through self-education on and off the job

The concept of self-education may be interpreted variously depending on one's
perspective. In the broadest sense it could include all types of self-initiated learning
experiences that geographical educators undertake during their professional lives.
However, in an attempt to separate it from the situated learning experiences in
formal training, the preference here is to focus on non-formal learning experiences
that educators practise as they carry out their professional business. Such experiences may be spontaneous responses to the urgent need to solve a pedagogic
problem, e.g. how to conduct a debriefing session at the conclusion of a simulation
exercise, or they may be deliberate, planned experiences which occur over a period
of time, e.g. learning how to generate a thematic map using a particular piece of
software. The maximization of technology by geographical educators does not
usually occur through sitting through endless formal training sessions. Rather, it
occurs through an introduction to the technology followed by extensive individual
practice. Often a considerable amount of trial-and-error will occur as the geographical educator grapples with learning how to use the Internet or a similar technology.

The power of self-education for learning is its personal nature and the self-
motivation that it engenders. Not all geographical educators are 'techno-freaks',
but those who believe that newer electronic technologies can facilitate learning
both in geography and as geographical educators will drive themselves to know
about multimedia education and learn to incorporate it in their geography classes.
Learning about such technologies in one's non-work environment can certainly
encourage many a geographical educator to attempt to transfer competencies and
strategies to formal learning situations.

iii   Practising personal values

Geographical educators have placed considerable emphasis on the importance of
social and environmental values in the curricular and policy documents, e.g.

International Charter on Geographical Education (IGU.CGE 1992). Generally, these have been couched in terms of the values it is hoped that learners will develop rather than those that geographical educators will practise. The ideal situation would be for the geographical educators have developed and practised these values in their personal lives. If the learning done by the student is to promote a concern for the environment, an appreciation of the landscape and an empathy for people in other cultures, it will be authenticated (Larsson 1996) if the geographical educators practise their own similar values in the formal learning experience.

People incorporate their personal values into their learning experiences consciously and subconsciously. The challenge for geographical educators is to do so consciously or intentionally. Promoting the belief in a sustainable world can be talked about by geographical educators in their classes. However, it is grasped more meaningfully by both the educator and his or her students when evidence of actual practice of such a value is demonstrated in the educator's personal life. The extent of commitment to the value will likely be enhanced by people in both these roles.

iv   *Applying theory and practising skills*

An interesting thing appears to have happened in school Geography as the result of the emphasis on enquiry learning. In the learning, the understanding and application of geographical theory has been largely replaced in post-industrial countries by the process of geographical enquiry, and the development of skills tends to be an acontextualized experience. This may well reflect what geography has been learned by educators in their pre-service training and the orientations promoted by their university tutors. Somehow, learning to apply theory and using skills as bases for developing geographical understandings need to be highlighted in the learning and professional preparation of geographical educators if they are going to be able to develop comprehensive explanations for events from a geographical perspective.

Geographical educators who have understood their theory will maximize such understanding though direct experience, e.g. in fieldwork, and indirect experience, e.g. viewing a videotape of slum development in a large South American city. Learning how to explain the landform formation on a fieldtrip in the local region or the morphology of a large slum environment is what geographic educators develop as they apply their theoretical understandings to practice or real-world situations.

v   *Learning through problem-solving*

Inquiry learning has been mentioned previously. It, and its predecessor scientific method, have been used by geographical educators as important stimuli for justifying the use of problem-solving in formal education. Problem-solving has increased its popularity in professional education through the concept of problem-solving and the recognition in the education and training worlds of problem-solving as a key competency. One of the challenges for geographical educators is to work out the extent to which they support inductive, experiential learning and deductive learning. Problem-solving as a learning approach is grounded in the search for solutions through data-gathering, to formulate meaning, i.e. to make a decision based on reasoned judgements about the data gathered (e.g. to decide on the extent to which recycling of household products is practised in an urban area), or through testing a hypothesis about some geographical phenomenon, e.g. the velocity across a stream at different places along its course.

The importance of experience should not be underestimated in learning to solve problems. Everyday expressions of seemingly trivial activities can be very helpful, e.g. finding one's way around a large shopping complex, deciding on which slope to plant a particular fruit tree or choosing when to go for a jog when holidaying in a country with an equatorial climate, especially if you come from a mid-latitude country. Geographical educators do learn to improve their decision-making skills by reflecting on such everyday experiences and transferring such competencies to their professional work.

vi Learning through interacting with others

Have you ever wondered why geographical educators congregate at conferences or symposiums? In most cases it is to learn more about their professional area by interacting with their colleagues. It is often why at geographical education conferences the practising educators prefer to attend workshops and demonstrations so that they can reflect on their own practice and learn to do things better. Often, geographical educators come to such conferences with a number of their own problems or challenges in mind which they will want to discuss with colleagues or visiting experts in order to improve their own practice.

Within the context of this professional practice, geographical educators have more immediate reasons for interacting with other professionals. They may not be able to operate a computer simulation properly and so they will seek help from the technology co-ordinator. They may not know the route for a particular field trip and so they will need to consult a colleague in the staffroom during recess. They may also need to obtain permission to order a new set of textbooks for the revised curriculum. In each of these cases the geographical educator will interact with another person before making a final decision, hopefully learning from each of these experiences.

vii Learning through offering leadership to others

An opposite way in which geographical educators learn is by leading their peers in professional activities. The learning that comes from preparing a presentation or demonstration for other geographical educators is an important example of experiential learning. Structuring a presentation about improving global understanding by using the Internet or organizing a workshop or visualizing environments from interpreting maps both involve careful reflection and decision-making by the person doing the presentation. Quite often it is associated with geography and for pedagogic learning. Such learning is confirmed during the presentation if it has been communicated effectively and clearly.

Experienced geographical educators will also learn by mentoring less experienced colleagues. It might be assumed that the person being mentored is the one who will do all the learning. However, that is not necessarily so, even though it is expected that he or she will do most of the learning. The experienced geographical educator may have to relearn a particular geographical theory or technique in order to explain and apply it to his or her junior colleague. For example, this person may not have used the theory of spatial diffusion for some years and has to relearn some of its finer aspects before communicating with a junior staff member.

Such leadership can be a very empowering process for both types of participants: for the experienced educator it can improve one's self-esteem, communication and planning skills and for the inexperienced educator it means learning more and learning it more effectively.

viii   Learning through open lateral planning

Geographical educators, like all professional educators, are prone to look beyond their comfort zone and to want to utilize different types of learning activities with their students. Teaching the same concepts and skills year after year using the same sort of strategies can become boring even to the most dedicated geographical educator. Educators go to conferences, read relevant professional journals, seek out people who have been identified by colleagues as 'innovators', and are generally searching for fresh ideas both to maintain motivation and to update their professional approaches.

The idea of learning from open lateral planning is based as much on adopting a very open mindset to the teaching of geography as it is of implementing innovative activities in geographical education. The geographical educator needs to develop a willingness and commitment to search for new ideas outside his or her field of study, to take the context of teamwork from a manufacturing plant (the idea of a self-managed work team) and transform it into the concept of autonomous study groups doing library research on a geography topic. There is no limit to the extent to which lateral thinking and planning can be used in the educational experience.

ix   Learning by being an advocate for colleagues

Geographical educators are professional educators. While their role of teacher is emphasized most frequently, they do occupy a range of roles which have an advocacy aspect to them. It is these roles that come into focus in this instance and from which they extend their professional learning. Such roles may include subject co-ordinator, executive member of a professional association and member of a curriculum development committee.

As subject co-ordinator in a school, a geographical educator undertakes to represent the views of his or her teachers in school-wide planning, development, management and performance. This role involves considerable interaction with members of the geography teaching staff, to understand their views in order to advance them in the wider school or community context. For example, justification of the expenditure on fieldwork within a school's budget may necessitate the subject co-ordinator developing and making a strong case that has been empowered by the whole geography teaching team.

As executive member of a professional association, e.g. the Geographical Association, it is often necessary to plead or defend the case for and of geography at times when government policy is changing on aspects of education, e.g. the case for geography as a core subject in the UK school curriculum. Geographical educators, sometime with expert advice, learn how to defend and promote their subject against any adverse changes. The advocacy exercised by geographical educators in relevant curriculum committees is more one of their professional area based on their own experiences in it. Such advocacy in curriculum development stems from the successes and failures of these educators in their own teaching, their philosophy of geography and education, and their discussions with colleagues on the best way to approach a proposed change.

x   *Learning through formal training*

All geographical educators will have experienced formal training prior to beginning their professional lives. They were educated and trained to become geography teachers or university tutors. Many of these educators accept the challenge to upgrade their qualifications by undertaking further formal training, and have received higher university awards. Additionally, they attend, largely in their own time, a range of specially designed programmes organised by local education authorities and professional associations. These experiences were all selected to promote professional learning in geography and education. They continue to be the accepted, credentialed pathway for becoming a geographical educator. However, once people become geographical educators, then formal training becomes less significant as a means of learning in one's work.

xi   *Learning through quality assurance*

The concept of quality assurance can be applied to geographical educators in a general way since one of their professional goals is to improve themselves as educators and to improve the learning that they facilitate. The aspect of learning which is evident here occurs through their reflection on their performance, discussing its positive and negative aspects and making decisions on ways to improve it. Such a reflective process can be very instructive if the geographical educators know what criteria they need to make judgements about their professional performance, e.g. effectiveness of their teaching, relevance of the learning that they promote to the students' lives, willingness to change to accommodate recent developments and ability to operate in an educational team.

Conclusion

This initial consideration of geographical educators' learning in their professional work indicates that it is a topic that should be considered very seriously from the perspective of the health of the world's geographical education. While we place very heavy emphasis on how students learn in geographical education we tend to forget about the concept of lifelong, experiential adult learning as it applies to professional geographical educators. As in all workplaces, the need to promote a smart-thinking and efficient workforce is necessary in geographical education at school and university levels. The promotion of 'new capitalist' aspects to the nature of the education that these professionals accept and promote can help to increase the smartness of geographical educators. It is initially a matter of working out what these ideas mean for geographical educators and then working out how to facilitate their development in their work contexts.

References

Andresen, L., Boud, B. and Cohen, R. (1995) 'Experience-based learning', in G. Foley (ed.) *Understanding Adult Education and Training*, Sydney: Allen & Unwin, pp. 207–19.

Bailey, P. and Fox, P. (eds) (1996) *Geography Teachers' Handbook*, Sheffield: Geographical Association.

Bednarz, S., Bettis, N., Boehm, R., de Souza, A., Downs, R., Marran, J., Morrill, R. and Salter, C. (1994) *Geography for Life: National Geography Standards*, Washington, DC: National Geographic Research and Exploration.

Billett, S. (1996) 'Situated learning: bridging sociocultural and cognitive theorising', *Learning and Instruction*, 6(3): 263–80.

Boud, D., Cohen, R. and Walker, D. (eds) (1993) *Using Experience for Learning*, Buckingham: SRHE and Open University Press.

Brookfield, S. (1986) *Understanding and Facilitating Adult Learning*, Milton Keynes: Open University Press.

Caffarella, R. and O'Donnell, J. (1991) *Self-directed Learning*, Nottingham: University of Nottingham Department of Adult Education.

Candy, P. (1991) *Self-direction for Lifelong Learning: A Comprehensive Guide to Theory and Practice*, San Francisco: Jossey-Bass.

Foley, G. (ed.) (1995) *Understanding Adult Education and Training*, Sydney: Allen Unwin.

Gerber, R. (1996) *Analysis of how workers learn in their jobs at the James Hardie Building Materials Division*, mimeo.

Gerber, R. and Lidstone, J. (1996) *Developments and Directions in Geographical Education*, Clevedon: Channel View Publications.

Gerber *et al.* (1995) 'Self-directed learning in a work context', *Education and Training*, 37(8): 26–32.

GTA (nd) *Geog and its value and place in the curriculum*, Melbourne: GTAV.

Hammond, M. and Collins, R. (1991) *Self-directed Learning: Critical Practice*, London: Kogan Page.

Hargreaves, A. (1994) *Changing Teachers, Changing Times: Teachers' work and culture in a postmodern age*, London: Cassell.

IGU CGE (1992) *International Charter on Geographical Education*, Brisbane: International Geographic Union Commission on Geographical Education.

Larsson, S. (1986) 'Learning from experience: teachers' conceptions of changes in their professional practice', *Journal of Curriculum Studies*, 19(1): 35–43.

Larsson, S. (1993) 'Self-directed learning in a work context: a short presentation of a project, its aim and method', paper presented at ESREA Seminar on Adult Education and the Labour Market, Ljubljana, Slovenia.

Larsson, S. (1996) *On meaning of life-long learning*, mimeo.

Lidstone, J. (1996) 'Professionalism in geographic education' in R. Gerber and J. Lidstone (eds) *Developments and Directions in Geographical Education*, Clevedon: Channel View Publications.

Marsden, W. (1995) *Geography 11–16: Rethinking Good Practice,* London: David Fulton.

Van der Schee, J., Schoenmaker, G., Trimp, H. and van Wetrhenen (eds) (1996) *Innovation in Geographical Education*, Utrecht: IGU CGE/Centre for Geographic Education, Free University, Amsterdam.

Williams, M. (1988) 'Continuing education for geography teachers', in R. Gerber and J. Lidstone (eds) *Developing Skills in Geographical Education*, Brisbane: International Geographic Union Commission on Geographical Education..

23 Action research for a new professionalism in geography education

Michael Naish

What is the use of research?

Teachers commonly have a healthy scepticism about research. Research is what goes on elsewhere, outside and beyond school. It is undertaken by experts who make use of teachers, schools and children to undertake their research. The research thus undertaken is directed at enhancing the qualifications of the student researcher or improving the curriculum vitae of the academic researcher. It is commonly perceived to be largely irrelevant to the needs of the practising teacher and is usually reported in somewhat inaccessible journals and books, not normally the everyday reading matter of hard-pressed teachers.

Fien (1992) points out that most research in geography education is of the empirical, process–product type. In empirical research the researcher is the actor, who poses hypotheses to be tested by the setting up of controlled experimental situations. Empirical research is positivistic in style and concerned with the processes of teaching and learning and the product of such processes. There is, as Fien points out, rather less of the interpretive mode of research in geographical education. In interpretive research, the ethnographic researcher observes the subjects of the research – the actors, often using a case-study approach in her or his search for illuminative evidence and information. In Fien's view, such research could offer 'rich descriptions of the thoughts, practices and problems of teachers' (ibid.: 267).

A third style of research, educational action research, developed in the UK and elsewhere from the mid-1970s, offers the possibility of research activity which is yet more immediately relevant to the needs of teachers and students and can thus contribute directly to the professional standing of teachers and teaching and to enhancement of the education of our students.

What is educational action research?

Educational action research is research undertaken by the practising teacher as a response to an issue or problem that is a matter of concern to that teacher. The purpose of undertaking the research is to try to get at the nature of the issue or problem, to explore its roots and causes and to plan and implement possible ways and means of dealing with it. The effects of implementing these ways and means are then evaluated and this may lead on to further attempts to refine the action, further reflection on the issue or problem and so on. Thus one could say that the basic characteristics are that it is undertaken by the practitioner and is mainly concerned to produce an effective action plan to deal with a situation or condition. Some examples may help to develop these ideas.

Example 1 Developing a teaching unit

Jeannette Kayes was dissatisfied with the part of her GCSE (General Certificate of Secondary Education) course for 14- to 16-year-old students (Kayes 1992). In particular, she was concerned 'that the Work and Employment part of the course was male biased, concentrating on manufacturing industry and traditionally male jobs. When teaching this it felt "other worldly" even to me and I was very conscious that I was not teaching it as well as the rest of the course' (p. 18). Kayes felt that she had little personal interest in this aspect of the course from an academic point of view, and she therefore set out to develop the unit to include more interesting, more demanding work for the pupils and to stimulate her own interest.

She decided to focus the unit on women's work in the global economy. She prepared the unit and taught it to her class while monitoring the experience to enable her to reflect on a series of questions for investigation. These were:

A   In terms of pupils

    1   Do pupils learn the subject content and therefore become more aware of the work women do?

    2   How do pupils react to the feminist content, and does there seem to be a difference in how girls and boys react?

    3   Do pupils' reactions to the feminist content change from the beginning to the end of the work?

    4   Does the subject content affect their performance in examination terms?

B   In terms of the unit

    1   Was the unit successful in terms of the pupils' results, and was there any gender pattern in the results?

    2   Was the unit successful in terms of the pupils' interest and enjoyment?

C   In terms of the rest of the GCSE

    1   What recommendations can be made to improve the rest of the GCSE course, especially the Work and Employment section?

    2   How can feminist geography be used in schools in the light of examination syllabuses and the National Curriculum?

In addition to analysis of the pupils' performance in assessment terms, a participant observer role was adopted in investigating and reflecting upon these questions, and the teacher kept a diary for a term, administered questionnaires to the pupils and interviewed pupils. She found that pupils had become more aware of the work women do. Four of the twenty pupils changed their opinions during the course of the work. Three boys became more positive about the role of women in the world of work, while one girl became rather negative towards equal opportunities issues. The majority of the boys expressed positive outcomes and the girls increased in confidence in class during the work. The study strengthened the researcher's resolve to develop more enquiry approaches in her teaching and learning strategies, and she gained in confidence with regard to integrating some aspects of feminist geography into the GCSE course.

Example 2 Developing the role of homework

P.J. Sweasey (1989) was concerned about the nature and role of homework in her large, mixed comprehensive school. Her feeling was that not enough care went into the setting of homework and that it was not being used to its full potential for the educational benefit of the students.

The researcher reviewed the literature on the topic and investigated current views using questionnaires to be completed by children, parents and fellow teachers. She also interviewed a number of families, a deputy headteacher and the head of geography in the school. The homework policies of some neighbouring schools were also examined.

Homework was seen to be occasionally irrelevant, frequently boring, often poorly designed and sloppily executed. It was seen as a chore to complete and a chore to mark. It was thought to appeal to the brightest students and to alienate the weakest. Homework set to improve individual study skills was done best by those who needed least improvement. Homework could provide the opportunity for the ability gap to be widened by the varying levels of support in the home.

As a response to these findings, the researcher produced a trial local studies unit with an integral homework scheme. The work was divided into sections and students in Year 7 (11- to 12-year-olds) were required to select their own route through the unit. Thus they were given an element of choice as to the order in which they undertook the sections and whether they treated them as classwork or homework. Pupils were expected to undertake at least thirty minutes of homework per week. Instructions and resources were provided for the work. Six teachers were involved with the large mixed-ability group of children, and pupils recorded their progress on specially prepared sheets.

The unit was carefully evaluated and a generally positive response was noted from the pupils, but the work did raise other issues, such as how to support the less able in this freely structured work. An increased level of competitiveness between pupils was noted and the researcher wished to go on to question whether this was (a) desirable and (b) beneficial for all pupils.

Example 3 Implementing the National Curriculum

The Education Reform Act of 1988 established a National Curriculum for England and Wales. The National Curriculum was fundamentally subject-based and Geography was included as one of the Foundation Subjects, to be taught to all children from age 5 to 16. Subject Working Groups were set up, which recommended to the Secretary of State for Education the Programmes of Study (PoS) and Statements of Attainment (SoA) for each subject. The PoS basically set out what was to be taught and the SoA listed what was to be assessed. The Secretary of State, working through the National Curriculum Council, had the last word on the final details of the PoS and SoA which were published as Statutory Orders for each subject (DES 1991).

The challenge for teachers was the translation of the Orders into a working curriculum for their particular school and pupil situation. For primary school teachers in particular, this was no mean task, since many lacked subject expertise for a number of the subjects included in the curriculum, and most lacked knowledge and experience of curriculum planning, development and evaluation.

Sue Dunkerley, studying at the time for a Master's degree in geography education, set out to monitor the implementation of the Geography National Curriculum in a primary school (Dunkerley 1992). She was strongly supported by the school in this endeavour and adopted the role of an external consultant or facilitator. Thus she was able to develop her research role as participant observer. She collected background information on the school and its catchment area, attended relevant staff meetings at the school when the geography element of the curriculum was being discussed, and worked with the teacher whose role it was to lead the development of the Geography curriculum in line with the Statutory Orders. She also made a collection of media cuttings at this time of rapid change, and attended meetings, such as those organized by the Geographical Association, which were relevant to the task.

During this work, the researcher mounted a simple questionnaire survey of the level of geographical background of the staff and their view of the nature of geography and its educational value. She maintained a journal in which she reflected on the process of developing the Geography curriculum, audio-taped the meetings, and encouraged the teacher responsible also to maintain a journal.

In her review of her findings, the researcher noted the significance of the fact that the whole school staff had been involved in the development through the staff meetings. The value of adopting a whole-school approach was clear. The level of awareness of the role and potential of Geography in the curriculum had increased as a result of the need to implement the National Curriculum requirements. The level and quality of resourcing, in terms of learning resources, had also improved. Dunkerley noted that the role of the participant observer, taking an active role in the development from an external perspective, required great sensitivity.

Example 4 Developing the curriculum at a national scale

The Geography 16–19 Project was a national project, funded for most of its lifetime (1976–85) by the Schools Council. The project worked with teachers and students in England, Wales and Northern Ireland to develop the Geography curriculum for 16- to 19-year-olds (Naish *et al.* 1987). It was set up as a direct response to analysis of the nature of the Geography curriculum in the mid-1970s, since it appeared that that curriculum was not fulfilling the educational potential of the subject. In particular, there was concern about the content of the subject in the 16 to 19 curriculum, where it tended to be largely influenced by and dependent upon developments in academic geography at higher education level. The tendency was for a significant time-lag between changes at the research frontier and changes at 16 to 19 level. These changes were largely mediated through examination boards, which were subject to institutional and historical inertia.

A second major concern was that the pedagogy of Geography courses for 16- to 19-year-olds was largely expository, thus limiting the range of skills being developed by students. Thirdly, the significance of attitudes and values in decisions about the use of space was largely unrecognized in Geography courses for the age group, as was the educational potential of involving students in active values enquiry into issues, questions and problems about the use of space. Thus the potential of Geography as a medium for the education of young people was seen to be largely unfulfilled and in need of consideration and development.

From the very beginning, it was the intention of the project to work with practising teachers in developing the Geography curriculum. Such intentions are encapsulated in the aims of the project, which were:

- to involve teachers and lecturers in a reconsideration of the objectives, content and teaching methods of Geography courses for the 16 to 19 age group; and
- by means of this involvement, to help them appreciate their role as curriculum developers.

In order to further these aims, the project team set up what they called 'a system for involvement' in the earliest stages of the project. Working through the Schools Council, pilot groups of teachers were set up in thirteen local authorities in England and Wales. These groups consisted of teachers from a range of establishments within each authority and they were led by a co-ordinator, usually from higher education and supported by their headteacher or principal and by the local authority advisory service. Some funding was made available to ensure that teachers could have reprographic facilities and travel to meetings locally and nationally. Each member of the three-person central project team was allocated a selection of these pilot groups and travelled regularly to work with the groups. At a later stage, single associate schools or colleges were nominated in a further twelve authorities, including two schools in Northern Ireland.

Working with this system for involvement, the project conducted an analysis of the current situation within Geography education for 16- to 19-year-olds, researched the needs of the students, and reviewed the significant rapid changes taking place in the subject at the time (late 1970s). On the basis of this research phase, they put forward broad aims for Geography in the 16 to 19 age range. In order to put these aims into operation, the system of team and teachers moved on to produce a framework for the Geography curriculum designed to help promote the construction of syllabuses and the preparation of teaching materials to support such syllabuses. The framework proposed an approach to Geography, dubbed by the project 'the people–environment approach', an active, enquiry-based approach to teaching and learning, to include values enquiry, and guidelines on selection of content and scale of study.

Continuing to work with its system of involved teachers, the project moved on to produce innovative courses for the Advanced level of the General Certificate of Education and other national examinations for 17-, 18- or 19-year-olds, all based on the curriculum framework. Teachers engaged with the team in the production of pilot materials to support these courses and undertook trials of the materials. The teachers were also critically involved in the development of the courses, their implementation and evaluation. When it came to the further dissemination of the project, the pilot teachers played a key role in conferences designed to introduce colleagues to what the project had to offer. Their role as change agents continued significantly in helping to establish and develop working groups of teachers in local areas meeting to discuss issues, develop materials and assessment items, and generally enhance each other's professional development.

Characteristics of action research

These examples demonstrate some further characteristics of educational action research. The, first is that action research is often *collaborative*. In the case of Examples 1 and 2, the researchers were students on a postgraduate degree course, working with a university-based supervisor and having the opportunity to share their ideas with fellow students in both formal and informal situations. In Example 3, the researcher, in addition to working with her supervisor and fellow students, also worked with the staff of the school and with one teacher in particular. In Example 4, the project team established its network of involved schools and colleges in order to undertake a large-scale collaborative action research enterprise.

The second characteristic is that the research in each of the examples was of a *critical* nature. In Example 1, it was concerned with problems of gender bias as this is commonly manifested in mixed classes in mixed-sex schools. For example, adolescent boys may frequently dominate lessons in such classes, demanding the attention of both male and female teachers and excluding girls from oral participation in the lesson. The research arose through a critical appraisal of this situation. It was also critical of the content of the unit, which previously to the research development had been mainly concerned with a view of work that states that most work and the most important work is undertaken by men. In Example 2, the research was based on a critique of the nature and quality of homework being set and undertaken in geography. In Example 3, the nature of the Geography Orders in the National Curriculum became subject to critical analysis by the researcher and the teachers. In Example 4, a critique of quality of Geography in the 16–19 curriculum and of the failure of geography to achieve its educational potential was the starting point for the large-scale project.

The third characteristic is that the research was *concerned with social situations*, the nature of such situations and ways in which conditions might be changed for the better. In Example 1, the social situation is that of the mixed-sex classroom, where certain gender characteristics were observed and questioned. In Example 2, the experimental unit questioned the conventional roles of teachers and pupils and the role of the home in the development of learning and as a place for learning. In Example 3, the critical role of the whole staff in the primary school was considered and the significance of whole staff involvement in curriculum renewal was emphasized. Journal entries in the reporting of the research opened up many important points about the nature of collaborative work. In Example 4, the role of teachers as curriculum developers and therefore the power of teachers relative to other elements of the education system was fundamentally under examination and development as teachers were involved in key areas of the work of the project.

The fourth characteristic is that the examples illustrate well the thinking of *reflective teachers* (Schön 1983). In Example 1, the researcher was aware of the limitations of her original approach to the unit, of the social situation in her classroom, and of the gender bias which can pervade much of the geographical content of the school curriculum. She set up an experimental situation which enabled her to reflect further on these situations and develop a possible approach to dealing with some of these. Her reflection upon the actual research led her on to recognize further issues and questions for analysis and possible treatment. Similar reflective activity on the part of the teacher can be observed in Examples 2 and 3, while in Example 4, reflection upon the process and product of the geography curriculum for 16- to 19-year-olds was deliberately called for by the project team and stimulated by the situation of team members and teachers working together on all aspects of the project's development.

A fifth characteristic is that, in each of the examples, the research was *systematic,* divided into clear phases, which included planning, implementation, reflection, analysis and reporting (through a dissertation or through publications). It is this systematic approach to action research, together with the fact that such research is *made public*, or shared through discussion with others, that distinguishes action research from simply what teachers do as a matter of good practice. Of course it *is* good practice to take a critical view of what one is doing, to develop new units or fresh approaches to units and to evaluate these in terms of student and teacher activity and involvement. To undertake such activities in purposeful, explicitly acknowledged, systematic research of the kind described above, may be a productive way of helping to develop the reflective skills of the professional teacher.

This notion of the reflective practitioner and of the teacher as researcher takes us on to a consideration of the origins and development of action research in education.

The origins and development of action research

In recent years a great deal has been written about action research. It is clearly a fashionable mode of research and its popularity is reflected in the number of books and articles produced through the 1980s and early 1990s. Many writers trace the origins of the genre to the work of social psychologists in group dynamics, and of Kurt Lewin in particular (Lewin 1948), stressing his concern for practical situations of social conflict. Lewin felt that where a community was prepared to study the results of its own social action, remedial efforts could be introduced. The notion of action following study is clear at this early stage and Lewin developed change experiments to allow groups, with the guidance of external consultants, to develop objective and detached means of examining the foundations of their own biases. Basic to his approach was the idea of action cycles which include analysis, fact finding, conceptualisation, planning, implementation and evaluation of action (McKernan 1991). Lewin pulled together ideas about the process of scientific enquiry developed in the late nineteenth century (Buckingham 1926) and the work of John Dewey on stages in reflective thinking (Dewey 1910, 1929, 1938) to develop a credible theory of action research so that it began to be recognized as an innovation in social inquiry. For Lewin, research should help solve social problems and 'research that produces nothing but books will not suffice' (Lewin 1948: 203).

It was Stephen Corey who led the post-war drive for educational action research as part of the movement for social reconstruction that characterized the years following the Second World War (Corey 1953). Corey believed that curriculum practice could be significantly developed and improved if teachers themselves were involved in research and development. The enthusiastic drive to use action research as the general strategy for curriculum change and development in the 1950s, characterized by teachers and schools co-operating with outside researchers, was overtaken in the 1960s by the research, development and dissemination movement which tended to isolate teachers from the process and involve them only as potential targets of the dissemination.

In the 1970s, the work of Lawrence Stenhouse (Stenhouse 1975) led to a renaissance of the action research approach through his promotion of the idea of the teacher as researcher. Stenhouse directed the Humanities Curriculum project (1967–72) which was concerned with a process model of curriculum with profound implications for the role of the teacher in the discussion of controversial issues amongst groups of adolescent students. In the process model, the curriculum is not 'a body of predetermined static content, to be reproduced via the pedagogical process. Rather it is the selection and organisation of content within a dynamic and reflective pedagogical process and is therefore constantly evolved and developed through it' (Elliott 1991: 16). Thus the role of the teacher, working with a particular group of students, is paramount in determining the day-to-day, week-to-week character of the curriculum. With the dominance of content provision removed, the door is opened for consideration of important questions such as the relative roles of teacher and learner and the appropriateness, relevance and significance of the content being considered at any particular time.

Under pressure of time, the Humanities Curriculum project team devised packs of resource materials to act as evidence to be fed into student discussions. The team then began to study the pedagogical situation within which the materials were being used by teachers. The importance of fostering self-reflection on the part of the teachers soon became clear if they were to gain in confidence and competence in developing an appropriate pedagogy rather than rely upon the critique provided by the outsiders – the project team. The potential of self-reflective practice for the generation of theory from the basis of practice became clear, and the importance of reflection upon practice as an element of professionalism received a further boost (Elliott 1991). On the basis of his experience with the Humanities project, Stenhouse clarified his view of the teacher as researcher. This is clearly stated in his influential book *An Introduction to Curriculum Research and Development* (1975) where his thesis is that teaching ought to be based on research undertaken by the teacher, who develops the curriculum by means of study of and evaluation of teaching episodes and approaches, thus improving her or his own work as understanding develops.

John Elliott, who was a member of Stenhouse's Humanities Curriculum Development Project team, has since played a leading role in proselytising educational action research. From 1973 to 1975, he and Clem Adelman led the Ford Teaching Project, sponsored by the Ford Foundation (Elliott and Adelman 1976). In this project, forty teachers in twelve schools undertook action research into the problems of implementing enquiry approaches in their classrooms. In Elliott's view (Elliott 1991), most curriculum projects in the 1960s and 1970s had espoused an enquiry approach to learning but had assumed that all that was needed to implement such an approach was the provision of supporting curriculum materials. His experience on the Humanities Project had suggested that this was far from the case, and the Ford Project offered teachers the opportunity to explore the issues through their own teaching and thus to generate 'diagnostic and practical hypotheses' which would help to develop a pedagogical theory. Triangulation approaches were employed in reflecting upon the practices of the teachers as Elliott and Adelman recorded lessons on tape or tape/slide and then interviewed the teachers and a sample of students about the recorded lessons. The interviews themselves were recorded and these recordings then discussed again with the teachers and students. Hypotheses generated through this triangulation approach were then circulated to other teachers involved in the project and used as the basis of discussion in meetings across project personnel. This led to further experimentation as teachers went on to try to assess how far the hypotheses could stand up to scrutiny from the perspective of their own teaching. Thus the teachers were encouraged to reflect on their practices in the light of the theory they had themselves helped to generate.

Efforts to create networks of researchers interested in action research and to disseminate ideas are illustrated by the setting up of CARN (the Classroom Action Research Network) in 1976 and of NARTAR (the National Association for Race Relations Teaching and Action Research). In 1990, the first world congress on action research, action learning and process management was held in Australia. The number and frequency of publications on action research have increased dramatically in recent years and attempts have been made to restructure award-bearing courses for teachers to support and encourage action research in schools (Elliott 1981).

How is action research undertaken?

Several writers offer advice on how to undertake action research. Some helpful examples are Elliott (1991), who includes a chapter entitled 'A practical guide to action research' in his interesting general review of the genre. Jean McNiff's *Action Research: Principles and Practice* (1988) contains sections on 'How to start an action research study' and on 'Making sense of the data' (McNiff 1988). James McKernan's comprehensive book *Curriculum Action Research* (1991) is a *Handbook of Methods and Resources for the Reflective Practitioner.*

Most writers make considerable play of elegant models of action research, each refining the other in efforts to encapsulate the essence of the process. All stress the cyclical nature of the endeavour, from the simplicity of McNiff's attempt to model Lewin's approach (Figure 23.1), to the more complex efforts of Elliott (1991) (Figure 23.2). The four basic activities in Lewin's approach are planning, acting, observing and reflecting, and this can lead on to revised planning, further action, observation and reflection, as indicated in Figure 23.1.

Kemmis (1980) elaborated Lewin's simple model, suggesting that research begins from an initial idea which is subjected to reconnaissance largely consisting of fact finding. This leads to the statement of a general plan which can be broken down into a series of steps for action. The first action step is implemented and then evaluated and this can lead to an amended plan with related steps. The researcher then spirals into implementation of action step 2, evaluation of step 2 and reconsideration in an amended plan, and so on – the cyclical, spiral process continues.

Elliott (1991) wished to refine this model by acknowledging that completion of the first cycle may cause a shift in the initial, or general idea. He considers that reconnaissance should be analytical as well as concerned with fact finding, and that each action step should be monitored as it is undertaken as well as being subjected to subsequent evaluation. These considerations led him to propose the model shown in Figure 23.2.

At this stage it may help to consider a hypothetical example of the application of this model.

Identifying the initial idea   The teacher is concerned that students at an early stage in her 16–19 course in geography are reluctant to talk. The amount, level and quality of their oral contributions is limited.

Reconnaissance   In order to be more clear about the situation, the teacher analyses the situation further and feels that:

- students' oral responses are poor when she poses questions in class;
- students have little to contribute towards discussion;
- students' oral responses are short and undeveloped;
- oral work is normally expected in whole-class situations;
- better performance is noted when students are in small groups.

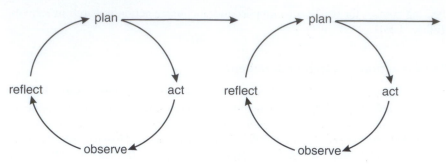

Figure 23.1   Action research cycles

Source: McNiff (1988).

She undertakes some reading on group work and language in learning. She puts forward hypotheses that:

Oral/discussion work will improve and make more of a contribution to student learning if:

- students are put into more challenging situations;
- students are encouraged to develop a fuller knowledge base;
- students are given more stimulating tasks to complete;
- students are given access to appropriate and relevant evidence in the form of learning resources and data.

Preparing the general plan   The teacher now re-states the initial idea with more clarity – she is anxious to improve students' oral work since she believes that student talk is vital for effective learning. Her general plan is to try to devise activities that will motivate the students to make more effective use of spoken language in their geographical studies.

She plans action steps:

- Action step 1 Set up a groupwork situation where students have to investigate certain aspects of an issue and report back on the completion of the task.
- Action step 2 Involve students in a role play which will enable them to take on a particular role in order to discuss an issue of spatial and environmental significance.
- Action step 3 Involve the students in the production of a videotaped report on a local people–environment issue.

The teacher considers what resources she will need to implement these action steps, decides who else may be involved in the activity, for example the media resources officer and the general public in action step 3. She thinks into the question of whether any ethical questions may be raised by the activities which could require sensitive attention.

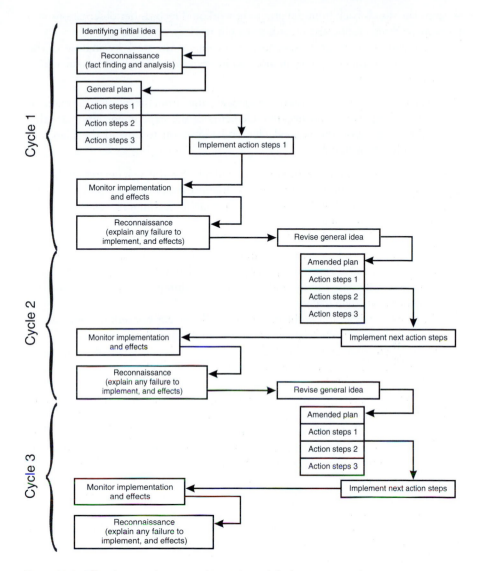

Figure 23.2 Elliott's revised version of Lewin's model of action research

Source: Elliott (1991).

Implementation of action step 1 The teacher plans the group work, decides how to monitor and evaluate it and then puts it into practice with the group of students.

Monitoring the implementation The teacher monitors the implementation of action step 1 by keeping a log of her work in preparation, of the actual teaching of the session and the students' learning, and of the evidence of their learning. During the teaching sessions she stands back from the groups at work and records her observations as a participant observer. She also records groups at work on audio tape.

At the end of the teaching sessions, she evaluates the work by analysis of the tapes, by using a student questionnaire and interviews, and by her own subjective evaluation of the events.

Reconnaissance The teacher uses the evidence gained from the monitoring exercise to consider the positive and negative elements of the experiment. She uses this analysis to help revise the general idea and moves on to amend the plan and proceed with action step 2.

An enormous range of techniques is available for the teacher-researcher to employ in the monitoring, analysis and evaluation stages of an episode of action research. McKernan (1991) describes forty-eight techniques, classified and grouped into the following:

- Observational and narrative research methods, e.g. participant observation, case studies, diaries, journals, photography, video/audio taping, rating scales.
- Non-observational, survey and self-report techniques, e.g. questionnaires, interviews, attitude scales.
- Discourse analysis and problem-solving methods, e.g. content analysis, document analysis, episode analysis, brainstorming, group discussions.
- Critical-reflective and evaluative research methods, e.g. triangulation, lesson profiles, student/teacher evaluation forms, critical trialling.

Elliott (1991) offers a simpler list consisting of diaries, profiles (e.g. lesson profiles), document analysis, photographic evidence, tape/video recordings and transcripts, using an outside observer, interviewing, running commentary, shadow studies (shadowing a participant), checklists, questionnaires, inventories, triangulation and analytic memos recorded at critical stages.

An important element of action research is sharing the experience and findings with colleagues, and this may be done informally, within the context of the researcher's institution, or more formally as a publication or a presentation at a conference or meeting. McNiff makes the point that the evidence in the form of tapes, photographs, videos or written reporting is available for consultation, and the teacher can say 'Look, I have evidence!' (McNiff 1988).

One of the key problems of action research is the question of how teachers are to find the occasion and the time to undertake activities that will distinguish their research from the kind of good practice which one would normally expect of teachers who evaluate their teaching in a reflective manner and reorganize their work on the basis of such evaluation. A study by Kwan and Lee (1994) invited geography teachers in Brisbane and Hong Kong to respond to a questionnaire survey investigating their knowledge of and involvement in action research. Only nine teachers responded, thus suggesting that action research is a low priority for them. Of the nine who responded, only four claimed to be undertaking action research, and it was clear that they had only recently discovered the idea. Three of the four provided only brief descriptions of the salient characteristics of action research while the fourth provided a fair description. The nine teachers described the main barriers to undertaking action research as:

- time constraints;
- heavy workload;
- lack of familiarity with techniques;
- lack of support and recognition from the school.

In the United Kingdom, the radical revolution in education undertaken by the Conservative governments of the 1980s and 1990s has placed new demands on teachers which have increased their workload considerably, especially in the amount of paperwork which has to be undertaken. Such bureaucratic demands militate against the proper activity of the reflective practitioner and it is the commonplace view of many teachers that it is difficult in the present situation to find time for the preparation and evaluation of their teaching. The phenomenon is by no means limited to the United Kingdom, as is indicated in Lidstone's (1994) reflections on becoming professional.

There is little doubt that at present, action research takes place mainly where teachers are released from normal teaching and administrative duties in some way, such as for in-service activities, or where the occasion is provided, usually through enrolment on a course in higher education, often at diploma and Master's level.

There is also little doubt that a key opportunity for action research is provided by in-service activities, including both short courses and award-bearing courses. Good practice would involve the in-service provider and the teacher in working together to isolate key issues and problems in the teacher's practice. This would lead to the setting up of action research activities to investigate these issues and problems and to endeavour to improve practice. It is increasingly common to find in-service courses of this nature developing. The key feature is to ensure that any required coursework is related to this kind of enquiry.

A new professionalism

The notion that involvement in critical action research may lead to an enhanced professionalism for teachers has been with us for some time. The Schools Council Geography 14–18 project team embraced the idea in the structure of their work, which involved the setting up of groups of teachers in various parts of the country, who worked on an analysis of the contemporary situation of the geography curriculum (Hickman *et al.* 1973). The thesis was developed that the main gatekeeper militating against improvement of the curriculum was the style and approach of public examinations. A cycle of curriculum underdevelopment was described in which teachers taught to achieve maximum success for their students in public examinations. If such examinations demanded mainly recall of factual information as a measure of success in learning geography, then this militated against the development of more enquiry-based approaches to teaching and learning such as might broaden the range of skills and abilities being developed by students through their geographical studies. It followed that curriculum change should be approached through a drive for new approaches in the design and requirements of the public examination syllabuses and an experimental examination for 16-year-olds became the main focus of the project's work.

The involvement of teachers in the discussions which led to this approach and then in the development of school-based elements of the courses, their trial and evaluation, was seen as a key element of the professional teacher's role, and to develop this role would lead to a new professionalism for the geography teacher.

These ideas are taken forward in Fien's important paper of 1992, where he calls for involvement of geography teachers in critical action research of a collaborative nature, the collaboration being with university-based tutors who would act as 'critical friends, sponsors and co-participants' of the teacher-researcher. The research would be critical in the sense put forward by Carr and Kemmis (1986), influenced by the kind of critical social science envisaged by Habermas (1972; see also McCarthy 1978). It would have, as its central concern, the role of providing a critique of and challenge to 'the personal beliefs and the ideological and structural contexts that constrain desirable practices in teaching' (Fien 1992: 268). The ultimate aim would be to make such desirable practices more possible to achieve.

Some writers concerned to discuss the nature of professionalism emphasize the potential of action research to enhance professional behaviour. Kemp (1977) analyses the competencies required in occupations, such as teaching, that require problem solving and decision making in complex situations. He suggests that learning from reflection upon experience is a key cognitive competence. In a group of competencies concerned with motivation, eliciting feedback on one's own performance is seen as a key ability. Action research is likely to enhance such abilities or competencies and thus form a vital element in maintaining and developing the professional status of teachers.

Carr and Kemmis (1986) suggest the following three distinctive features of professionalism:

1   Professions base methods and procedures on theoretical knowledge and research.
2   Members of a profession have dominant commitment to the well-being of their clients.
3   Members have the individual and collective right to make autonomous, independent judgements regardless of external, non-professional controls and constraints with regard to particular decisions in particular situations.

At the time of writing, the professional status of teachers as viewed within this definition is under prolonged and active attack in the United Kingdom through the legislation of the Education Reform Act and through the National Curriculum that forms the central element of the Act. While nothing can be done to diminish the commitment of teachers to the well-being of their students, theoretical knowledge and research is being disregarded and teachers are being denied their individual and collective right to make autonomous, independent judgements regardless of external controls. Movements to control the training of new teachers also militate against the professional status of teachers. A key element of the professions is normally considered to be the links with higher education in the training of members of the profession, yet at the present time we witness attempts to break the link with higher education in the training of teachers and base such training entirely in schools. In the National Curriculum the role of the teacher is reduced to that of 'delivery' of the prescribed curriculum. The content of the curriculum is set out in the programmes of study contained in the Statutory Orders for each of the subjects that make up the National Curriculum. Teachers have little choice in the selection of content, while in the assessment of the pupils, stress is placed on externally set Statutory Assessment Tasks (SATs).

For the teacher committed to action research and thus to enhanced professionalism, this Fordist, conveyor belt, strait-jacket curriculum can offer little hope of an enabling education for our children. The review undertaken by the School Curriculum and Assessment Authority (SCAA) in 1993–94 (Dearing 1994) offers little scope for fundamental improvement of this situation, although marginal improvements are included. The professional role of teachers will need to be reconsidered radically if education that will genuinely offer the opportunity for the development of autonomous thinking individuals is to be re-established. The effective growth of action research as a means to a new professionalism should assist considerably in this process and should help to provide the opportunity for geography to begin to move towards the achievement of its true educational potential once again.

References

Alexander, R.J. and Ellis, J.W. (eds) (1981) *Advanced Study for Teachers*, Teacher Education Study Group, Society for Research into Higher Education, distributed by Naferton Books.
Buckingham, R.B. (1926) *Research for Teachers*, Silver Burdett Co.
Carr, W. and Kemmis, S. (1986) *Becoming Critical: Education, Knowledge and Action Research*, The Falmer Press.
Corey, S. (1953) *Action Research to Improve School Practices*, Columbia University, Teachers' College Press.
Dearing, R. (1994) *The National Curriculum and Assessment. Final Report*, School Curriculum and Assessment Authority.
DES (1991) *Geography in the National Curriculum (England)*, Department of Education and Science, HMSO.
Dewey, J. (1910) *How We Think*, D.C. Heath.
—— (1929) *The Sources of a Science of Education*, Horace Liveright.
—— (1938) *Logic: The Theory of Inquiry*, Henry Holt.
Dunkerley, S.M. (1992) 'The implementation of National Curriculum Geography in one primary school', unpublished MA dissertation, Institute of Education, University of London.
Elliott, J. (1981) 'The teacher as researcher within award-bearing courses', in R.J. Alexander and J.W. Ellis (eds) *Advanced Study for Teachers*, Teacher Education Study Group, Society for Research into Higher Education, distributed by Naferton Books.
—— (1991) *Action Research for Educational Change*, Open University Press.

Elliott, J. and Adelman, C. (1976) *Innovation at the Classroom Level: A Case Study of the Ford Teaching Project*, Open University Press.

Fien, J. (1992) 'What kind of research for what kind of teaching? Towards research in geographical education as a critical social science', in D. Hill (ed.) *International Perspectives on Geographic Education*, Center for Geographic Education, University of Colorado at Boulder/Rand McNally.

Habermas, J. (1972) *Knowledge and Human Interests*, Heinemann.

Haubrich, H. (ed.) (1994) *Europe and the World in Geography Education*, Papers for the International Geographical Union Commission on Geographical Education Meetings in Berlin and Prague, 1994, Geographiedidaktische Forschungen Band 25, Hochschulverband für Geographie und ihre Didaktik e. V. (Selbstverlag).

Hickman, G., Reynolds, J. and Tolley, H. (1973) *A New Professionalism for a Changing Geography*, Schools Council Geography 14–18 Project, Schools Council.

Hill, D. (ed.) (1992) *International Perspectives on Geographic Education*, Center for Geographic Education, University of Colorado at Boulder/Rand McNally.

Kayes, J. (1992) 'Taking equal opportunities in school a step further: an evaluation of a subject-focused response', unpublished MA dissertation, Institute of Education, University of London.

Kemmis, S. (1980) 'Action research in retrospect and prospect', mimeo presented at the Annual General Meeting of the Australian Association for Research in Education, Sydney.

Klemp, G.O. (1977) *Three Factors Success in the World of Work: Implications for Curriculum in Higher Education*, McBer & Co.

Kwan, T. and Lee, J. (1994) 'A reflective report on an action research towards understanding conceptions of action research held by geography teachers', in H. Haubrich (ed.) *Europe and the World in Geography Education*, Geographiedidaktische Forschungen Band 25, Hochschulverband für Geographie und ihre Didaktik e. V. (Selbstverlag).

Lewin, K. (1948) *Resolving Social Conflicts*, Harper.

Lidstone, J. (1994) 'Becoming professional: geographers and environmental education', keynote address delivered at International Geographical Union Regional Conference, Prague, 1994.

McCarthy, C. (1978) *The Critical Theory of Jürgen Habermas*, Hutchinson.

McKernan, J. (1991) *Curriculum Action Research. A Handbook of Methods and Resources for the Reflective Practitioner*, Kogan Page.

McNiff, J. (1988) *Action Research:*
 Principles and Practice, Macmillan Education.

Naish, M., Rawling, E. and Hart, C. (1987) *Geography 16–19: The Contribution of a Curriculum Project to 16–19 Education*, Longman.

Stenhouse, L. (1975) *An Introduction to Curriculum Research and Development*, Heinemann.

Schön, D. (1983) *The Reflective Practitioner*, Temple Smith.

Sweasey, P.J. (1989) '"Homework with Humanity". A study of homework in geography and humanities in secondary schools', unpublished MA dissertation, Institute of Education, University of London.

Index